Roadmapping Extended Reality

Scrivener Publishing
100 Cummings Center, Suite 541J
Beverly, MA 01915-6106

Publishers at Scrivener
Martin Scrivener (martin@scrivenerpublishing.com)
Phillip Carmical (pcarmical@scrivenerpublishing.com)

Roadmapping Extended Reality

Fundamentals and Applications

Edited by

Mariano Alcañiz

*Department of Biomedical Engineering at the Polytechnic
University of Valencia, Spain*

Marco Sacco

*Institute of System and Industrial Intelligent Technologies
for Advanced Manufacturing STIIMA, Lecco, Italy*

and

Jolanda G. Tromp

*Center for Visualization & Simulation, Computer Science Department,
Duy Tan University, Viet Nam*

&

*Human-Computer Interaction, Computer Science Department,
State University of New York, Oswego, NY, United States of America*

Scrivener
Publishing

This edition first published 2022 by John Wiley & Sons, Inc., 111 River Street, Hoboken, NJ 07030, USA and Scrivener Publishing LLC, 100 Cummings Center, Suite 541J, Beverly, MA 01915, USA
© 2022 Scrivener Publishing LLC
For more information about Scrivener publications please visit www.scrivenerpublishing.com.

Wiley Global Headquarters

111 River Street, Hoboken, NJ 07030, USA

For details of our global editorial offices, customer services, and more information about Wiley products visit us at www.wiley.com.

Limit of Liability/Disclaimer of Warranty

Library of Congress Cataloging-in-Publication Data

ISBN 978-1-119-86514-8

Cover image: Pixabay.Com
Cover design by Russell Richardson

Set in size of 11pt and Minion Pro by Manila Typesetting Company, Makati, Philippines

Printed in the USA

10 9 8 7 6 5 4 3 2 1

Contents

Foreword

It is my honor to present this book about extended reality (XR) technologies and application areas. Extended reality is part of the Information and Communication Technology domain and includes virtual reality and mixed reality, the latter including augmented reality and augmented virtuality, as defined in the reality–virtuality continuum of Milgram and colleagues in 1994. In spite of its numerous already existing applications, XR has incredible societal potential; therefore, Europe must invest much more than it currently does. To this aim, bundling a vision about what the future of XR should be seemed a prerequisite.

The EuroXR Association was founded in 2010 as a continuation of the work in the European Union funded FP6 Network of Excellence INTUITION (2004–2008). It is an umbrella organization gathering not only individuals, but also national chapters and associations, large companies, small-to-medium enterprises (SMEs), as well as research institutions, universities, and laboratories. In November 2020, the EuroXR Association launched the XR Open Forum. This initiative aims to organize regular meetings with EuroXR members, but is also widely open to external experts, to brainstorm on the new actions that our association could lead on, with the aim to increase the awareness of Europe in the Extended Reality domain. This book presents the EuroXR Delphi consensus study results and a wide variety of XR technology reviews and XR application areas—the first outcome of the XR Open Forum initiative of the EuroXR Association.

Therefore, as the new president of EuroXR, it is a great pleasure to first congratulate the editorial team of this book, namely, Pr. Mariano Alcaniz Raya (Director LabLENI, Universitat Politècnica de València, Spain), Dr. Marco Sacco (Past president of EuroXR, Head of CNR-STIIMA subsidiary in Lecco, Italy), and Dr. Jolanda G. Tromp (Consultant to EuroXR Association for the Delphi consensus study; Director Center for Visualization and Simulation, Duy Tan University, Vietnam; Visiting Assistant Professor, State University of New York in Oswego, NY, USA;

visiting researcher, 3D DIANA research lab, University of Malaga, Spain). More widely, I want to express my genuine gratitude to the renowned scientists and experts who contributed chapters to this great project that the association has decided to undertake. This book allowed EuroXR members and many external collaborators to work together to achieve something bigger, and we are happy to underline once again the importance of collaboration in such a scientific and advanced technology field. I also thank Beatrice Palacco (EuroXR Communication Manager), Yves Geunes, X3D webdeveloper, and John Bottoms, 3D Internet consultant, who helped the editorial team so much and contributed to the Delphi consensus study, and I thank all the EuroXR association member volunteers and respondents who generously contributed their time and knowledge to the Delphi consensus study and this book.

This book is based on an internal report to the European Commissioners charged with future technology investment portfolio, and aims to deliver a synthetic but strong overview of the state-of-the-art in XR as of today. Over the past 11 years, the EuroXR Association has developed many friendly relationships with international XR experts, specifically to serve within the international expert committees of our annual conferences. Therefore, it was quite natural for the EuroXR Association to collect the latest views of international XR experts and share its vision with anyone working in the XR area. We really hope that everywhere in the world, our vision of XR will be useful for scientists to expand research questions and address new challenges, for providers and new companies to set new goals and envisage next steps, and for end-user analysts to be able to specify more complex needs and/or target many more people.

Dr. Patrick Bourdot
President of EuroXR (European Association of Extended Reality –
https://www.euroxr-association.org/)
Research Director at CNRS; Co-Head of VENISE team (Virtual & Augmented
Environments for Simulation & Experiments – http://www.limsi.fr/venise/),
University of Paris-Saclay, France

Preface

Recently, according to the Gartner Hype Cycle, extended reality (XR) technologies have graduated from being described as mature technologies and are now entering the plateau of productivity. Several leading tech giants are announcing that they will focus their future on the upcoming "metaverse." While the "metaverse" is too new to define, there is a clear consensus about XR's (VR/AR/MR) importance. This book offers a comprehensive overview of the technological aspects of XR and discusses the main challenges and future directions in the field. It is divided into two parts. The first part, "XR Technologies," covers the main technological aspects of XR. The chapters in this section review and discuss relevant fundamental concepts of XR, the actual state-of-the-art, and future challenges. The second part, "XR Applications," focuses on a wide range of applications, including a future roadmap. All in all, this book, which is geared towards a wide multidisciplinary audience of academic and industry stakeholders as well as government agencies and non-profit organizations, offers a snapshot of the state-of-the-art of XR and addresses the necessary requirements for its application.

The three main aspects that were holding XR technologies back from mainstream adoption—price, cables, size—have been overcome. However, there are many aspects of XR technologies currently being explored and developed that still need urgent research in terms of security, privacy, health and safety, long-term effects, addiction risks, and age-related developmental concerns; therefore, our aim is to inform all readers of these open issues and challenges. The main benefit of technology roadmapping is to summarize information to inform and direct technology investment decisions. There are currently a great number of interdisciplinary researchers and developers working in the XR R&D field focused on identifying critical technologies and technology gaps and identifying ways to leverage R&D investments.

The intended audience of this book includes XR enthusiasts, researchers, developers, students, and practitioners at large institutes and companies, SMEs, etc. To serve this audience in the best way possible, the book has been divided into two sections. The first section, "XR Technologies," provides a scientific overview of the technologies and discusses technical state-of-the-art aspects of XR. This section starts with a chapter that describes a Delphi consensus study amongst XR experts to gauge their opinion on the future of XR. Then, subsequent chapters address the following topics: digital narratives, haptic interfaces, audio interfaces, visual interfaces, software platforms, human perception engineering, XR & AI, XR open standards, and human factors. In the second section, "XR Applications," a practical overview is given of the various application areas that have been found promising for innovation with XR solutions, and informs readers of the potential return on investment. Subsequent chapters in this section cover the following topics: neurorehabilitation, retail and marketing, industrial training and maintenance, human resources skill training, and surgery. A brief summary of each chapter of the book follows.

- Chapter 1 describes the Delphi consensus study financed by the EuroXR Association into the state-of-the-art of XR R&D, which gathered information from more than 400 international XR practitioners as input for a dedicated panel of 7 invited XR experts for the Delphi consensus seeking process, who formulated 42 consolidated forecasting statements after 2 consensus rounds, regarding future directions, challenges and a roadmap for XR, created based on their responses.
- Chapter 2 sets forth that it is of utmost importance to address the central role of narrative as one of the main factors contributing to the expressive and representational potential of XR technologies in many domains of application.
- Chapter 3 sets forth that haptic technologies are still under-exploited in XR applications, which makes it all the more important to understand the obstacles that remain to be overcome in terms of technology and applications.
- Chapter 4 sets forth that immersive audio is a very active research area with many potential applications in XR and that there is huge potential in this field, which is underrepresented in the area of XR, and should therefore be included in any future research roadmap on the topic.
- Chapter 5 discusses the main approaches visual interfaces are following these days to attain the goals fixed by the different brands in the XR field, along with a short overview of future technologies with the potential to become the state-of-the-art in the next few years.

– Chapter 6 sets forth that the evolution of spatial computing is driving the adoption of a new 3D software ecosystem
known as the metaverse, a new paradigm that will require a
whole new set of software platforms.
– Chapter 7 proposes the foundations of a new field known as
perception engineering to unify and guide XR research in
human perception, focusing on the current state and potential shortcomings of human perception and XR research,
and setting goals for the field to aspire to concerning best
practices, inclusivity, and open-source modular technology.
– Chapter 8 highlights the challenge of merging Extended
Reality and Artificial Intelligence to build a synergic collaboration between technologies to support and preserve a
humancentric vision.
– Chapter 9 sets forth that the convergence of XR technologies creates a computing paradigm shift by facilitating a
new 3D interactive multi-user experience accessible anywhere via the internet. This future 3D internet will have
certain requirements: it needs an XR enabling internet
backbone, based on interoperability, open standards, created together in open source academic-industry cross-
disciplinary collaboration, including urgent regulation to
mitigate the inherent risks to privacy and security of XR
technologies. The challenges and roadmap for the near and
mid-term XR Backbone developments are discussed.
– Chapter 10 presents an overview of human factors/ergonom-
ics (HF/E) issues associated with XR regarding user experience models defined in early virtual reality (VR) research,
including several recommendations for future research.
– Chapter 11 presents the state-of-the-art concerning the use
of XR technologies in the rehabilitation of neurological disorders, concluding that they are a promising tool to address
the challenges presented by motor/physical rehabilitation
and cognitive training programs. However, several improvements for future developments related to devices and human
factors are also addressed.
– Chapter 12 explores the use of XR technologies as a very
promising tool to examine various customer behavioral patterns in dynamic, complex, and realistic situations that will
enhance our knowledge of new models of buyer-product

and buyer-seller relationships. It also sets forth that it is necessary to provide a standard framework that will allow the creation of controlled laboratory situations to study the factors that affect the acceptability of new products and retail spaces and the influence that the different elements that surround consumers have on their decisions.

- Chapter 13 describes recent research results that present XR as a promising solution for assembly, training, and maintenance tasks in Industry 4.0. However, before XR becomes widely used, the industry must overcome several challenges like 2D and 3D data standardization challenges, authoring tools, and new interfaces among others.
- Chapter 14 emphasizes that XR is a very important tool for assessing training skills of the 21st century that companies need to address the strategies they use to develop their human resources in terms of knowledge and leadership. In this chapter, the latest developments in XR technology and organizational sciences are examined. It introduces the concept of XR-based behavioral biomarkers (XRBB) which can be obtained for the evaluation of skills using a neuroscientific organizational paradigm based on implicit brain processes measured through psychophysiological signals and behavior of subjects exposed to complex social conditions replication using XR interfaces.
- Chapter 15 shows the current state of XR technologies in surgery, highlighting their strengths and weaknesses, showing examples of implementations, and outlining the future work that should lead to overcoming current weaknesses and result in giving surgeons efficient and effective tools for their work.

Lastly, contact information gathered from this book's many contributors is presented to facilitate direct discussions between readers and leading research and industry professionals interested in XR technologies.

Mariano Alcañiz
Marco Sacco
Jolanda Tromp

Future Directions for XR 2021-2030: International Delphi Consensus Study

Jolanda G. Tromp[1,2*], Gabriel Zachmann[3], Jerome Perret[4] and Beatrice Palacco[5]

[1]*Center for Visualization & Simulation (CVS), Duy Tan University, Da Nang, Viet Nam*
[2]*3D DIANA Research Group, E.T.S.I. de Telecomunicacion, University of Malaga, Malaga, Spain*
[3]*CGVR Lab, University of Bremen, Bremen, Germany*
[4]*Haption, Laval, France*
[5]*EuroXR Association, Brussels, Belgium*

Abstract

XR has been put forward as one of the "Essential Eight" key enabling technologies of the 21st century. Together, they are expected to drive the digital transformation that has started only recently in many areas of business, daily life, and leisure. Importantly, XR has the potential to play a major role in supporting the achievement of several if not all 17 Sustainable Development Goals set forth by the UN. The path towards realizing the full potential of XR technologies needs to be clarified in order to make informed decisions about research and development agendas, investment, funding, and regulations. In order to provide insights into the best approach to further develop XR towards its full potential, the EuroXR Association initiated a study using the well-established Delphi consensus method, drawing on the expertise of independent senior XR experts to formulate future directions for XR R&D. The results are presented in terms of a roadmap for the future of XR, identifying the prerequisites to clear the path for this, and clarifying the roles and responsibilities for the XR research community, the XR business community, and the government and regulation bodies. The main findings of our XR roadmap are summarized into a number of specific areas for the stakeholders to act upon, in order to push the cutting edge of XR and be part of the early-adopters who have this key enabling technology at their disposal throughout industry, education and society.

Corresponding author: Jolanda.tromp@duytan.edu.vn

Mariano Alcañiz, Marco Sacco and Jolanda G. Tromp (eds.) Roadmapping Extended Reality: Fundamentals and Applications, (1–34) © 2022 Scrivener Publishing LLC

Keywords: Extended reality, Delphi method, XR Roadmap, XR and 17 SDGs

1.1   Introduction

Leaders, governments, companies, educational institutions, researchers, and members of the general public aim to understand and anticipate the opportunities offered by new technologies. Of particular interest are emerging technologies that are expected to have a transformational or high impact potential. Currently the synergy of a number of technology developments is converging with such transformational potential, referred to as the "Essential Eight" Key Enabling Technologies (KETs) that are transforming the way we organize work, education, communication, socialization, information access, and our identity (see Figure 1.1):

1. **Augmented Reality (AR):** location-based, multi-sensory, window between real and virtual;
2. **Virtual Reality (VR):** real-time interactive 3D Computer Graphics (CG), collaborative design spaces, simulation, testing, and optimization spaces;
3. **Artificial Intelligence (AI):** big data analytics, machine learning (ML), micro and macro process analysis, and optimization;
4. **5G Cloud Computing:** decentralization, mobile computing;
5. **Blockchain:** cybersecurity, privacy, and trust;
6. **5G Internet of Things (5G IoT):** high-speed connectivity between IT and Operational Technology (OT), smart cyber-physical twins;
7. **Drones:** autonomous and semi-autonomous robots and virtual agents
8. **3D Printing:** additive manufacturing.

Extended Reality (XR) technology solutions consist of various combinations of the KETs, using VR, AR, Mixed Reality, and 360° interactive 3D

AR   VR   AI   5G Cloud   Blockchain   5G IoT   Drones   3D Printing

Figure 1.1 The essential eight key enabling technologies. Illustration by: Maxelante Bussemaker.

scanned real world spaces and objects, to provide an interface to interact with remote machines or view 3D computer generated visualizations and simulations, and display augmentations and big data results dynamically, facilitating and facilitated by the other current KETs. XR provides the online 3D communication and interaction space, similar to how AI provides the underlying intelligence for the behaviors of cyber-physical IoT systems, 3D CG spaces, and VR/AR user interactions. XR facilitates the embodiment of the interactions, the space in which the activities are situated, providing a spatial context to the information. While AI has recently been prioritized by many governments and companies, XR has not been prioritized as much yet.

The innovations that the current KETs are predicted to enable are expected to greatly change our local and global societies because they will allow us to optimize the time needed to get things done, and the way we do it, and in the process creating a multi-billion industry. The increased interest can already be witnessed by the plethora of research publications, business reports, and forecasts about the anticipated opportunities of the KETs that have been produced recently and are rapidly increasing in volume [1–23]. The early adopters of novel solutions using XR in combination with AI and IoT will be able to optimize their product or service design via big data analysis using Machine Learning (ML) and this will enable them to gain a rapid advantage [5, 24–27].

These days, advancements in eye and hand-tracking capabilities are built into XR headsets and allow for psychophysiological measurements of the user while interacting with the XR experience. This information is used to analyze customer engagement, and what is more, it can be tested and quantified, thus allowing calculations to measure Return-On-Investment (ROI) to be based on actual time and motion studies with quantitative data [15]. There is clearly a huge potential advantage in being able to save users and institutions time and money, accelerate development processes, measure user engagement to personalize their experience, facilitate communication and collaboration better than a videoconference, and enable a rapid iteration of new business models with increasingly more optimized processes and profitable ROI.

To better understand where funding for future XR applications research and development will be best allocated to facilitate the cutting-edge advantages, the EuroXR Association conducted a consensus survey among global XR experts using the Delphi consensus seeking method. This chapter summarizes the results.

1.2   XR and the Delphi Study Forecast

The Delphi method is an interactive multi-stage forecasting procedure where specific experts identify technical developments and trends in an iterative process to achieve clarification and consensus [28–32]. The method was developed by the RAND Corporation to generate scenarios for long-range strategic planning in the 1950–1960s and became a widely accepted approach to facilitate the development of reliable group opinions using expert panels [33, 34]. It was developed to structure time-consuming group opinion seeking processes, among a set of experts by getting them to participate in a panel, and seek consensus on future developments for complex problems, using participative inquiry that has its roots in humanistic psychology [35]. The Delphi forecast consists of statements formulated by the group of domain experts regarding the topic that is being studied.

A core benefit of the Delphi method is the opportunity to provide domain experts an anonymous place to express different opinions and reach consensus within a structured asynchronous and synchronous text-based information exchange setting. The domain experts express and share views in the group, directly or mediated by the Delphi organizers, depending on the online consensus tool interface and design of the study [36–38]. Since the start of the COVID-19 pandemic, the frequency of use and popularity of using consensus tools via the internet such as online Delphi have risen considerably. The full description of the Delphi study reported here can be found in [39].

The preparation for the Delphi consensus process starts with an open survey to collect topics regarding the theme of the Delphi from the wider forum of experts. These themes provide the basis for the initial forecast statements. The Delphi consensus seeking process itself uses a group of specifically selected participants, a panel of domain experts. The panel of experts is asked to assess and rewrite the statements until they can fully agree with the contents. Typically, for Delphi studies, depending on budget and time available, the consensus seeking rounds are repeated until a minimum of 70% consensus has been achieved for each statement by the panel.

The preparation survey that aims at collecting the starting points for the Delphi statements was distributed via the EuroXR Association (www.euroxr-association.org), the VRISI network (www.vrisi.de), and other international XR professional groups, and many members of these lists forwarded the invitation to their mailing lists, such as the German and the French VR/AR/XR Association. Respondents were invited to nominate themselves for the Delphi XR Expert panel. Eighty-two respondents submitted a response to the online survey; however, of those 82, 40 had to be discarded because they were very incomplete, leaving 42 complete records for our analysis. On average, it took respondents 1 hour to reply to the survey. There were 24 academics in the sample, 18 employed in business, and four of these respondents stated that they were both involved in academia and business. They are from 15 different countries. In the previous waves, they worked 42 years in XR R&D, and there is some visibility of the previous waves of the VR/AR development over the years, as illustrated in the Gartner Hype Cycle [1] in the clusters of respondents' number of years involved in XR R&D; the current influx of newcomers in the field was found. A similar cluster distribution was found in the age brackets in which the respondents fit, showing the normal distribution in age that one would hope and expect for a field that has been in existence for more than 30 years. Forty-one out of forty-two respondents are members of one or more professional XR membership groups. There were 9 women (21%) and 33 men (79%) in the sample, and they are aged between 25 and 75. The original full set of 82 records (before excluding the abandoned/incomplete responses) showed a similar ratio of female/male respondents of 16 females (22.2%) and 58 males (75%) and 2 respondents who preferred not to share their gender information (2.8%)—the latter showing the growing trend of more openness towards non-binary gender orientation, and gender orientation diversity is also reflected in the XR community and the Delphi sample group.

Twelve participants for the Delphi XR expert panel were selected from the anonymized list of self-nominated respondents for the Delphi panel of the first survey, based on the following selection criteria: >35 years old to ensure significant amount of experience in XR, Senior position in their respective organization (e.g., professor, team leader, etc.), active position in academia or industry, actively working in XR, and gender balance 50/50 was attempted by inviting additional female experts.

This Delphi study consisted of two rounds of consensus seeking. For the first round, 43 Delphi statements were prepared based on an exhaustive content analysis of the initial open survey and a literature review, with an estimated time of 1 hour to respond to complete it. Participants were asked to read each of the statements and decide in what way they agree/disagree with them and correct it, if it did not reflect their opinion. The aim of this Round 1 survey was for each participant of the XR panel to rewrite the statements in such a way that it is fully in line with their opinion. The statements were followed by a four-point scale to indicate their agreement with the statement as follows: Strongly Disagree, Disagree, Agree, Strongly Agree, and an open response box asking them to rewrite the statement in case they could not fully agree with it.

The survey was open for 7 days, and reminder emails were sent out with an extension of the deadline by a few days in order to maximize the number of responses. Seven experts responded in total: 7 male and 0 female respondents, working in multiple, diverse, and different areas of the XR R&D field: Industry 4.0 (43%), 3D interaction (14%), Mitigating cybersickness (14%), Optics (14%), Personalized interaction (14%), Virtual tours (14%), XR for business, (14%), XR for training (14%), and XR UXUI (14%).

The statements were initially grouped into four overarching themes relevant to creating a technology roadmap: the market, the enabling environment, human capital, and the innovation ecosystem, further defined as:

- **XR Market:** statements regarding the position of the XR market and statements are related to building XR development skills and awareness for different Technological Readiness Levels (TRL).
- **XR Enabling Environment:** statements regarding leadership in terms of standards for XR R&D.
- **Human XR Capital:** statements regarding building XR development skills and awareness for different TRL.
- **XR Innovation Ecosystem:** statements relating to the XR development platforms: middleware/real-time 3D engines.

Of the 43 statements of Round 1, 28 statements had full consensus, leaving 15 statements with less than 70% consensus to be improved by the expert panel in Round 2. The statements from this first round of consensus seeking and the comments and rewrites from the panel members are reused for the next round of consensus seeking, after a reconciliation of each statement by the Delphi study designers. The reconciliation consists of removing any overlap introduced by the multiple and diverse rewrites from each of the panel members, coordinated by the Delphi study designers.

Round 2 of this Delphi was the final round. During this round, a final effort to find consensus for the 15 statements that were not fully agreed yet was sought, and additionally all statements were analyzed in terms of their importance and urgency. Round 2 closed with a total of 42 statements accepted, and one statement really had the panel divided (R2 Q12, in XR Enabling Environment). During the final round of the Delphi, the statements were weighted by the panel in terms of importance and urgency. In many statements, the respondents already explicitly expressed urgency or priority or strong agreement in the statement, or it was added at the request of one or more of the panel members. To visualize the collective opinions of importance/urgency on the statements the scores placed in colored columns in the tables below:

- Column A: extremely important/totally agree/extremely urgent
- Column B: very important/strongly agree/very urgent
- Column C: important/agree/urgent

1.2.1 XR Market

These are statements regarding the position of XR in the market, and statements are related to building XR development skills and awareness for different TRLs.

XR market statements	A	B	C
1 XR technologies are a strategic source of competitiveness, and their development must be strongly supported. (R2 Q31)	7		
2 Focus on the potential market share in creating 3D asset libraries specific to Industry 4.0 use-cases, to help speed up XR development, because many industry use-cases are early-adopters of high-precision manufacturing using XR Industry 4.0 solutions, and the Industry 4.0 use-case specific 3D assets are expected to become of interest world-wide. (R2 Q9)	5	1	
3 Urgently support the development of industry specific XR Development Asset stores, with high quality shareware assets that are available for developers under a sustainable non-profit business model, crowd-sourced, no-cost, or low-cost. (R2 Q25)	5	1	
4 It may or may not be too late for newcomers to catch up on the global consumer XR input/output device manufacturing market, because there are many big companies producing consumer XR input/output devices, but stakeholders should explore this direction. (R2 Q14)	3	2	1

5 XR developers and stakeholders can capture the market by prioritizing research into XR Customer eXperience (CX) measurements and psychophysiological user behavior data. (R2 Q11)	2	4	
6 With several global companies interested in monetizing users' data, more research into General Data Protection Regulation (GDPR) is needed, specifically regarding protection and regulation of XR users' personal and psychophysiological data, and because the GDPR may not cover all legal aspects; additionally, a complete classification of the psychophysiological data should be made, and this will be especially important for BCI solutions. (R2 Q15)	2	3	1
7 XR technologies are essential for the development and success of Industrial Data and Clouds. (Q48)		7	
8 Facilitate the market uptake of XR applications for healthcare by establishing more flexible rules for experimentations and by creating a funding instrument dedicated to the certification process. (R2 Q19)		6	

Based on these statements, it is clear XR is part of the KETs, has been used in the manufacturing industries for decades, and is now entering many new sectors due to its consumer-grade availability. Consequently, all experts in the Delphi XR panel unanimously and strongly agreed that XR is of strategic importance. It is now important for many areas of industry, business, health, science, and environment, and will be in the future for many more.

With respect to spurring on "supporting" markets and technologies (statements 2, 3, 4), such as input/output devices and 3D assets, the Delphi XR panel experts suggest that newcomers should be prepared to invest heavily to catch up with global developments; otherwise this might be wasted effort, since global XR developments are extremely fast-paced and dynamic in this area. However, there is an opportunity to develop use-case specific tailored solutions for future XR markets.

XR offers serious potentials for multinational companies to intrude on people's privacy and monetization of user data, and could, potentially, cause serious issues with respect to society as a whole (statements 6 and 8). Therefore, the experts feel that regulating the applications of XR is an important task for governments, regulators, and end-users.

1.2.2   XR Enabling Environment

These are statements regarding leadership in terms of regulations, standards, and TRLs of participants and institutes for XR R&D.

XR enabling environment statements	A	B	C
9 Urgently fund R&D and standardization work towards the cybersecurity of XR technologies, especially personal XR devices that are going to be part of the mobile phone. (R2 Q44)	7		
10 Make available and subsidize easily accessible prototyping solutions for R&D and end-user invention support in electronics and optics R&D and testing, including facilities such as publicly accessible design and manufacturing spaces and 3D printing equipment for rapid-prototyping of XR hardware designs by XR end-users, in order to foster diversity in the designs based on real end-user UXUI XR experiences, and enabling an end-user driven evolution in input/output solutions, in a short cycle of human-centered design–implement–test–redesign. (R2 Q23)	3	2	1
11 Support XR R&D for input/output devices that go well beyond the currently developed devices, for instance, climate input/output devices (wind, rain, etc.), olfactory IO devices (providing scents), hand tracking, and use-case specific haptic devices, including standards for these new items. (R2 Q35)		7	
12 Make funds more accessible for facilitating innovation via new XR labs and independent developers by increasing the success rate of proposals and by providing active help and support with the application process. (R2 Q41)		7	
13 Orientate on how to prioritize, support, and facilitate access to state-of-the-art XR technologies for the development of multi-user, remote collaboration XR solutions, as this involves multiple institutes collaborating, coordinating, and doing (their part of) a R&D project together. (R2 Q46)	3	3	1
14 Promote the collection of rules of best practice concerning the licensing of intellectual property rights in the field of XR, covering in particular the amounts of the royalties, the criteria of exclusivity, and the periods of validity, and encourage coordinated, open access to code which has been developed with public funding. (R2 Q20)	3	2	1

15 Create specific funding programs where strategic results (e.g., source code, 3D assets) will be made accessible for free to certain third parties, e.g., SMEs/research institutes, to extend the impact of government-funded progress and enter the market using crowd-sourced testing. (R2 Q24)	3	2	1
16 If the government were to partner with existing commercial XR platform vendors and/or provide subsidized bulk access to commercial XR platforms and assets, then this could create a strong bias in competition depending on the partnership format; however, sharing standard APIs and providing more affordable access to commercial platforms may be beneficial. (R2 Q7)	2	3	1
17 Focus more on preventing the widening of the digital divide by being more inclusive of countries with a low TRL and by coordinating the allocation of XR human capital and XR development resources, in a strategic manner that strengthens leadership and competitiveness in the global XR R&D sector. (R2 Q10)	2	3	1
18 Promote standardization of 3D scene description format, and also for immersive audio, other XR content, and devices. (R2 Q47)	1	6	
19 Finance projects dealing with legal issues in XR technologies. (R2 Q45)		7	
20 Help improve continuation and reuse of outstanding R&D results, help share, and help increase visibility of XR project results. (R2 Q49)		7	
21 New version: Negotiate towards the standardization and open source access of commercial XR SDKs and encourage their adoption in Horizon Europe projects. (R2 Q12b)		4	2

Four XR Panel members preferred the new version of statement 21 (R2 Q12); however, two of them continued to prefer the initial version. One respondent did not reply.

Q12a Old version: [n]egotiate access to the source code of commercial XR SDKs for [..] XR labs and developers.

Research and innovation give us the tools to shape our future and the reality in which we want to live. This notion is reflected in the unanimous agreement of the Delphi panel members that looking towards the envisioned usage scenarios of XR towards 2030, standards and regulations regarding cybersecurity are of the utmost importance and fall directly in the realm of the government (statements 9 and 19). Lacking such regulations, uptake and proliferation of XR as an enabling technology could be seriously hindered.

There is also a strong opinion among the Delphi XR panel experts that investing in radically novel devices and input/output modalities could put the early adopter ahead of the curve (statement 11). Of course, such efforts must be accompanied by researching the respective fundamental principles and algorithms, in terms of human factors, interaction paradigms, physically based interaction, size, weight, and power consumption for each novel use-case.

Another important aspect is the funding process itself: all Delphi XR panel experts are of the opinion that funding processes need to be streamlined, simplified, and—above all—the success rates need to be improved. Otherwise, only research labs and SMEs with a high TRL who already have a wealth of XR tools and resources for proposal writing at their disposal will have success when applying for funding.

1.2.3   Human XR Capital

These are statements regarding building XR development skills and awareness for different Technological Readiness Levels of the XR R&D developers.

Human XR capital statements	A	B	C
22 Create more long-term XR R&D projects to facilitate long-term fundamental research, long-term teamwork, skills exchange, and continuity of XR R&D skills development, especially in the areas that are very cutting-edge for XR technology breakthroughs. (R2 Q32)		7	
23 Promote, subsidize, and facilitate access to state-of-the-art XR equipment for end-users and the general public; it should also help raise awareness and understanding of the possibilities and potentials, and inspire potential start-up ideas, in order to stimulate next generations to include XR technologies in their ideas and innovation proposals. (R2 Q33)		7	

24 Promote the creation of scientific councils in high-tech XR companies and act to facilitate the participation of researchers in these bodies, for example by creating dedicated funding instruments. (R2 Q37)		7	
25 Develop specific support for the optimization of academic-industry collaboration for XR R&D projects because the type of knowledge exchange needed for XR development may affect the success of the collaboration in unknown ways, and improvements could be made in terms of better management of XR researchers' creative capacity, adjustments to the incentives structure, senior management support and strong leadership focused on rapid XR R&D skills development, and more recognition of skills achieved. (R2 Q38)		7	
26 Widely disseminate and promote XR R&D research of best practices for successful XR knowledge-transfer cycles within academic-industry collaborations and focus on how to maximize capacity to absorb the new XR skills and XR project output, and integrate the new XR technology solutions into the value chain. (R2 Q39)		7	
27 Focus more on helping to allocate XR competencies, support mobility of XR experts for international skills exchange, and training of developers at labs and companies for all XR stakeholders, including virtual (pandemic solutions) and real networking events. (R2 Q40)		7	
28 XR solutions will help reduce the time-intensive requirements of building physical prototypes dramatically, bringing ideas and innovations to life and products to market far more quickly, although there is still much improvement needed of the XR development pipeline, the learning curve and time needed, and the number of experts available. (R2 Q50)		7	
29 Finance R&D regarding the detection, measurement, correction, and protection against discrimination of sexual, ethnic, and economic minorities, in the use of XR technologies. (R2 Q18)		6	
30 Prioritize, organize, and subsidize XR developers training and affordable train-the-trainer educational events at all educational levels, to address the current and imminent shortage in skilled XR developers and instructors. (R2 Q22)	2	4	

To advance research and innovate, people, their minds, expertise, knowledge, and skillsets are clearly the most important factor for success. Investment in research and skills development (statements 22, 23, and 27) and transfer of knowledge and skills (statements 24, 25, and 39) are strongly and unanimously recommended by the Delphi XR panel experts. Important ideas here are long-term funding of fundamental research, novel instruments to facilitate smooth flow of information between companies and academia (statement 25), and fostering public understanding of XR technologies.

1.2.4   XR Innovation Ecosystem

These are statements relating to XR Development Platforms: middleware/game-engine.

XR innovation ecosystem statements	A	B	C
31 Urgently promote the development of WebXR technologies. (R2 Q36)	7		
32 To strengthen leadership and competitiveness, more research is urgently needed towards the development and exploitation of B2B applications using XR, more open databases, and more business for the XR field in general. (R2 Q42)	7		
33 Urgently understand/create/adopt worldwide standards and support solutions for low-cost, reusable, interoperability solutions for integrations of domain specific data such as BIM, scientific simulations, etc., and these solutions should be best practices in industrial R&D projects, be independent from the current mainstream XR software companies, and make it as efficient as possible to plug into the currently most used interactive XR platforms. (R2 Q26)	5	1	
34 Foster research into how to make XR technologies and designs more accessible to all diverse user groups, exploring how to include more than the currently targeted market-segment (male, educated, English speaking consumers), making sure that communication is unbiased and checking contents for localization, and using AI to automate adaptations where possible. (R2 Q21)	4	2	

35 Engage and provide full support to startups, SMEs, scale-ups, and manufacturers of XR components, such as Zeiss, Bang & Olufsen, STMicroelectronics, etc., in order to spur on the development of XR devices, since breakthrough innovations generally come out of startups and combinations of parts and components from diverse manufacturers (while those components are expensive), and use market calls for R&D and XR startups, so that market-driven companies and solutions will grow and create breakthrough innovations. (R2 Q28)	4		2
36 Urgently support R&D to expand and improve the XR development pipeline in terms of asset types, complexity of data and ontologies, and to improve interoperability between the different asset formats used in different industries. (R2 Q27)	3	3	
37 Urgently improve the support for XR R&D scaling up of its innovators and SMEs and reduce the currently existing notable scaling-up gap for XR tech scale-ups and unicorn companies (European governments so far offer less in comparison to the United States and China). (R2 Q8)	2	4	
38 Give more support to individual XR startups directly, to bring them into the XR ecosystem and help with commercialization of ideas, help with market entry, and generally make seed money for XR startups more easily accessible. (R2 Q16)	2	4	
39 It is important to fund projects that investigate methods to establish anonymity when using XR technologies, but it should also fund projects to achieve strong identification and authentication in a secure manner in cases where applications need it. (R2 Q17)	2	4	
40 XR technologies have the potential to provide a strong and adequate response to the problem of carbon emissions, by making remote work and interactions between people more efficient, thus reducing the need for personal or professional travel, and developments for solutions into this direction should be prioritized, especially as a response to pandemic-related travel restrictions and precautions. (R2 Q34)		7	
41 Focus the R&D in XR technology in order to establish strategic leadership and competitiveness in the global XR R&D sector: in terms of hardware, the focus should be on human factors, interaction paradigms, ergonomics, customization, form factor, technology vs size, weight, and power consumption, and in terms of software, the focus should be on applications and SW platforms built on top of de facto market standards (IOS, Android). (R2 Q13)		6	

Since the world will become more and more digitally connected, a big theme in this category is the interplay between XR and the internet/WWW (31, Q42, Q26, Q27). This is relevant both for academia as well as industry, and funding should focus on XR standards, data pipelines, cloud storage and edge computing for XR, seamless and fluid switching of devices, settings, and environments.

Europe is a diverse, multicultural, and multi-economic union of nations, and the Delphi XR panel experts recommend expanding funding to level the playing field both for diverse groups of population as well as for diverse nations with highly different economies, and there is a huge difference in market power between the international, global players (such as Google and Facebook) and aspiring start-ups and scale-ups (think David v. Goliath). Governments should urgently help SMEs by simplifying the funding schemes, helping with commercialization efforts.

1.3   Key Enabling R&D Prerequisites, Concerns and Targets

After Round 2 of the Delphi consensus process, a deeper analysis of the statements revealed 6 additional themes that emerged from looking for similarities among statements. In order to further understand the implications of the statements, they were re-examined, analyzed, and grouped according to additional important commonalities, and the following overarching themes were identified: 1) Speed up XR Development, 2) Support XR Research to Market, 3) XR Standardization Concerns, 4) XR Business Concerns, 5) XR & the 17 Sustainable Development Goals, and 6) XR Collaboration and Knowledge exchange, further discussed in the following sections.

1.3.1   Statements on Speeding Up XR Development

These statements (statements 40, 41, 32, 36, 9, 13, 46, 27) prioritized establishing an XR market share, and various suggestions on how to achieve this were made, which are summarized below. Additionally, the statements cover the need for skills development, access to complex XR configurations for R&D, and awareness raising of the possibilities of the new technologies. According to the XR panel of experts, there are three critical areas that need to be addressed to speed up XR development and, thus, stay at the international cutting edge of the technology development:

- Easier and more funding for training, connecting people, and developing competencies in XR; this needs to be done both on the experts' and researchers' level as well as on the students' level.
- Easier access to XR hardware and platforms for educational institutions on all levels.
- Better support for start-ups and scale-ups to enter a highly dynamic and competitive market, better support for researchers to get access to funding, and higher acceptance ratios of proposals to improve success rates and reduce researchers' application time investments.

1.3.2   Statements on Supporting XR Research to Market

There are a number of statements (statements 31, 37, 38, 39, 42, 45, 19, 34, 8, 11, 16, 23) that prioritized concerns for more support for academic-industry knowledge exchange, making XR research results more visible to potential end-users, addressing the legal issues regarding collecting privacy sensitive data via XR UIs, and creating XR end-user UX prototyping facilities. The Delphi XR panel identified two issues that should be addressed to improve the transfer of research into sustainable XR businesses in the market:

- Two-way knowledge and skills exchange between academia and companies should be improved. This could be done, for instance, by funding long-term scientific council boards in companies and by better support for researchers' creative capacities, adjustments to incentive structures, and promotion of best practices for knowledge transfer and XR integration into value chains.
- Fund projects dealing with the multitude of legal issues around XR technologies, which can be a significant barrier to market entrance, especially for SMEs. In particular, legal issues around XR products and research in the health sector should be addressed and simplified by the government, since these can be a real obstacle to innovation in that sector.

1.3.3   Statements on XR Standardization Concerns

In terms of standardization, the XR Panel prioritized concerns regarding XR health and safety standards, cybersecurity, accessibility for all, and interoperability XR development skills training (statements 44, 48, 51, 18, 47, 26, 21, 17, 22). An important step for widespread adoption of XR technologies is standardization. This relates to data exchange standards, facilitating exchange of virtual scenes and communication between XR systems at runtime. It also relates to research into human factors regarding long-term use of XR, which can then be turned into best practices and standards to ensure users' safety and health. Furthermore, standards regarding the security of XR systems and users' data, especially in light of the massive, organized security breaches lately and the massive monetization of user's data, are urgently needed to facilitate widespread adoption of XR.

1.3.4   Statements on XR Business Concerns

There are a number of statements that express the need for business-oriented measures (statements 8, 9, 11, 13, 16, 19, 31, 37, 45, 48). These statements can be grouped in four categories:

- **Regulations:** The government is an effective player for regulations. Regulations can be restrictive for businesses (e.g., experimentation in healthcare), but they can also act as protection for companies with respect to other global players (e.g., legal issues).
- **Strategy:** The role of the government is also to define strategic orientations in order to foster the creation of strong industrial sectors (e.g., Industrial Data and Clouds). There is a need to think broadly (Q48), but also to be aware of the detailed roadmap (statement 41).
- **Funding:** The financing conditions of companies in Europe are less favorable than those in Asia or in the USA. Funding is not only needed for start-ups, but also innovators, high-tech SMEs, scale-ups, and unicorns.
- **Knowledge:** The technology transfer from academic research to business is difficult because of the differences of culture and organization. A legal framework and incentives is needed for mobility between research and industry.

1.3.5   Statements on the 17 Global Sustainable Development Goals

Statements about XR and the 17 Global Sustainable Goals (17 SDGs) were collected in Round 0, 1, and 2 of the Delphi, and the respondents listed a number of XR solutions for the 17 SDGs, because they have a large bearing on global, international goals, and considerations regarding priorities are influenced by the urgency for the solutions for the 17 SDGs. These results are presented in full below.

40 XR technologies have the potential to provide a strong and adequate response to the problem of carbon emissions, by making remote work and interactions between people more efficient, thus reducing the need for personal or professional travel, and research and developments for solutions into this direction should be prioritized, especially as a response to pandemic-related travel restrictions and precautions. (R2 Q34)

41 XR researchers and the government should prioritize XR validation research by systematically mapping out the wide variety of XR use-cases specific to diverse end-users and globally, including commitment to the

17 Global Sustainable Development Goals (17 SDGs), XR health & safety, human factors and ergonomics for long-term use in serious XR applications, and age- and gender-related issues. (R0 Q43)

28 XR solutions will help reduce the time-intensive requirements of building physical prototypes dramatically, bringing ideas and innovations to life and products to market far more quickly, although there is still much improvement needed of the XR development pipeline, the learning curve and time needed to reach proficiency, and the number of experts available. (R2 Q50)

42 What XR developments will help reduce the CO2 emissions by half by 2030 and to neutral by 2050 (R1 Q30):

- Visualizations of consequences of the 17 SDGs risks and strategies,
- Virtual prototyping and testing,
- Virtual access to healthcare, education, work, and colleagues,
- Soft skills and diversity training in XR,
- Empowering low TRL members to leapfrog to 21st century ecological, economic, and social levels,
- Device-less interaction to lower manufacturing of interfaces (reducing the number of materials needed to build them and pollution by less shipping),
- Increase remote meetings and showrooms,
- Educational applications to raise awareness,
- Remote field services, using XR, leveraging remote operations, and reducing the carbon footprint,
- More collaborative applications,

- Immersive training by enhancing quality content development and global deployment using XR to reduce time spent, travel demands, and decreasing after training problems,
- Increase remote training and education with XR experience,
- Develop individual assistance using AI applications (medical, education, etc.),
- Integrate XR applications in transport systems.

XR technologies in conjunction with the other KETs have great potential to realize many of the 17 SDGs. For instance, SDG 3 (Good Health and Well-Being) can be helped through adoption of XR in healthcare, e.g., long-distance, immersive telemedicine to provide health services to rural areas; or by using XR gamification to fight obesity, which is quickly becoming the predominant health risk in industrial countries. For SDG 9 (Industry and Innovation), XR has been and will continue to be an important tool in industry, especially for the development of new products in all phases of the product life cycle. XR will become an increasingly important tool to improve resilience of infrastructure, in particular using telepresence for remote inspection and maintenance (e.g., bridges, pipelines, wind parks, aircraft, etc.). XR will play an important role in pursuing SDG 13 (Climate Action): true, immersive, and interactive telepresence will help reduce the number of business travels substantially. At the same time, it will contribute to SDG 9 by allowing worldwide distributed companies to communicate more efficiently. SDG's 14 (Life below Water) and 15 (Life on Land) will take advantage of XR technologies by creating all kinds of immersive digital twins of ecosystems that will help scientists improve their understanding of those ecosystems; they will also help local authorities to take sustainable decisions; and they will help the general public to better appreciate the value of those ecosystems. XR technologies can help SDG 4 (Quality Education) by providing relatively inexpensive tools for developing countries to leapfrog into modern business and industrial processes.

1.3.6   Statements on Collaboration and Knowledge Exchange

Collaboration is a process that needs to be fostered. On the one hand a multidisciplinary and multicultural team gives a broader view and wider potential pool of ideas from the different team members, across cultures and countries. On the other hand, there may be unfamiliar issues, such as different company or cultural styles of collaboration, or having one shared language that all team members speak sufficiently fluently cannot always be achieved. In addition to that there are different terminologies for different development fields involved. This can create a source of misunderstandings that must be discussed, and solutions put in place in advance. The following statements were recommendations towards addressing the need to develop collaboration success factors quality assurance, as a prerequisite for advancing to the cutting edge of XR developments:

13 Orientate on how to prioritize, support, and facilitate access to state-of-the-art XR technologies for the development of multiuser, remote collaboration XR solutions, as this involves multiple institutes collaborating, coordinating, and doing (their part of) an R&D project together. (R2 Q46)	3	3	1
27 Focus more on helping to allocate XR competencies, support mobility of XR experts for international skills exchange, and training of developers at labs and companies for all XR stakeholders, including virtual (pandemic solutions) and real networking events. (R2 Q40)	7		
26 Widely disseminate and promote XR R&D research of best practices for successful XR knowledge-transfer cycles within academic-industry collaborations and focus on how to maximize capacity to absorb the new XR skills and XR project output, and integrate the new XR technology solutions into the value chain. (R2 Q39)	7		
25 Develop specific support for the optimization of academic-industry collaboration for XR R&D projects, because the type of knowledge exchange needed for XR development may affect the success of the collaboration in unknown ways, and improvements could be made in terms of better management of XR researchers' creative capacity, adjustments to the incentives structure, senior management support and strong leadership focused on rapid XR R&D skills development, and more recognition of skills achieved. (R2 Q38)	7		
22 Create more long-term XR R&D projects to facilitate long-term fundamental research, long-term teamwork, skills exchange, and continuity of XR R&D skills development, especially in the areas that are very cutting-edge for XR technology breakthroughs. (R2 Q32)	7		
12 Make funds more accessible for facilitating innovation via new XR labs and independent developers by increasing the success rate of proposals and by providing active help and support with the application process. (R2 Q41)	7		

In order to address the shortage of XR developers, it is recommended that more is done to be inclusive about access to the new technology information, tools, and education, by creating technology spaces that are open to the general public where anyone with an interest in new technologies, or ideas for XR solutions, can come to explore the latest hardware/software and build a prototype. A recommendation is made to develop free to attend XR knowledge exchange centers, showcasing project results, with workshops and international trainers and knowledge exchange visiting researchers, and knowledge multiplier train-the-trainer workshops. What is more, achieving the synergy of diversity from intercultural knowledge exchange, cross-cultural collaboration, and interdisciplinary innovation success needs to be put first on the agenda, and the results from previous projects should be exhibited to raise TRL awareness for future generations, and study all collaboration and knowledge exchange success factors specific to XR R&D.

1.4   Future Research Agenda and Roadmap

The Delphi XR panel experts were asked to describe the state of XR, in terms of current (i.e., 2021), the near future (i.e., ~2023), 5 years from now (~2025), and ~10 years from now (i.e., ~2030). They suggested a rich collection of future trends on how XR will be used by those milestones; see Table 1.1 for the details. Together these items form an impression of the XR roadmap and research agenda ahead, and the identification of the prerequisites that need to be satisfied to embark on this roadmap and fulfill this research agenda. The prerequisites are summarized and discussed below in terms of explicit roles and responsibilities for the XR research community, the XR business community, and the government and regulatory bodies, respectively. This is followed by an overview of the near-term challenges: funding of high-risk and long-term XR R&D, novel regulations regarding XR usage, novel XR funding instruments, accessibility, and democratization for XR, with a comprehensive overview of the legislation and regulations necessary to clear the path to the future of XR and the XR roadmap envisioned here.

The challenges for the growth of XR for the industry as a whole, and specifically for the XR research community, the SME XR developer and early-adopter community, as well as the government and legislators, can be summarized in terms of roles and responsibilities as follows:

Table 1.1 Timeline for the XR R&D roadmap.

2021	1. Remove the following barriers to XR prototyping: a) Development of competencies in XR necessary. b) More research into making collaborative virtual environments usable. c) Standardization in the use of XR needed: virtual menus, functional buttons in devices such as joysticks, interaction with devices, etc. d) Access to public and private immersive labs and equipment at large scale needed. e) Interoperability improvements. f) Full replacement of the current engineering pipeline needed. 2. Inclusiveness of XR technologies and how XR could improve life quality, 3. Develop XR devices with **humanitarian** standards, 4. Increase IA in the development of new applications, 5. Support data communications platforms (data centers, satellites, and fiber) to transport information with security survey and best transportation of data, 6. Research in HCI and Human Factors topics, which require working with users, which has been banned for more than one year, 7. Field Services as massive adoption and training to enhance even more the use of XR, 8. Industrial applications and training, 9. Tele-existence, Remote collaboration.
2023	Huge investment needed from EC and nationally for XR R&D and manufacturing of: 1. HMD display hardware solutions, without cables, stand-alone (Wi-Fi to cloud). 2. XR-UI gesture-driven and specific use-cases for BCI-driven solutions for fully inclusive Accessibility. 3. Shared, accessible API-Open source XR development platform, 4. Cheap and easy access to XR development tools (and training?), 5. Continuous transfer of deployable apps from project demonstrators. 6. Integration of XR with CS, Human–Computer Interaction, Maths, Psycho-neuroscience, and Social Science. 7. Automatic content creation for XR solutions combinations of AI and IoT for support of the XR developer's work of professional applications. 8. XR content for interactive movies and remote presence and interactions,

(Continued)

Table 1.1 Timeline for the XR R&D roadmap. (*Continued*)

		9. Non-intrusive UI solutions, Multi-sensory UI solutions, gesture-based solutions, ultra-realistic haptic bodysuit, 10. XR data computed in the cloud. 11. Earth-wide system with XR HMDs tracked for collaboration between systems. 12. Increase our knowledge of Human Factors issues of XR, integrations of XR with HCI best practices.

	2025	1. Finding solutions for hardware challenges posed by ubiquitous XR for head mounted displays (XR-HMDs) is prioritized.
		2. XR and AI integrations need to take place by developing a deep link between XR, AI, ML, CS, HCI, Math, Psycho-Neuroscience, and Social Science, and by resolving the ethical issues. Using AI to:
		  a) Automate decisions, while promoting user-centered decision-making, completing the XR experience by simplifying selected tasks,
		  b) Improve the form factor and usability of the XR devices and support correct modeling,
		  c) Speed up content creation via non-intrusive UI solutions, including automatic BCI-XR content creation,
		  d) Highly usable, safe professional use cases, interactive movies, and remote presence apps (tourism, etc.),
		  e) Integrated academic-industry commercialization of XR research and development results.
		3. Technology breakthroughs are needed for:
		  a) Hardware solutions for XR head mounted displays (XR-HMDs),
		  b) Multi-sensory devices that simplify body tracking, non-intrusive devices that collect UI, information less intrusive and less cumbersome to use than ultra-realistic haptic bodysuit UI solutions,
		  c) XR content creation via experimental BCI and novel HCI solutions,
		  d) XR-UI via experimental BCI and novel HCI solutions.

	2030	1. XR and AI will be combined to create an intelligent, human-centered, harmonious experience and tool for humans 2. The essential public debate around personalization and privacy concerns is better understood; good efforts to clarify the advantages to the user, solutions of user-centric opt-in/out of personal data-collection are available at various levels and are generally accepted. 3. XR apps will be deployed on smartphones much more than today, seamlessly integrated with sophisticated (physiological) sensors and other electronic devices, enabling new communication solutions for work and social life.

(*Continued*)

Table 1.1 Timeline for the XR R&D roadmap. (*Continued*)

4. Personal XR devices that will be fully connected to our smartphones and complement the use of it.
5. Developments are underway for devices that replace the smartphone, which will be even more ubiquitous in use than smartphones, for work and social life as they are less intrusive, and more comfortable and lightweight, dedicated to specialized applications.
6. Multi-sensory XR (haptics, sound, smell, and taste) with automatic body and gesture tracking by cameras will be developed.
7. Multi-sensory, haptic body suits, with high-resolution, automatically created avatars adapted to the anthropomorphic parameters of the user.
8. The user interface will be predominantly driven by markerless, camera-based tracking of gestures, body, and eyes. This will utilize cameras that are either integrated directly in the headsets or distributed throughout rooms or workspaces to allow for larger and more precise tracking.
9. Developments are rapidly advancing for thought-driven UIs (brain–computer interfaces).
10. Regulations protecting privacy, minorities, and ethics with regards to XR as a whole and brain–computer interfaces are in place.
11. Business models to deploy XR in various application areas have been proven successfully, many more business models are emerging, and further systematic efforts to establish business models in more application areas are underway.
12. XR apps for professional use will be widely available and widely in use. Manufacturing industries (the forerunners) continue to use all types of XR and have XR integrated well into their development workflows. Other sectors, e.g., health and medicine, inspection and maintenance, autonomous and remote driving, and many more have adopted XR.
13. Telepresence and virtual collaboration in common virtual spaces are being taken up by many industries.
14. Telemedicine (for general physicians) and teleconsultation (in the operating room) will be feasible and accepted by both professionals and citizens.
15. XR movies have matured but will remain a niche market.
16. Videogames, home remodeling using VR/AR, and first-person XR visits to remote places (virtual tourism) are dominating the consumer market.

1.4.1   XR Research Community Roles and Responsibilities

- Improve transfer of technology from research to market. It is still not efficient enough and too many startups still fail for lack of sufficient incubation periods and guidance.
- Improve collaboration between academia and industry outside of funded projects; review the incentives for industry to engage in such collaboration.
- Engage large industrial players in XR technologies.
- Lobby for improvements and a higher success rate of XR R&D project proposals, and support for the complex application process.
- Lobby for better understanding for the need for long-term funding for high-risk, fundamental research
- Lobby to change the mindset regarding the fact that failure of research projects is not an option.
- Lobby for multinational long-term funding.

1.4.2   XR Business Community Roles and Responsibilities

- Improve the difficult access to seed money for startups.
- Improve the lack of scale-up funding.
- Coordinate and initiate base technologies (hardware and software) for XR R&D that are currently not being developed yet.
- Lobby to improve the regulations and bureaucracy, which hamper business development.
- Develop a strong cloud solution including storage and compute services.
- Lobby to improve the rigid rules for experimentations in healthcare, and the issues regarding the certification process that is different for each country.

1.4.3   Legislative and Government Bodies Roles and Responsibilities

- Increase funds necessary for seed money for startups.
- Increase funds necessary for scale-up funding.
- Improve current regulations and bureaucracy that are hampering business development with XR solutions.

- Foster and finance strong leadership for the development of a digital platform for XR, big data analytics, and R&D needs.
- Review the healthcare solutions with XR and other KET solutions that are being slowed down by rigid rules for experimentations in healthcare, and by a complex certification process.

1.5   Near-Term Challenges

The main findings of our XR roadmap in terms of near-term future challenges can be summarized as follows: there are four priority areas to act upon, in order to remain at the cutting edge of XR R&D and have this Key Enabling Technology at disposal throughout industry and society. These four priority areas are: 1) Funding of high-risk and long-term XR R&D technologies, 2) Novel regulations regarding XR Usage, 3) Novel XR funding instruments, and 4) Accessibility and Democratization for XR R&D. These four priority areas are further described below.

1.5.1   Funding of High-Risk and Long-Term XR R&D Technologies

1) The race towards the ultimate XR display is still going on; while the US and Japan are currently ahead of Europe in that area, it is still not too late for newcomers to enter this market. However, massive investment in R&D is needed to develop novel display technologies and bring the newcomers ahead of the current contenders. There are many opportunities to do so: light field displays, super-high resolutions, combining headsets with 5G, integrated systems combining display with cameras with computer, light-weight form factors, etc.

2) Research into natural user interfaces (NUIs), especially camera-based, both for mobile XR as well as room-sized XR applications. Such NUIs will usually involve physically based simulation of the interactions among virtual objects.

3) R&D into collaborative XR applications, both collocated as well as remote; this includes telepresence, telemedicine, remote driving, and many more; this also requires fundamental research into data compression, latency mitigation, and dynamically updating avatars.

4) Other modalities are still under-researched, such as audio, haptics and force-feedback, sound synthesis, temperature, and airflow. This should be tackled on the level of both hardware and algorithms.

5) In order to break free from dependency on specific commercial providers of software platforms, invest in development of open-source software platforms. There exist promising candidates already. Such new software platforms (game engines/real-time engines) should adhere to established standards (e.g., OpenXR) proposed by international standard developing organizations such as the Khronos group.

6) Since virtual and augmented technologies are directly associated with spatial computing, it is natural that XR will play an important role in the exploration, visualization, and interaction with digital twins. This is already being done in the manufacturing industries for developing new prototypes, but it can and should be utilized in many other digital twins.

1.5.2   Novel Regulations Regarding XR Usage

1) GDPR for XR: Privacy and security could be seriously breached by providers of XR technologies on all levels, utilizing AI in combination with eye-tracking, user-behavior, and many other physiological factors. The government is called upon to establish clear regulations that will prevent that from happening without users' explicit consent.

2) Regulations should be established that will allow for worldwide research and deployment of XR applications in healthcare and medicine, without going through all national regulatory bodies, or at least that should be greatly simplified. Otherwise, companies will first target markets where regulations are straightforward, and probably move their business to those locations altogether.

3) In the long term, when XR will have become an everyday tool, regulations should be devised that ensure our humanitarian values of protection against discrimination of sexual, ethnic, religious, and economic minorities.

1.5.3   Novel XR Funding Instruments

1) Provide more funding instruments for long-term, multinational projects. There are already many opportunities for multinational funding, which is good, but none of them are really long term.

2) Create better incentives for industry and businesses to engage in high-risk projects together with academia; so far, companies are not willing to engage in high-risk projects that might, by definition, fail; also, researchers in academia are unwilling to take risks in funded projects, since that would jeopardize their funding contracts.

3) Create funding instruments that will level the playing field for all countries in international collaborations, for the long-term future. So far, it is pretty much impossible for countries with lower technological standards to catch up with the richer countries.

4) In order to foster exchange of ideas between academia and industry/businesses, there should be funding or other incentives for companies to bring experts from academia into advisory boards or other consulting roles for long periods of time.

5) There should be funding schemes [in Europe between the FET-type and the RIA-type], for XR R&D, which might not have commercial application areas until 5–10 years later.

6) Funding schemes are needed that help startups and scale-ups to enter the market and establish a user base; especially mid-term to long-term focus is needed to compete with Chinese competitors.

1.5.4   Accessibility and Democratization for XR R&D

For XR technologies to go mainstream, advances in hardware, software, novel developer partnerships, and democratic access to the latest XR technology solution for researchers and developers together with representative end-users are vital. However, for many countries and communities, XR developers face serious barriers to developing prototypes: lack of access to the R&D tools, prototyping centers, education, startup opportunities, and resources that many cannot afford [40]. Democratization of XR R&D access means improving support for development of XR ideas, commercialization plans, and venture capital. The following areas, identified through the Delphi study as well as supported by the literature review, need to be addressed:

1) Low Technological Readiness Level (TRL) becomes a bottleneck in the ability to take advantage of XR to drive innovations of product, production, and business models, risking that the digital divide grows wider even faster.

2) The skills gap to perform and expand XR R&D exists to different degrees, not only in XR but also for all Key Emerging Technologies. This has two dimensions: a quantitative one (overall dearth in supply compared to demand) and a qualitative one (mismatch in skills supply and demand) [9, 41]. Consequently, a strategic plan is needed to foster XR skillsets on all levels, from beginner through to highly specialized experts, and in a multitude of different sub-areas, ranging from hardware to fundamental XR algorithms and methodologies, to XR software platforms (e.g., game engines) to vertical applications markets.

3) Many universities have already begun to integrate some XR courses in their curricula, but complete study programs are still rare, and resources, both teaching staff and student labs, are scarce. Online XR training could be a solution, but only to a point, because of the high costs associated with the equipment and software, and the complexity of the R&D XR pipeline, made more difficult by the rapid changes in the development tools. Teaching using XR technologies itself is helpful in closing the gap [2, 14] and essential to support non-XR educators who want to use XR in their curriculum. The need for XR tech support is similar to how network and system administration support became an important and vital service when the PC went mainstream, and XR tech expertise will be an important and crucial skill for jobs and employment in the future.

4) The availability of skilled XR developers is obviously a prerequisite for companies and countries to get to or stay at the cutting edge of the XR technology R&D. Especially with fast-paced, highly innovative areas like XR, governments should support educational institutes to provide XR R&D educations as part of life-long learning and knowledge exchange opportunities [41].

5) Accessibility for all, diversity, and inclusion for XR users and XR developers are important topics because XR has the potential to include people with disabilities, to assist and employ them in ways that have not been possible before. There are a range of disabilities that will need to be considered in making XR accessible, such as auditory, cognitive, neurological, physical, speech, and visual diversities. Understanding XR itself presents various challenges that are technical. To add to this, many designers and authors may neither know nor have access to people with disabilities for usability testing and may not have ways of understanding accessibility-related user needs to create requirements from. To make accessible XR experiences and development tools for all, there is a need to understand XR interaction design principles, accessibility semantics, and assistive technologies, which all represent "basic" complexities, as well as understand exactly what type of diversity user needs need to be met [42].

6) Global and local governments and regulatory bodies should provide legal support and guidance so that users' GDPR rights, their privacy, and the exploitation of users' behavior are managed according to humanitarian standards. Even today, users could potentially be identified uniquely based on their IP address, eye gaze tracking, and many other psycho-physiological measurements (e.g., heart rate, pupil dilation, etc.). All these data could be utilized to the advantage of the users and XR skills development; however, there are also serious potential ethical, legal, and societal implications, such as security and privacy, targeted advertising, manipulation using fake information, monetization, and many more [25].

7) The government should investigate the addictive potential of XR, especially among the young and adolescent generations, and provide appropriate regulations and the development of dedicated institutes for support and treatment, to protect these groups.

8) Overall, there is the need for scientists from all areas to embrace XR technologies as a tool and to reach out to XR researchers to form interdisciplinary collaborations. Cultural barriers are often cited as inhibiting factors to successful collaboration and different organizational cultures resulting in a mismatch between business and university strategy, time scale, expectations, failure to agree on IP terms, and contrasting

views on liabilities. It is important to consider the invisible costs of knowledge transfer in the international cross-cultural setting. The government needs to foster such cross-cultural interdisciplinary collaborations through suitable measures included in the funding programs and stimulate fundamental further research into how to take cross-cultural business and academia knowledge transfer issues into account and provide solutions for any potential barriers, including those originating from cross-disciplinary cultural differences and business and academia cultural differences.

9) Interdisciplinary efforts between XR researchers and researchers from other areas should also be created to help the cause of the 17 Sustainable Development Goals. This can be spurred on by the government by developing appropriate funding programs specifically targeted at such collaborations and by including XR in funding programs targeted at the 17 SDGs.

In conclusion, XR has the potential to transform our societies and the workplace in almost all areas of communication, personal life, business, and industry. Especially when XR is blended and combined with AI, robotics, and 5G, it could become a disruptive technology transforming government, science, industry, and leisure. The government and all stakeholders are called upon to ensure this is to the benefit of all humankind.

Acknowledgments

This Delphi study was made possible by funding from the EuroXR Association, and the help of many volunteers, including the respondents to the surveys and the members of the Delphi XR Panel and the analysis team. The authors thank everyone for sharing their valuable time, important professional expertise, interesting insights, and efforts to respond to the surveys.

References

1. Fenn, J. and Linden, A., *Gartner's Hype Cycle Special Report for 2005*, Gartner, Inc, USA, 2005. https://www.gartner.com/en/documents/484424/gartner-s-hype-cycle-special-report-for-2005, ID: G00130115.

2. Davies, A., Fidler, D., Gorbis, M., *Future Work Skills 2020*, Institute for the Future for the university of Phoenix Research Institute, USA, 2011, https://www.iftf.org/uploads/media/SR-1382A_UPRI_future_work_skills_sm.pdf

3. Baciu, C., Opre, D., Riley, S., New way of thinking in the era of virtual reality and artificial intelligence working paper, 2016. DOI: 10.13140/ RG.2.1.3986.6483, retrieved from: https://www.researchgate.net/publication/ 303818717_A_New_Way_of_Thinking_in_the_Era_of_Virtual_Reality_ and_Artificial_Intelligence.

4. Schwab, K., *The Fourth Industrial Revolution*, World Economic Forum (WEF), 2016.

5. Schwab, K. and Davis, N., *Shaping the Future of the Fourth Industrial Revolution: A Guide To Building A Better World*, World Economic Forum (WEF), Penguin House, USA, 2018.

6. Schwab, K. and Zahidi, S., *The Global Competitiveness Report: How Countries Are Performing On The Road To Recovery, Special Edition 2020*, World Economic Forum, Switzerland, 2020. https://www.weforum.org/reports/ the-global-competitiveness-report-2020.

7. Bezegova, E., Ledgard, M.A., Molemaker, R., Oberc, B.P., Vigkos, A., *Virtual Reality And Its Potential For Europe*, ECORYS, Brussels, Belgium, 2017, https://xra.org/wp-content/uploads/2020/07/rs-vr-potential-europe-01.pdf.

8. Hall, S. and Takahashi, R., Augmented and virtual reality: the promise and peril of immersive technologies, in: *McKinsey Report*, 2017, https://www. mckinsey.com/industries/technology-media-and-telecommunications/ our-insights/augmented-and-virtual-reality-the-promise-and-peril-of- immersive-technologies.

9. Armstrong, K., Parmelee, M., Santifort, S., Koziol, K., Greenberg, R., Schwartz, J., Tetrick, R., *Preparing Tomorrow's Workforce For The Fourth Industrial Revolution For Business: A Framework For Action*, Deloitte Global & The Global Business Coalition for Education, 2018. https://www2.deloitte. com/content/dam/Deloitte/global/Documents/About-Deloitte/gx-prepar- ing-tomorrow-workforce-for-4IR.pdf.

10. Hadwick, A., *VRX XR Industry Insight Report 2019-2020*, vr-intelligence, 2019, https://s3.amazonaws.com/media.mediapost.com/uploads/VRXindustryreport. pdf.

11. NEXT-NET, Next horizons for European supply chains: strategic research and innovation agenda. *NEXT-NET Consortium, European Commission, Horizon 2020*, 2019.

12. Capgemini, Augmented and virtual reality in operations: a guide to invest- ments, Capgemini Research Institute, research report, p. 1, 2019. https://www. capgemini.com/wp-content/uploads/2018/09/AR-VR-in-Operations1.pdf.

13. Accenture, *Waking Up To A New Reality: Building A Responsible Future For Immersive Technologies*, G20, Young Entrepreneurs Alliance (YEA, 2020), https://www.accenture.com/_acnmedia/Accenture/Redesign-Assets/ DotCom/Documents/Global/1/Accenture-G20-YEA-report.pdf.

14. Bucea-Manea-Tonis, R., Bucea-Manea-Tonis, R., Simion, V.E., Ilic, D., Braicu, C., Manea, N., Sustainability in higher education: the relationship between work-life balance and XR e-learning facilities. *Sustainability*, 12, 5872, 2020. doi:10.3390/su12145872, https://www.mdpi.com/2071-1050/12/14/5872.

15. Coltekin, A., Lochhead, I., Madden, M., Christophe, S., Devaux, A., Pettit, C., Lock, O., Shukia, S., Herman, L., Stachon, Z., Kubicek, P., Snopkova, D., Bernardes, S., Hedley, N., Extended reality in spatial sciences: a review of research challenges and future directions. *ISPRS Int. J. Geoinf.*, 9, 439, 2020. doi: 10.3390/ijgi9070439, https://www.mdpi.com/2220-9964/9/7/439/pdf.

16. Doolani, S., Wessels, C., Kanal, V., Sevastopoulos, C., Jaiswal, A., Nambiappan, H., Makedon, F., A review of extended reality (XR) technologies for manufacturing training. *J. Technol.*, 8, 77, 2020.

17. Schreer, O., Pelivan, I., Kauff, P., Schäfer, R., Hilsmann, A., Chojecki, P., Koch, T., Wiegratz, R., Royan, J., Deschanel, M., Murienne, A., Launay, L., Verly, J., D4.1: Revised landscape report, final report "extended reality for all". *XR4ALL Consortium*, 2020.

18. Qualcomm, *The Mobile Future of Extended Reality (XR)*, Qualcomm Technologies, Inc, USA, 2020. https://www.qualcomm.com/documents/mobile-future-extended-reality-xr.

19. Kallman, A., XR in today's reality. *Integrated Systems Europe*, 2021, https://www.iseurope.org/the-big-read-xr-in-todays-reality/.

20. Lee, M.J.W., Georgieva, M., Alexander, B., Craig, E., Richter, J., *State of XR & Immersive Learning Outlook Report 2021*, ISBN: 978-1-7348995-1-1 Immersive Learning Research Network, Walnut, CA, 2021.

21. XR association, A new reality in immersive technology (XR): insights and industry trends, research report, XR Association (XRA), Washington, USA, 2021. https://xra.org/research/a-new-reality-inimmersive-technology-xr-insights-and-industry-trends/.

22. Ziker, C., Truman, B., Dodds, H., Cross reality (XR): challenges and opportunities across the spectrum, in: *Innovative Environments In STEM Higher Education*, *Springerbriefs In Statistics*, Ryoo, J. and Winkelmann, K. (Eds.), 2021.

23. Luigies, R. and van den Hurk, K., VR4REHAB innovation blueprint, interreg North-West Europe programme, Research report, 2021, https://docplayer.net/215521416-Vr4rehab-innovation-blueprint.html.

24. Fernandez-Matias, E. and Eurofound, *Automation, Digitisation And Platforms: Implications For Work And Employment*, Publications Office of the European Union, Luxembourg, 2018, https://www.eurofound.europa.eu/sites/default/files/ef_publication/field_ef_document/ef18002en.pdf.

25. Müller, J., *Enabling Technologies For Industry 5.0: Results Of A Workshop With Europe's Technology Leaders*, European Commission, ISBN 978-92-76-22048-0, Luxembourg, 2020, doi: 10.2777/082634.

26. Butt, J., A strategic roadmap for the manufacturing industry to implement industry 4.0. *Designs*, 4, 11, 2020. doi : 10.3390/designs4020011.

27. Peruffo, E., Rodriguez Contreras, R., Mandl, I., Bisello, M., *Game-Changing Technologies: Transforming Production And Employment In Europe*, Eurofound Office of the European Union, Luxembourg, 2020.

28. Gelernter, D., Abelson, J., Forest, P.G., Eylesa, J., Smith, P., Martin, E., Gauvin, F.P., Deliberations about deliberative methods: issues in the design and

evaluation of public participation processes. *Soc Sci. Med.*, V57, p239–251, 2003.

29. Keeney, S., Hasson, F., McKenna, H., *The Delphi Technique In Nursing And Health Research*, Wiley-Blackwell, John Wiley & Sons, USA, 2011.

30. Landeta, J. and Barrutia, J., People consultation to construct the future: a Delphi application. *Int. J. Forecast.*, 27, 1, 134–151, 2011.

31. Förster, B. and Gracht, H.A., Assessing Delphi panel composition for strategic foresight — a comparison of panels based on company-internal and external participants. *Technol. Forecast. Soc Change*, ISSN-e 1873-5509, Vol. 84, 1, 215–229, 20142014.

32. Kezar, A. and Maxey, D., The Delphi technique: an untapped approach of participatory research. *Int. J. Soc Res. Methodol.*, Routledge, United Kingdom, 19, 2, 143–160, 2016. http://dx.doi.org/10.1080/13645579.2014.936737.

33. Helmer-Hirschberg, O., *Analysis Of The Future: The Delphi Method*, RAND Corporation, USA, 1967, https://www.rand.org/pubs/papers/P3558.html.

34. van Bracht, R., Piller, F., Kleer, D., Predicting the future of additive manufacturing: A Delphi study on economic and societal implications of 3D printing for 2030. *Technol. Forecast. Soc Change*, 117, 2, January 2017. DOI: 10.1016/j.techfore.2017.01.006.

35. Reason, P., Three approaches to participative inquiry, in: *Handbook Of Qualitative Research*, N.K. Denzin and Y.S. Lincoln (Eds.), pp. 324–339, Sage, Thousand Oaks, 1994.

36. Goluchowicza, K. and Blind, K., Identification of future fields of standardisation: an explorative application of the Delphi methodology. *Technol. Forecast. Soc Change*, 78, 9, 1526–1541, November 2011. doi.org/10.1016/j.techfore.2011.04.014, https://isiarticles.com/bundles/Article/pre/pdf/1037.pdf.

37. Aengenheyster, S., Cuhls, K., Gerhold, L., Heiskanen-Schüttler, M., Huck, J., Muszynska, M., Real-time Delphi in practice — a comparative analysis of existing software-based tools. *Technol. Forecast. Soc Change*, 118, C, 15–27, 2017.

38. Conea, C. and Unnib, A., Achieving consensus using a modified. Delphi technique embedded in Lewin's change management model designed to improve faculty satisfaction in a pharmacy school. *Res. Soc Admin. Pharm.*, 16, 12, 1711–1717, December 2020, doi: 10.1016/j.sapharm.2020.02.007. Epub 2020 Feb 19.

39. Tromp, J.G., Perret, J., Zachmann, G., Palacco, B., *EuroXR Delphi Report*, Euro XR Association, Brussels, Belgium, May 2021.

40. Crisanti, A., Pavlova, E., Krantz, J., *The VC Factor: Data-Driven Insights About VC-Backed Start-Ups In Europe*, Invest Europe, Luxembourg, 2015.

41. Butter, M., Hartmann, C., Gijsbers, G., de., M., Horizon 2020: key enabling technologies (KETs), booster for European leadership in the manufacturing sector, in: *Directorate-General For Internal Policies, Policy Department A, Economic and Scientific Policy*, 2014Study for the ITRE Committee, 2014.

42. XR accessibility user requirements W3C working group note 25, research report, World Wide Web Consortium (W3C), international working group, August 2021, 2021. https://www.w3.org/TR/xaur/.

Digital Narratives in Extended Realities

**Luis Emilio Bruni*, Nele Kadastik, Thomas Anthony Pedersen
and Hossein Dini**

*Augmented Cognition Lab, Department of Architecture, Design and Media Technology,
Aalborg University, Aalborg, Denmark*

Abstract

XR technologies are increasingly considered as expressive media with special qualities for narrative representation. In this chapter, we chart some of the major challenges inherent in the implementation of digital narratives in XR. For this purpose, we consider the intersections between different research domains like classical and post-structural narratology, cognitive narratology, literary studies, computer science, game research, cognitive science, and particularly interactive digital narratives (IDN) and storytelling. As with IDN, many of the challenges of implementing narratives in XR have to do with the trade-offs between interactivity and immersion. In this direction, we aim to contribute to the bridging between the IDN and XR research domains. We elaborate on specific issues in IDN that may require particular care in XR, such as agency, embodiment, narration, "point of view technologies," artificial agents, and AI. Additionally, we provide examples of different application domains in games, serious games, cultural experiences, healthcare, and immersive journalism. To conclude, we highlight the eminent role of narrative cognition in XR and suggest a roadmap for combining XR technologies, cognitive sciences, advanced biometric signals processing, and storytelling techniques for investigating ways we interact cognitively with stories and the effects of XR narratives on the human emotional-cognitive system.

Keywords: Extended realities, interactive digital narratives, storytelling, immersion, interactivity, narrative cognition

---

**Corresponding author*: leb@create.aau.dk

Mariano Alcañiz, Marco Sacco and Jolanda G. Tromp (eds.) Roadmapping Extended Reality: Fundamentals and Applications, (35–62) © 2022 Scrivener Publishing LLC

2.1   Introduction

When speaking about the expressive and representational potential of XR technologies, in its many domains of application, it is of the utmost importance to address the central role of narrative in these new kinds of media platforms and technologies. In an attempt to chart the major challenges to the implementation of digital narratives in XR, it is necessary to consider the intersections of different research domains like classical and post-structural narratology, interactive digital narratives (IDN), interactive digital storytelling (IDS), cognitive narratology, literary studies, computer science, game research, and, of course, XR research more generally.

As a discipline, "Narratology" is a fairly recent academic endeavor; however, the term is retrospectively applied to works that can be traced as far back to Aristotle. Thus, narratives have been implicit all along the history of humankind as a central element for the construction of individual and collective meanings. In the last four decades, narratology has increasingly moved from mainly concerning itself with the structure of written literary fiction towards including narratives within the range of other disciplines such as psychology, cognitive sciences, communication studies, and pedagogics. This has meant that while in the past narrative was seen as predominantly concerned with communicating fiction and stories, today narrative is widely considered as a fundamental cognitive mode for organizing human experience [1–7]. This turn has many implications for the development of XR; both as a medium for narrative representation and for XR experiences in general. In other words, XR technologies are becoming privileged media for new kinds of narrative representation, and at the same time, the "narrative cognitive mode" is becoming a suitable framework for investigating user experience in immersive simulations [8].

In the last two decades, the challenges of narratives in digital media have been debated as a trade-off between immersion and interactivity, or between author control over the narrative and "user agency." These are two faces of the same coin, which have to do with how the possibilities for interaction may interrupt the "flow" of being immersed in a narrative world, or how the agency afforded to the audience can compromise the coherence of the narrative intended by the author. This issue has been widely discussed in IDN as the "narrative paradox" [9–12]. However, it is important to notice that the term "immersion" has a wider range of connotations in IDN than in the XR domain. In the former, it has come to mean more specifically "narrative immersion," that is, how do we get involved with the story and its world (including but not limited to its perceptual and spatial aspects). This puts the notion of immersion in relation with terms such as engagement, imaginative involvement, suspension of disbelief, emotional response, and suspense. On the other hand, in the XR domain, immersion has been mostly considered from the technological, spatial, and perceptual point of view, establishing a difference between the psychological and perceptual aspects of "presence" and the immersive qualities of the technology [13].

As we will see, the major challenges of narratives in the XR domain still have to do with interactivity, immersion, and their trade-offs. It turns out that many discussions in IDN also apply to, and are relevant for, narratives in XR. However, it is also important to point out that not all digital narratives in XR are or need to be interactive. Furthermore, there may be certain issues of IDN that are specific to XR implementations and thus require particular care in this regard. It is therefore a goal of this chapter to stimulate the bridge between these two domains of research.

2.2   XR and Interactive Digital Narratives (IDN)

Koenitz et al. [14] have identified three non-mutually exclusive "evolutionary trajectories" in the advent of interactive digital narratives. The first trajectory, based on text, originates in the 1960s and has evolved through (text-based) fiction games in the 1970s to Hypertext Fiction in the early 1990s. The second trajectory has more emphasis on the audio-visual dimension that leads, for example, to interactive movies, multilinear TV shows, and experimental art installations. The third trajectory includes complex narrative designs that take advantage of the innovative potential of technological advances that increase multimodal representational possibilities, AI capabilities, and the increase in storage and processing capacity. This latter trajectory not only encompasses video games, and the most sophisticated audiovisual IDNs, but certainly also includes the rapidly expanding possibilities of the whole range of XR technologies.

Perhaps the first important distinction that needs to be made for narratives, regarding interactive media such as XR, is the distinction between "linear" and "nonlinear" narratives. The former refers to an uninterrupted, or continuous, delivery of narrative material in a given medium where the author controls the order in which the events, or blocks of information, are presented to the audience. On the other hand, in the case of "nonlinear" narratives, this order can be altered by introducing interactive elements that allow the user (or audience) to make choices, or take actions, which may influence the linear organization of those events. Even though interactivity in narratives is not a phenomenon that arose exclusively with the advent of digital technologies, it has been widely recognized (especially in the field of IDN) how digital technologies have taken the possibilities of interactive narratives into a new level [15, 16]. This is particularly pertinent to XR, as industry and labs around the world continue to develop sophisticated interface technologies for mixing the real and the virtual in innovative ways—exploring a multiplicity of multimodal displays, interactive affordances, and possibilities for embodiment and disembodiment. This is giving rise to new "post- symbolic" languages that incorporate gestures, emotions, and even cognitive processes (as, e.g., in BCI). As claimed by Knoller and Ben-Arie [17], this trajectory of increasingly rich interfaces calls for a reexamination of the IDN's heritage and current practice in relation to these new developments, as these technological platforms provide new multimodal and interactive modes for meaning-making [18].

2.2.1   Interactivity

When considering XR technologies as narrative media, the interaction between the user and the virtual world changes the role of the users from external observers of images to active participants within a virtual world [19]. The wide range of opportunities for interactivity in XR poses many challenges to the representation of intelligible and coherent narratives—as it has been the case in IDN when granting the user large amounts of freedom to explore the virtual world and interact with the story through the many different kinds of affordances. Even though narratives in XR can be considered as a specific case of IDN, relatively little research has been done to investigate narrative structures and implementations associated with IDN in XR [20].

   In this regard, it is important to consider the distinction between the interactivity inherent to the medium and the interactivity of the narrative itself [15]. The former consists of all the affordances and technological support that the given platform can provide (e.g., haptic devices, tracking technologies, programmable features, AI, etc.). The latter—the interactivity intrinsic to the "work" itself—has to do with designing and creating a narrative that can use those technological affordances, which in turn empower the user to influence the linear representation of the narrative in such a medium. As Ryan [15] claims, all interactive narratives require a reasonably interactive medium, but not all interactive media necessarily mediate narratives.

   From a technical (i.e., non-narrative) perspective, the interactivity of the XR medium can be generally described by three different types of "physical" interactions possible in a virtual or mixed environment: Viewpoint Motion Control (or travel), Selection, and Manipulation [19–23]. Viewpoint Motion Control refers to the ability of the user to translate and rotate the point of view (sometimes referred to as "point-of-view" technologies, or more generally, tracking technologies). Selection has to do with the ability to purposefully select objects in the virtual or mixed environment. Finally, Manipulation regards actual interaction with selected objects in such environments, e.g., the ability to pick up, rotate, examine, move, open, etc., including locomotion and self-body perception. Aside from these "physical" interactions with the environment, it has also been proposed that "system control" is a separate form of universal 3D task and consists of "changing the mode or state of the system, often through commands or menus" [22].

On the other hand, the interactivity of the narrative in XR needs to be considered as intimately related to the user's placement and relation to the storyworld, and the amount of agency afforded to the user [24]. Regarding this placement, the user can be considered as being internal (e.g., being a specific character in the storyworld), or external, being situated outside the diegesis of the world, entailing an omniscient presence, understanding, or perspective. Regarding the amount of agency afforded to the user, the interactivity of the narrative can additionally be considered as either exploratory or ontological. In exploratory interaction, the user has no lasting influence on the storyworld, whereas in ontological interaction, "the storyworld evolves as a result of the interaction" [24].

Besides the perspective (internal/external) and agential (exploratory/ontological) categorizations of interaction with a narrative, Ryan [15] also describes four additional types of narrative interaction based on the degree of intentionality and freedom granted to the user. First, there is reactive interactivity, in which the user does not express any intentionality and the system simply reacts to the presence of the user or to any other environmental variable. Second, there is random selection, in which the user makes a choice, however without any real knowledge of the consequences or strategic value of the choice. Third, there is purposeful selection, in which the user is conscious of his choices and selects with the expectation of certain outcomes. Finally, there is productive interactivity, considered the fullest kind of interaction, in which the user leaves a personal and durable mark in the storyworld or makes a non-prescripted contribution to the development of the narrative. All these kinds of interactivity are not mutually exclusive and can work in concomitance. The possibility of making selections (randomly or purposefully) is what determines the possibility of branching narratives and can be combined with affordances (either of the user or the system) to alter the world or the story itself.

One of the main design challenges for narratives in XR is to harmonize the interactivity of the medium with the interactivity of the narrative, and actually consider them in unity. The different types of interactivity of the medium can potentially all be applicable with the different types of interactivity of the narrative, but the approach for their individual implementation will differ with the specific design requirements.

2.2.2   Immersion

In the last two decades, the term "immersion" has had different connotations in the XR and in the IDN domains. While in the field of XR the term has sometimes been used interchangeably with "presence," in his seminal work, Slater [13] suggests a distinction between the two. While presence would refer to perceptual and psychological responses to the system, immersion would be directly related to some qualities of the technology. In order to avoid confusion between immersion as "the person's response to the VE (Virtual Environment) system," the term "system immersion" has been proposed to more accurately describe "the extent to which the actual system delivers a surrounding environment, one which shuts out sensations from the 'real world'" [25]. On the other hand, in the IDN domain the term "immersion" has a wider range of connotations than in the XR field [26–29]. In IDN, immersion has come to mean more specifically "narrative immersion," which can be described as "an engagement of the imagination in the construction and contemplation of a storyworld" [29]. This description suggests that we can view the phenomenon of immersion as a continuously evolving "mental model of the narrative world" [30], that is, how do we get involved with the storyworld (including but not limited to its perceptual and spatial aspects). This brings the construct into close relation with a series of other terms such as engagement, imaginative involvement, emotional response, suspension of disbelief, and suspense [27, 31–33]. In this sense, narrative immersion can be further subdivided into, "spatial," "temporal," and "emotional" immersion, based respectively on three important aspects of narrative experience: settings, plot, and characters [24, 29]. These aspects should not be considered individually, but as working together in concert and enhancing each other.

Spatial immersion regards our reaction to the settings or the "place" of the narrative, which—independent of any narrative medium (written literature, theater, film, games, or VR)—is always a major component in situating the action, the epoch, and the characters in play. This is no less true for the new narrating possibilities in the different XR platforms, given that *place* in VR and AR narratives also have "an important influence on the emotional experience of the audience" [34], and should therefore be seen as an additional "agentic player" [35]. Furthermore, there has been an increasing interest in the design and implementation of "storyworlds" even before the definition of characters and plot relations [36–39]. The multiple spatial design possibilities in XR, which may combine real and synthetic spaces and props, as well as innovative ways to situate the participants in such virtual or mixed environments (e.g., VR, AR, MR, geolocation apps), brings new challenges and opportunities for representing such settings with narrative considerations. The narrative spatial requirements, sense of presence and realism, will be different for diverse XR platforms given the specific levels of transparency and seamlessness of their interfaces. Ultimately, spatial immersion correlates to the spatiality of the display (a sense of being surrounded; sense of depth, and the tracking of the point of view) [24], but narratively speaking, it depends also on its congruence and significance to the action.

Temporal immersion encompasses the narrative effects of curiosity, surprise, and suspense. It can therefore be regarded as the aspect of the story that keeps the user captivated and moving forward. It can be considered together with spatial immersion, when the user feels an incentive to explore the environment of the storyworld, and through this exploration experiences both curiosity about what is about to happen, i.e., suspense as well as surprise. The progression of narrative time distils the field of the potential, selecting one branch as the actual, and confining the others to the realm of the forever virtual. In turn, this selection generates new ranges of virtualities [15, 24]. The most suspenseful situations chart the future into a fan of diverging, but reasonably computable, outcomes [15]. In other words, narrative design constrains the horizon of possibilities in the virtual world. Suspense increases as the range of possibilities decreases. However, there must be a "structured horizon of anticipation" [40], delineated by our knowledge of the characters/agents, their contexts, goals, plans, and desires [15, 24]. In narrative, there is a subtle dialectic relation between the building of suspense and the suddenness of surprise, which can be seen as a dynamic shift between expectation and "un-expectation" in the uncertainties of the structured horizon of anticipation. Contrary to the projection towards the future implied by suspense, surprise is usually associated with the unmet expectations of the "here and now." Every increase of (unexpected) information that reduces (or increases) uncertainty may have an element of surprise [41]. Temporal immersion is also related to the level of narrativity involved in the experience that is staged in the particular

XR application. If the scripted activity involves a plain sequential action, the temporal development may have a low level of narrativity. Such level of narrativity will increase as the events show causal relations that get cognitively linked by a process of emplotting [6]. The highest levels of narrativity are obtained when the events and actions are organized in a plot that unfolds in the form of a dramatic arc, including a conflict, a rising action, a climax, and a resolution. Dramatic narratives pose the greatest challenges to IDNs in XR due to the "narrative paradox," [11, 12] which implies the difficulty of scripting a coherent dramatic arc while affording large degrees of freedom and agency to the user.

Emotional immersion revolves around the idea that the user develops empathic emotions towards synthetic characters in the storyworld and forms bonds and relations to these [24]. Independently of the level of narrativity of the events represented or enacted in the XR, emotional immersion will be in relation to the significance that those events and actions may have to the participant. This significance may be dependent on the resonance or invested interest the users have for the events, and/or on the bonds that they may develop with characters, agents, or other participating users. The better these affective dispositions are prompted by the narrative, the stronger the emotional involvement of the participants will be [42]. Emotional immersion is related to the temporal dimension via the anticipatory nature of empathic reactions. The stronger the emotional immersion is, the more the users will hope for some outcomes and fear others, the more intensely they will experience empathic distress and pleasure, and the more likely they will in retrospect appreciate or learn from the experience [42].

A final aspect that can be considered as an element of narrative immersion is *epistemic immersion*. This aspect can be regarded as "the desire to know" [29]. It is regarded to be quite simple to achieve in an IDN, e.g., in the form of classical mystery stories or problem solving. With epistemic immersion, the user is encouraged to explore and try to work out the story of the narrative using clues or smaller scattered segments of the story.

2.2.3   Environmental Storytelling

The logic of *Environmental storytelling* (ES) may be a source of inspiration for the implementation of narratives in the newest XR technologies. In ES the environment is utilized as the narrative discourse, i.e., a tool for organizing and structuring the narrative material to be mediated through the physical (or virtual) space of the environment [43, 44]. Thus, in delivering the intended narrative, ES relies heavily on the users exploring and discovering the narrative by interpretation of nonverbal elements placed in (or built into) the environment. These elements are often designed as "cause-and-effect" elements, which provide, what would otherwise be a static environment, with a sense of temporality, i.e., showing that something has occurred. In this way, ES tries to engage the user in both "spatial," "temporal," and "epistemic" immersion by creating an environment that is both visually captivating as well as cognitively engaging, which brings about the effects of curiosity and suspense.

By considering narratives "less as stories" and more as "spaces" ripe with narrative possibility," Jenkins [45] articulated two strategies for implementing narratives in the logic of environmental storytelling: *embedded narratives* and *emergent narratives* [45]. *Embedded narratives* inserts narrative information into the environment, as it focuses on the user exploring and piecing together the story from small story clues. As such, embedded narratives focus mainly on epistemic and spatial immersion. However, as mentioned, they also engage us temporally, as the information embedded in the environment should convey a timeline of what has happened in order to make the epistemic aspects of the narrative work. On the other hand, *Emergent Narratives* spontaneously arise from the actions of the user(s) and are thus not pre-scripted or pre-structured. The storyworld is an environment filled with narrative potential by the designer, but the actual narratives that emerge are based on the audience's actions and interpretations of what happens in this space.

2.2.4 Agency

Agency in XR refers to the cause/effect relationship between the user and the virtual environment. It has been described as the experience of controlling one's own actions and the consequences that might follow [46]. Agency gives the user the ability to make choices and to see and enjoy the results of those choices. When a narrative is involved in the experience, agency specifically encompasses the users' ability to control aspects of the narrative, or even contribute to it. This could be typically manifested in many kinds of affordances that imply "action verbs" (e.g., run, jump, shoot, etc.), possibilities for choices and decision-making, but also the capacity for navigation through the storyworld, possibilities for customizing an avatar or creating characters, changing points of views (perspective-taking), building things, or adding narrative elements and content.

Extrapolating Mateas's [47] reasoning from the context of interactive drama to the current narrative perspective in XR, interactors experience agency when the dramatic elements that are made available in the virtual storyworld are commensurate with the material constraints and the many affordances offered by the XR interfaces in the immersive environment. A failure to fine-tune a coherent mapping between interaction affordances and the sense of narrative closure will result in a decreased sense of agency.

Even though in the context of XR high levels of agency are usually an uncontested desideratum, for the sake of narrative coherence and intelligibility, "run-amuck agency" should arguably be avoided. Too much power or freedom may compromise the possibility to instantiate a narrative and/ or impede the development of a dramatic arc; e.g., the interactor will get rid of the antagonist too early, solve all the major problems prematurely, and therefore erase all the drama [48].

The growing toolbox of affordances, props, embodiment, and sensorial multimodal possibilities of XR offer many opportunities for enabling users in the roles of protagonists or witnesses with high degrees of agency. If used coherently with the narrative design, increased agency can become a compelling resource for interactive storytelling.

2.2.5   Embodiment, Narration, and "Point of View Technologies"

XR technologies present challenges with embodiment in two directions, and both can be related to challenges or opportunities in the narrative realm. On the one hand, some XR technologies can be considered as a disembodying technology, replacing the user's real body with a body image that transfers the agency to a digital avatar [15, 24]. At the same time, an important part of XR research is the development of more immersive interfaces for embodiment, where the participation of the physical body and corporeal freedom is considered a primary concern. Both issues have a bearing with the classical narratological problems of "narration," "focalization," and the perspective of the narrative—i.e., how such enacting conditions place the user in first- or third-person perspective, and how omniscient these perspectives can become and be implemented in the storyworld.

In classical narratology, the term "narration" refers to the person or the entity we perceive to be the source of whatever is being told. Closely related, "focalization" tends to refer to the point of view that we as audience can infer the narrator instantiates. Building on the work of Genette [49, 50], who considered focalization as a way of controlling the flow and accessibility of narrative information, Bal [51] categorized focalization as either *internal* or *external*, i.e., the narrator is either an active character in the narrative (therefore with the same amount of knowledge of that character) or is non-active in the narrative, which may entail both omniscient narrators as well as spectating narrators. In this sense, Bal considers focalization as very closely related to "narration" and the "point-of-view."

This close connection between "narration" and "focalization" has given rise to many discussions on the interrelations and overlaps of these two terms, leading to considerations and permutations of different roles for the author, the narrator constructed by the author, the entities the narrator is talking to (i.e., the narratees), and the real audience [49–53]. These complex relations can get even more entangled, or blurred, when XR as a medium introduces what can be called "point-of-view technologies" [15, 24] (e.g., tracking the user perspective in VR), together with other embodiment affordances offered by XR technologies and the agency possibilities that come with IDN logic.

Ryan [24] covers part of the issue when she marks the distinction between internal and external kinds of interactivity (see previous descriptions on *Interactivity*), i.e., how the interactor can be placed in the immersive storyworld as external to it (third-person, birds-eye view), or how the user can be placed internal to the story diegesis in a sort of first-person or second-person perspective. With the agency and roleplaying capacity of XR media, such first-person perspective is quite different from the first-person perspective that can be achieved in linear narratives, in which the character is not driven by the user. While the agency afforded to the interactor correlates directly to the nonlinearity of IDN, his or her representation in the virtual storyworld relates to the embodiment possibilities of digital avatars and self-body representation in the virtual environment. Interface devices such as data gloves, wired bodysuits, MoCap, Kinect, etc., not only immerse the user in a virtual environment but can also place him as an actor in the story with his own agency and perspective of what is being narrated.

Whether the user acts from first-person perspective, with more or less self-body representation (e.g., limbs, whole body, etc.), or from a third-person perspective (e.g., being disembodied into an avatar), the author/designer will need to define how to best place and empower the user as a narrator or character (be that as spectator or active agent). In linear narratives, the author can play with the (constructed) narrator's awareness of self as a storyteller and his or her self-consciousness in influencing the outcomes of what is happening in the storyworld.

Additionally, it is useful to categorize the form of "narrative information" that is being narrated (or focalized), as either *imperceptibles* (i.e., internal elements that cannot be directly perceived, such as thoughts and emotions) or *perceptibles* (i.e., externally perceivable elements, such as actions, appearances, conversations, etc.) [51]. For XR though, it becomes a challenge to imagine how such predefined internal focalization and imperceptibles might be conveyed or transmitted to the user. In fact, if we utilize the term "focalization" from the perspective of point of view, then we can argue that the more agency the user has, the more internal the focalization necessarily will be. By this, the problem of embodiment and focalization in XR falls into the narrative paradox, i.e., the freedom of movement and interaction granted to the user complicates the control of the flow of narrative information from the author point of view.

Considering the user through the lens of narration and focalization can inform the design of both the interaction modalities afforded to the user, and the general form of the narrative representation, according to the intentions of the author and the goals of the system that is being designed. Thus, in XR it becomes important to consider the difference between the narrative intended by the author and the narrative perceived by the user. Bruni and Baceviciute [12] termed this gap the "Author–Audience Distance," which is regarded as a function of "narrative intelligibility," in turn defined as "the process in which the audience receives or generates meaning in a way that is close to what is intended, desired or expected by the author." In this perspective, the more interactive freedom or agency afforded, the more the story will be open for interpretation. In other words, narratives in XR that place the user as a first-person active participant in the storyworld (i.e., internal focalization and internal/ontological interactivity) might easier instantiate more open or emergent stories, while placing the user as a spectator to the unfolding events (external focalization and external/exploratory interaction) can more readily convey a more didascalic or didactic story [12].

2.2.6   Agents and AI

In immersive simulations, IDN, and narrative games, computer-controlled agents and nonplaying characters (NPCs) have been considered to be an important factor for achieving high levels of presence, immersion, and suspension of disbelief. This has to do with both a) the design of the agents and b) the modeling of its intelligent and adaptive behavior. Therefore, the problem of designing and programming believable and intelligent characters gets entangled with the challenges of designing branching narratives that adapt or respond to user input.

In order to provide the user with a desired feeling of agency, i.e., that the user's choices and actions have (or feel like having) a real influence in the outcomes of the narrative, the AI that drives the branching narrative—usually referred to as "drama manager" [54–59]—needs to include a credible response repertoire for each interactable NPC deployed in the storyworld, which is consistent with the set of trajectories in which the narrative can unfold. In the case of XR implementations, the multimodal representation of virtual characters poses further challenges in terms of believability and what has been called "the uncanny valley" [60, 61].

With believable "life-like" agents requiring the ability to do "several intelligent activities in parallel" [56], advances in AI for computer-controlled characters becomes a key issue for providing narrative coherence, to orient users' actions, and to provide narrative hooks and closure [14]. In order to implement believable NPCs and agents in XR-IDNs, an appropriate and sufficient model of human behavior still needs to be developed, as well as their integration as characters in the drama manager and the storyworld. As pointed out by Ryan [29], emotional immersion relies also on the interaction with artificial characters and the believability of this interaction. One could argue that another form of immersion (closely tied with emotional immersion) is *social immersion*, which would then be experienced through the users' ability to suspend their disbelief in relation to the social realism and coherence in their engagement with the agents present in the storyworld.

2.3   Domains of Applications

While the expressive and representational power of the XR media is still largely unexplored with respect to IDN, the past few years have witnessed an increasing demand and interest for immersive narrative experiences in a number of fields and domains. These include entertainment, healthcare, education, culture, museology, journalism, and many more. Although it is beyond the scope of this chapter to give an exhaustive overview of all of them, it is nevertheless pertinent to highlight some relevant examples.

2.3.1   Games

Perhaps one of the most apparent application domains that has introduced a variety of novel solutions and applications involving XR-IDN is entertainment. The entertainment sector has had a predominant role in introducing immersive technologies to the wider audiences and in bringing down the costs of the technology [62, 63]. In this context, it has helped push the boundaries of IDN in XR. Moreover, the technological aspects,

XR technologies in video games have enabled the implementation of more captivating stories.

We can consider some of the popular and unique narrative-based VR games such as "Lone Echo" [64], "Tokyo Chronos" [65], "Altdeus: Beyond Chronos" [66], and the highly popular "Half-Life: Alyx" [67]. "Lone Echo" is a popular story-based VR single-player role-playing experience, developed by Ready At Dawn. While the game is well equipped with a number of impressive features, including the game's locomotion system, Lone Echo also demonstrates how storytelling in VR requires going beyond just the interaction afforded by the technology and the game mechanics–challenging and adapting narrative elements for this new type of storytelling. "Altdeus: Beyond Chronos" and "Tokyo Chronos" are both narrative VR games that can be referred to as "virtual reality visual novels"; both games are heavily story-driven and feature multiple-choice decision points that have an impact on the game and its ending. Moreover, it has been suggested [68] that Altdeus, with its 15–20 hours of gameplay, features one of the largest branching storylines in a VR game to date. Lastly, "Half-Life: Alyx" (HLA) needs to be mentioned, perhaps as the currently most celebrated story-based VR game. HLA builds on the Half-Life 2D video game series and is similar to its antecedent—a first-person shooter (FPS) .

In comparison to the growing number of successful story-driven VR games, AR and MR experiences with a compelling storyline are currently more rare to come by. However, in the past few years, the increasing appeal of location-based storytelling across different media has challenged game designers and developers to explore this medium further. Building on the popular British stop motion franchise of the same name, "Wallace & Gromit: The Big Fix Up" [69, 70] is a recent narrative XR game experience that makes use of a variety of media formats to involve and engage fans. As described by the creators, the story plays out using "multi-user AR gameplay, character phone calls, comic strips, and extended reality (XR) portals." Another mixed-reality experience released in 2020 for the Magic Leap platform is "The Last Light" [71]. Rather than a game, the experience is a short film that plays out on real-life objects in front of the user.

2.3.2   Serious Games

The growing importance of narrative in XR outside the industry of entertainment is exemplified by the growing domain of serious games.

XR serious games make use of "serious storytelling" and are increasingly used in pedagogics and training across a diversity of areas [63]. Moreover, growing evidence suggests that incorporating rich immersive digital narratives in VR serious games can support more enhanced learning outcomes than non-immersive and non contextualized virtual environments [72, 73]. In 2020 BBC Studios and PRELOADED launched an educational AR app "Micro Kingdoms: Senses" [74] for the Magic Leap platform. The app is a type of interactive documentary in which the user can (while wearing the Magic Leap's AR glasses) explore and interact with different types of insects while the experience is being narrated.

Another form of application of XR-IDN in serious games is through pervasive games. Pervasive games can be referred to as technology mediated location-based experiences, bridging the physical and the digital worlds using mobile devices or other types of wearables, designed for multiplayer interaction [75]. While pervasive games found their way to the general public through successful games such as Pokemon Go in 2016 [76], there is ample ground to suggest that the future of IDN pervasive games lies largely in serious games [77]. When talking about IDN in pervasive serious games, it is essential to highlight the crucial role of narrative in delivering these experiences, "[T]hese experiences must be linked by a coherent narrative, a common thread in the story, which is responsible for conveying the author's intention and directs the user's interactions for their use" [78].

Another key challenge in XR serious games relates to obtaining a better understanding of players' behavioral responses, as more elaborate understanding could result in more effective storytelling, particularly in terms of integrating more complex narratives and characters, but also help improve the overall game experience [73, 79].

2.3.3 Cultural Experiences

Mobile-based IDN also holds potential in engaging different audiences in cultural activities and experiences. While the incentives for incorporating MR, VR, and AR in museums and cultural heritage sites have in the past been perhaps more focused on the technology, Holloway-Holloway-Attaway and Rouse [80] point out that the current shift is much more focused on embodiment and directly enhancing the visitor experience. Moreover, Katifori et al. [81] argue that in respect to designing and producing effective storytelling experiences for XR in the cultural domain, there is still a long way to go as "lack of standard methodologies, guidelines, and appropriate authoring tools specifically designed to support cultural institutions in developing mobile interactive storytelling experiences has been an impediment to the integration of interactive storytelling in museum practices and cultural heritage in general" [81]. Nevertheless, the rising trend in encouraging visitors to become active participants in the creation of cultural experiences has highlighted the potential role of XR systems in engaging and better establishing visitors' relationships between physical and virtual spaces and artefacts, and has already resulted in numerous noteworthy examples.

In 2011–2014, an EU-funded project, CHESS—Cultural Heritage Experiences through Socio-personal interactions and Storytelling [82]—investigated the possibilities of IDS using XR technologies for creating more personalized on-site visitor experiences. The project allowed for producing "branching narratives which interweaved informational content with storytelling elements combined in a coherent plot via a graph based authoring tool" [81, 83]. The CHESS project served as the foundation for a more recent EU Research and Innovation (RIA) action named EMOTIVE (Emotive virtual cultural experiences through personalized storytelling). The EMOTIVE project examined methods and tools for supporting cultural and creative industries in creating Virtual Museums, relying on 'emotive storytelling' and using XR technologies [84]. Moreover, a recent story-based project created for the visitors of Changdeok Palace in South Korea, a UNESCO-recognized World Cultural Heritage site, makes use of AR technology to allow visitors to explore South Korean legends. In addition to providing information about the palace, the app also offers the visitors to experience "situational plays based on history at buildings within the compound, royal court dances and traditional games" [85].

2.3.4   Healthcare

Although still considered a relatively new area of research in healthcare, IDN has been considered as a useful tool for various health interventions in both adult and pediatric care, particularly for counseling and therapy purposes [86–89]. Additionally, IDNs have been studied as a tool for the education and training of health professionals [90]. In the adult population, digital storytelling has been studied more among older adults, suggesting it as promising for improving mood, enhancing memory, supporting social connectedness, and promoting personalized care, among others [86]. In pediatrics, its potential is similarly highly regarded in the psychosocial domain, providing a way for children and adolescence to make better sense of their experiences of illness [87]. More recently, IDN is also being explored through the integration of immersive technologies. While not always driven by a carefully constructed narrative, Virtual Reality has demonstrated compelling results in the frames of pediatric healthcare and rehabilitation, including children's pain management and anxiety [91, 92], treatment of specific phobias [93], and cerebral palsy [94], among others. It has been proposed that through its immersive qualities, VR as a storytelling medium can support changing concepts of the self more quickly and easily than in real life [95]. Moreover, it has been suggested that controlled VR environments could provide more effective means for training and building communication skills that could be generalized to real-world experiences [96], but also allow children to more effectively engage with background narratives [97]. While XR-IDN in healthcare can in many ways still be considered in its infancy, recent findings and growing interest suggest its potential for applying a more person-centric approach in healthcare, and thus help promote more active participation in the treatment process.

2.3.5   Immersive Journalism with XR

Incorporating XR technologies for telling nonfiction stories has introduced new possibilities for involving audiences in current events. Described as a hybrid form blending journalism, video games, and cinema, it allows people to gain first-person experiences of news events, locations, and situations described in news stories [98, 99]. The fact that in the center of immersive journalism lies experience, rather than presentation, sets it apart from traditional journalism and thereby establishes itself as a new field of journalism [99]. However, while the proponents of immersive journalism often see it as the future, there nevertheless exists some disagreement regarding the development and direction for these new forms of interactive narratives in journalism.

2015, when The New York Times launched their VR-app in collaboration with Google (distributing one million Google Cardboard headsets to the newspaper's subscribers), in many ways marks the year when immersive journalism was introduced to larger audiences. The app allowed readers to *experience* a documentary about the global refugee crisis through three independent stories [100]. The success of the project naturally exceeded all expectations; however, it was the level of emotional involvement and engagement of the readers that came to mark VR in immersive journalism as an "empathy machine" [101–104]. Jones [101] argues that seeing VR merely as an empathy machine is restrictive in the development of immersive journalism stories. Acknowledging that VR can undoubtedly introduce new perspectives and allow readers to become active participants in the story, the author highlights that it should not be seen as the central aspect for VR in immersive journalism, "[A]lthough it can be an invaluable medium to generate reflection and new perspectives, the argument that the experience is of the same value and has the same effect as the contextualised lived experience of the subject is reductive" [101]. While the use of technology can offer viewers spatial immersion, it does not in fact always guarantee narrative immersion: "In journalism, it is necessary to consider in which cases the immersive experience is the best vehicle to achieve the aim of making people care about what happens in the world" [105]. It is essential to recognize the unique considerations for integrating XR technologies into journalistic storytelling, such as establishing the role of the viewer and their capacity for agency, or issues around different journalistic formats for spatial narrative [105].

2.4   Future Perspectives

The future challenges in XR could be broadly categorized into technical and creative [106], the latter including more specifically the narrative aspects. This overlaps with our previous distinction between interactivity of the medium and interactivity of the narrative. In this direction, research will be needed in order to harmonize the different types of interactivity and affordances of the medium with the different types of interactivity and design requirements of the narrative.

Some of the challenges of XR as an expressive medium for authors of fictional works have to do with the development of new narrative techniques that adapt to the technological developments. "Whilst the progress in graphics and physics is no less than astonishing, the same cannot be said for the larger challenge of creating specific narrative forms to produce compelling and captivating experiences ... The narratives and characters they host remain shallow, static and lacking in believability, dramatic engagement and narrative development in comparison" [107].

As hinted above (in Section 2.2), further research will be needed on the trade-offs between different forms of immersion (spatial, temporal, emotional, epistemic) and all the different forms of interactivity (both from the technological and the narrative points of view). This will bring new questions about the role of agency and its influence in the mediation of narrative content and the fulfillment of specific narrative goals as the new platforms evolve. These trade-offs between agency and control over the narrative's coherence will be dependent on the domains of applications and the role played by the narrative in the design of the system [12]. In XR, such agency will count with many technical possibilities for embodied interaction. From the narrative perspective, this will bring new challenges and opportunities in terms of how to include the user in the narration process, i.e., issues of focalization, perspective taking, points of view, etc. The social aspects implicit in the interaction with AI-guided agents will also bring interesting questions in terms of design, immersion, and narrative intelligibility and closure.

All this means that the evolution of XR will inevitably require a better understanding of the technology as a medium, highlighting the nontechnological aspects of experience, as well as the eminent role of *narrative cognition* as a fundamental human cognitive mode for organizing and mediating experience. The combination of XR technologies, cognitive sciences, advanced biometric signals processing, and storytelling techniques will allow us to investigate the ways we interact cognitively with stories and the effects of the narratives on the human emotional-cognitive system [8]. Given the many different domains of applications for interactive narratives in XR and its specific requirements in terms of multimodality and embodied cognition, research in narrative cognition will be necessary to aid the development of communication strategies to use effectively the narrative mode in order to harness its potential beneficial applications in XR media. With the enhanced importance of embodiment, perception, cognition, and action in XR research, the "enactive approach" to cognition [108, 109] and HCI [110, 111] could prove to become a renewed source for inspiration to investigate the subject's situatedness in the emerging mixed and extended realities[1]. This is particularly the case when implementing or investigating narrative cognition in XR systems. An enactive approach to narrative cognition would allow us to pay attention to the embedded levels of analysis that go from the physiological to the phenomenological levels. As a matter of

---

[1]Even though the "enactive approach" to novel HCI interfaces was considered very promising at the beginning of VR/AR research, it was somehow abandoned on the way and considered only marginally by a handful of researchers.

fact, XR-IDN—considered as experiential systems [112]—incorporate live action in performative environments, which include sensorimotor coupling, proprio- and self-perception, movement and gesture tracking, immersion, multimodality, role-playing, and intersubjective interactions with others and with artificial agents (and their designers). This will require new methodologies for the investigation of narrative cognition and its multifarious implications. By studying key cognitive processes and affective states elicited by narratives in XR systems, we will be able to assess the use of narratives as rhetorical devices in many different domains of applications, such as, e.g., education, pedagogics, health, ecology, culture, and entertainment. However, with the growth of XR as potential narrative media, it will also be essential to discern and be able to identify the intentional and unintentional, beneficial and deleterious, uses of XR narratives for rhetorical purposes. As mentioned, the use of the narrative mode of communication has been extended into many beneficial domains of applications, but can also potentially be utilized in cases of indoctrination and manipulation. In this regard, more research will be necessary in order to understand how narrative rhetoric mediated with the emerging XR technologies potentially could be misused—e.g., by manipulating affective dispositions, either into liking, caring, and loving or into disliking, resenting, and hating—as the users get situated in ubiquitous narrative trajectories, either as spectators or as active agents.

It is likely that in the next few years we will witness a surge in transmedia storytelling driven by the convergence of XR technology. Jenkins describes transmedia storytelling as "a process where integral elements of a fiction get dispersed systematically across multiple delivery channels for the purpose of creating a unified and coordinated entertainment experience," in which every medium contributes to the unfolding of the story [37]. Nevertheless, transmedia storytelling is not anymore considered to be exclusively in the domain of fiction and entertainment. The combination of IDN with location-based technology and pervasive gaming has already resulted in a diversity of concrete applications in culture, health, and fitness [14]. More advanced geo-localization techniques (including indoor tracking) together with innovative XR could expand the possibilities of transmedia storytelling, integrating the narrative with physical and digital environments in different domains and contexts of application. A growing number of news media outlets are already applying or starting to consider transmedia strategies as a better way to connect and involve their audiences [113]. In this direction, an interdisciplinary network of researchers and practitioners (INDCOR) was recently constituted to advance the use of interactive digital narratives to represent highly complex topics, and prospect its applications in broad usage by media producers and the general public [114].

The convergence of XR systems with ubiquitous transmedia narratives in many domains of our lives requires urgent ethical and cultural considerations that cannot be neglected. As we increasingly engage in the process of interfacing our body–minds with more fully immersive, pervasive, multimodal, representational, enactive, hyper-interactive environments, filled with narratives and rhetorical devices, the users—under constant and ever-increasing cognitive pressure from the multimodal overload of content, choices, and interactions—may come to experience difficulties in discerning the *ontological boundaries* between fiction and reality, or between factuality and fakeness. In susceptible target groups (e.g., children), the increased mimetic possibilities of impersonating characters and personas portrayed in transmedia worlds and other types of (story)worlds can elicit "pseudo emotional" responses that tend to become real as these ontological boundaries get blurred by the aggregation of transmedia products and contents of different types and nature. This could potentially affect the users' emotional balance and their capacity for discerning the boundaries of reality, their patterns for suspension-of-disbelief, the adoption of belief and value systems, and vulnerability to intended or unintended rhetorical devices or persuasive campaigns. It would therefore be important to research whether XR media brings about qualitative changes in terms of its representational and rhetorical capacity, which, in turn, can have effects on the user's own criteria and capacity for judgment and discernment [18].

As we tried to show in this chapter, the future research agenda for further investigating narrative involvement in extended reality systems presents a myriad of opportunities across a wide spectrum of disciplines, and social and commercial sectors. It will thus be useful to bridge the XR technical domains with the almost three decades of research in interactive digital narrative, interactive digital storytelling, computational narrative, and cognitive narratology, among others. Besides some of the mentioned technical and narrative aspects involving immersion, interactivity, agency, embodied interaction, narration, focalization, perspective taking, social aspects, AI-guided agents, etc., it will be important to keep in sight the social, cultural, and ethical aspects of XR-IDN design in the many promising application domains.

References

1. Polkinghorne, D.E., *Narrative Knowing And The Human Sciences*, State University of New York Press, Albany, NY, 1988.

2. Barthes, R. and Duisit, L., An introduction to the structural analysis of narrative, in: *New Literary History*, pp. 237–272, 1975.

3. Bruner, J., *Acts of Meaning*, Harvard University Press, Cambridge, 1990.

4. Bruner, J., *The Narrative Construction Of Reality*, vol. 1-21, Critical inquiry, 1991.

5. Bruner, J., *Life As Narrative. Social Research: An International Quarterly*, JHU Press, Baltimore, MD, pp. 691–710, JHU Press, Baltimore, MD, 2004.

6. Ricoeur, P., *Time And Narrative*, vol. 1, University of Chicago Press, Chicago, 1984.

7. Cortazzi, M., *Narrative Analysis. Language Teaching*, pp. 157–170, Cambridge University Press, Cambridge, 1994.

8. Bruni, L.E., Dini, H., Simonetti, A., Narrative cognition in mixed reality systems: Towards an empirical framework. *International Conference On Human-Computer Interaction*, pp. 3–17, 2021.

9. Aylett, R., Narrative in virtual environments—Towards emergent narrative. *Proceedings Of The AAAI Fall Symposium On Narrative Intelligence*, pp. 83–86, 1999.

10. Aylett, R. and Louchart, S., *Towards A Narrative Theory Of Virtual Reality. Virtual Reality*, pp. 2–9, Springer, 2003.

11. Louchart, S. and Aylett, R., Solving the narrative paradox in VEs—Lessons from RPGs. *International Workshop On Intelligent Virtual Agents*, pp. 244–248, 2003.

12. Bruni, L.E. and Baceviciute, S., Narrative intelligibility and closure in interactive systems. *International Conference On Interactive Digital Storytelling*.

13. Slater, M., *A Note On Presence Terminology*, 3, 1–5, Presence connect, 2003.

14. Koenitz, H., Ferri, G., Haahr, M., Sezen, D., Sezen, T.I., Introduction: A concise history of interactive, digital narrative, in: Interactive Digital Narrative: History, Theory and Practice, 11–21, Routledge, New York, NY, 2015.

15. Ryan, M.L., *Narrative As Virtual Reality: Immersion And Interactivity In Literature And Electronic Media*, JHU Press, Baltimore, MD, 2001.

16. Si, M., Thue, D., André, E., Lester, J., Tanenbaum, J., Zammitto, V., Preface. *Interactive Storytelling Fourth International Conference On Interactive Digital Storytelling*, 2011.

17. Knoller, N. and Ben-Arie, U., The holodeck is all around us—Interface dispositifs in interactive digital storytelling, in: *Interactive Digital Narrative History, Theory And Practice*, H. Koenitz, G. Ferri, M. Haahr, D. Sezen, T.I. Sezen (Eds.), pp. 51–66, Routledge, New York, NY, 2015.

18. Bruni, L.E., Sustainability, Cognitive technologies and the digital semiosphere. *Int. J. Cult. Stud.*, 18, 103–117, 2015.

19. Bowman, D.A. and Hodges, L.F., Formalizing the design, evaluation, and application of interaction techniques for immersive virtual environments. *J. Vis. Lang. Comput.*, 10, 37–53, 1999.

20. Dooley, K., Storytelling with virtual reality in 360-degrees: A new screen grammar. *Stud. Australas. Cinema*, 11, 161–171, 2017.

21. Bowman, D.A., Chen, J., Wingrave, C.A., Lucas, J., Ray, A., Polys, N.F., Li, Q. *et al.*, New directions in 3d user interfaces. *Int. J. Virtual Real.*, 5, 3–14, 2006.
22. LaViola Jr., J.J., Kruijff, E., McMahan, R.P., Bowman, D., Poupyrevet, I.P., *3D User Interfaces: Theory And Practice*, Addison-Wesley Professional, Boston, MA, 2017.
23. Flavián, C., Ibáñez-Sánchez, S., Orús, C., The impact of virtual, augmented and mixed reality technologies on the customer experience. *J. Bus. Res.*, 100, 547–560, 2019.
24. Ryan, M.L., Narrative as Virtual Reality 2: Revisiting immersion and interactivity, in: *Literature and Electronic Media*, JHU Press, Baltimore, MD, 2015.
25. Slater, M., Measuring presence: A response to the Witmer and Singer presence questionnaire. *Presence*, 8, 560–565, 1999.
26. Heim, M., *The Metaphysics Of Virtual Reality*, Oxford University Press on Demand, New York, NY, 1993.
27. Cairns, P., Cox, A., Nordin, A.I., Immersion in digital games: Review of gaming experience research, in: *Handbook Of Digital Games*, M.C. Angelides and H. Agius (Eds.), pp. 337–361, John Wiley & Sons, Ltd, Hoboken, NJ, 2014.
28. Ermi, L., Fundamental components of the gameplay experience. *Analysing Immersion, DiGRA*, 3, 1–14, 2005.
29. Ryan, M.L., From narrative games to playable stories: Toward a poetics of interactive narrative. Storyworlds. *A J. Narrative Studie*, 1, 43–59, 2009.
30. Ryan, M.L., Narratology and cognitive science: A problematic relation. *Style*, 44, 469–495, 2010.
31. Steuer, J., Defining virtual reality: Dimensions determining telepresence. *J. Commun.*, 42, 73–93, 1992.
32. McMahan, A., Wolf, M.J.P., Perron, B., Immersion, engagement, and presence: A method for analyzing 3-D video games, in: *The Video Game Theory Reader*, pp. 67–86, Routledge, New York, NY, 2003.
33. Green, M.C., Brock, T.C., Kaufman, G.F., Understanding media enjoyment: The role of transportation into narrative worlds. *Commun. Theory*, 14, 311–327, 2004.
34. Ding, N., Zhou, W., Fung, A.Y.H., Emotional effect of cinematic VR compared with traditional 2D film. *Telemat. Inform.*, 35, 1572–1579, 2018.
35. Kukkakorpi, M. and Pantti, M., A sense of place: VR journalism and emotional engagement. *Journalism Pract.*, 15, 785–802, 2021.
36. Jenkins, H., *Convergence Culture: Where Old and New Media Collide*, New York University Press, New York, NY, 2006.
37. Jenkins, H., Transmedia storytelling 101. Confessions of an Aca-fan, 2007. https://henryjenkins.org/blog/2007/03/transmedia_storytelling_101.html.
38. McDowell, A., *PD4C21 - Production Design For The 21st Century*, Kosmorama, 2017. https://www.kosmorama.org/en/kosmorama/artikler/pd4c21-production-design-21st-century
39. Ryan, M.L. and Thon, J.N., Storyworlds Across Media: Toward a Media-Conscious Narratology. University of Nebraska Press, Lincoln, NE, 2014.

40. Carroll, N., The paradox of suspense, in: *Suspense: Conceptualizations, Theoretical Analyses, And Empirical Explorations*, P. Vorderer, H.J. Wulff, M. Friedrichsen (Eds.), pp. 71–92, Routledge, 1996), New York, NY, 2013.

41. Bruni, L.E., Baceviciute, S., Arief, M., Narrative cognition in interactive systems: Suspense-surprise and the P300 ERP component. *International Conference on Interactive Digital Storytelling*, pp. 164–175, 2014.

42. Zillmann, D., Mechanisms of emotional involvement with drama. *Poetics*, 23, 33–51, 1995.

43. Carson, D., Environmental storytelling: Creating immersive 3D worlds using lessons learned from the theme park industry, 2000a. Gamasutra.com, https://www.gamasutra.com/view/feature/3186/environmental_storytelling_.php.

44. Carson, D., Environmental storytelling, part II: Bringing theme park environment design techniques to the virtual world, 2000b. Gamasutra.com, https://www.gamasutra.com/view/feature/3185/environmental_storytelling_part_.php?print=1.

45. Jenkins, H., Game design as narrative architecture. in: First Person, N. Wardrip-Fruin, P. Harrigan (Eds.), pp. 118-130, MIT Press, Cambridge, MA, 2004.

46. Kong, G., He, K., Wei, K., Sensorimotor experience in virtual reality enhances sense of agency associated with an avatar. *Conscious. Cogn.*, 52, 115–124, 2017.

47. Mateas, M., A preliminary poetics for interactive drama and games. *Digit. Creat.*, 140–152, 12, 2001.

48. Miller, C.H., Digital storytelling: A creator's guide to interactive entertainment. *Elinor Actipis*, 2008.

49. Genette, G., *Narrative Discourse: An Essay In Method*, vol. 3, J.E. Lewin (Ed.), Cornell University Press, 1972), Ithaca, NY, 1980.

50. Genette, G., *Narrative Discourse Revisited*, J.E. Lewin (Ed.), Cornell University Press, 1983), Ithaca, NY, 1988.

51. Bal, M., *Narratology: Introduction To The Theory Of Narrative*, C. van Boheemen (Ed.), University of Toronto Press, Toronto, 1985.

52. Phelan, J., Why narrators can be focalizers—and why it matters, in: *New Perspectives On Narrative Perspective*, van Peer, W. and Chatman, S. (Eds.), pp. 51–64.

53. Prince, G., A point of view on point of view or refocusing focalization, in: *New Perspectives On Narrative Perspective*, van Peer, W. and Chatman, S. (Eds.), pp. 43–50, 2001.

54. Mateas, M., *An Oz-Centric Review Of Interactive Drama And Believable Agents*, vol. 297-328, Artificial intelligence today, Berlin, Heidelberg, 1999.

55. Mateas, M. and Stern, A., Towards integrating plot and character for interactive drama, in: *Socially Intelligent Agents*, pp. 221–228, 2002.

56. Mateas, M. and Stern, A., Façade: An experiment in building a fully-realized interactive drama. *Game Developers Conference*, 2003.

57. Yu, H. and Riedl, M.O., Data-driven personalized drama management. *Ninth Artificial Intelligence And Interactive Digital Entertainment Conference*, 2013.

58. Moallem, J.D. and Raffe, W.L., A Review of Agency Architectures in Interactive Drama Systems. *2020 IEEE Conference On Games (CoG)*, 2020.

59. Utsch, M.N.R., Pappa, G.L., Chaimowicz, L., Prates, R.O., A new non-deterministic drama manager for adaptive interactive storytelling. *Entertain. Comput.*, 34, 2020.

60. Mori, M., The uncanny valley. *Energy*, (In Japanese), 7, 33–35, 1970.

61. Mori, M., MacDorman, K.F., Kageki, N., The uncanny valley [from the field]. *IEEE Robot. Autom. Mag.*, 19, 98–100, 2012.

62. Muñoz-Saavedra, L., Miró-Amarante, L., Domínguez-Morales, M., Augmented and virtual reality rvolution and future tendency. *Appl. Sci.*, 10, 322–345, 2020.

63. Ziker, C., Truman, B., Dodds, H., Cross reality (XR): Challenges and opportunities across the spectrum, in: *Innovative Learning Environments in STEM Higher Education*, pp. 55–77, 2021.

64. Ready at Dawn, Lone echo, 2017. https://readyatdawn.com/game-list/lone-echo/.

65. MyDearest Inc., Tokyo chronos, 2019. https://tokyochronos.com/en/.

66. MyDearest Inc., Altdeus: Beyond chronos, 2021. https://altdeus.com/en/.

67. Valve, Half-life: Alyx, 2020. https://www.half-life.com/en/alyx.

68. Oculus, Pilot a Mech as you Explore a Branching Narrative, 2020, Oculus Blog, https://www.oculus.com/blog/pilot-a-mech-as-you-explore-a-branching-narrative-in-sci-fi-visual-novel-altdeus-beyond-chronos/"

69. Wallace & Gromit, Fictioneers Ltd.,: The big fix up, 2020. https://www.thebigfixup.co.uk/.

70. Spangler, T. and Wallace and Gromit, First augmented-reality animated experience to launch this fall, Variety, 2020. https://variety.com/2020/digital/news/wallace-gromit-augmented-reality-free-app-1234614685/.

71. Magic Leap Studios, The last light, 2020. https://world.magicleap.com/en-us/details/com.magicleapstudios.lastlight.

72. Checa, D. and Bustillo, A., A review of immersive virtual reality serious games to enhance learning and training. *Multimed. Tools Appl.*, 79, 5501–5527, 2020.

73. Irshad, S. and Perkis, A., Increasing user engagement in virtual reality: The role of interactive digital narratives to trigger emotional responses, in: *Proceedings of the 11th Nordic Conference on Human-Computer Interaction: Shaping Experiences, Shaping Society (NordiCHI '20), Association for Computing Machinery*, pp. 1–4, 2020.

74. BBC Studios and PRELOADED, Micro kingdoms: Senses, 2020. https://preloaded.com/bbc-earth-micro-kingdoms/.

75. Oppermann, L. and Slussareff, M., Pervasive games. *Entertain. Comput. Serious Games*, 9970, 475–520, 2016.

76. Niantic Inc., Pokemon GO, 2016. https://pokemongolive.com/en/.

77. Hauge, J.B., Söbke, H., Ştefan, I., Stefan, A., Applying and facilitating serious location-based games. *International Conference on Entertainment Computing*, 2020.

78. Arango-López, J., Valdivieso, C.C.C., Collazos, C.A., Vela, F.L.G., Moreira, F., CREANDO: Tool for creating pervasive games to increase the learning motivation in higher education students. *Telemat. Informat.*, 38, 62–73, 2019.

79. Malegiannaki, I. and Daradoumis, T., Analyzing the educational design, use and effect of spatial games for cultural heritage: A literature review. *Comput. Educ.*, 108, 1–10, 2017.

80. Holloway-Attaway, L. and Rouse, R., Designing postdigital curators: Establishing an interdisciplinary games and mixed reality cultural heritage network. *Adv. Digit. Cult. Herit.*, 10754, 162–173, 2018.

81. Katifori, A., Karvounis, M., Kourtis, V., Perry, S., Roussou, M., Ioanidis, Y., Applying interactive storytelling in cultural heritage: opportunities, challenges and lessons learned. *International Conference on Interactive Digital Storytelling*, 108, 2018.

82. CHESS, The CHESS project, 2014. http://www.chessexperience.eu/.

83. Vayanou, M., Katifori, A., Karvounis, M., Kourtis, V., Kyriakidi, M., Roussou, M., Tsangaris, M. *et al.*, Authoring personalized interactive museum stories. *International Conference on Interactive Digital Storytelling*, 2014.

84. EMOTIVE, EMOTIVE project - Storytelling for cultural heritage, 2019. https://emotiveproject.eu/.

85. Arirang, C., Nexus Studios, 2020. https://nexusstudios.com/work/changdeok/.

86. Stargatt, J., Bhar, S., Bhowmik, J., Mahmud, A.A., Implementing digital storytelling for health-related outcomes in older adults, in: *Protocol For A Systematic Review. JMIR Research Protocols*, 2019.

87. Wilson, D.K., Hutson, S.P., Wyatt, T.H., Exploring the role of digital storytelling in pediatric oncology patients' perspectives regarding diagnosis, in: *A Literature Review*, SAGE Open, 2015.

88. Akard, T.F., Dietrich, M.S., Friedman, D.L., Hinds, P.S., Given, B., Wray, S., Gilmer, M.J., Digital storytelling: An innovative legacy-making intervention for children with cancer. *Pediatr. Blood Cancer*, 62, 658–665, 2015.

89. Baceviciute, S., Albæk, K.R.R., Arsovski, A., Bruni, L.E., Digital interactive narrative tools for facilitating communication with children during counseling: A case for audiology. *Lecture Notes Comput. Sci. (Including Subseries Lecture Notes Artif. Intell. Lecture Notes Bioinformatics)*, 7648, 48–59, 2012.

90. Moreau, K.A., Eady, K., Sikora, L., Horsley, T., Digital storytelling in health professions education: a systematic review, in: *BMC Medical Education*, pp. 1–9, 2018.

91. Won, A.S., Bailey., J., Bailenson, J., Tataru, C., Yoon, I.A., Golianu, B., Immersive virtual reality for pediatric pain. *Children*, 4, 52–67, 2017.

92. Arane, K., Behboudi, A., Goldman, R.D., Virtual reality for pain and anxiety management in children. *Can. Fam. Physician*, 63, 932–934, 2017.

93. Bouchard, S., Could virtual reality be effective in treating children with phobias? *Expert Rev. Neurother.*, 11, 207–213, 2011.

94. Chen, Y., Fanchiang, H.C.D., Howard, A., Effectiveness of virtual reality in children with cerebral palsy: A systematic review and meta-analysis of randomized controlled trials. *Phys. Ther.*, 98, 63–77, 2018.

95. Georgieva, I. and Georgiev, G.V., Reconstructing personal stories in virtual reality as a mechanism to recover the self. *Int. J. Environ. Res. Public Health*, 17, 26–51, 2020.

96. Bryant, L., Brunner, M., Hemsley, B., A review of virtual reality technologies in the field of communication disability: Implications for practice and research. *Disabil. Rehabilitation: Assist. Technol.*, 15, 365–372, 2020.

97. Parsons, T.D., Riva, G., Parsons, S., Mantovani, F., Newbutt, N., Lin, L., Venturini, E., Hall, T., Virtual reality in pediatric psychology. *Pediatrics*, 140, 86–91, 2017.

98. Toursel, A. and Philippe, U., Immersive journalism, a "new frontier" of information experience? *Braz. J. Res.*, 15, 336–357, 2019.

99. De la Peña, N., Weil, P., Llobera, J., Spanlang, B., Friedman, D., Sanchez-Vives, M.V., Slater, M., Immersive journalism: Immersive virtual reality for the first-person experience of news. *Presence*, 19, 291–301, 2010.

100. Ismail, I. and Solomon, B.C., The displaced. *New York Times*, 2015.

101. Jones, S., It's not just about empathy, in: *Immersive Journalism as Storytelling: Ethics, Production, and Design*, T. Uskali, A. Gynnild, S. Jones, E. Sirkkunen (Eds.), pp. 82–95, Routledge, New York, NY, 2021.

102. Sundar, S.S., Kang, J., Oprean, D., Being there in the midst of the story: How immersive journalism affects our perceptions and cognitions. *Cyberpsychol. Behav. Soc Netw.*, 20, 672–682, 2017.

103. Bujić, M., Salminen, M., Macey, J., Hamari, J., Empathy machine": How virtual reality affects human rights attitudes. *Internet Res.*, 30, 1407–1425, 2020.

104. Sánchez Laws, A.L., Can immersive journalism enhance empathy? *Digit. J.*, 8, 213–228, 2020.

105. Domínguez, E., Going beyond the classic news narrative convention: The background to and challenges of immersion in journalism. *Front. Digital Humanities*, 4, 1–11, 2017.

106. Skult, N. and Smed, J., Interactive storytelling in extended reality: Concepts for the design, in: *Game User Experience And Player-Centered Design*, pp. 449–467, 2020.

107. Koenitz, H., Ferri, G., Haahr, M., Sezen, D., Sezen, T.I., Introduction: Perspectives on interactive digital narrative, in: *Interactive Digital Narrative History, Theory and Practice*, pp. 1–8, Routledge, New York, NY, 2015.

108. Thompson, E., Sensorimotor subjectivity and the enactive approach to experience, in: *Phenomenology And The Cognitive Sciences*, pp. 407–427, 2005.

109. Varela, F.J., Thompson, E., Rosch, E., *The Embodied Mind: Cognitive Science And Human Experience*, MIT press, Boston, MA, 8, 1991.

110. Kaipainen, M., Ravaja, N., Tikka, P., Vuori, R., Pugliese, R., Rapino, M., Takala, T., Enactive systems and enactive media: Embodied human-machine coupling beyond interfaces. *Leonardo*, 44, 433–438, 2011.
111. Raymaekers, C., Special issue on enactive interfaces. *Interact. Comput.*, 21, 1–2, 2009.
112. Mechtley, B., Roberts, C., Stein, J., Nandin, B., Sha, X.W., Enactive steering of an experiential model of the atmosphere. *International Conference on Virtual, Augmented and Mixed Reality*, 2018.
113. Gambarato, R.R. and Tárcia, L.P.T., Transmedia strategies in journalism. An analytical model for the news coverage of planned events. *J. Stud.*, 18, 1381–1399, 2017.
114. INDCOR, INDCOR - COST Action CA18230: Interactive narrative design for complexity representations, 2019. https://indcor.eu/.

Haptic Interfaces

Jerome Perret

Haption, Laval, France

Abstract

Haptic technologies have the ability to transform the user experience by enhancing the sense of presence in XR. But if they have conquered our daily lives within the last 20 years, they are still under-exploited in XR applications. It is true that, since the turn of the millennium, they have not experienced any major technological or scientific breakthrough. It is all the more important to understand the obstacles that remain to be overcome, in terms of technology (actuators, physics simulation) and applications (vocational training, telemedicine, remote industrial maintenance).

Keywords: Haptics, telepresence, physic engine

3.1 Introduction

The term *haptics* designates, in this context, the technologies that make it possible to interact with a computer system through the sense of touch. We distinguish the tactile sense on the one hand, which mobilizes the nervous receptors present under the skin, and the kinesthetic sense on the other hand, which involves muscles and joints (more commonly referred to as *force-feedback*). With the exception of certain very specific uses, these two modalities are bidirectional (input and output) and often combined.

During the first two decades of the 21st century, haptics conquered everyday objects. From vibrators in smartphones to driving assistance in our cars, haptic technologies have demonstrated their usefulness and robustness. Thanks to mass production, the price of components has

Email: jerome.perret@haption.com

Mariano Alcañiz, Marco Sacco and Jolanda G. Tromp (eds.) Roadmapping Extended Reality: Fundamentals and Applications, (63–74) © 2022 Scrivener Publishing LLC

Figure 3.1 PS5 DualSense controller trigger mechanism. TronicFix (YouTube).

dropped dramatically, while also gaining in quality and performance. Today, high-quality haptic feedback is not limited to professional applications: for example, the controller of the PlayStation™ 5, released in November 2011, includes very powerful force-feedback triggers (Figure 3.1).

XR applications are not left out. Indeed, Augmented Reality takes advantage of the vibrators integrated in mobile devices to signal contextual events. On the Virtual Reality side, the controllers of immersive headsets all integrate haptic feedback components. And the main software platforms provide different types of interactions that exploit this equipment.

Europe occupies a very honorable place in scientific terms, thanks to top-notch teams, in particular: Munich in Germany, Pisa in Italy, Paris and Grenoble in France, and Delft in the Netherlands. The EuroHaptic Society organizes the international EuroHaptics conference every two years, of very good standard. In addition, the biennial ACTUATOR conference on actuation technologies offers significant space for haptic applications.

Economically, Europe is mainly present in the professional market, first, thanks to OEMs such as Valeo, Robert Bosch, and Continental, for the automotive market. Next, Europe (at large) has three manufacturers of "generic" force-feedback devices: Haption in France (Figure 3.2), Force Dimension in Switzerland, and MOOG in the Netherlands; but this market is still very confidential. Finally, Europe has many startups offering new concepts, with very mixed success.

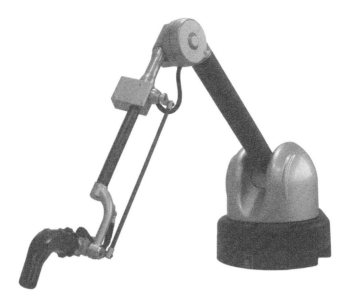

Figure 3.2 Virtuose™ force-feedback device. Haption.

3.2 State-of-the-Art

From the foundation of the concept of virtual reality (Sensorama [1]), haptic feedback is considered an integral part. The first notable scientific results dealt with force-feedback for a scientific application in virtual reality: the docking of molecules [2]. Until the early 2000s, most of the work concerned the development of force-feedback devices to interact with simple virtual environments [3]. It can be said without exaggeration that the scientific fundamentals of haptic interaction were already in place at the turn of the millennium: actuator control, transmission of forces, principles of stability, real-time physical simulation, and interaction metaphors.

Over the past two decades, progress has been largely incremental. The actuators have become more compact and more performant. The technical solutions for the transmission of forces, still largely dominated by the use of tensioned cables, use new materials, increasing efficiency. Control stability has benefited from the increased frequency of processors. New techniques for structuring algorithms have enabled significant gains in the complexity of virtual environments simulated in real time [4]. Interactions with haptic systems have become more intuitive and efficient. However, there has not been a major scientific or technological breakthrough.

Nevertheless, it would be wrong to think that haptics is no more than a technique for engineers, and that it suffices to integrate building blocks in order to compose an effective application. On the contrary: the lack of a major breakthrough does not come from the absence of barriers, but from the extreme complexity of this technology, which is too often misunderstood. Too often, newcomers to XR technologies tend to think of visual feedback as the one and only key, and focus most of their effort in this area. But many applications are inoperative without haptic feedback, and its integration poses open scientific problems, which can only be resolved after years of research.

3.3   Scientific and Technological Challenges

3.3.1   Actuation Technologies

A first challenge concerns the actuators, essential for carrying out a haptic interaction. Many types of actuators have been tested as part of prototypes, for example: shape-memory alloys, piezoelectric transducers, electroactive elastomers, and rheological fluids. Some of those technologies provide very high force density and bandwidth, but have dramatic limitations for haptics, e.g., nonlinearity, hysteresis, small working volume, and cost. Consequently, most haptic devices on the market today are equipped with electromagnetic motors. XR applications have different performance and quality requirements compared to mobile terminals and automotive equipment. However, the economic stakes are lower, and therefore, it is unlikely that the XR market will drive R&D in haptic actuators.

Organic molecules have conquered many domains of technology, thanks to their incredible versatility. Recently, the market breakthrough of OLED has shown that organic molecules are not only energy efficient, but that they can meet very high quality requirements. One can hope that organic molecules suitable for haptic actuators can be discovered or created, with similar benefits. Although some research has already been conducted in that direction [5], the field is largely unexplored.

3.3.2   Energy Efficiency

A second challenge, closely linked to the first, lies in energy consumption. Haptic feedback involves a transfer of mechanical energy, which comes from a source of electrical energy. Electromagnetic motors already have a good efficiency, and the gains to be expected from this side are limited.

However, the actuator of a haptic device is only used part of the time to apply mechanical power, and the rest of the time it only resists user action.

Energy recovery is well-known in the case of electric vehicles (cars, bicycles, rollers): instead of using friction for braking, the electric motor is used as a generator, and the current thus produced is fed back into the batteries. This technique has been recently introduced with some success in the robotic industry [9]. It can be argued that the power generated by haptic devices, even high-performance force-feedback devices, is not large enough to be worth collecting. However, the development effort is probably not excessive, and energy recovery can make a big difference for wireless devices. This could strengthen the competitiveness of certain actuation technologies, such as piezoelectricity, which lends itself particularly well to the generation of energy under the action of a finger pressure, for example.

3.3.3   Physics Simulation

A third scientific challenge is physical simulation in real time, at haptic frequency. In order to allow a natural and reliable haptic interaction, it is indeed essential to have the means to simulate the laws of physics, more or less simplified, at a frequency much higher than that of visual rendering, ideally close to 1 kHz. Real-time physical simulation has made colossal progress since the turn of the century to meet the needs of video games but also of previewing for special effects in cinema.

While the field of real-time physics simulation for video games is dominated by American players, Europe is well placed in the market of professional applications, e.g.:

- The SOFA framework is an open-source platform for physics simulation, initially launched in Boston but now developed mostly in Europe [8, 10]. Although generic, until now it found most of its application in healthcare, for surgery training (Figure 3.3). SOFA is especially recognized for the quality of the treatment of deformable objects using finite elements.
- The Swedish company Algoryx develops and sells a physics engine called AGX Dynamics, widely used for realistic simulation of complex industrial construction sites [11]. It provides specific modules for cables and wires, hydrodynamics, terrain, tires, etc. (Figure 3.4).
- The French research center CEA LIST develops the physics engine XDE, which is specially optimized for the simulation

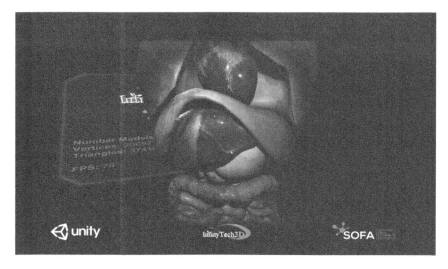

Figure 3.3 Internal organs simulation. Infiny Tech3D (YouTube).

Figure 3.4 Cable interaction in a subsea scenario. Algorix (YouTube).

of human avatars in real time for first-person ergonomic studies [12]. XDE is commercialized by the French company Light & Shadows (Figure 3.5).

Nevertheless, there are still few solutions capable of maintaining the performance necessary for a stable haptic interaction. The continuous increase in the power of microprocessors and the use of GPUs for high-performance

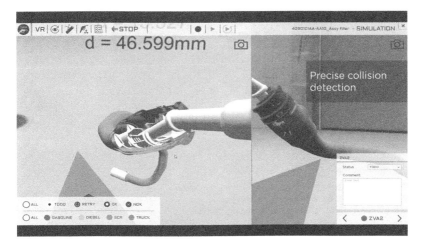

Figure 3.5 Simulation of nozzle insertion. Light & Shadows (YouTube).

computing is ineffective, the resolution of the equations of physics being difficult to parallelize. A hope could come from artificial intelligence techniques: just as AI can now improve the resolution of a computer-generated image, thus making it possible to increase the display frequency, it could be used tomorrow for managing the fine interactions with the simulated objects, the laws of physics being calculated at a coarser level, to guarantee the overall coherence of the virtual scene [13].

3.4 Application-Specific Challenges

3.4.1 Professional Training

Of all the applications of haptics in XR, professional training in virtual reality is the most important from an economic and societal point of view (Figure 3.6). Not all VR training topics need haptic feedback, on the contrary [6]. And some areas are already adequately covered, such as dental care, for example [7]. But some areas of expertise are largely without technical solutions for VR training—in the healthcare sector: emergency and field medicine, open surgery, obstetrics, and forensic medicine; in the handcraft and artistic sector: competitive sports, musical instruments, and industrial maintenance. All those cases pose two common challenges. The first one is the real-time interactive simulation of complex physical processes in ill-defined conditions. The second one is the transfer validity,

Figure 3.6 Virtual reality-based training of hand surgery. University of Regensburg.

i.e., the ability of the trainees to apply in real conditions the skills they have learned in the virtual environments.

3.4.2   Telemedicine

A second application is augmented reality for telemedicine. There can be no doubt that telemedicine, whose importance has been greatly boosted by the COVID-19 pandemic, will continue to expand in Europe and the rest of the world. To strengthen its effectiveness, it is essential to have better means of telepresence and communication between doctor and patient, including bilateral haptic interaction. Haptic feedback is essential to the physician for manual interventions such as palpation or mobilization, but also for using diagnosis equipment as in echography.

The challenges posed by this application concern the hardware, the real-time communications (5G), the public acceptability and confidence in the technology, and the integration into the care processes. Some of those challenges are more organizational than scientific or technological, but they can only be addressed within a comprehensive multidisciplinary approach.

3.4.3   Remote Maintenance

A third application is industrial remote maintenance with telepresence. European industry needs ever more flexibility and agility, while reducing environmental impacts. Remote maintenance provides an effective response by reducing intervention times and eliminating unnecessary travel. It can be carried out with or without human presence on site, but in both cases, haptic feedback is necessary. If a human operator is present at the remote site, then it is a question of using haptic guidance techniques for operations requiring manual expertise. On the contrary, if the operations are carried out by means of a robot, then it is necessary to implement telerobotic techniques with force feedback in order to guarantee the safety of the equipment and the quality of the result.

3.5   Future Research Agenda and Roadmap

In this section, we provide guidance elements for defining a research agenda and roadmap for each of the challenges defined in the previous sections.

3.5.1   Organic Molecules for Haptic Actuators

This challenge requires a long-term investment of multidisciplinary research, combining organic chemistry, smart materials, and multidomain physics. It also needs a tight connection between academic research and industry. If successful, it is likely to give Europe a significant competitive advantage, which could help regain leadership in the more general field of actuation technologies.

- Current TRL: 1–2
- TRL within 5 years: 5–6
- Time to TRL 9:   10 years

3.5.2   Energy Recovery from Negative Work in Haptic Actuators

While less significant in terms of market impact, this challenge is liable to give a competitive edge to European device manufacturers. While design elements and functionality have been central to purchasing decisions so far, environmental impact is gaining in importance.

- Current TRL: 3–5
- TRL within 5 years: 5–7
- Time to TRL 9:   8 years

3.5.3   Interactive Physics Simulation for Haptics in XR

Our analysis shows that a qualitative leap is possible, subject to bringing together the best teams from the academic world and companies within a major unifying project centered on the combination of artificial intelligence with digital modeling. Such a project will have spinoffs in many other areas: medical diagnosis, environmental impact studies, energy savings, waste treatment, etc.

- Current TRL: 3–5
- TRL within 5 years: 5–7
- Time to TRL 9:   8 years

3.5.4   Haptic Interaction for VR-Based Training

Vocational education and training, both initial and lifelong, are major societal and economic issues for Europe. As part of the digitalization process, XR technologies, and more specifically virtual reality, will play a key role in the future. Many SMEs and startups are already active in this field, but they face several difficulties. One of them lies in the complexity of the vocational training environment in Europe, which remains a national competence, with very heterogeneous certification and cost support processes. Another is the technological barrier to entry, in particular concerning haptic feedback, essential for all professions requiring manual skills.

In this area, it is crucial to create bridges between SMEs, research laboratories, and vocational training institutes.

- Current TRL: 3–5
- TRL within 5 years: 5–7
- Time to TRL 9:   8 years

3.5.5   Haptic Interaction for Telemedicine

The COVID-19 pandemic has had a positive effect on the uptake of telemedicine in Europe, with significant benefits for the care and quality of patient follow-up. Europe has thus made up part of its delay with respect to the USA and Asia. To go further, it is essential to improve the user experience and to offer new services. R&D work in the field of bidirectional haptic interaction must continue and be amplified for the purposes of: palpation, echography, muscle and joint mobilization, social exchange, etc.

In the medium term, these technologies will have a multifactorial impact: reduction of health costs, keeping dependent people at home, energy savings due to shorter travel distances, etc.

- Current TRL: 1–2
- TRL within 5 years: 5–6
- Time to TRL 9:   10 years

3.5.6 Haptic-Enabled Telepresence for Remote Industrial Maintenance

Telerobotics with force-feedback has been used in the nuclear industry for over 30 years, and many of the leaders in the field are based in Europe. With the rapid deployment of high-speed communications (including 5G) and the democratization of robotics, its application to remote industrial maintenance is coming. It still faces several difficulties, including standardization of interfaces, data protection, safety of people, and equipment, but this should be a low-hanging fruit for European industry. XR technology experts must get involved in this field and develop effective telepresence features with haptic feedback.

- Current TRL: 4–5
- TRL within 5 years: 6–8
- Time to TRL 9:   8 years

References

1. M.L. Heilig, Sensorama simulator. United States patent US3050870A, 1961.
2. Ouh-Young, M. and Brooks, F.P., *Force Display In Molecular Docking*, Ph.D. Dissertation, The University of North Carolina at Chapel Hill. Order Number: AAI9034744, 1990.
3. Massie, T.H. and Salisbury, J.K., The PHANToM haptic interface: a device for probing virtual objects, in: *Proceedings Of The ASME Dynamic Systems And Control Division*, 1994.
4. Weller, R., New geometric data structures for collision detection and haptics, in: *Springer Series On Touch And Haptic Systems*, ISBN 9783319010199. 2013.
5. Lipomi, D.J., Dhong, C., Carpenter, C.W., Root, N.B., Ramachandran, V.S., Organic haptics: intersection of materials chemistry and tactile perception. *Adv. Funct. Mater.*, 30, 1906850, 2020. https://doi.org/10.1002/adfm.201906850.

6. Vander Poorten, E., Perret, J., Muyle, R., Reynaerts, D., Vander Sloten, J., Pintelon, L., To Feedback or not to feedback—the value of haptics in virtual reality surgical training, in: *Proceedings Actuator 2014*, Bremen, Germany.

7. Steinberg, A., Bashook, P., Drummond, J., Ashrafi, S., Zefran, K., Assessment of faculty perception of content validity of PerioSim©, a haptic-3D virtual reality dental training simulator. *J. Dent. Educ.*, 71, 1574–82, 2008 Jan.

8. Faure, F., Duriez, C., Delingette, H., Allard, J. *et al.*, SOFA: A multi-model framework for interactive physical simulation, in: *Soft Tissue Biomechanical Modeling For Computer Assisted Surgery*, 2012.

9. Ghorbanpour, A. and Richter, H., Control with optimal energy regeneration in robot manipulators driven by brushless DC motors, in: *ASME 2018 Dynamic Systems And Control Conference*, DOI: 10.1115/DSCC2018-8972.

10. www.sofa-framework.org

11. www.algoryx.se/agx-dynamics/

12. De Magistris, G., Micaelli, A., Evrard, P., Andriot, C., Savin, J., Gaudez, C., Marsot, J., Dynamic control of DHM for ergonomic assessments. *Int. J. Ind. Ergon.*, 43, 2, 170–180, doi: DOI: 10.1016/j.ergon.2013.01.003 March 2013.

13. De, S., Deo, D., Sankaranarayanan, G., Arikatla, V.A., Physics-driven neural networks-based simulation system (PhyNNeSS) for multimodal interactive virtual environments involving nonlinear deformable objects. *Presence (Camb)*, 20, 4, 289–308, 2011 Aug. doi: 10.1162/pres_a_00054.

4

Immersive Sound for XR

Arcadio Reyes-Lecuona[1]*, Tifanie Bouchara[2,3] and Lorenzo Picinali[4]

[1]Telecommunication Research Institute (TELMA), Universidad de Málaga, Málaga, Spain
[2]CEDRIC, CNAM, Paris, France
[3]LISN, CNRS, Université Paris Saclay, Orsay, France
[4]Imperial College London, London, UK

Abstract

Sound plays a very important role in everyday life as well as in XR applications, as it will be explained in this chapter. Recent advances and challenges in immersive audio research are presented, discussing how, why, and to which extent there is potential for further development of these technologies applied to XR. The fundamentals of immersive audio rendering for XR are introduced before presenting the main technological challenges still open in the area. Finally, a series of future applications is presented, which the authors envision being examples of the potential of immersive audio in XR, and a research roadmap is outlined.

Keywords: Spatial audio, binaural spatialization, auralization, HRTF, immersive audio rendering

4.1 Introduction

Since the second half of the twentieth century, in the early days of VR, audio has been included together with graphics in almost every definition of what VR is and what VR technologies should deliver. Nevertheless, if we look at the research activities in this domain, most of the effort has been focused on the visual modality. Comparatively, audio and haptics have received much less attention by the XR scientific community in the last three decades. Figure 4.1 illustrates this by showing the number of

---

*Corresponding author: areyes@uma.es

Mariano Alcañiz, Marco Sacco and Jolanda G. Tromp (eds.) Roadmapping Extended Reality: Fundamentals and Applications, (75–102) © 2022 Scrivener Publishing LLC

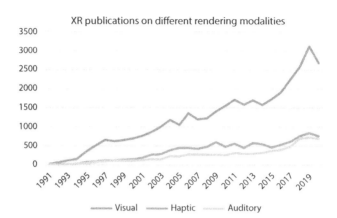

Figure 4.1 Number of publications reported by Scopus since 1991 in the field of XR for the Visual, Haptic, and Auditory modalities. The queries used for each curve are a combination of two parts, one common for every modality (*"Virtual Reality"* OR *"Augmented Reality"* OR *"Mixed Reality"* OR *"Extended Reality"*), and the modality-dependent term (*"graphics"* OR *"visual"* OR *"graphical"*) or (*"force feedback"* OR *"tactile"* OR *"haptics"* OR *"haptic"* OR *"touch"*) or (*"audio"* OR *"sound"* OR *"auditory"* OR *"acoustic"* OR *"acoustics"*), respectively.

scientific publications reported by Scopus in the area of XR related with those three modalities. As pointed out by Serafin *et al.* [1], it can be argued that sound is an under-used modality in XR, although this situation is changing and audio rendering and interaction research is slowly becoming more and more present in XR.

Looking at the multimodal rendering and interaction matters from a broader point of view, it is clear that sensory integration, describing richness and consistency of the presentation from different modalities, is a key factor when estimating the quality of the immersion [2]. So, it is not only a matter of including audio but of making it consistent with other stimuli as well. That necessarily involves carefully simulating spatial attributes of the audio rendering, which has been a research area of increasing interest in the past twenty years within the audio community. At this point in time, there are still several open technological challenges in spatial audio rendering for XR.

A further topic that is of major interest to the XR community, and in which audio has strong implications, gravitates around research on the concepts of presence, i.e., the sense of being in the virtual world, immersion, or plausibility (i.e., the illusion that the perceived events in the virtual environment are really happening). Since early research in this topic, sound has been taken into account and included in the classical instruments used to estimate the sense of presence, such as the Presence Questionnaire (PQ) [3]. More recently, a few studies have tried to explore the effect of spatial audio attributes on the perceived plausibility of the virtual scene [4, 5]. It is in fact true that research on how spatialized audio might affect the sense of presence is nowadays a major topic of interest, as demonstrated by the number of works on this topic presented in international research venues. An example of the latter is the Sonic Interaction in Virtual Environments (SIVE) workshop, which has been hosted within the IEEE Virtual Reality Conference for several years now. However, the influence of the auditory modality on presence still remains relatively unexplored if compared with its visual counterpart [1]. In this sense, the full potential of audio spatialization has not yet been fully explored and exploited within XR. In addition to its contribution to improving presence, audio can also influence the sense of co-presence (i.e., the sense of being together in the same shared virtual or augmented world), which is central in immersive collaborative applications.

Several other very relevant challenges exist related with audio and XR, encompassing research fields such as sound synthesis and sonic interactions, as well as technologies and techniques for audio production in the creative industries. However, an overview of these topics would require extensive space within the chapter, and, as they are in large part not specific to XR, we have taken the decision to focus mainly on the spatial aspects of sound rendering specifically applied to XR.

In Section 4.2, we overview the fundamentals of immersive audio rendering for XR for both headphones and loudspeakers, while in Section 4.3, we discuss the technological challenges specifically related with binaural audio (i.e., specifically processed for headphones listening). Section 4.4 focuses on several applications we envision for the future in this field, and Section 4.5 closes the chapter presenting a future research agenda and roadmap.

4.2   Immersive Audio Rendering for XR

Rendering a realistic and interactive audio environment requires to take the entire pipeline of immersive sound production into account [6]. First, produce a sound. It may be by playing a pre-recorded sound or by interactively synthesizing virtual sources, for instance through physics-based sound modeling (see [7] and [1] for a review). Second, place it in the virtual environment by simulating the sound wave propagation from the source to the listener's ears. This requires not only to model the acoustics of the environment but also to consider the position and orientation of the source and the listener, as well as their respective movements. Finally, render the sound directly to the listener. When dealing with binaural rendering, i.e., when processing immersive audio for headphones playback, this final step is often carried out by modeling the listener's physical characteristics, such as torso, head, and ears. The succession of these three processes can be referred to as "auralization" [8].

4.2.1   Fundamentals of Spatial Hearing and Binaural Rendering

Human beings are able, to some extent, to determine the position of a sound source in the surrounding environment, which is key to understand and react to what happens around them, be it virtual or real. To do so, they rely on different localization cues, which are influenced by several factors such as the size and shape of the listener's head, pinnae (i.e., the visible parts of the ear), and torso [9]. One of the main goals of spatial audio technologies for XR is to replicate these localization cues in a virtual environment to therefore improve the spatial features of each source (e.g., direction and distance) while maintaining the realism of the simulated soundscape.

Lateralization, i.e., determining the position of a sound source on the left or on the right, is mainly performed using time and level (amplitude) differences between the signals arriving at left and right ears (Interaural Time Differences—ITD and Interaural Level Differences—ILD, respectively). In order to be able to discriminate between front and back, or between above and below, the hearing system also infers direction from binaural and monoaural (i.e., involving both ears or one ear only) spectral variations. Indeed, the sound coming from a specific direction up to our eardrum is modified in a frequency-dependent manner by different acoustic interactions with our body, such as diffraction from head and torso, head shadowing, or reflections on the various parts of the pinnae. Those modifications, together with the interaural differences mentioned above, are described by a set of functions known as HRTFs (Head-Related Transfer Functions).

To simulate a specific direction of a sound source using headphones, one can therefore use the binaural synthesis process: the anechoic audio signal generated by the sound source is convolved with the appropriate pair of HRTFs (one for each ear) corresponding to the simulated direction [10].

As they are only measured in, or calculated from, anechoic environments, HRTFs contain only user-related properties but completely lack room-related ones. Yet, such information (i.e., reverberation) is very useful to improve the overall realism of the rendering, especially the externalization sensation [11]. Rather than using HRTFs, it is possible to use binaural room impulse responses (BRIRs), which contain additional information about the acoustics of the listener's environment. Such filters are more complex to measure and manage, mainly when scalability and flexibility are essential factors [12].

Finally, in addition to the direction of a sound source, listeners are also able to estimate its distance. This estimation is mainly based on the analysis of three factors: the overall level of the source (or level changes, in the case of movements closer or farther away), spectral balance between high and low frequencies (both as a monoaural and as an interaural cue), and reverberation effects, i.e., the ratio between amount of direct sound coming from the source and the amount of sound reflected on the various surfaces within the environment where the source and listener are located [9]. The simulation of these effects can be obtained through auralization, as described in the following section.

4.2.2   Auralization and Introduction to Room Acoustics

Beyond the simulation of sound source positions in the virtual space, to provide a sense of immersion, it is essential to also render the global acoustics of the environment where the sources and the listener are located.

A more synthetic definition of auralization is the process of "rendering audible, by physical or mathematical modelling, the sound field of a source in a space, in such a way as to simulate the binaural listening experience at a given position in the modelled space" [8]. It is therefore an artificial computer-aided process whose main goals, for interactive and immersive virtual environment systems, concern both the accuracy—i.e., the virtual auditory environment to sound realistic, possibly indistinguishable from the real one—and the computational efficiency of the complex real-time room acoustic simulation [13, 14]. This has been an explored research topic for decades, and many approaches have been proposed, which can be classified in four well-established categories [15, 16]:

- Synthetic reverberation using delay networks,
- Physical simulation of the propagation of the sound wave (solving the wave equation or using ray tracing simplifications),
- Convolution with measured or synthetic impulse responses,
- Virtual simulation of classical analogue reverberation techniques, such as vibrating plates, etc.

Auralization can be useful to simulate existing acoustical environments, create new ones, compare different architectural designs [17], or recreate lost ones [18].

4.2.3   Overview of Loudspeaker-Based Techniques

While headphones rendering may be very appropriate for individual applications, loudspeaker-based spatial sound reproduction may appear less intrusive, and therefore more appropriate to complement CAVE and video-projected XR systems. Allowing the users to interact more naturally without being isolated from each other also facilitates system-free communication between them within co-located multi-user applications. However, loudspeaker-based techniques do not allow separating the sounds addressed to each user as easily as headphones systems. Furthermore, they suffer from several limitations, including hardware and computational costs, and the size of the area where the users can interact with each other and experience a coherent sound simulation.

Three broad categories of loudspeaker-based audio techniques exist: multichannel amplitude-panning techniques, multichannel holophonic techniques, and loudspeaker-based binaural audio. While the two first categories rely on the use of multiple audio channels, each routed to a different loudspeaker of an array, the last category, in its most common implementations, only requires a pair of loudspeakers.

Initially developed to increase immersion in music and films through stereophonic systems, the first spatial audio loudspeaker-based techniques relied on amplitude panning principles. Those techniques have been extended to spatialize sound through different loudspeaker configurations such as quadraphony, ITU 5.1 Surround, or even 22.2 Surround. The main idea behind amplitude panning is to produce phantom sources between loudspeakers surrounding the listener through the use of level differences between those loudspeakers [19]. One of the most advanced solutions using amplitude panning principles is VBAP (Vector Based Amplitude Panning) [20], which allows one to use an arbitrary number of loudspeakers positioned in 2D or 3D setups. The principal limit of those techniques is the reduced sweet spot, i.e., the area where the listener can perceive a correct sound field reproduction. This of course limits the number of listeners that can simultaneously benefit from this audio rendering.

Holophonic solutions, on the contrary, are based on the physical reconstruction of the sound field in an extended listening area. Those techniques include Wave Field Synthesis (WFS) [21] and Higher Order Ambisonics (HOA) [22]. To generate an accurate sound field, WFS relies on the

Huygens-Fresnel principle stating that the wave front generated by a sound source can be recreated by the superposition of secondary audio sources (e.g., a linear loudspeaker array), which emit secondary wave fronts. While leading to very realistic spatial audio rendering with a fine spatial resolution, WFS is computationally intensive and suffers from limitations in real world due to the large number of required loudspeakers. HOA, which is based on the spherical harmonics decomposition of space, is to a certain extent less complex (both in terms of computing and hardware) than WFS, but potentially leads to lower spatial resolution, especially when lower orders are used [23].

While binaural audio is created for reproduction through a pair of headphones, it is also possible to use binaural on loudspeakers by taking some precautions. It is in fact essential that the left signal is delivered to the left ear only, and vice-versa for the right ear. When binaural signals are reproduced through loudspeakers, due to the wave travelling to both sides of the head, the left and right channels are not perfectly separated. The interference between the two channels is referred to as *cross-talk*, and in the case of binaural audio, it results in a significantly degraded spatial audio effect, as well as in an overall decrease in low-frequency content due to the phase-related cancellations caused by the ITDs. Cross-talk cancellation techniques exist, based on sets of inverse filters created for specific loudspeakers and listener position, which allow for the reproduction of binaural signals through loudspeakers. These techniques are often referred to as *transaural* audio rendering.

Recent research has looked into the design of techniques based on linear loudspeaker arrays (i.e., two or more loudspeakers arranged on a line, generally positioned in front of the listener) or multidriver sound-bars (i.e., a wide enclosure containing several loudspeaker drivers), which improved the robustness of the inverse filters [24], and allowed to adapt such filter in real time according to the position of the listener [25]. Devices and applications incorporating such technologies exist and are available to the general and professional public, even though evident limitations exist related with the complexity of the playback system (if compared with a simple pair of headphones) and with the robustness to the listener's head rotations.

4.3   Technological Challenges

As simplicity of implementation (both software and hardware) and portability are often highly desirable in XR, this section focuses only on the main technological challenges in the area of binaural audio.

4.3.1   HRTF Personalization for XR

Everyone perceives spatial sound differently thanks to the particular shape of their ears, torso, and head. High-quality simulations need therefore to be uniquely tailored to each individual in an effective and efficient manner. This is especially important in AR, where the virtual auditory simulations should ideally blend seamlessly with the real world. It is in fact true that, in an acoustic AR context, for example when using a playback device such as the BOSE Frames[1], listeners hear the surrounding soundscape through their own ears, and in order to create a virtual source that is indistinguishable from a real one, the rendering has to be highly personalized.

Therefore, binaural synthesis implies to first measure the individual HRTFs of each user for every possible direction. However, recording HRTFs is very time and resource consuming and is rather sensitive to measurement errors [26]. Therefore, XR applications often use generic or pre-measured HRTFs, such as those recorded from a dummy head mannequin, or those recorded from real people and stored in publicly available databases, e.g., CIPIC [27], LISTEN [28], and also SADIE [29] and ARI [30].

Unfortunately though, using non-individualized HRTFs have been known to have a major effect not only on sound sources localization accuracy (e.g. [31]), but also on perceptual attributes such as Coloration, Externalization, Immersion, Realism, and Relief/Depth, as defined in [32]. Various methods and techniques exist in order to improve the match between the HRTF used for the rendering and the one specific to the listener. These can be mapped in two separate groups: the first one based on system-to-user adaptation approaches and the second one on user-to-system adaptation approaches.

Looking at system-to-user adaptation, these methods aim to provide every individual with the best possible HRTF. In addition to acoustically measuring each listener's individual HRTF, personalization can be achieved using other approaches such as HRTF modeling, therefore synthesizing an individual HRTF starting from morphological geometric information about the ears of the listener [33, 34] possibly obtained from photographs or 3D scans [35]. Another common approach is to select a best fitting HRTF from a database of already-measured ones. This can be done using morphology-based methods [36, 37] or perceptual-based methods, for example looking at individual preference [38, 39], localization accuracy, or both [40, 41].

---

[1]https://www.bose.co.uk/en_gb/products/frames.html

User-to-system adaptation approaches look at the matter from the opposite point of view, therefore trying to train a listener to improve performances (e.g., localization accuracy) when using a non-individualized HRTF. Such approaches usually rely on perceptual training routines and have been proven to be successful also after just a few VR-based training sessions [42, 43].

Moreover, as users are continuously moving in the environment and rotating their head, an accurate and realistic XR system requires head tracking and the development of dynamic adjustment strategies to update the selection and interpolation of the appropriate HRTFs in real time according to the actual relative position and orientation of the listener from the source. This is even more important when using non-individualized HRTF in order to avoid externalization problems [44].

Finally, it is important to underline that, within an AR context, using a non-individual HRTF can cause additional problems if compared with VR scenarios, as users are already listening to sounds from the surrounding environment, which are filtered through their own HRTF. In this case, with the limited knowledge we currently have on the processes of HRTF adaptation and on the ability of our hearing system to retain two separate sets of HRTFs, it is very much preferable to use individual or at least highly personalized HRTFs.

While it is clear that several methods exist to tackle the matter of HRTF personalization, none of these yet represents the ultimate solution, especially in the context of audio for XR. A major issue is related with finding a standard way to determine how well these methods compare with each other, and the key to this is to establish a set of pertinent metrics to perceptually assess HRTFs, as well as to accurately describe the relationship between such metrics and the characteristics of the HRTF filters.

4.3.2   Real-Time Capturing and Rendering of Room Acoustics

As it has been introduced in Section 4.2, part of the sound spatialization process involves the simulation of how the environment modifies the sound emitted by the sources before arriving to the listener. Several approaches have been presented, including delay networks, physical simulations, and convolution with room impulse responses [15, 16]. However, none of them can be considered as an ultimate solution for the real-time and interactive geometry-dependent processes needed by XRs, in particular when considering acoustic AR and the needs to match the virtual environment with the real one.

Convolution-based algorithms can achieve a high degree of realism, but they are not flexible enough to simulate arbitrary (i.e., not known/measured in advance) positions and orientations of sound sources and listener within the acoustic environment. Having sets of spatial impulse responses (e.g., binaural, or using multichannel techniques such as Ambisonic) arriving from multiple directions to a fixed location, as it is usually the case when using BRIRs, these methods can deal relatively easily with head rotations. However, unless a very large number of measurements are taken or synthesized, they cannot accurately simulate movements of the listener around the room nor movements of the sound sources. There are techniques that can be used to simplify this, or at least part of it. For instance, the 3D Tune-In Toolkit [45] implements a BRIR-based virtual loudspeaker reverberation approach, which is very efficient with a large number of sound sources, allowing both head rotations and sources movements, but relying on certain approximations (e.g., the room is "locked" to the head of the listener). It has been shown [12] that these simplifications do not have significant perceptual implications when the direct path is rendered in the highest possible quality (i.e., direct HRTF convolution). Nevertheless, this and similar convolution-based methods are problematic when the listener changes dynamically position around the space. Solutions exist to allow listener's translations when using convolution-based reverberation approaches (e.g., [46]), but they require a lot of measured/synthesized data to be produced and stored, and they are not particularly efficient nor flexible (e.g., changing characteristics of the environment requires re-measuring/synthesizing all the impulse responses).

Flexibility is not a problem for computational acoustics methods based on physical simulations [13], but these often result in high computational costs, which is not usually affordable in real time and mobile applications such as XR.

Rendering techniques based on delay network approaches are computationally efficient, but their parameterization does not relay on physical attributes of the environment, making it difficult to realistically simulate the reverberation of a specific environment, especially when this has to match a real one.

It is therefore clear that this is a still open area of research, especially for the specific requirements of XR applications. Several promising research works are tackling these limitations. An example is the use of hybrid methods, such as Scattering Delay Network (SDN), which is a computationally efficient approximation of geometric ray tracing using a delay network structure to simulate propagation with digital waveguides [47]. An interesting area that could have significant impact on room acoustics simulations is hardware acceleration. Recent developments include *TrueAudio Next* by AMD, an SDK for GPU accelerated and multicore high-performance audio signal processing that supports efficient convolution algorithms [48]. More recently, NVIDIA has released *VRWorks Audio*, taking advantage of techniques developed for ray tracing algorithms in graphical rendering and adapting them to acoustic rendering [49]. These recent developments show the interest of major graphics card and processor-tech companies in the integration of 3D Audio processing techniques in XR applications.

It should not be forgotten that the final goal is to create for the user the illusion that the sound is being reproduced in a given environment. In this sense, there is still a lot to understand from the perceptual side of things. We need to understand what is perceptually relevant, and should therefore be rendered with a high level of accuracy, and what is not, and can therefore be simplified. For example, it is well known that it is more important to have high spatial accuracy when computing early reflections than the last part of the reverberation [50]. Nevertheless, more research is still needed in order to better understand the relationship between the physical attributes of reverberation and the listener's perception, ultimately aiming at modeling such mechanisms, as it has already been extensively attempted when looking at localization accuracy [51].

All these techniques are intended to simulate a specific virtual environment that can be the simulation of a real environment or of a completely new one. As introduced in the previous section, in the case of audio AR, it is especially important to capture the room acoustic characteristics in order to blend virtual and real sounds and make the virtual ones plausible in the real environment. However, XR applications are especially demanding in terms of requirements for this task, as these acoustical characterizations should be rendered in real time, and for all possible locations and orientations of sound sources and listeners. Research showed that it is possible to extract some acoustic features from simple recordings of sounds within the environment [52]. However, this information is far from being enough for rendering a virtual reverb that matches the real one. Another approach consists in capturing the room geometry using artificial vision techniques [40] and use it to simulate the acoustics of that specific environment. The main challenge remains to capture the acoustical properties of the different surfaces. Considering the relevance and potential impact of this research area, and the tremendous advances done in the field of machine learning in the recent years, it is possible to see how the two could work together aiming to achieve real-time room acoustic characterization for interactive XR applications.

4.3.3   Evaluation of 3D Audio Technological Improvements

A key open challenge in the domain of immersive audio for XR is to find a standard way to quantify how well methods and technologies compare with each other. This matter is related both to the need to establish a set of pertinent metrics to assess immersive audio rendering, and with the complexity and time-consuming nature of experiments involving subjects, which dramatically limits the possibilities in terms of experimental conditions.

Regarding the first task, extensive work has already been done on the standardization of assessments in the field of audio quality, for example when looking at telecommunications and lossy compression. Equivalent work though still has to be carried out in the domain of immersive audio, and it is evident that any advancement in this area will need to rely on a coordinated and concerted effort across different research groups. Looking at the second task, a potential solution could be found in the use of auditory models, in particular binaural ones. These integrate computational simulations of human binaural auditory processing, which in certain cases can be used to predict listener's responses to immersive audio signals. They have already been used in the past to rapidly perform substantial evaluations, which would be too long and extensive to be implemented as auditory experiments [12, 53]. Tools such as the Auditory Modelling Toolbox [51] are excellent resources for this purpose, organizing models in an accessible and consistent manner, and allowing researchers around the world to freely use them and, if possible, further contribute to their development by sharing novel evaluation data.

4.3.4   Web and Networked Solutions

Thanks to the recently released *WebXR API* specification [54] (which has superseded the former WebVR), it is now possible to build XR applications that run directly in a web browser. The possibility of including 3D audio within these applications is supported by the *Web Audio API* [55], which is also part of the Web standards. An example of a 3D binaural audio application running on the web is the *PlugSonic* suite [56], which will be introduced in the next section. Besides the not yet fully explored possibilities of building consumer applications to be distributed through the web and run in either desktop, mobile, or XR specific device, like an HMD, this technology opens a full avenue of opportunities for research. Conducting

Internet-based experiments has been of interest for some years, especially in disciplines such as psychology, due to the possibility to access to massive amounts of participants. This has significantly increased in popularity during the COVID-19 pandemic, as the availability of experimental subjects for lab-based experiments was severely limited, when not impossible. However, experiments over the internet present a series of important weaknesses, mainly based on the lack of experimental control, which can threaten the experiment reliability and internal validity. In the case of 3D audio, there are specific challenges that should be addressed, such as coping with the diversity of audio equipment and setups, with signal/noise control within the environment, with latency issues (for example when performing head-tracking) and low computational efficiency. Pushed out of necessity, the scientific community has made a great effort to improve the methodology for conducting web-based audio experiments during the pandemic, but there is a lot still to be done in order to exploit the enormous potential of Internet to conduct experiments.

Another big opportunity for the XR industry and research communities is the advent of 5G technology. 5G is a wireless communication infrastructure that could satisfy the specific demanding requirements of XR services and applications, more specifically high bandwidth and very low latency [57]. Focusing on the audio component of these XR applications, it is particularly interesting the possibility of adapting the rendering algorithms with high computational cost to be partially run in the network. In this sense, the simulation of the environment acoustics could benefit very much from 5G and edge computing, specifically considering the requirements of real-time interactivity. Some efforts have already been made in this direction [58], but there is a big potential still to be explored regarding this technology, which is not fully deployed yet.

4.3.5 Authoring Tools

To extend the use of the audio modality in XR projects, it is essential to offer optimized authoring tools for the design, editing, and processing of the sonic content of the virtual environment. Those tools should be designed and developed for two distinct populations: expert sound designers, to allow them to work with sounds directly immersed in the environment; and users non-expert in sound design or in XR, for example those who need to frequently renew or personalize the auditory content of their application—such as therapists, trainers, or museum curators.

Considering the first group, the majority of professional editing and mixing tools for XR are actually audio engines, such as Wwise[2] or Fmod[3], initially developed in the game industry to create and integrate the sound part of virtual environments. They allow to manipulate a lot of sound parameters (temporal evolution, frequency content, adjustment of the audio effects, spatial curves of attenuation of the various parameters, etc.) but necessitate to alternate between the VR environment editing tool (like Unity), also in 2D with a 3D view, and a third-party 2D application for sound editing only. Worse than that, they require switching between 2 devices to get an immersive audio preview, from computer/monitor for editing, to HMD (Head Mounted Display) plus audio headsets for listening and checking.

Immersive authoring tools, i.e., tools to create and edit immersive content directly while immersed in the XR world, already exist for the visual modality—for instance in the video game and animation industries (e.g., with the app *One Man Movie* [59]), or for CAD activities [60]—to allow the 3D animator to better understand the relationships between the objects of the 3D scene (distance/occlusion/lights). 3D animators can modify the objects directly in the virtual reality environment, being themselves equipped with a VR headset and immersed in the center of the 3D scene. It is now time to extend those tools to the audio modality to allow a direct manipulation of the sound properties and a better consideration of the spatial relationships between objects and sound effects. To our knowledge, only one recent tool, Dear Reality's *DearVR Pro* plugin and its accompanying *Spatial Connect*, is now available to bridge the gap between the mixing and the production environment. Developed as a plugin, it offers the ability to profile and debug audio directly from inside a VR headset. Questions about how to optimize interactions for immersive audio mixing and what will be the emerging design processes to produce the immersive auditory content can now be explored.

4.4   Envisioning Applications

After having carried out a review of the main technological challenges in the area of immersive sound for XR, in this section, we present a series of use cases in application areas that we believe are very relevant to this topic and have a high potential to generate future impact.

---

[2]https://www.audiokinetic.com/fr/products/wwise/
[3]https://www.fmod.com/

Besides the challenges already mentioned in the previous section, it is important to note that the applications described below also require significant technological advancements, as well as a deeper understanding on auditory and multisensory perception mechanisms.

4.4.1   Use Case 1: Audio for Immersive Collaborative Work and Videoconferences

More and more applications have been developed that allow several users to work together to achieve complex tasks. Users can be co-situated (i.e., located in the same physical space) or be geographically separated and work remotely. These applications have become even more essential during the COVID pandemic, not only in a professional context but also for supporting personal and social relationships, for instance through videoconferencing systems. In this context of collaboration, the audio modality is definitely a priority.

Firstly, it is the primary modality for communication between users (voice). Audio has been proven to enhance coordination, for instance on XR remote assistance applications where a remote expert is helping a field worker (e.g., emergency repair assistance of an aircraft engine or a car; see [61] for a review). In such context, audio spatialization and sonic immersion are of primary importance as they are known to facilitate communication and improve speech intelligibility [62]. This is particularly relevant for videoconferencing systems, be it immersive 3D systems or just 2D videoconferencing. Indeed, the use of spatial audio improves the user experience by allowing spatial separation between the various attendances within the meeting and ensuring the externalization of their voices as defined in Section 4.2. This should also improve the sense of co-presence (the feeling that others are with us in the same shared virtual space) by simulating that the voices of all attendants are placed in the same acoustical space (see information about the auralization process described in Section 4.2). Moreover, enabling full 3D spatialization, we can imagine virtual meetings where different conversations might take place at the same time, as in a party, but without the need of isolating every single conversation as fully private. This would open enormous possibilities for immersive virtual social meetings.

Secondly, audio can be employed to maintain a form of awareness of what others are doing when co-working on a shared task. Sonification (the use of non-speech audio to convey non-audio information) can be useful to better understand each task carried out by the others, but the design of sound feedback, while being a generic HCI topic more than specifically related to XR problematics, might still be improved [63]. More interestingly, 3D audio technologies can be used to "place" a collaborator outside the field of view when visual interactions are not required, in such a way it is still possible to hear them and understand where they are, without overloading the visual channel.

Finally, immersive audio sound design can have a major impact on the interactions and relationship between co-users, but further research on the topic is needed to determine in what extent. Indeed, to the best of our knowledge, no study has determined precisely how auralized sounds modify the interaction behavior between two virtual collaborators. A previous study [64] suggests that the spatialization of sound, localized or not to the position of the virtual avatar, has an influence on the relationship and interactions between two immersed collaborators, but the nature of this influence remains to be determined. Additionally, studying the role played by the sound modality in terms of co-presence and relationship to others will allow the community to optimize the design of sound feedback for collaborative immersive applications. This would also improve the possibility for every user to simultaneously perceive and interact with the shared auditory (or multisensory) virtual environment with the same quality. These questions will be particularly important in emergent applications where collaborators might be equipped with heterogenous immersive systems; for instance, some of the users co-situated in a shared CAVE could remotely work with users equipped with XR headsets or even AR tablet solutions.

4.4.2   Use Case 2: Inclusivity and Assistive Technologies for Visually Impaired and Blind Users

As for other digital technologies, it is essential for the XR community to focus on creating an inclusive digital world where everyone, even people with disabilities, has the opportunity and the agency to experiment immersion, and connect and interact with others in virtual or augmented environments. With this goal in mind, everyone should ultimately benefit from XR technologies.

To do so, it is important that accessibility is considered since early design stages of XR applications, either designing inclusive and universal applications, or creating new assistive technologies that can suit individual needs and help in everyday life.

Audio XR can definitely help to achieve this goal, both for rendering standard audio content and for conveying non-audio information through the auditory sense, i.e., through sensory substitution. This can have a major impact for individual with disabilities, for example when looking at XR applications dedicated or accessible to visually impaired and blind (VIB) users [65]. XR can be used for learning in safer conditions; for instance, audio and VR have been used for Orientation and Mobility Training Courses where VIB children learn how to explore their environments efficiently, effectively, and safely, sometimes through 3D serious games [66, 67]. Furthermore, audio AR and VR have often been proposed as assistive technologies to help VIB users to navigate in real life [68] or to learn the spatial configuration of an environment before being physically introduced to it [46, 69, 70].

Finally, audio rendering could help making VR games more inclusive and accessible, for example by carefully designing and managing user interfaces, making extensive use of auditory displays and immersive audio techniques.

In order to achieve these goals, significant improvements to available tools and technologies are still needed. An area that would benefit from major advancements is the design process for audio-based accessibility-focused tools, which should involve all stakeholders (including VIB end users, developers, carers, etc.) and include extensive formative and summative evaluation stages.

4.4.3   Use Case 3: From Hearing Aids to Hearing Devices

Hearing aids have been around for decades. From the first analogue hearing aids, which were basically simple frequency-dependent amplifiers, to the miniaturized digital ones, which sit completely inside the ear canal, the technological advancements have been the key for such devices to become a viable solution for hearing impairment. We are though still far from sufficient uptake; the majority (80%) of adults aged 55–74 years who would benefit from a hearing aid do not use them [71]. The combination of very recent advancements in the areas of Machine Learning, Virtual and Augmented Reality, Internet of Things, and Spatial Signal Processing has the potential to foster a disruptive change in how technology is used to improve the life of hearing impaired listeners and, why not, also of individuals with normal hearing, well beyond what is possible with current hearing aids [72]. Let's imagine a future where hearing can be assisted and augmented by earbuds or AR glasses, connected to smartphones, Bluetooth speakers, and voice-activated devices and applications; where these will automatically fit to the individual's hearing sensitivity, and continuously adapt to the various contents and scenarios, in order to always meet the needs and preference of the listener; where the spatial attributes of the surrounding soundscapes can be enhanced and modified, in order to be able to hear who talks on the other side of the table, or to focus on the sounds of nature around us.

4.4.4   Use Case 4: Rehabilitation/Monitoring/Clinical Disorders

Beyond assistive and rehabilitation applications for hearing and visually impaired people, some others worth mentioning XR applications exist for health and well-being. While XR has been used for therapeutic purposes for several years (see [73]), those applications often focused on motor rehabilitation and visual modality. Yet, audio interaction and auditory displays offer several opportunities thanks to audio advantages (e.g., rhythm and temporal resolution, 360° perception...), beginning with the ability of audio to reinforce VR pain management [74].

Moreover, combining audio and XR allows the development of new digital tools for creative and artistic therapies, known to be effective and engaging [75]. For instance, new studies are now exploring how to combine VR and music therapy to help autistic children to relax [76]. Indeed, XR offers the opportunity to train everyday abilities in a safer context where the environment is controllable, so people can re-adapt themselves progressively to the presence of stressful sources.

The auditory modality is also clearly more relevant when treating symptoms of perceptual disorders related to the auditory modality, be it hearing disorders (e.g., hearing impairments) or multisensory integration disorders (e.g., as appearing in schizophrenia [77] and autism [78]). For instance, mid-age hearing loss (presbyacusis) was found to be the highest factor correlated to the increase of the risk to develop early onset dementia [79]. Using XR-based auditory and cognitive training could therefore be a key to prevent or reduce/delay the symptoms of such disorders [80].

Audio can also help to assess and support rehabilitation of syndromes for which other senses are impaired (e.g., visual, tactile, or proprioceptive disorders) while the auditory perception remains relatively preserved. For instance, patients affected by Unilateral Spatial Neglect (USN—a syndrome occurring after a stroke) are unable to attend to visual and haptic stimuli on one side of their body, while they can still detect, but not correctly localize, sounds. Therefore, as suggested in [81], audio immersive interfaces could be a key component in XR rehabilitation and assessment approaches, which have already been designed for USN but based on haptic and visual technologies only [82].

Finally, XR offers the opportunity to simulate the symptoms of given disorders/diseases to allow other people to better understand the difficulties of living with such impairments.

For instance, in the 3D Tune-In project [83], VR-based simulations were used to demonstrate to normal hearing individuals how hearing loss could compromise everyday activities, and how a hearing aid could improve this.

4.4.5   Use Case 5: Immersive Sonification

Immersive analytics is an emerging field that focuses on taking advantage of XR technologies to display, organize, and make sense of large datasets by allowing users to interactively and immersively explore them [84]. Up to now, immersive analytics has focused mainly on visualization. However, the total amount of information that should be displayed and integrated can be very high for certain tasks. Being able to convey more information, without visually overloading the users, could be achieved by making use of immersive sonification, i.e., representing the data through spatialized non speech sounds.

It is in fact true that hearing abilities (fine temporal and spectral resolution, patterns detection and recognition, 360° spatial listening and localization, simultaneous listening of several sound streams) and the inherent multidimensionality of sound (each sound has multiple properties that can be assigned to independent variables, or combined to reinforce the perception of a single variable) make sonification particularly suitable for representing spatial data around the user, or multiple parameters simultaneously, and possibly assist/integrate visual analyses of complex data.

The use of sonification in immersive analytics is very recent, and only a few studies have been conducted yet, all leading to promising results. For instance, the presence of sound have proved to enhance the structural understanding of a neuroscience data network in [85], have been used to help in immersive molecular docking [86, 87], computational fluid dynamics [88], and stock market monitoring [89], and to facilitate audience understanding of complex phenomenon involved in time perception in an art/science installation [90].

Research is though still needed in order to move forward in this topic, and further optimize immersive sonification for various uses. For example, questions inherent to sonification itself (i.e., independently from immersion) remain unanswered. Even if some guidelines have been already outlined [91], sonification is still a young field and we are still far away from a formal design methodology. For instance, studies have still to be carried out to determine and document the sound parameters to choose to best represent every type of data. Furthermore, the context of immersion helped raising a lot of new questions and issues. Following the work of [92], initiated to determine how natural locomotion would change the contribution of sound in a multimodal immersive analytic applications, the next step is to study the interplay between sonification and immersive interactions. Finally, in the context of big data analysis, technological issues are also likely to appear due to the number of sound sources to generate (play or synthesize) and spatialize. This will push the audio algorithms and technologies to their computational limits and make the associated challenges even more critical (see Sections 4.2 and 4.3 of this chapter).

4.5   Future Research Agenda and Roadmap

Immersive audio is a very active research area with many potential applications in both AR and VR. In this chapter we have discussed why we believe there is a huge potential in this field, which is underrepresented in the area of XR, and should therefore be included in any future research roadmap on the topic. Summarizing the technological challenges and research areas of interest in immersive audio research, which have been exposed along this chapter, we outline here our recommendation for a research agenda.

4.5.1   Short Term Areas of Interest

- In the near future, personalization of HRTF will be of great interest for both research and industry. Further effort should be made exploring different approaches to allow affordable techniques for obtaining individual HRTFs, surpassing acoustic measurements as the gold standard. Effective (i.e., realistic), scalable (i.e., parameterizable), and optimized (i.e., light computational cost for real-time use) rendering of room acoustics is another area that will significantly contribute to the advance and commercial success of near future XR systems.

- Linked to the previous item, technological advancements cannot move significantly forward without a better understanding of how the human spatial hearing system works, of what elements of the HRTF are psychoacoustically relevant in terms of spatial hearing and individualization, of what virtual room acoustics processes are audible and important for a given space and source position, etc. This knowledge will allow us to measure/estimate whether a simulated immersive audio experience is suitable and of sufficient quality for a given individual/scene/task.

- AR systems are currently in constant improvement and the development of high-quality transparent audio reproduction devices will be a key element in this evolution.
- Immersive audio for the Web and other networked solutions is another area where a great effort should be made in the near future, especially when looking at real-time systems and applications where latency is of primary importance (e.g., head tracking).

Overcoming these challenges, real and virtual auditory worlds could be seamlessly blended and applications such as videoconference and collaborative work programs with personalized immersive audio, as well as use cases of immersive sonification, might be feasible enough to become a reality.

4.5.2   Mid- to Long-Term Research Opportunities

- Auditory models will contribute both to better understanding human spatial hearing mechanisms and to facilitate the assessment and validation of methods and technologies for immersive audio in XR. This can be addressed using an analytical approach as well as a data-driven AI-based approach. Models will be more reliable and accurate the more we understand human perception and could be used at the same time to improve research about perceptual mechanisms.
- The development of authoring tools optimized for immersive audio should be fostered by investing in standardization and interoperability. Some good initiatives born in Europe, such as the SOFA standard, are good starting points that should be repeated and extended. Per se, this is potentially a goal achievable in the short term, but it is unlikely that such standards can effectively become benchmarks until they are extensively and consistently employed across the academic and industry communities.

- Another key future research topic relates to moving beyond sensory perception, towards exploring and understanding the mechanism by which immersive audio, and its different rendering choices and parameters, can impact how, for example, users interact and communicate in XR systems and environments.

In the mid-term, we foresee that immersive audio will be more and more used in XR applications for rehabilitation, monitoring, and treatment of clinical disorders, as well as an assistive technology for visually impaired users. Furthermore, AR immersive audio technologies might soon have a major impact on the hearing aids domain, possibly driven forward by research on hearing augmentation and, more specifically, by the superseding of the traditional hearing aid concept, towards the more extensive notion of hearing devices.

Acknowledgments

The research and writing of this text were partially financed by the Spanish National Project SAVLab (Grant No. PID2019-107854GB-I00 / AEI / 10.13039/501100011033) and the French FUI 25 United-VR project.

References

1. Serafin, S. *et al.*, 'Reflections from five years of sonic interactions in virtual environments workshops'. *J. New Music Res.*, 49, 1, 24–34, 2020. doi: 10.1080/09298215.2019.1708413.
2. Schubert, T., Friedmann, F., Regenbrecht, H., 'Embodied presence in virtual environments', in: *Visual Representations and Interpretations*, pp. 269–278, Springer, London, 1999.
3. Witmer, B.G. and Singer, M.J., 'Measuring presence in virtual environments: A presence questionnaire'. *Presence*, vol, 225–240, 1998.
4. Bailey, W. and Fazenda, B.M., 'The effect of visual cues and binaural rendering method on plausibility in virtual environments'. *144th Audio Eng. Soc. Conv. 2018*, May 2018.
5. Bergstrom, I., Azevedo, S., Papiotis, P., Saldanha, N., Slater, M., 'The plausibility of a string quartet performance in virtual reality'. *IEEE Trans. Vis. Comput. Graph.*, 23, 4, 1352–1359, Apr. 2017. doi: 10.1109/TVCG.2017.2657138.
6. Savioja, L., Huopaniemi, J., Lokki, T., Väänänen, R., 'Creating interactive virtual acoustic environments'. *J. Audio Eng. Soc*, 47, 9, 675–705, Sep. 1999.

7. James, D.L., Langlois, T.R., Mehra, R., Zheng, C., 'Physically based sound for computer animation and virtual environments', in: *ACM SIGGRAPH 2016 Courses*, New York, NY, USA, pp. 22, 1–8, 2016, doi: 10.1145/2897826.2927375.

8. Kleiner, M., Dalenbäck, B., Svensson, P., 'Auralization—an overview'. *J. Audio Eng. Soc*, 41, 11, 861–875, Nov. 1993.

9. Blauert, J., *Spatial Hearing - The Psychophysics of Human Sound Localization*, 2nd edition, MIT Press, Cambridge, 1996.

10. Møller, H., 'Fundamentals of binaural technology'. *Appl. Acoust.*, 36, 3, 171–218, 1992. doi: https://doi.org/10.1016/0003-682X(92)90046-U.

11. Giller, P.M., Wendt, F., Höldrich, R., 'The influence of different BRIR modification techniques on externalization and sound quality', in: *EAA Spatial Audio Signal Processing Symposium*, Paris, France, pp. 61–66, Sep. 2019, doi: 10.25836/sasp.2019.20.

12. Engel, I., Henry, C., Amengual Garí, S.V., Robinson, P.W., Picinali, L., 'Perceptual implications of different Ambisonics-based methods for binaural reverberation'. *J. Acoust. Soc Am.*, 149, 2, 895–910, 2021.

13. Savioja, L. and Svensson, U.P., 'Overview of geometrical room acoustic modeling techniques'. *J. Acoust. Soc Am.*, vol, 708–730, 2015, doi: 10.1121/1.4926438.

14. Savioja, L. and Xiang, N., 'Introduction to the special issue on room acoustic modeling and auralization'. *J. Acoust. Soc Am.*, 145, 2597, 2019. [Online]. Available: https://asa.scitation.org/doi/10.1121/1.5099017.

15. Välimäki, V., Parker, J.D., Savioja, L., Smith, J.O., Abel, J.S., 'Fifty years of artificial reverberation'. *IEEE Trans. Audio Speech Lang. Process.*, 20, 5, 1421–1448, Jul. 2012. doi: 10.1109/TASL.2012.2189567.

16. Välimäki, V., Parker, J., Savioja, L., Smith, J.O., Abel, J., 'More than 50 years of artificial reverberation'. *Proc AES 60th Int. Conf*, pp. K–1, 2016.

17. Katz, B.F.G., Thery, D., Boccara, V., 'Auralization uses in acoustical design: a survey study of acoustical consultants'. *J. Acoust. Soc Am.*, 145, 3446, 2019. [Online]. Available: https://asa.scitation.org/doi/full/10.1121/1.5110711.

18. Postma, B.N.J. and Katz, B.F.G., 'Creation and calibration method of acoustical models for historic virtual reality auralizations'. *Virtual Real.*, 19, 3, 161–180, Nov. 2015.

19. Theile, G. and Plenge, G., 'Localization of lateral phantom sources'. *J. Audio Eng. Soc*, 25, 4, 196–200, Apr. 1977.

20. Pulkki, V., 'Virtual sound source positioning using vector base amplitude panning'. *J. Audio Eng. Soc*, 6, 45, 456–466, 1997.

21. Berkhout, A., Vries, D., Vogel, P., 'Acoustic control by wave field synthesis'. *J. Acoust. Soc Am.*, 93, 2764–2778, May 1993. doi: 10.1121/1.405852.

22. Daniel, J., *'Spatial Sound Encoding Including Near Field Effect: Introducing Distance Coding Filters and a Viable, New Ambisonic Format'*, May 2003.

23. Wierstorf, H., Raake, A., Spors, S., 'Assessing localization accuracy in sound field synthesis'. *J. Acoust. Soc Am.*, 141, 2, 1111–1119, 2017. doi: 10.1121/1.4976061.

24. Elliott, S.J., Cheer, J., Choi, J.-W., Kim, Y., 'Robustness and regularization of personal audio systems'. *IEEE Trans. Audio Speech Lang. Process.*, 20, 7, 2123–2133, 2012.

25. Gálvez, M.F.S., Menzies, D., Fazi, F.M., 'Dynamic audio reproduction with linear loudspeaker arrays'. *J. Audio Eng. Soc*, 67, 190–200, 4, 2019.

26. Andreopoulou, A., Begault, D.R., Katz, B.F.G., 'Inter-laboratory round robin HRTF measurement comparison'. *IEEE J. Sel. Top. Signal Process.*, 9, 5, Special Issue on Spatial Audio, 895–906, 2015. doi: 10.1109/JSTSP.2015.2400417.

27. Algazi, V.R., Duda, R.O., Thompson, D.M., Avendano, C., 'The CIPIC HRTF database', in: *Proceedings of the 2001 IEEE Workshop on the Applications of Signal Processing to Audio and Acoustics (Cat. No.01TH8575)*, pp. 99–102, 2001, doi: 10.1109/ASPAA.2001.969552.

28. 'Listen HRTF Database'. [Online]. Available: http://recherche.ircam.fr/equipes/salles/listen/index.html.

29. Armstrong, C., Thresh, L., Murphy, D., Kearney, G., 'A perceptual evaluation of individual and non-individual HRTFs: a case study of the SADIE II database'. *Appl. Sci.*, 8, 11, 1–21, 2018. doi: 10.3390/app8112029.

30. 'ARI HRTF database'. [Online]. Available: https://www.kfs.oeaw.ac.at/index.php?view=article&id=608&lang=en.

31. Wenzel, E.M., Arruda, M., Kistler, D.J., Wightman, F.L., 'Localization using nonindividualized head-related transfer functions'. *J. Acoust. Soc Am.*, 94, 1, 111–123, 1993. doi: 10.1121/1.407089.

32. Simon, L., Zacharov, N., Katz, B.F.G., 'Perceptual attributes for the comparison of head-related transfer functions'. *J. Acoust. Soc Am.*, 140, 3623–3632, Nov. 2016. doi: 10.1121/1.4966115.

33. Katz, B.F., 'Boundary element method calculation of individual head-related transfer function. II. Impedance effects and comparisons to real measurements'. *J. Acoust. Soc Am.*, 110, 5, 2449–2455, 2001.

34. Stitt, P. and Katz, B.F.G., 'Sensitivity analysis of pinna morphology on head-related transfer functions simulated via a parametric pinna model'. *J. Acoust. Soc Am.*, 149, 4, 2559–2572, 2021. doi: 10.1121/10.0004128.

35. Greff, R. and Katz, B.F.G., 'Round Robin comparison of HRTF simulation results : preliminary results', in: *Audio Eng Soc Conv 123*, New York, USA, pp. 1–5, 2007, [Online]. Available: http://www.aes.org/e-lib/browse.cfm?elib=14246.

36. Geronazzo, M., Peruch, E., Prandoni, F., Avanzini, F., 'Applying a single-notch metric to image-guided head-related transfer function selection for improved vertical localization'. *J. Audio Eng. Soc.*, 67, 6, 414–428, 2019.

37. Zotkin, D., Hwang, J., Duraiswaini, R., Davis, L.S., 'HRTF personalization using anthropometric measurements', in: *Workshop on Applications of Sig Proc to Audio and Acoustics*, pp. 157–160, 2003, doi: 10.1109/ASPAA.2003.1285855.

38. Katz, B.F. and Parseihian, G., 'Perceptually based head-related transfer function database optimization'. *J. Acoust. Soc Am.*, 131, 2, EL99–EL105, 2012.

39. Andreopoulou, A. and Katz, B.F.G., 'Investigation on Subjective HRTF rating repeatability', in: *Audio Eng Soc Conv 140*, Paris, pp. 9597, 1–10, Jun. 2016, [Online]. Available: http://www.aes.org/e-lib/browse.cfm?elib=18295.

40. Kim, C., Lim, V., Picinali, L., 'Investigation into consistency of subjective and objective perceptual selection of non-individual head-related transfer functions'. *J. Audio Eng. Soc*, 68, 11, 819–831, 2020.

41. Zagala, F., Noisternig, M., Katz, B.F., 'Comparison of direct and indirect perceptual head-related transfer function selection methods'. *J. Acoust. Soc Am.*, 147, 5, 3376–3389, 2020.

42. Steadman, M.A., Kim, C., Lestang, J.-H., Goodman, D.F., Picinali, L., 'Short-term effects of sound localization training in virtual reality'. *Sci. Rep.*, 9, 1, 1–17, 2019. doi: 10.1038/s41598-019-54811-w.

43. Stitt, P., Picinali, L., Katz, B.F.G., 'Auditory accommodation to poorly matched non-individual spectral localization cues through active learning'. *Sci. Rep.*, 9, 1, 1063, 1–14, 2019. doi: 10.1038/s41598-018-37873-0.

44. Hendrickx, E., Stitt, P., Messonnier, J.-C., Lyzwa, J.-M., Katz, B.F., De Boishéraud, C., 'Influence of head tracking on the externalization of speech stimuli for non-individualized binaural synthesis'. *J. Acoust. Soc Am.*, 141, 3, 2011–2023, 2017.

45. Cuevas-Rodríguez, M. *et al.*, 'The 3D tune-in toolkit – 3D audio spatialiser, hearing loss and hearing aid simulations', in: *2018 IEEE 4th VR Workshop on Sonic Interactions for Virtual Environments (SIVE)*, pp. 1–3, 2018, doi: 10.1109/SIVE.2018.8577076.

46. Picinali, L., Afonso, A., Katz, B.F., 'Exploration of architectural spaces by blind people using auditory virtual reality for the construction of spatial knowledge'. *Int. J. Hum. Comput. Stud.*, 72, 4, 393–407, 2014.

47. De Sena, E., Haciihabiboğlu, H., Cvetković, Z., Smith, J.O., 'Efficient synthesis of room acoustics via scattering delay networks'. *IEEE Trans. Audio Speech Lang. Process.*, 23, 9, 1478–1492, 2015. doi: 10.1109/TASLP.2015.2438547.

48. Wakeland, C., 'AMD TrueAudio Next-The right next step for audio on VR', AMD, 2016. [Online]. Available: https://gpuopen.com/wp-content/uploads/2016/07/TAN_whitepaper_2016.pdf.

49. Patait, A., 'VRWorks audio SDK in-depth | NVIDIA developer', 2017. Accessed: May 30, 2021. [Online]. Available: https://developer.nvidia.com/vrworks-audio-sdk-depth.

50. Brinkmann, F., Gamper, H., Raghuvanshi, N., Tashev, I., 'Towards encoding perceptually salient early reflections for parametric spatial audio rendering', *148th Convention*, 2020, June 2-5, Online 2020.

51. Søndergaard, P. and Majdak, P., 'The auditory modeling toolbox', in: *The Technology of Binaural Listening*, J. Blauert, (Ed.), pp. 33–56, Springer, Berlin, Heidelberg, 2013.

52. Antonacci, F. *et al.*, 'Inference of room geometry from acoustic impulse responses'. *IEEE Trans. Audio Speech Lang. Process.*, 20, 10, 2683–2695, 2012. doi: 10.1109/TASL.2012.2210877.

53. Brinkmann, F. and Weinzierl, S., 'Comparison of Head-Related Transfer Functions Pre-Processing Techniques for Spherical Harmonics Decomposition', 2018, Accessed: Nov. 10, 2020. [Online]. Available: https://www.aes.org/e-lib/browse.cfm?elib=19683.

54. The World Wide Web Consortium (WC3), 'WebXR device API'. Accessed: May 30, 2021. [Online]. Available: https://www.w3.org/TR/webxr/.

55. The World Wide Web Consortium (WC3), 'Web audio API'. Accessed: May 30, 2021. [Online]. Available: https://www.w3.org/TR/webaudio/.

56. Comunitá, M., Gerino, A., Lim, V., Picinali, L., 'Web-based binaural audio and sonic narratives for cultural heritage', in: *Conference on immersive and interactive audio*, p. 14, Mar. 2019.

57. Curcio, I., Gunkel, S., Stockhammer, T., 'State-of-the-art of extended reality in 5G networks', 2019.

58. Iwaya, Y. and Katz, B.F.G., 'Distributed signal processing architecture for real-time convolution of 3d audio rendering for mobile applications', in: *Lecture Notes in Computer Science (including subseries Lecture Notes in Artificial Intelligence and Lecture Notes in Bioinformatics)*, vol. 11162, pp. 148–157, Oct. 2018, doi: 10.1007/978-3-030-01790-3_9.

59. Galvane, Q., Lin, I.-S., Christie, M., Li, T.-Y., 'Immersive Previz: VR Authoring for Film Previsualisation', New York, NY, USA, 2018, doi: 10.1145/3214822.3214831.

60. Okuya, Y., Gladin, O., Ladevèze, N., Fleury, C., Bourdot, P., 'Investigating collaborative exploration of design alternatives on a wall-sized display', in: *CHI 2020 - ACM Conference on Human Factors in Computing Systems*, Honolulu, United States, pp. 1–12, Apr. 2020, doi: 10.1145/3313831.3376736.

61. Wang, P. et al., 'AR/MR remote collaboration on physical tasks: a review'. *Robot. Comput. Integr. Manuf.*, 72, 102071, 2021. doi: https://doi.org/10.1016/j.rcim.2020.102071.

62. Baldis, J.J., 'Effects of spatial audio on memory, comprehension, and preference during desktop conferences', in: *Proceedings of the SIGCHI Conference on Human Factors in Computing Systems*, New York, NY, USA, pp. 166–173, 2001, doi: 10.1145/365024.365092.

63. Cidota, M., Lukosch, S., Datcu, D., Lukosch, H., 'Workspace Awareness in Collaborative AR Using HMDs: A User Study Comparing Audio and Visual Notifications', New York, NY, USA, 2016, doi: 10.1145/2875194.2875204.

64. Chen, W., Clavel, C., Férey, N., Bourdot, P., 'Perceptual conflicts in a multi-stereoscopic immersive virtual environment: case study on face-to-face interaction through an avatar'. *Presence*, 23, 4, 410–429, 2014. doi: 10.1162/PRES_a_00209.

65. Zhao, Y., Cutrell, E., Holz, C., Morris, M.R., Ofek, E., Wilson, A.D., 'SeeingVR: a set of tools to make virtual reality more accessible to people with low vision', in: *Proceedings of the 2019 CHI Conference on Human Factors in Computing Systems*, New York, Association for Computing

Machinery, NY, USA, pp. 1–14, 2019, [Online]. Available: https://doi.org/10.1145/3290605.3300341.

66. Allain, K. *et al.*, 'An audio game for training navigation skills of blind children', in: *2015 IEEE 2nd VR workshop on sonic interactions for virtual environments (SIVE)*, pp. 1–4, 2015.

67. Thevin, L., Briant, C., Brock, A.M., 'X-road: virtual reality glasses for orientation and mobility training of people with visual impairments'. *ACM Trans. Access. Comput. TACCESS*, 13, 2, 1–47, 2020.

68. Csapó, Á., Wersényi, G., Nagy, H., Stockman, T., 'A survey of assistive technologies and applications for blind users on mobile platforms: a review and foundation for research'. *J. Multimodal User Interfaces*, 9, 4, 275–286, 2015.

69. Griffin, E., Picinali, L., Scase, M., 'The effectiveness of an interactive audio-tactile map for the process of cognitive mapping and recall among people with visual impairments'. *Brain Behav.*, 10, 7, e01650, 2020.

70. Guerreiro, J., Ahmetovic, D., Kitani, K.M., Asakawa, C., 'Virtual navigation for blind people: building sequential representations of the real-world', in: *Proceedings of the 19th International ACM SIGACCESS Conference on Computers and Accessibility*, New York, NY, USA, pp. 280–289, 2017, doi: 10.1145/3132525.3132545.

71. McCormack, A. and Fortnum, H., 'Why do people fitted with hearing aids not wear them?'. *Int. J. Audiol.*, 52, 5, 360–368, 2013.

72. Mehra, R., Brimijoin, O., Robinson, P., Lunner, T., 'Potential of augmented reality platforms to improve individual hearing aids and to support more ecologically valid research'. *Ear Hear.*, 41, Suppl 1, 140S, 2020.

73. Hayre, C.M., Muller, D.J., Scherer, M.J. (Eds.), *Virtual Reality in Health and Rehabilitation*, CRC Press, Boca Raton, 2020, [Online]. Available: https://www.taylorfrancis.com/books/edit/10.1201/9780429351365/virtual-reality-health-rehabilitation-christopher-hayre-dave-muller-marcia-scherer.

74. Johnson, S. and Coxon, M., 'Sound can enhance the analgesic effect of virtual reality'. *R. Soc Open Sci.*, 3, 27069646, 150567–150567, 2016.

75. Yinger, O.S. and Gooding, L., 'Music therapy and music medicine for children and adolescents'. *Child Adolesc. Psychiatr. Clin. N. Am.*, 23, 3, 535–53, Jul. 2014.

76. Andersen, L., Serafin, S., Adjorlu, A., Andersen, N., 'Singing in Virtual Reality with the Danish National children's choir', Oct. 2019, [Online]. Available: https://hal.archives-ouvertes.fr/hal-02382500/document#page=247.

77. Percie du Sert, O. *et al.*, 'Virtual reality therapy for refractory auditory verbal hallucinations in schizophrenia: a pilot clinical trial'. *Schizophr. Res.*, 197, 176–181, Feb. 2018. doi: 10.1016/j.schres.2018.02.031.

78. Bauer, V., Bouchara, T., Bourdot, P., 'eXtended Reality for Autism Interventions: The importance of Mediation and Sensory-Based Approaches', to appear in *Journal of Autism and Developmental Disorders*, 2022. Preprint available at : https://arxiv.org/abs/2106.15983.

79. Livingston, G. *et al.*, 'Dementia prevention, intervention, and care'. *Lancet*, 390, 10113, 2673–2734, 2017.

80. Frost, E., Porat, T., Malhotra, P., Picinali, L., 'A novel auditory-cognitive training App for delaying or preventing the onset of dementia: participatory design with stakeholders'. *JMIR Hum. Factors*, 7, 3, e19880, Sep. 2020. doi: 10.2196/19880.

81. Bara, T.-G., Guilbert, A., Bouchara, T.B., 'A new step to optimize sound localization adaptation through the use of vision', in: *AES International Conference on Audio for Virtual and Augmented Reality*, Seattle, United States, Aug. 2020, [Online]. Available: https://hal.archives-ouvertes.fr/hal-02922711.

82. Ogourtsova, T., Souza Silva, W., Archambault, P.S., Lamontagne, A., 'Virtual reality treatment and assessments for post-stroke unilateral spatial neglect: A systematic literature review'. *Neuropsychol. Rehabil.*, 27, 3, 409–454, Apr. 2017.

83. Eastgate, R., Picinali, L., Patel, H., D'Cruz, M., '3d games for tuning and learning about hearing aids'. *Hear. J.*, 69, 4, 30–32, 2016.

84. Skarbez, R., Polys, N.F., Ogle, J.T., Bowman, D.A., 'Immersive analytics: theory and research agenda'. *Front. Robot. AI*, 6, 82, 2019. doi: 10.3389/frobt.2019.00082.

85. Papachristodoulou, P., Betella, A., Verschure, P., '*Sonification of Large Datasets in a 3D Immersive Environment: A Neuroscience Case Study*', pp. 35–40, Jan. 2014.

86. Ferey, N. *et al.*, 'Advances in human-protein interaction—interactive and immersive molecular simulations', in: *Protein-Protein Interactions— Computational and Experimental Tools*, Cai, W. and Hong, H. (Eds.), 2012.

87. Férey, N. *et al.*, 'Multisensory VR interaction for protein-docking in the CoRSAIRe project'. *Virtual Real.*, 13, 4, 273, 2009.

88. Vézien, J.-M. *et al.*, 'Multisensory VR exploration for computer fluid dynamics in the CoRSAIRe project'. *Virtual Real.*, 13, 4, 257–271, 2009.

89. Chabot, S. and Braasch, J., 'High-density data sonification of stock market information in an immersive virtual environment'. *J. Acoust. Soc Am.*, 141, 5, 3512–3512, 2017.

90. Polydorou, D., Ben-Tal, O., Damsma, A., Schlichting, N., 'VR: time machine', in: *Human-Computer Interaction. Human Values and Quality of Life - Thematic Area, HCI 2020, Held as Part of the 22nd International Conference, HCII*, vol. 12183, pp. 294–306, 2020, doi: 10.1007/978-3-030-49065-2_21.

91. Hermann, T., Hunt, A., J.G. Neuhoff, (Eds.), *The Sonification Handbook*, Logos Publishing House, Berlin, 2011, [Online]. Available: https://sonification.de/handbook/.

92. Bukvic, I., Earle, G., Sardana, D., Joo, W., '*Studies In Spatial Aural Perception: Establishing Foundations For Immersive Sonification*', 2019.

Visual Interfaces in XR

Rubén Mohedano* and Julio Chaves

LIMBAK, Madrid, Spain

Abstract

In the mixed reality (MR) continuum, all headsets comprise a visual interface featuring at least two parts: a display engine (containing the information to be displayed to user) and an optical train/combiner (directing and transforming the display information to achieve the required visual experience by users). The type of displays and optics used in each case vary a lot, depending on whether the devices are augmented reality (AR) only, virtual reality (VR) only, or something in between. Even in each one of these specific segments, the visual interfaces can vary as well, depending on the strategy of each approach, which might prioritize some features over others. Among the different features to be considered, the field of view, angular resolution, size/total track length and weight, contrast/efficiency, image quality, eye-box, and costs outstand. In the AR-only limit, contrast/efficiency, image quality, eye-box, costs, and size/weight often prevail over other considerations, while on the VR-only side, the field of view, cost, and resolution are king, with size/weight slowly coming into play in recent solutions. This chapter briefly discusses the main approaches visual interfaces are following these days to attain the goals fixed by the different brands in the extended reality (XR) field, along with a short overview of future technologies with potential to become the state of the art in the mid and long run.

Keywords: Optics, display, field of view, angular resolution, total track length, efficiency

5.1 Introduction

This chapter is focused on the visual interfaces of near-to-eye (NTE) systems, and do not cover other forms of augmented reality or virtual reality

---

*Corresponding author: rmohedano@limbak.com

Mariano Alcañiz, Marco Sacco and Jolanda G. Tromp (eds.) Roadmapping Extended Reality: Fundamentals and Applications, (103–134) © 2022 Scrivener Publishing LLC

experiences (such as those based in direct view through smartphones and the superposition of synthetic contents, or VR "caves").

NTE systems project the information of a display panel magnified onto a user's eyes by means of an optical system. Depending on the angle subtended by the information projected, the nature/complexity of the information, and the overlap, or not, with the actual scene surrounding the user, the system can have the form of:

- Smart glasses, rather simple information, shown under a narrow angle, eye-wear where the actual scene prevails over the digital information
- AR/mixed reality headsets, complex contents under medium-wide angles, where the prevalence of digital and actual information can change and depends on the application
- VR, showing complex digital contents under a very wide angle to provide the presence experience and blocking all light from a user's surroundings

The history of NTE systems is not short. However, the definite push to these technologies came when Facebook bought the Oculus VR company for $2 billion, opening new possibilities for affordable VR headsets accessible to the general consumer. This chapter is mostly focused on systems developed in the boom XR period 2014–2021.

After an introduction of basic concepts that are the key for the understanding of NTE visual interfaces, this chapter briefly explains the main building blocks of these systems, and afterwards deepen on the special features (the type of displays and optics used in different approaches) of AR and VR systems that make them unique, and different from each other, within the MR spectrum.

At the end of the chapter, we review technological alternatives with potential to become a game-changer in future XR systems.

5.2   Definitions

The following concepts (and the corresponding acronyms) are key to understand the current chapter and XR in general.

5.2.1   Field of View (FOV)

Angle subtended by the synthetic image as seen from the eye. The FOV determines the apparent size of such synthetic information, and it is very important in VR to achieve the presence feeling. The FOV is often beyond 90° in VR, and varies in the smart-glasses (~20°) to AR (up to 50°) continuum.

5.2.2   Angular Resolution

The angular distribution of synthetic image pixels, greatly influencing the experience. It is measured in pixels per degree (ppd) and should be benchmarked against the human eye's maximum angular resolution, which is 60 ppd (although resolutions above 40 ppd are often considered indistinguishable from 60 ppd for the eye).

5.2.3   Optical Efficiency

Light flux leaving the optic over the light flux from display entering the optical system. This value has an impact on system autonomy (for standalone devices) and contrast (for see-through optical combiners in AR). It can achieve values in the range of 90% for single-lens VR systems or below 10% in pancake optics or complex waveguide AR systems.

5.2.4   Eye Relief (ER)

Distance from a pupil to the first optical surface in front of it. This value is often beyond 18 mm to allow for the usage of prescription glasses in VR systems.

5.2.5   Total Track Length (TTL)

Distance from the display panel to a user's pupil that determines, eventually, the size of the headset. Eye relief is therefore embedded in the TTL.

5.2.6   Input and Output Pupils

In optics, the input and exit pupils are virtual apertures in the optical system such as only rays that pass through this virtual aperture can enter and exit the system, respectively.

5.3   Visual Interfaces Building Blocks

In the MR continuum, all headsets have at least two parts in common: a display engine (containing the display panel with information to be displayed to the user and, in some cases, some illumination and or projection optics) and an optical train, directing and transforming the display engine information to achieve the required visual experience by users. In the case of optical see-through MR systems, this optical system is called a "combiner" because it should be able to combine the synthetic and real scene images. There is a wide range of different MR systems offering different experiences. On one end of the range, we have the smart-glass systems, generally a monocular, lightweight device that is able to show a limited (in terms of performance, FOV, aesthetics…) amount of information to users. Other, more complex, high-end MR systems are stand-alone, binocular optical see-through systems featuring advanced performance features including wide FOV, head and hands tracking, surroundings recognition, and improved connectivity and computing capabilities. On the VR end of the continuum, we can mention tethered, wide FOV (fully immersive), high-angular-resolution devices including haptics and a range of advanced features, including eye-tracking, for example. The next sections show examples throughout the entire continuum, with more emphasis on the binocular high-performance AR and VR systems.

5.3.1   Display Engine

The simplest display engine possible is the display panel itself. Many VR systems are based on liquid crystal display (LCD) panels using integrated backlights in a monolithic part facing the optical train, imaging the panel images onto a user's pupil with the required FOV. In other, more complex systems, especially in optical see-through AR headsets, the display engine has to, additionally:

1) Include an illumination system in case the panels are non-emissive
2) Include some kind of "relay optics," to form an exit pupil fitting with the entrance pupil of the optical combiner that comes after, and make sure its aspect ratio is compatible with the pupil expansion scheme utilized by the system to achieve the eye-box at the exit of the optical combiner

Regarding the panel displays, we can find:

1. Direct-view panels (used in smartphone systems, LCD or AMOLED (active-matrix organic light-emitting diodes), with sizes ranging 2.0–5.5 in. in diagonal and achieving

500–850 PPI). These displays are used in VR headsets because achieving the required wide FOV and presence feeling is easier with large panels.

2. Micro-display panels, in sizes from 0.2 to 1.0 in. with better resolutions than direct-view panels, varying in the range 2000–3500 PPI. These panels are more common in see-through AR headsets, where lightweight, sleek form factors and thin optical combiners are best met with small displays. For these systems, the efficiency is very critical because the panels' information has to compete with the scene surrounding the user, and particularly has to compete with daylight sometimes.

5.3.2   Optical Train

The optics in AR/VR systems in charge of producing the actual visual experience vary in form and approach, but all aim to image the panel images (object plane, or o-plane) onto a virtual, image plane (i-plane) located away from the user, at an apparent distance (typically, 1–2 m) and under an FOV that depends on the choice and strategy of every brand. Optical architectures in MR include a choice of lenses, mirrors, waveguides, prisms, and sometimes more special systems, including diffractive surfaces or holographic, polarization, and Fresnel schemes.

VR often requires a wider FOV, to make sure that the experience is really immersive and the users feel the presence on the synthetic world. For most display panels, stretching the pixels throughout a wide FOV leads to rather low angular resolution, in pixels per degree, and to the chicken-wire (also known as screen-door) effect. Achieving the right combination of FOV and image quality requires a rather long (>50 mm) total track length (distance from display to pupil) when conventional, rotationally symmetric lenses (the simplest optical train available) are used, which, in turn, imply very bulky headsets. More sophisticated systems, based on light-folding, multi-channel free-form lenses or the pancake configuration (discussed below) enable shorter TTL (<30 mm typically) devices, without giving up the FOV or image quality.

FOVs are often narrower in AR systems but difficult to achieve anyway, provided these systems need to be stand-alone, lightweight, and sleek, which, in practice, means the usage of small micro-displays. As we will see below, the size of display has a direct influence on the FOV achievable when the room for the optical train is limited. In optical see-through AR systems, the combiner optics often struggles to show the AR content when competing with the daylight. Contrast, brightness, and a system's optical efficiency are the key to face that situation.

5.4   Visual Interfaces in VR

VR systems feature a set of lenses or mirrors (in the simplest case, one single lens) that project the image coming from a display panel onto the eye with the desired characteristics: three dimensional (3D), correct magnification, and wide FOV to provide the immersion feeling, image quality, etc. All commercial headsets released along the years by sales leaders Facebook-Oculus, HTC, and SONY PSVR are based in one single lens. Since there is no need to show a user's surroundings directly (these can be shown through cameras, though), the optics and display can be placed directly in front of the user's eyes, and the headset is often designed perfectly fitting face shapes to prevent the entry of stray light.

The choice of display and lens-projection system define the size of the headset and its main performance features (image quality, resolution, eye-box, FOV, efficiency). The market has been dominated so far by solutions based on rather conventional (rotationally symmetric lenses) optical systems, but new devices based on multi-channel free-form optics or light-folding lenses based on polarized light are drawing some attention lately.

5.4.1   VR Display Panels

Basic geometrical calculations involving the physical laws that rule the optics science, and considering the large FOV needed to produce the "presence" or "immersion" feeling introduced above. It is straightforward that VR requires panels often larger than those found in AR (or, alternatively, a tiling of small panels next to each other, adding up to achieve the required size of FOV).

Along with smartphones acting as displays (as in the case of the top-seller Samsung Gear VR, by Oculus, back in 2017), the top-seller VR headsets have featured in the past both large LCD and OLED displays, with increasing pixel count from 640×800 (Oculus DK1, 2014) to 2448×2448 (HTC Vive Pro 2, Vive Focus, 2021) with sizes ranging 5.7 in. (one display for both eyes, Oculus DK2) to 2.1 in. in diagonal. The evolution of displays in pixel count is shown in Figure 5.1.

Oculus quest 2 uses a single near-4K LCD display, which means effective $1,832 \times 1,920$ resolution served up per eye.

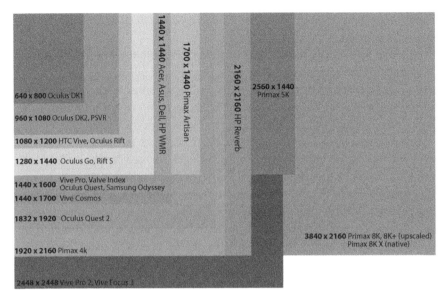

Figure 5.1 Evolution of pixel count in VR displays along the years (Night1, Dzid, JeffyP -Own work, Comparison chart of per-eye headset resolutions, CC BY-SA 4.0, Created: 13 May 2021).

5.4.2 Basics of VR Lens

VR optics may take a variety of configurations and sizes; however, they all have in common facing a display and generating a virtual image under a wide FOV, to produce the immersion or presence feeling. The said virtual image should be visible even as the eye rotates to gaze in different directions or when the VR headset moves relative to the eye, as the headset may displace while being used or when removed and put back on. The limited space allowed for the optics; the wide FOV, along with higher tolerances in the relative position of the eye and optic (larger eye-box, as defined above), put increasing demands on the already-demanding imaging capabilities of the said optic, leading to serious challenges in optical design.

The simplest configurations found in the market these days may be a solid convex lens facing a display placed at a distance smaller that the focal distance of the lens, so that the system generates a virtual image at a distance of about 1.5 m or so. These lenses have a tendency to form a good image quality at the center but show degrading performance at wider angles. When the lens forms a good image quality at the center of the FOV but the screen resolution is such that the virtual images of its pixels are larger than what the eye can resolve, the said pixels will be discernible. The dark areas around the emitting regions of each pixel will also be visible, leading to a "screen-door effect" or "chicken-wire effect" that degrades the viewing experience.

At wider angles, the image quality of the lens will degrade. And so does the acuity of the human eye, or how many cycles per degree the eye can resolve at wider angles (to the line through the center of the eye and the center of the pupil). In general, steps may be taken to try and adapt the behavior of the lens to that of the human eye within the FOV [1].

Another phenomenon that may occur in convex lenses when used in VR headsets is the color separation of images formed by the red, green, and blue pixels of the display at wide angles due to chromatic aberration. This contributes to the degradation of the perceived image quality at wider angles. Again, some measures may be taken to mitigate these effects, such as trying to correct the chromatic aberrations through optic design or by modifying the software running in the device to shift (distort) the red, green and blue images differently to counter the chromatic aberration of the optic.

As referred above, one important aspect of a VR optic is the ability to provide a region in which the eye may move and still perceive a good image quality. The said region is typically called the eye-box as it may be conceived as a box into which the eye pupil should be confined. As the eye moves and rotates inside the said box, not all light it receives has equal importance. In particular, for a particular pupil position and orientation, only one direction of the light will be perceived with high resolution: the axis through the center of the eye and the center of the pupil ("gazing direction"). As the angle of the incoming light increases with respect to said axis beyond 3° only, the ability of the eye to discern image quality decreases rapidly and so does the need for those rays to form a good image quality.

5.4.3   Long and Short Focal Distance Configurations

As referred above, the simplest VR optic is a converging lens coupled to a display. This is illustrated in Figure 5.2 where a lens L images a point D on the display to a virtual image point V. The Short Focal Distance Configurations eye then focuses the light appearing to come from V to a point E on the back of the eye where a real image is formed and seen. The distance TTL from the eye to the display is the Total Track Length, while the distance ER from the eye to the lens is the Eye Relief.

This configuration is again illustrated in Figure 5.3a.

Achieving a wide FOV with good image quality using a lens is quite challenging from the optical design point of view. Typically, this is addressed by adding extra optical elements.

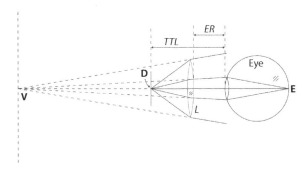

Figure 5.2 A lens as a VR optic.

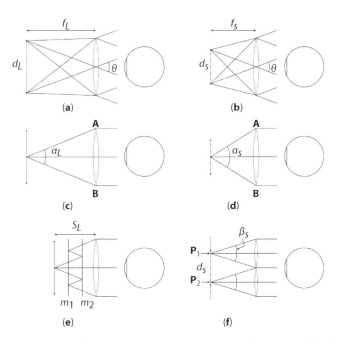

Figure 5.3 VR optics configurations. Figure 5.3 VR optics configurations. The challenge of reducing the size of a VR system by means of a conventional, rotationally symmetric lens is shown in (a), (b), (c) and (d). The lens in (b) and (d), which works with a smaller display panel (dS<dL), located closer to the lens (fS<fL) and then reducing the size of the headset, needs more power to bounce the light and produce the same FOV (θ) the longer focal length system in (a) and (d) produces. This introduces aberrations and poorer image quality in the system, unless some other approach is used, such us light folding (e) or multi-channel approaches (f).

The single lens configurations also result in bulky headsets (something undesirable in wearable devices) because the display should be located far from the lens to let it do its job, increasing the TTL. A significant reduction in size may be achieved by replacing the lens with a long focal length f_L with another lens with a short focal length f_S and coupling it to a smaller display with smaller pixels, as illustrated in Figure 5.3b. The resulting configuration could still emit light within the same cone θ, resulting in the same FOV, and the resolution could be made the same in both cases. However, assuming that aperture **AB** is maintained, the reduction in focal length from f_L to f_S results in an increase of the numerical aperture, as the cone of light captured by the optic increases from angle α_L to α_S, as illustrated by the comparison of Figure 5.3c and Figure 5.3d. This creates new challenges for the optical design that is now more difficult.

The configuration of Figure 5.3a is then easier to design but bulkier, while the configuration in Figure 5.3b is more compact but harder to design. In order to improve on these configurations, one needs to find a way to make the configuration of Figure 5.3a more compact or the configuration of Figure 5.3b easier to design.

One straightforward option to reduce the weight of the system is to reduce the size of the lens itself, making it a Fresnel lens. This, however, has a moderate effect on compactness since the focal distance tends to outweigh the lens thickness as a contribution to the total thickness of the system.

In the case of improving Figure 5.3a, one needs to reduce the depth of the device from f_L to s_L. This may be achieved by using "folded optics" in which light is reflected back and forth between mirrors m_1, m_2, as illustrated in Figure 5.3e.

In the case of improving Figure 5.3b, one needs to reduce the angle of the light captured by the optic from a large value α_S to a smaller value β_S, easing the optical design process. This may be achieved by splitting the optic in two channels as illustrated in Figure 5.3f. Now each channel deals with a smaller amount of light, and rays are more "paraxial," easing the design process. However, now two different points P_1, P_2 on the display share the same information since their light is emitted in the same direction by both optics. For that reason, in order to maintain the FOV and resolution, the display size d_S may have to be increased both in the size and number of pixels.

In the case of improving Figure 5.3a, a possible configuration for "folded optics" is as illustrated in Figure 5.14. In this example, the light from a micro-display panel enters the optic through a refractive surface s_1, suffers TIR (total internal reflection) at a surface s_2, is reflected at a mirror s_3,

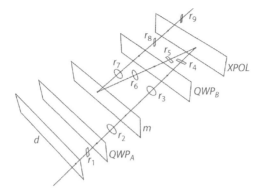

Figure 5.4 Working principle of a pancake optic.

refracts at surface s_2, and finally reaches the eye. These types of optics may also be used for AR by making s_3 a half-mirror and adding a see-through compensator.

If polarization control is allowed as a degree of freedom in the system, then much more compact optics may be achieved but with a much lower efficiency [2–4]. Figure 5.4 shows the working principle of such a device, called a pancake.

A display d emits linearly polarized light, shown in as vertically polarized r_1. It crosses a quarter-wave retarder plate QWP_A becoming circularly polarized r_2. A part of the said light crosses half-mirror m as light r_3 crosses another quarter wave retarder plate QWP_B, becoming linearly polarized light r_4, shown as horizontally polarized. It is then reflected by the reflective polarizer film $XPOL$ as light r_5. It crosses quarter-wave retarder plate QWP_B, becoming circular polarized light r_6, which is again partially reflected at half-mirror m, becoming light r_7. It again crosses quarter-wave retarder plate QWP_B, becoming linearly polarized light, now in the vertical direction, crossing polarizer $XPOL$ (a reflective polarizer) as light r_9 leaving the system. As is implicit in this description, reflective polarizer $XPOL$ reflects horizontally polarized light, but transmits vertically polarized light.

The quarter-wave retarder plate QWP_A may be placed on the display so that the display itself emits circularly polarized light. Quarter-wave retarder plate QWP_B may be laminated on a lens or on polarizer $XPOL$, leading to different possible configurations.

The devices designed according to this principle may be made compact and with a good image quality. However, this comes at a price of a low efficiency. Note that when light crosses half-mirror m from r_2 to r_3, half of the light is lost. And when light is reflected at half-mirror m from r_6 to r_7, half the light is again lost. Therefore, these two processes reduce the available light to 0.5 × 0.5 = 0.25, or ¼ of the light. Aside from these losses, there are also extra losses at the polarizers and other optical elements. When plastic parts are present, birefringence should be low in order to avoid modifying the polarization of the light as it crosses the said plastic parts.

Figure 5.5 shows an example of a pancake design. It follows the principle illustrated in Figure 5.4 where the light from a display d crosses a half-mirror m, is reflected at a polarizer $XPOL$ (that includes a QWP) back to the half-mirror m and back to the polarizer, that it now crosses forming an image seen by the eye. In its path, light also crosses a series of refractive lenses used to improve image quality and adjust image magnification.

Going back to the case of improving Figure 5.3b, if multi-channel optics are used, each channel deals with a much smaller numerical aperture, making it easier to design and improving the overall image quality, since rays are more paraxial in each lens channel. This has an important impact, especially for wider viewing angles, as needed in VR optics. For this reason, multichannel optics tend to have an overall better image quality across the wide FOV, making them a powerful approach.

Figure 5.6 illustrates the working principle of a multi-channel optic. Lens L_A images point **A** of the display to virtual point **V**. Lens L_B images point **B** of the display to the same virtual point **V**. The eye pupil captures

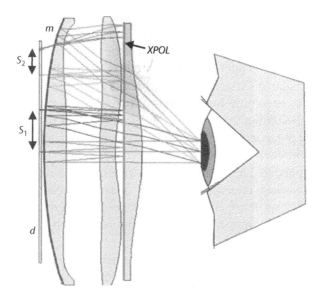

Figure 5.5 Pancake optic with human eye adapted resolution: higher at the center of the FOV and lower at its periphery.

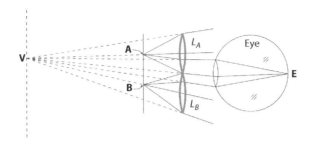

Figure 5.6 Working principle of a multi-channel optic.

light coming through lenses L_A and L_B, all appearing to come from virtual point **V**. The said light is focused to **E** at the back of the eye where a real image is formed and made visible. The information of virtual image point **V** is duplicated on the display at points **A** and **B**. As the eye rotates, it may capture light coming only through lens L_A. For those directions, there will be no duplicity of information on the display.

Multi-channel optics also differ from single-channel optics in the eye-box. Referring to Figure 5.7, the eye-box is the region R in which the eye pupil p may move and still see the virtual image V properly through lens channels L_A and L_B.

Lens L_A is associated with portion a of the display, while lens L_B is associated with portion b of the display. It is said that a and b are the clusters of lenses L_A and L_B, respectively. The eye pupil should not move to a position where ray r_4 is visible. This would allow the pupil to see a point of cluster b through lens L_A, leading to cross-talk. Cluster b has the information for lens L_B and not for lens L_A. Region R should then be below ray r_2 crossing the bottom edges of cluster a and lens L_A. Also, the eye pupil should not move to a position where ray r_3 is visible. This would allow the pupil to see a dark region beyond the end of cluster a of the display. Region R should then be above ray r_1, crossing the top edges of cluster a and lens L_A.

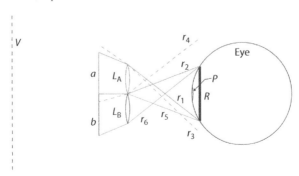

Figure 5.7 Eye-box of a multichannel optic.

A similar reasoning may be applied to rays r_5 and r_6 through lens L_B and the pupil range region R should be above ray r_5 (symmetrical to r_2) and below ray r_6 (symmetrical to r_1). This sets the edges of R at the intersections of rays r_2 and r_6 and rays r_1 and r_5. The actual pupil range region may extend (with variable size) to the left and right of R.

Figure 5.8 shows an example of one such optic with two channels [5]. In this case, those two channels image two separate displays whose virtual images partially overlap forming a complete image of VR being displayed. The larger, main optical element L closer to the eye splits the light in two channels. Each of the said channels has some extra lenses in a move "conventional" configuration, which includes diffractive doublet lenses for image quality and chromatic correction. This multi-channel approach may be taken one step further by increasing the number of channels to, say, four. Also, each channel may be folded combining the compactness advantages of a multi-channel with those of a folded optic.

This type of configuration is illustrated in Figure 5.9 where light from four different portions of the display is combined into a single image shown to the eye. Each channel shows a folded configuration, leading to a compact design. As the eye rotates, different portions of the display become visible through the different channels, as shown on the right of Figure 5.9.

As the number of channels covering the aperture increases to a large number, the optic becomes a lens array. The focal length of each channel diminishes, making the system more compact, but the said focal length reduction has a dramatic effect on the reduction of the resolution the system is able to attain. Also, the display now has a substantial amount of repeated information, which is duplicated for different channels whose virtual images overlap to form the overall virtual image.

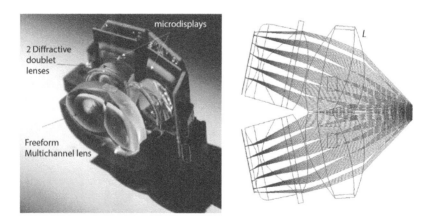

Figure 5.8 Two-channel VR optic designed for two displays.

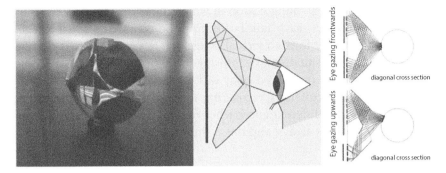

Figure 5.9 Four-channel VR optic. As the eye rotates, different portions of the display become visible.

Lanman and Duebke [6] worked on a very compact, pioneer arrangement, based on mini-lens arrays able to reduce the NTE size radically, at the expense of the angular resolution, limited by the amount of repeated information in the display panel.

In order to recover the lost resolution, one needs to resort to other degrees of freedom in the system. As an example, if the lenses are small enough for several of those to fit into the human eye pupil, several of these

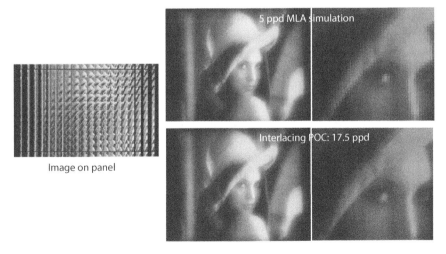

Figure 5.10 The optic as a lens array configuration with many channels often has the drawback of low resolution, owing to the need of displaying redundant images in the panel (left). However, part of the resolution can be recovered (as shown in the bottom center and right images, shot through an actual prototype, compared to the top pictures, which are 5ppd simulations of the same images) by means of interlacing, an optical approach patented by LIMBAK based on a sub-division of mini lens in the array in different clusters able to project the pixels in the virtual image so they do not overlap.

may be interlaced in a configuration in which the lens array is "split" into different lens families, each family forming the complete virtual image. However, each family forms a virtual image that is slightly shifted relative to the others. In this situation, the information shown in Figure 5.10, compared to the original one, the display will be slightly different for the different families of microlenses, recovering a part of the lost resolution [7].

Combinations of different approaches may be used to help recover the lost resolution of lens arrays, and this is the subject of current research.

5.4.4   Eye Tracking and Human-Eye Resolution Adapted Designs

As the VR headset user looks in different directions within the VR scene, his or her eyes move within a volume called the eye-box. The optic must be able to provide good image quality within said eye-box. However, at each moment, the eye pupil only occupies a small portion of said eye-box and this may be used to improve the image quality. One may, for example, increase the focal length of the optic, increasing its resolution. This will decrease the size of the eye box, but if the pupil position can be tracked, the image shown on the display may move via software so that the eye box follows the pupil in its movement.

This method may be used for different optical configurations, for example, that in Figure 5.9. However, now, the visible areas of the display may overlap for different eye positions. In order to avoid cross-talk between channels, the images show on the display for the different channels may be moved on the display, following the movement of the eye.

The human eye has a variable resolution, being higher in the gazing direction and lower at peripheral angles. Also, people have a higher tendency to look forward within a limited range of eye rotations. These characteristics of the human vision may be used to improve the overall image quality of a device by adapting it to the said characteristics. In particular, one may design an optic whose resolution is higher at the center of the FOV and decreases toward peripheral angles where the eye is unable to resolve a high-resolution image. In practice, this means that the central portion of the FOV uses a large portion of the display while the peripheral region of the FOV uses a relatively smaller portion of the display with the resulting decrease in peripheral resolution.

This principle may be adapted to different optical configurations by designing an optic with a variable focal length, being higher at the center and lower at the periphery of the FOV. One such example is shown in Figure 5.5 where central red and blue fields reach the display d separated by a large distance s_1 between them, while peripheral fields green and magenta reach the display d separated by a shorter distance s_2. Note that the colors of the light rays in the figure are for illustration purposes only and are unrelated to the characteristics of the light rays they represent. The central portion of the FOV (where the human eye has a higher resolution) comprised between the directions of fields red and blue is then matched with a large portion of the display s_1, resulting in a higher perceived resolution. However, the peripheral portion of the FOV (where the human eye has a lower resolution) comprised between the directions of fields green and magenta is matched with a small portion of the display s_2, resulting in a lower perceived resolution.

5.5   Visual Interfaces in AR

AR is achievable with all VR headsets, provided that they feature a couple of cameras to capture the user surroundings and therefore replace the function of the eyes, which cannot see through the headset. This approach has been named *"video see-through"* or *"digital see-through"* elsewhere. These systems show the same general challenges discussed in the VR section above (and therefore will not be discussed here) and add others related to the cameras. Among the latter, we can mention that 1) the resolution of camera sensors and display should match if possible to make synthetic and real contents offer identical pixels per degree, 2) camera optics should be compact to avoid increasing the headset TTL, and 3) the system should try to work out the parallax problem, coming from the fact that the camera entrance pupil is shifted with regard to actual user pupils. These systems will not be discussed in detail here to avoid redundancy with the contents of VR, which entirely apply to them.

As VR systems, *optical see-through* AR visual interfaces are based on a set of lenses or mirrors projecting the image coming from a display panel onto the eye with the desired characteristics (magnification/FOV, image quality, etc.). However, along with the correct projection of virtual contents, the arrangement of optical parts, and the nature of lens and mirror surfaces and coatings, should be compatible with optical see-through to let the users see the scene around them.

This projection system that not only shows the synthetic content but allows optical see-through as well is often named *"optical combiner."* It defines the size of the headset and its main performance features (eye-box, FOV).

Depending on the type and number of bounces the light coming from panels follow before hitting the eye, we can classify the different optical see-through AR architectures in three main groups: the pioneers, free-space combiners, and TIR prism combiners, and the state-of-the-art waveguide optics, with the latter being the most complex but showing better performance features, except for efficiency. Compared to waveguide optics, free-space and prism combiners tend to be cheaper, and often offer better contrast (light transmission efficiency from display is higher) at the expense of being thicker/heavier unless a part of the FOV is sacrificed. The Eye-box can be limited also in these two types of systems.

5.5.1 AR Display Panels

Micro display panels are available in different technologies, including LTPS (low temperature polisilicon) LCD, LCoS, micro-active-matrix organic light-emitting diode (mu-AMOLED), micro-inorganic light-emitting diode (i-LED), and Digital Light Processing (DLP) MEMS. The efficiency of these systems vary from 3 to 50%, depending on the technology, with DLP MEMS being the brightest. Although color-sequential displays are more efficient than color-filter displays, the former can produce color breakup when the user's head moves quickly. LCD and OLED panels usually work as true RGB color panels, whereas LCoS and DLP panels are usually color-sequential displays. Due to their high brightness, high efficiency, high reliability, and small pixels, inorganic LED arrays on Si backplanes (commonly referred to as micro-iLED micro-displays) have gained a lot of attention lately.

Various head mounted display (HMD) systems (Intel Vaunt, North Focals, and HoloLens V2, for instance) feature *scanning display engines* these days. These systems are bright, very efficient with laser illumination, and small (thanks to their limited etendue), which in turn provide high contrast. Besides, they enable different types of optical foveation/resolution increase by smartly combining gaze tracking and switching the pixels in the angular space in specific custom ways.

Other headsets are trying *diffractive display systems*. Laser-based phase panel display engines (i.e., dynamic holographic projectors) have recently been applied to HMD prototypes due to their high brightness (light is redirected through diffraction rather than being absorbed as with traditional panels) and can provide a per-pixel depth display to solve the vergence-accommodation conflict [8].

Due to partially unsolved challenges in the real-time calculation of the computer-generated-hologram (CGH) pattern, laser speckle, a small exit pupil, and high cost, their implementation in HMD products is limited though. However, dynamic holographic displays based on phase panels remain a good architectural option for tomorrow's small-form-factor, high-FOV, high-brightness, and true-per-pixel-depth HMDs.

5.5.2   Free-Space and TIR Prism Combiners

Free-space combiners consist of one or several optical components, including mirrors and lenses, aligned in an optical train that is able to project the display panels, in general either located at the temple or at the forehead, onto the eyes of the user. In this type of combiners, most of the light-ray paths from a panel to a pupil occur in air. This approach has been used in military applications and helmets [9] for a long time. There are several types of free-space combiners, the simplest ones including one single-plane 50% reflective mirror and others comprising up to three components.

For instance, the system in Figure 5.11 comprises a micro-display at the forehead, emitting light downwards through a lens and toward a 50%-reflectivity flat mirror tilted 45° that bounces the light toward the user's pupil. The combination of display size and lens shape produce the synthetic scene and FOV, and the half-transmittance of the mirror allows for a direct view of the surroundings. This configuration was used by AR glasses such as ODG-R7 in 2015.

The function of the lens + flat mirror can be made by a single curved reflector, like in the system schematically shown in Figure 5.12, with the panel located at the temple. These curved reflectors, in the high-end configurations, embed a set of holographic (North Focals in 2019) or Fresnel reflectors, which enable better performance features and are lightweight.

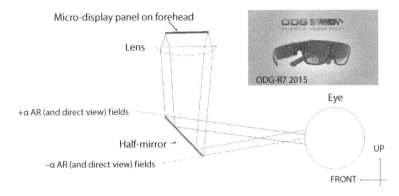

Figure 5.11 Free-space combiner based on a lens and a 50% reflectance mirror. This approach was used by ODG-R7 in 2015.

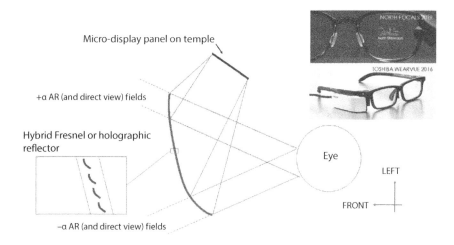

Figure 5.12 AR free-space combiner based on one single curved mirror.

This approach has also been applied in basic AR systems with the direct projection of large smartphone-like displays located at the forehead.

Another common approach is based on the so-called "bird bath" (utilized in the Google glass [10], for instance, although this case was a particular case of free-space combiner, since all elements where embedded into an optically dense medium) which includes a reflective collimation lens working with an additional flat combiner, like the example of Figure 5.13.

The efficiency of free-space optical combiner varies depending on the architecture: 50% for a single partial mirror, 12.5% for a birdbath reflector

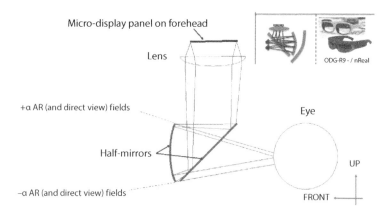

Figure 5.13 Birdbath configuration in a free-space combiner.

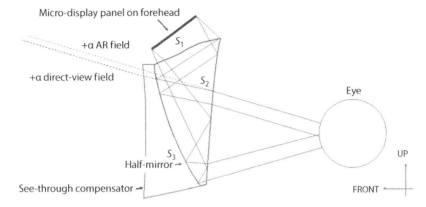

Figure 5.14 Schematic view of a Free-form prism optical combiner.

with three passes through partial mirrors, and 25% for a three-reflector design in which one is a full mirror.

One important family of combiners optics is that of the *free-form TIR-prim combiners*. The availability of freeform diamond-turning machines with 5 degrees of freedom axes in the last 20 years has boosted the research on these devices [11, 12]. These machines, which are becoming quite standard in most optical manufacturing shops, can produce direct cuts of plastic lenses or metal inserts for injection molding in mass production). The basic free-form prism combiner includes three surfaces, with at least two being free-form: 1) a semi-transparent/mirrored surface 2) a TIR surface right in front of the eye and 3) a refractive surface in front of display (see Figure 5.14). TIR prism combiners require one additional prism, bonded to the original one, to compensate for the see-through distortion. Both can be injection molded and later cemented together, which increases the optics thickness and weight, especially for large FOVs over 30–40°. Alternatives have been proposed with tiled prism combiners to bring various FOVs together.

Single-TIR-Bounce Prism Combiners are the quite common in AR and can be found in different devices, such as an early Canon AR headset, and more recently on Lenovo Daystar AR, NED Glass X2, and many others, thanks to the easy access to both free-form prism design and fabrication. More complex devices showing more than one TIR bounce aim to achieve thinner AR headsets or smart glasses [13].

5.5.3 Waveguide Optics Combiners

In this group, we found devices where the number of bounces in the TIR propagation of light is high, and the devices turn into optical guides working as periscopes with a single entrance pupil and often many exit pupils.

Apart from the guide section itself, a waveguide combiner consists of the input and output couplers. These can be either simple prisms, micro-prism arrays, embedded mirror arrays, surface relief gratings, analog holographic or resonant waveguide gratings, and meta-surfaces. Waveguide combiners have been used outside the AR field for years, in tasks such as planar optical interconnections [14] and LCD backlights.

5.5.3.1   Exit Pupil Expansion (EPE)

The simplest waveguide combiners are flat and do not need an exit pupil expansion, but hardly attain FOV > 20° and only fit with smart glasses. Flat waveguides can use different extraction schemes, including a single curved semi-transparent mirror (Epson Moverio) or flat holographic outcouplers. A flat semi-transparent mirror in a bird-bath configuration was used in the Google glass, as mentioned before. Extraction mirrors can be multiplied to increase the eye-box. Fracturing metal mirrors into individual pieces is another option (LetinAR waveguide combiner). These alternatives are shown, schematically, in Figure 5.15.

In curved waveguides, designs are more difficult because the extraction mirror facets have to counter the lens effect every TIR bounce produces in the propagation.

Larger FOV in binocular designs often requires one-dimesional (1D) or two-dimensional (2D) pupil expansion. 1D allows achieving >10 mm eye-box horizontally without the need of IPD adjustment. 2D can be utilized in case an easier vertical fit is desired as well. In this way, AR glasses not only can fit viewers with a larger range of inter-pupillary distance but also can provide greater compatibility for viewers with various face shapes and nose height.

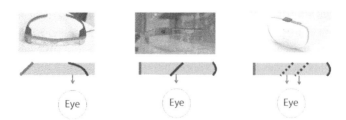

Figure 5.15 Simple flat waveguide combiners based on curved embedded mirror (Epson Moverio, left), bird bath (Google glass, center) and bird bath + fractured embedded mirrors (LetinAR, right).

Systems using 1D pupil expansion need a display engine that is able to generate an input pupil sufficiently large in the non-expanded direction, which has an impact on the size of the engine, but achieves good imaging and color uniformity along the entire eye-box. This is the case of the Lumus LCoS-based display engines. If the light engine is located at the forehead, the input pupil should be large horizontally, and the pupil expansion occurs vertically. In case the display engine is at the temple, the input pupil is large in vertical and the expansion occurs along the horizontal axis.

2D pupil expansion enables smaller light engines, which will not have the burden to generate the 2D eye-box by themselves (owing to etendue limitations, they cannot). In this case, the display engine can produce a small circular or square input pupil. Combiners featuring 2D EPE can use one guide per color, or two guides for the three colors, and even one single guide for all. Materials also vary, and depending on the approach, eye-box, color uniformity, efficiency, and the FOV vary.

There are different approaches to achieve 2D EPE, like using two similar systems with an embedded set of parallel beam splitters in series and orthogonal to each other, so the pupil expansion occurs first in the X direction and later in Y, as shown at the left of Figure 5.16 [15, 16], using 90°-turn gratings. This approach is used in Digilens, Nokia, Vuzix, HoloLens, and MagicLeap One.

Another approach is using a grating in front of the display engine able to "scatter" the light already in 2D fan (the grating "grooves" now become "pillars"), which will flood a large area output coupling grating able to expand the exit pupil already in X and Y, as shown in Figure 5.16, right. This approach [17] is used in the BAE Q-Sight combiner or the WaveOptics Ltd. Phlox 40-deg combiner (now EnhancedWorld Ltd.). It is not easy for one grating area to take care of all the 2D expansions and preserve the total output luminance and uniformity among the exit pupils. However,

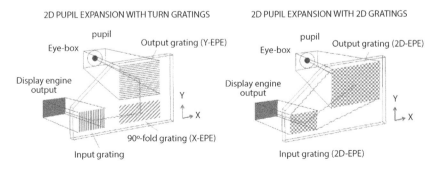

Figure 5.16 2D EPE schemes, using turn gratings (left) and 2D gratings (right).

using two grating areas instead of three potentially reduce light loss during transportation, and, moreover, the final output grating can have more area to increase the eye box size. The eye box size of the WaveOptics 40-degree FOV module can reach around 19×15 mm^2, the largest among all similar products in the market.

5.5.3.2   Incouplers and Outcouplers Strategy

There are several technologies compatible with in- and outcoupling of the light when travelling from the display engine to the user's eye: on the one hand, there are couplers based on refractive/reflective features (geometric waveguides), and on the other, we have diffractive/holographic gratings (diffractive waveguides). The most common couplers these days are embedded half-tone mirrors in geometric waveguides and thin volume holograms, slanted surface relief gratings, in diffractive waveguides. These offer different combination of coupling efficiency, color uniformity over the eye-box and FOV, mass production costs, and size/weight.

In geometric waveguide, coupling is a relatively straightforward combination of reflection and transmission mechanism through transflective mirrors, but they tend to be bulky sometimes with a quite tedious manufacturing procedure (since the ratio reflection/transmission should vary along the guide). Lumus is one of the companies working in this approach and has achieved 50° FOV with a technology compatible with the look of conventional eyewear and offering good contrast values.

In diffractive waveguide, in- and outcoupling is carried out by planar diffraction gratings, for instance [18], based on features whose size is in the range of visible wavelengths (micro–nanoscale). In these features, which have in general flat faces, light splits into multiple diffraction modes, both transmissive and reflective: the power and angle of each mode depend on the tilt and period of the grating. Other values (such as refractive index, specific feature geometry, and thickness) allow emphasizing some preferred modes over others, in particular, those whose diffraction direction is the one we need. The Bottom line is we are bouncing the light as desired (particularly, we need to make sure that the propagated light can be bounced by TIR along the guide) but using an overall (macroscopically) planar surface, saving space and material. It is important to stress a given

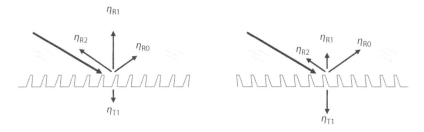

Figure 5.17 Example of slanted surface relief gratings. The orientation of gratings with respect to incoming light help emphasizing certain modes over others, to produce in-coupling, out-coupling or turn gratings.

grating will bounce different colors in different angles, producing color dispersion, both in the reflections and in the transmission modes.[1]

Diffractive waveguide couplers, compared over geometric couplers, offer more flexibility in design and manufacturing. They can be achieved by state-of-the-art semiconductor micro-/nano-fabrication techniques (surface relief gratings, like the ones schematically shown in Figure 5.17), or by laser interfering holographic technique (holographic gratings), acting on a film located on top of the waveguide substrate. Geometric waveguides need traditional molding, cutting, gluing and multi-layer coating (varying along the waveguide) processes, which compromise yield and scalability, with the corresponding impact on costs.

Diffractive waveguides show other problems, though. One is color non-uniformity across the whole FOV (rainbow effect). In order to mitigate the color dispersion issue, the most common approach is to use three waveguides for red, green, and blue color bands, respectively, each layer having its own grating parameters optimized for one color only. This reduces the color non-uniformity across the eye box, but cannot totally cancel it (since each waveguide still transports multiple colors rather than a single wavelength). In order to achieve thinner devices, most brands are trying to work with two guides rather than three, either using light engines with narrower bandwidths RGB (laser) and grating features able to handle RGB in one single guide [Dispelix].

---

[1]Geometric refraction also produces color dispersion, due to the variation of refractive index with wavelength, but geometric reflections are free of this chromatic problem.

5.6   Future Research Agenda and Roadmap

5.6.1   Future Visual Interfaces in VR

5.6.1.1   Pancake-Type Optics

The current development of VR optics involves improvements in its different components: display, electronics, software, optics, eye tracking, … Each of these areas have specific challenges.

Regarding the optics, there are different aspects that have room for improvement and are the subject of current research.

New configurations of pancake-type designs are currently under investigation. These architectures need low birefringence materials in order to avoid changes in light polarization as it travels back and forth inside the optic. This should ideally be achieved in the mass production of injection-molded optics but remains as a difficulty with an impact on costs and a subject of further research.

The two surfaces that act as reflectors are a semi-transparent mirror and an *XPOL*. In order to provide flexibility in the optical design process, both of these components should be shaped. Semi-transparent mirrors may be made as curved shapes, but that is still a difficulty for the *XPOL* and *QWP* components very few suppliers can handle these days.

5.6.1.2   Multichannel Optics

Multichannel optics have the potential to combine compactness and high resolution in a device that has high efficiency. However, by including many small components, these optics have challenges in manufacturing. Precision in the case of multichannel optics involves not only the form factor of every lens in the array (that can be orders of magnitude tighter than the accuracy required in conventional optics, considering the small size of every optical channel, specially in mini-lens arrays) but also the alignment of different lenses in the optical train with respect to each other.

5.6.1.3   Built-In Myopia and Astigmatism Correction

VR optics generate a virtual image some distance away. However, for people with myopia, the said image may be at a distance that is too far to focus. In that case, the VR headset needs a procedure to bring the virtual image closer so that the user is able to see it properly. This ability to adjust the distance to the virtual image may be achieved by moving internal parts in the optic, for example, moving the display closer or further away to/from the optic, or moving some of the optical components in the optical train. Another option is to have lenses that can be replaced so that each person would put in the headset a lens that would correct the image for his or her myopia condition. Aside from myopia, some people also have astigmatism, and this is an additional challenge for the optic. Ways to correct for these cases of imperfect vision are also the subject of the current investigation.

5.6.1.4   Visual Comfort and Enhanced User-Experience

Different people have different interpupillary distances, and this means that, in many cases, the distance between optics for the two needs adjustment for each person. Ideally, the eye-box would be so large that no adjustment is needed. This, however, may be challenging to include in the optical design, given all other constraints that need to be met. New research may help alleviate this need for adjustment, improving the user experience.

VR headsets typically show content on a virtual plane some distance away (about 1.5 m or so). Slightly different images are shown to both eyes, creating a 3D sense of depth. However, the 3D objects may be at a different distance than the virtual plane where the said virtual images are formed. This difference in distance from the virtual plane to the position of the virtual 3D objects results in a vergence-accommodation mismatch, which may be uncomfortable. Different strategies may be tried to alleviate this inconvenience, including having the ability to show virtual image planes at different distances, showing curved virtual images, or adjusting the position of the virtual plane to the average depth of the objects shown in the VR scene.

Pancakes can also improve resolution by applying passive foveal super-resolution and by using an advanced combination of lens materials and stacks to make it compatible with small (<1 in. diagonal) high-pixel-count displays. So far, there are no optics in the state of the art that are able to produce the required >90° FOV with such small displays, and the opportunities for any architecture either to handle the FOV and resolve the pixels are obvious.

Other way to improve resolution is using pupil-tracking. In multi-channel optics, this allows for a reduction of duplicated pixels along the panel. Finally, increased FOV can greatly improve the user experience, which will benefit from emulating what happens with human vision in real life. The efforts in such direction will probably be based on additional low resolution display panels with projection optics closer to the sides of temples.

5.6.2   Future Visual Interfaces in AR

5.6.2.1   *Video See-Through Headsets*

The main challenge in this case is working out the parallax problem that comes from the headset cameras being a few millimeters ahead of the actual user pupils. This causes a wrong perception of the scene, which is particularly cumbersome if we need to manipulate objects with hands close to us. Fixing this problem is of particular interest in applications such as surgery or training of all kinds when the tasks involve manipulating objects nearby.

Apart from the correction of parallax, the camera optics should be as thin as possible, in order to avoid adding up to the total track length, which impacts the headset size, as discussed several times in this chapter.

Current trends seem to push this option over optical see-through systems, thanks to the benefits discussed before. However, the loss of eye-contact is the major drawback, and a complex feature to deal with some major brands are probably trying to fix.

5.6.2.2   *Optical See-Through Headsets*

One way to sort out the future research lines in AR comes from benchmarking the current challenges in the field against the two main building blocks in AR, to find out what the latter can do to address and tackle these challenges. The main demands in AR are:

1. lowering the costs
2. improving the headset aesthetics/size
3. increasing the eye-box
4. controlling the color separation
5. increasing the FOV
6. improving the contrast
7. enhancing image quality
8. increasing the lifetime to be able to achieve stand-alone headsets

The two main building blocks are display engine and waveguide optics. Table 5.1 below shows how each building block can be improved to have a positive impact on each of the challenges listed. The ideas on the table can inspire future research topics in this area.

Indeed, we can withdraw future research lines in the intersection cells, assigning the highest priority to those that appear more often in the table because they help in addressing several challenges at once. According to this criteria, future research should put more emphasis on:

Table 5.1 Main challenges future AR headsets will face, benchmarked against the two main building blocks. In the intersection cells, we can collect possible future research lines.

		Building block	
		Display engine	**Combiner optics**
Challenge	Lower costs	Lower cost-yet high PPI micro-displays High-production-yield display engines	Advanced SINGLE waveguides taking care of RGB Cost-effective in and out-couplers
	Size/aesthetics	Miniaturization of display engine illumination and projection optics using free-form optics	Curved waveguides, optical design able to counter the lens power introduced by curvature
	Eye box	Projection optics using free-form optics	Advanced EPE schemes
	Color separation/ fringes	Laser based displays, narrower bandwidth RGBs	Advanced SINGLE waveguides taking care of RGB
	FOV	Advanced free-form Projection optics	
	Contrast	i-LED displays for more brightness but achieving the required ppi	better gratings? better waveguides?...
	Image quality	Higher ppi displays Advanced optics manufacturing	
	Battery lifetime	More efficient (nits/watt) displays Smart computing adapted to scenes	More efficient optics

- High-PPI + high production yield (low cost) + high brightness + low consumption micro-displays
- Free-form illumination optics able to shrink the size of the display engine module while improving its performance (eye-box, FOV, image quality…)

- Advanced single waveguides handling RGB to reduce costs and improve aesthetics, able to meet the FOV goals
- Advanced in and out couplers for better efficiency and performance, able to lower manufacturing costs as well
- Curved waveguides

However, dynamic holographic displays based on phase panels remain a good architectural option for tomorrow's small-form-factor, high-FOV, high-brightness, and true-per-pixel-depth HMDs.

References

1. P. Benitez, J.C. Minano, D. Grabovickic *et al.*, Imaging optics adapted to the human resolution. Patent 10,690,813 B2, filed in January 2015 and issued June 2020.
2. J.L. Russa, Infinite optical image-forming apparatus. United States of America Patent 3,443,858, filed in February1966, granted in May 1969.
3. Huxford, R.B., Wide-FOV head-mounted display using hybrid optics. *Proc. SPIE 5249, Optical Design and Engineering*, 2004, https://doi.org/10.1117/12.516541.
4. Narasimhan, B.A., Ultra-compact pancake optics based on ThinEyes® super-resolution technology for virtual reality headsets. *Proc. SPIE 10676*, Digital Optics for Immersive Displays, 106761G, 21 May 2018, https://doi.org/10.1117/12.2315688.
5. Buljan, M., Narasimhan, B., Benítez, P. *et al.*, Ultra-compact multichannel freeform optics for 4xWUXGA OLED microdisplays. *Proc. SPIE 10676*, Digital Optics for Immersive Displays, 1067607, 21 May 2018, https://doi.org/10.1117/12.2307452.
6. Lanman, D. and Luebke, D., Near-eye light field displays. *ACM Trans. Graphics (TOG)*, 32, 1–10, 2013, doi: 10.1145/2508363.2508366.
7. P. Benitez and J.C. Miñano, Immersive compact display glasses. United States of America Patent 10,432,920 B2, Filed 2013-11-25, granted October 2019.
8. Maimone, A., Georgiou, A., Kollin, J., Holographic near-eye displays for virtual and augmented reality. *ACM Trans. Graphics*, 36, 1–16, 2017, 10.1145/3072959.3073624.
9. Melzer, J., Brozoski, F., Letowski, T., Harding, T., Rash, C., Guidelines for HMD design, in: *Helmet-Mounted Displays: Sensation, Perception and Cognition Issues*, pp. 805–848, Chapter: Chapter 17, U.S. Army Aeromedical Research Laboratory, Fort Rucker, Alabama 36362-0577, 2009.
10. M.I. Olsson, M.J. Heinrich, D. Kelly, J. Lapetina, Wearable device with input and output structures. United States of America Patent US20130044042A1, filed 2011-08-18, issued September 2011.

11. Hua, H., Cheng, D., Wang, Y., Liu, S., Near-eye displays: state-of-the-art and emerging technologies. *Proc. SPIE 7690*, 769009, 2010.
12. Hua, H., Past and future of wearable augmented reality displays and their applications. *Proc. SPIE 9186*, Fifty Years of Optical Sciences at The University of Arizona, 918600, 20 October 2014, https://doi.org/10.1117/12.2063946.
13. C. Gao, H. Hua, Y. Lin, Ergonomic head mounted display device and optical system. United States of America Patent US20120162549A1, filed 2010-12-24, granted 2016-05-24.
14. Michael Miller, J., de Beaucoudrey, N., Chavel, P., Turunen, J., Cambril, E., Design and fabrication of binary slanted surface-relief gratings for a planar optical interconnection. *Appl. Opt.*, 36, 5717–5727, 1997.
15. S. Robbins and D.D. Bohn, Two-dimensional exit-pupil expansion. Patent US8736963B2, filed 2012-03-21, granted May 2014.
16. Kress, B. and Shin, M., Diffractive and holographic optics as optical combiners in head mounted displays. *UbiComp 2013 Adjunct - Adjunct Publication of the 2013 ACM Conference on Ubiquitous Computing*, pp. 1479–1482, 2013, 10.1145/2494091.2499572.
17. Cameron, A., Optical waveguide technology & its application in head mounted displays. *Proceedings of SPIE*, vol. 8330E, p. 12, 2012, 10.1117/12.923660.
18. Levola, T. and Laakkonen, P., Replicated slanted gratings with a high refractive index material for in and outcoupling of light. *Opt. Express*, 15, 2067–74, 2007, 10.1364/OE.15.002067.

XR and Metaverse Software Platforms

Lorenzo Cappannari[1][*] and Antony Vitillo[2]

[1]*AnotheReality, Milan, Italy*
[2]*New Technology Walkers, Turin, Italy*

Abstract

The evolution of spatial computing is driving the adoption of a new three-dimensional (3D) software ecosystem known as the metaverse, a new paradigm that will require a whole new set of software platforms. The authors group them under five categories: (1) enabling platforms: core platforms enabling the rest of the Extended Realities (XR) software ecosystem, including operating systems, digital stores, real-time engines and frameworks, world tracking and mapping, and cloud rendering; (2) content platforms: allowing the acquisition, creation, and management of all 3D content populating the metaverse, such as digital twins or virtual environments; (3) human-centered platforms: a very specific type of content related to human representations and virtual beings; (4) utility platforms: focus on tools that allow populating the metaverse with applications and utility-related use cases, such as new search engines and new low-code application platforms; and (5) application platforms: focus on specific vertical application field, mainly covered in other sections of this book. The authors do highlight potential future development within each category, and suggest a prioritization of investments on the following platforms: (a) Web real-time engines, (b) augmented reality-cloud platforms, (c) low-code/no-code platforms, (d) virtual beings, and (e) massive networking services.

Keywords: Metaverse software platforms, content creation platforms, digital twin platforms, virtual beings platforms, low-code utility platforms

*[*Corresponding author:* lorenzo@anotherreality.io

Mariano Alcañiz, Marco Sacco and Jolanda G. Tromp (eds.) Roadmapping Extended Reality: Fundamentals and Applications, (135–156) © 2022 Scrivener Publishing LLC

6.1   Introduction

6.1.1   Toward the Metaverse

The year 2020 represented a pivotal year in the evolution of the new paradigm of spatial computing. During the pandemic emergency, the world society has experienced the following key trends:

1. The adoption of XR interfaces, finally reaching a wider distribution beyond research and Business to business (B2B) markets. The reference goes here to the rapid adoption of virtual reality (VR) consumer stand-alone devices such as the Oculus Quest 2, and the massive consumer adoption of augmented reality (AR) interactions in advertising and content creation, projected to reach 1 billion active users by 2022 [1].
2. The maturing phase of other enabling emerging technologies now considered holistically as part of a spatial computing ecosystem. The reference goes here to the different applications of artificial intelligence (AI; computer vision, voice recognition, prediction), IoT and robotics, distributed ledgers (going beyond cryptocurrencies, thanks to Non Fungible Tokens (NFTs)), and edge computing.
3. The sudden digital transformation of the global society, imposed by the Covid-19 emergency, forced the adoption of traditional/two-dimensional (2D) digital tools, at the same time showing their limitations—like the lack of realistic human interactions and of a shared digital space.

The collision of the above brought back to the public debate the concept of metaverse as the evolution of the actual bidimensional digital ecosystem. The word metaverse has many synonyms, each of them focusing on a specific take on the subject: Magicverse [2], Mirrorworld [3], and AR Cloud [4] are focusing on their capabilities of augmenting the real world; Spatial Internet and Spatial Web are focusing on their network-based infrastructural nature; Omniverse [5] and Multiverse are focusing on their capability of grouping together different ecosystems and worlds. In all its declinations, the metaverse remains a collective virtual shared space, created by the convergence of virtually enhanced physical reality and physically persistent virtual space. In this chapter, we will examine XR software platforms as the software ecosystem enabling the metaverse, the core software infrastructure of the upcoming three-dimensional (3D)-based and spatial computing paradigm.

6.1.2   Towards the Metaverse Ecosystem

Software platforms are major pieces of software under which various smaller application programs can be designed to run. XR software platforms are divided into five different categories or layers:

1. Enabling platforms. Core software platforms that enable the rest of the XR software ecosystem, including operating systems, digital stores, real-time engines and frameworks, world mapping and tracking, and cloud rendering.
2. Content platforms. Platforms that allow the acquisition, creation, and management of all 3D content populating the metaverse, such as digital twins or virtual environments.
3. Human-centered platforms. Platforms managing the very specific type of content related to human representations and virtual beings. Given the relevant implications of a digital representation of humans within a collective space focused on digital human-to-human interactions, the metaverse, this type of content has been grouped in a separate category.

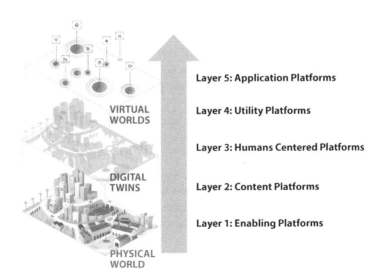

Figure 6.1 The spatial computing/metaverse software platforms ecosystem. The figure summarizes the whole section 6.1.2.

4. Utility platforms. Platforms that focus on the tools that allow populating the metaverse with applications and utility-related use cases, such as new search engines and new low-code application platforms.
5. Application platforms. Platforms that focus on a specific application field. This category will be mainly covered in other chapters of this book.

The five categories can be seen as logic layers of software, moving from the core computing power toward real use cases and applications of technology.

6.2   Enabling Platforms

The first layer groups all software platforms that enable all other software to run; it is therefore the layer comprising all basic tools on which the other layers are based.

6.2.1   Operating Systems

Every AR and VR device, exactly like any other hardware device, has its own operating system. The operating system is a software layer that lets all other applications running on the device interact with the underlying hardware, bridging the software and the hardware. At the current stage, XR operating systems are mostly a counterpart of the ones that are available on the mobile market. Most headsets (e.g., Oculus Quest, HTC Vive Focus) run a modified version of Android, but there are some notable exceptions anyway, like Microsoft HoloLens running on Windows 10 Holographic (from Windows Core OS).

It is reasonable to envision that in the future, all XR operating systems will further evolve, allowing users to better exploit the physical space around them (there will be a transition from 2D frontal interfaces to 3D interfaces all around the user) and offering more natural interfaces (that will let the user use his/her gaze, his/her hands, and his/her voice to interact with the system), to the point that they will eventually become personal—like 3D personal assistants, helping the user to perform specific tasks [6].

6.2.2   Digital Stores

On top of the immersive operating system run applications, and the digital stores where users can find and purchase them. At this stage, every XR hardware producer offers its own digital store: Facebook has the Oculus Store, Pico the Pico Store, Microsoft the Windows Store, and so on. There are also notable cases where a single store is available on multiple devices, such as Viveport being available on several Chinese headsets (from HTC, Pico, iQiYi, etc.). Some stores are dedicated to specific segments, like the VIVE Business AppStore, only to enterprise-oriented experiences. Looking at the AR ecosystem, still mobile driven, Google Play Store and Apple Store are the digital stores of reference.

It is reasonable to envision that in the future, these stores will become smarter, proposing to us the applications we may be interested in, and that will include gamification mechanics to keep the users hooked in. With socialization being a key aspect of immersive realities and digitalization in general, an evolution towards multiplayer features is expected from digital stores.

6.2.3   Real-Time Engines and Frameworks

In order to develop the applications that users can launch on their AR/VR devices, most content creators use what are called "game engines": software applications that let teams of professionals with different backgrounds (developers, 3D artists, designers, etc.) collaborate together to create 2D or 3D applications. Since in the XR space, they are not only used to develop games, they are generically referred to as "real-time engines." The most famous engines are Unity and Unreal Engine, but other alternatives, like the open-source Godot Engine, do exist. Most of these engines run on a personal computer/Mac, but recently, some Web-based alternatives that let people create immersive applications running completely within a browser are coming to light: Amazon Sumerian and MetaVRse are two notable examples of this kind. There are also simplified engines specialized in the creation of the popular AR filters that are in use on smartphones, like Lens Studio and Spark AR Studio. Many gaming studios also have their own custom engines, like Valve, using its Source game engine. Within game engines, developers can use plugins and existing libraries to speed up their workflows. For instance, in Unity, it is possible to use the XR Interaction Toolkit, MRTK, MARS, to develop faster XR experiences by providing the interaction layer out of the box.

It is reasonable to envision that in the future, game engines will offer compatibility with more platforms, so that in the same game engine, it will be possible to create software for more headsets, and more functionalities. It is expected that all basic layers of tracking and interactivity, in the next few years, will be offered either by game engines directly or by development frameworks built on top of them [7]. Also, bigger attention toward web-based engines is expected, like WebXR: current web engines and frameworks are either too simple (e.g., AR.js) or too expensive (e.g. Sumerian, The 8th Wall). There is clear need for a valid web-based alternative, affordable and feature rich, enabling the foundations of the Spatial Web.

6.2.4 World Mapping and Tracking

XR devices, being spatial, need to perceive and understand the space around them. They need to assess environment and the context the user is in, and also track the user behaviors, providing immersive mixed reality functionalities. The long-term vision is that there will be a system that:

- understands exactly the space around the user, in order to let virtual and physical elements properly interact with each other
- understands the context, perceiving exactly what both the user and the people around him/her are doing
- is able to share easily data from one user to the other, so that both can operate in a common context
- understands the intentions of the user in a natural way

This is the so-called "AR Cloud" [4]. Thanks to a constantly updated digital twin of the real world, it is possible to create digital elements that coexist in a persistent and shared way in every location of the world, for all people of the world. It will allow for the full blending of real and virtual elements in everyday life. The AR Cloud encompasses problems of networking, tracking, AI, 3D meshes, information management, and possibly IoT and also includes non-technical issues like privacy (Can a company own the environmental data about my private physical places?) and ownership (Can someone put a persistent virtual element on top of my private space?). At this stage, no company has delivered a fully functioning version of the AR Cloud, but all major companies (Google, Apple, Microsoft, Facebook, etc.) are working on it, each one holding a specific advantage in a field (e.g., Google already owns a map of the whole world with Google Maps; Microsoft can already create shared mixed reality experiences with Spatial Anchors). There are also open efforts toward the AR Cloud: the Open AR Cloud Consortium is working on an AR-Cloud that is open, connected, and accessible [8].

6.2.5   Cloud Rendering

To make sure everyone wears XR glasses all the time, every day, these pieces of hardware must be fashionable and lightweight. Yet, it is a difficult present challenge to create something that is lightweight and that, at the same time, can perform heavy calculations to show realistic virtual elements. One of the possible solutions lies on cloud rendering: all the heavy calculations (graphical rendering, AI calculations) are performed in the cloud and then streamed to the XR device, which will basically just need a display and a wireless network adapter. There are already many companies working in this direction: NVIDIA, Microsoft, and Plutosphere are some notable examples. The encoding/decoding part of this system is already working well; what is lacking is a distributed edge cloud network to guarantee that the streaming latency stays below 15 ms, in order to offer a comfortable user experience [9].

6.2.6   Future Projections for Operating Systems

While operating systems and digital stores today are under complete control of foreign hardware manufacturers, EU companies have room to innovate in sectors like:

1. Web-based real-time engines and frameworks
    While a stand-alone runtime engine that can compete with Unity and Unreal seems a hard reach at this stage, the market is currently lacking a reliable web-based real-time engine that:
    - Can run completely on the web
    - Is open and not locked to any particular platform, allowing developers to deploy the engine on their own servers, and to publish their web apps on hostings of their choice
    - Offers a similar interface to the one of its stand-alone counterparts, flattening developers' learning curve
    - Offers a level of functionalities similar to the one of its stand-alone counterparts
    - Can be extended by everyone with plugins and frameworks
    - Is compatible with most browsers, devices, and AR/VR technologies
    - Produces immersive web software that is modifiable and follows the WebXR standards
    - Is affordable for developers

Given the ever-growing importance of the Spatial Web, such an engine could become an important tool to let more developers create web-based immersive content, accelerating the growth of the technology. Together with the engine, frameworks and middlewares that let developers create their experiences faster shall also be created (e.g., User Interface (UI) elements, tracking facilities, input libraries). This set of tools could become the de-facto standard for the development of WebXR content.

2. AR Cloud

As seen in the previous analysis, many companies are already working on the AR Cloud [4], widely considered the foundation of a consumer-ready mixed-reality paradigm. Such a strategic infrastructure mixing physical and digital assets should see a strong public regulation, just like any other telecommunication infrastructure. Also, the time is ripe for European companies to create their own systems, with solutions ideally based on the paradigms proposed by the Open AR Cloud Consortium [8]. A system able to reconstruct an updated digital twin of the mesh of the world using data from multiple sources is needed. Such sources may be:

• Satellite photos, street-view photos, and videos, already owned by some companies or available in open databases
• The live camera stream of any user device (e.g., smartphone), that can update the digital twin in real time, updating the data of every physical location in real time

The system should be able to understand the physical environment surrounding the users, and use these data to update a shared mesh of the world, keeping a strong focus on sensible user data privacy. Also, a data ownership environment shall be evaluated, therefore defining the concept of the "digital ownership of a physical place".

3. Cloud rendering solutions

Cloud rendering is the network foundation that will allow the size and weight reduction of XR wearable hardware. A forward-looking ecosystem shall take the following features in consideration:

• 5G/6G connection widely available
• A streaming framework, composed of client and server counterparts, able to stream the real-time rendered videos of 3D interactive elements. This infrastructure shall provide high-quality visuals while using the lowest bandwidth possible and the lowest latency; it must be open,

customizable, and multi-cloud for maximum flexibility and scalability.

- A network of edge servers installed in key locations, allowing latencies below 15 ms

6.3   Content Platforms

The current evolution of the web has shown that customer-generated content is one of the key drivers of adoption for a new software platform. However, while TikTok and the like represent the final step of over 200 years of evolution of 2D media content acquisition and editing tools, in XR, we are basically starting from scratch. With the content moving from 2D first to 3D first, there is a growing need for software platforms allowing the acquisition, creation, and management of the 3D content populating the metaverse.

6.3.1   Content Acquisition

2D media content became ubiquitous, thanks to the diffusion of mobile phones and social media. With the evolution of the metaverse, a similar trend for 3D content is expected, thanks to the embedding of tools like LiDAR and other laser scanning technologies within consumers' personal devices. New iPhones' LiDAR capabilities are already pushing the development of easy-to-use 3D measurement and 3D model acquisition tools, but the results are still not quite accurate [10]. At the same time, startups like Threedy.ai are using computer vision and machine learning algorithms to recreate realistic 3D models from 2D photos, with a certain degree of accuracy [11]. For both content creation technologies (scanning and computer vision), the outcome is still not optimized enough for a wide consumer market. In fact, as laser scanning tools were born for professional usage, the output media file is usually too detailed and not optimized for 3D real-time usage. The ecosystem is therefore still lacking a solid tool that is able to acquire a 3D model of an object or environment fully ready to be imported within interactive virtual worlds or applications, without requiring any technical manual rework.

6.3.2   Content Creation and Management

Content creation platforms are those technical or semi-technical tools that allow 3D content creation from scratch, or from a subset of ready-made layouts or templates. They target different types of content creators: from skilled creators, requiring complex tools in order to produce high-end pieces of content often for community reuse (think of AR filters, for example), to casual creators, closer to traditional consumers creating content and requiring simpler tools based on prefabricated templates. Since 3D content has been widely used by the media industry during the past 20 years (in gaming, movies, and advertising), there is already a wide array of tools available for industry professionals. Technical and professional software platforms like Adobe 3D Studio Max or Blender are paired with less technical and more easy-to-use 3D content creation tools verticalized by use case. All these platforms are used today to create XR 3D content.

It is reasonable to envision that more easy content creation platforms will sprout together with the massive adoption of the metaverse, both generalist ones and the others more focused on specific use cases or applications. These authoring platforms will represent at the same time 3D management tools, allowing not only content creators to enhance virtual worlds with their own custom content in the long term but also platform holders to evolve their worlds without requiring the intervention of a developer—the same function that CMS and backend platforms have for traditional 2D websites.

There are 3D content creation tools embedded within specific virtual worlds that can be more or less complex to use, depending on the target user. A casual creator expects an extremely easy user experience, and usually, entertainment virtual worlds like Minecraft, RecRoom, and Roblox do provide to their players tools to create their own 3D content starting from already existing elements to be used within the game ecosystem, while other virtual worlds like VRChat allow more freedom and control over the 3D content creation, requiring the use of more technical tools (Unity, Blender, etc.) and therefore targeting more skilled creators. Some other tools, often very content specific (think of Unreal Metahuman, an avatar-only creation tool), do offer a higher level of complexity and quality of the content created, are easy to configure but yet are purely aiming at the skilled creators' market. In the XR world, there are already several easy-to-approach 3D content creation platforms usable directly in VR, like Dreams, Quill, Tiltbrush, Masterpiece VR, or SculptVR, but they require good artistic skills from the user to produce high-quality results. There are also creator platforms focused on AR content like Adobe Aero, Snap Lens Studio, and SparkAR, mostly focused on AR filters on simple AR content.

6.3.3   Content Distribution

3D-first content distribution ecosystems are going to evolve. The market-places of 3D content are already available within game engines like Unity and Unreal, themselves slowly evolving as comprehensive ecosystems for skilled creators. Independent marketplaces of 3D contents are also already available on the Web, like Sketchfab, Turbosquid, or Google Poly (now deprecated).

Startups like EchoAR are also deploying 3D-first cloud content management system solutions, unifying back-end-as-a-service with a content delivery network (CDN) infrastructure, enhancing the deployment of content-based solutions with low-leatency access through different regions and geographies [12]. We expect more and more integrated solutions like this to pop up in the future.

6.3.4   Future Projections for Content Platforms

Professional 3D creation tools are already fairly established, whereas we see a growing need for:

1. Automatic content acquisition tools
    With the mass adoption of the metaverse, there will be a growing need for user empowerment to easily import 3D content from the physical world. In order to do that, there will be a growing need of applications that allow:
    *   Automatic 3D content acquisition and optimization, in order to create a seamless import from the physical world to the virtual world without the need for further technical manipulations. This will imply easy content acquisition and automatic optimization to make them compatible with the new real-time 3D standards.
    *   Automatic 2D-to-3D content conversion and optimization tools, which will allow the transformation of traditional 2D media like photos and videos into real-time-ready 3D objects and environments.
2. Content creation tools
    Content creation tools will further evolve toward two different directions, both needing further research in order to adopt the right languages and standards. Developers in this space can take advantage of the experience accumulated within the video game

world. Two main categories of content creation tools are going to be needed:

- Casual creators' tools. Just like it happened in the social media scenario, where advanced 2D video-first content editing tools are allowing people to self-express in new creative ways (think of TikTok's video editor), there will be a higher need for easy-to-use 3D editors for prosumers. They will allow users to easily populate virtual worlds with their own content and personalize it to match their self-expression needs.
- Skilled creators' tools. At the same time, there will be a growing need for more complex content-based creation tools, targeting creators, allowing them to evolve virtual worlds with more complex applications and tools (see Low-Code/No-Code Platforms under Utility Platforms).

6.4 Human-Centered Platforms

AR and VR are digital realities in which the user can become a virtual version of himself/herself. Inside them, he/she can interact with other digital humans, which can be controlled by real people or by AI.

6.4.1 Avatar Creation

When dealing with the concept of digital identities, the first issue is how to represent oneself within in a virtual world. This is usually done via an avatar, even if experimentations are being done to stream the 3D volumetric video of the user, using tools like DepthKit. Every social VR experience offers an avatar creation tool: for instance, VRChat and Altspace VR offer their avatar editors, so that every user can create the avatar that he/she prefers. Facebook has launched its Avatars, featuring several customizations in order to serve people from diverse backgrounds [13]. Most of the proposed avatars feature a cartoonish style, but there are exceptions, like Epic Games' MetaHuman Creator [14]. Most of them offer only humanoid characters, while VRChat offers the user complete freedom to be everything he/she wants (e.g., a dog, a car). If some work has been done to create a shared visual identity, little work has been done until now to create a true digital identity shared among all the applications in the metaverse, a complete representation of oneself interoperable through different virtual worlds.

6.4.2   Realistic Interactions

Even the most realistic of avatars would be useless without proper communication capabilities. When we communicate in the real world, we don't only use our voice, but we also perform many macro and micro gestures that result into meaningful forms of communication. There is a strong need of improvement in this direction. Users should be able to have their faces, with all their micro-expressions, translated into the virtual world of their choice. Also, movements and body posture, together with hand gesticulation, shall be available.

Facebook is working on all these features with its Full-Body Codec Avatar project, not expected to be released commercially before 5–10 years [15]. A more practical approach, for now, is exploiting headsets with facial tracking sensors (e.g. HP Reverb G2 Omnicept Edition) and tracking units (e.g., Vive Tracker, Tundra Tracker), applied on the legs and waist to represent all body movements. Current results are mediocre, and there are a lot of improvements that are still needed to truly express ourselves in VR.

6.4.3   Virtual Beings

In the metaverse, many avatars will not represent real people, but will be controlled by AIs, in what are today called "virtual beings." This is a clear evolution of the current voice-only digital assistants (e.g., Siri) or textual chatbots: soon, interaction will become 3D, immersive, and carried on with more natural means of communications. Virtual beings are an open topic of research, and there are not many valid examples on the market as of today. Magic Leap promised a virtual assistant called Mica [6], but failed to deliver on its promises; more interesting is the work of Fable Studio with its Lucy, a virtual character already able to talk with people, take part to events (she took part in some panels at the Sundance Festival [16]), and remember her experience with other beings she has interacted with. In fact, she has been reported to be able to create a human bond with the people she interacts with.

Developers can already create a simple version of virtual beings with Amazon Sumerian, which lets you create digital avatars that can speak using the AI services offered by AWS [17], or by mixing some avatar creator tools with GPT-3 AI to give them speaking capabilities. Fable Studio is also offering the possibility to selected developers to have access to its Virtual Beings Studio, which is the suite of tools that have been used to create Lucy and her companion virtual humans.

6.4.4   Future Projections for Human-Centered Platforms

Virtual beings are estimated to become an extremely profitable market, yet its maturity is still on an early stage, opening the way to many research opportunities.

1. Powerful avatar management tools
   Everyone should be able to express their true self in the metaverse, being able to create an avatar that truly matches his/her needs. This can have two meanings: (a) the ability to create a realistic self-representation in an affordable and easy way; (b) the ability of creating non-human avatars, building on top of one the key characteristics of VR technology—that of experiencing what is impossible in real life, such as the embodiment of any object or animated figure. On top of creation tools, easy avatar animation tools are also required, replicating users' physical movements with great detail, and avatar interoperability, allowing a user to keep his/her own digital identity consistent through the metaverse.

2. Digital identity systems
   Since users are going to spend progressively more and more time in the metaverse, they will need systems to manage a digital identity. In real life, every country tracks citizens' data, and different countries have conventions to share these data (e.g., the passport); there will be a need to create similar mechanisms also in users' digital life. Avatar interoperability systems are going to be a substantial starting point, yet also, conventions on data tracking, sharing, and ownership are going to be needed. For example, activities performed in a specific virtual world (e.g., a bond I have created with another avatar, like a marriage), avatar-related tools' interoperability and cross-worlds porting, virtual currencies, etc. Blockchain technologies will be key in the development of common virtual identity frameworks.

3. Virtual beings' platforms
   The final goal of virtual beings' research is to become virtually indistinguishable from real humans. This requires heavy research in:
   - Avateering realism technologies, to make the appearance of a virtual being similar to a physical person, avoiding the "uncanny valley" [18] effect
   - AI and ML so that the virtual being is not only able to speak naturally with other people but also able to

remember the past history with every other real or digital person, and behave with that person accordingly

- Artificial Intelligence (AI) and Machine Learning (ML) so that the virtual being understands the context inside which he/she is, so that he/she can trigger specific actions (e.g., help the user).
- Behavioral studies and expression, so that the virtual being understands and adapts his/her behavior according to the context, throughout all his means of expression, being words and other kinds of body language
- Ethical studies and legal implications (e.g., reliving a dead person in VR, or what the consequences of harassing a virtual being are), making sure that we build a sustainable and ethical future also inside the metaverse

6.5   Utility Platforms

The world is a complex environment, and so will be its virtual counterpart, the metaverse. More and more physical products will become virtual, and this trend will unlock new use cases, new digital economies, and new applications. This completely new ecosystem, in order to become widely used and properly scalable, will need a whole new set of flexible, interoperable utility platforms and tools. Nowadays, most of the tools used to create XR-based applications come either from the gaming industry, that shares the same 3D-based software ecosystem, or from some vertical developments funded by technology corporations.

6.5.1   Services

Virtual worlds have been around since the raising of the massive multiplayer online role-playing games (MMORPG [19]), which do effectively represent the forerunner of the metaverse. Such entertainment environments created a huge digital economy, and they allowed the birth of new vertical services and utilities for developers, many of them based in the cloud. The most typical services for Virtual World developments are already available for game programmers, but we expect a further verticalization toward more generalist use cases with the evolution of spatial computing. Today's most relevant services platforms are:

- Networking: the barebone technical layer that allows the implementation of multiplayer technologies, synchronizing the state of the world to all the actors, routing messages, and events, providing servers and resources, and development SDKs as well.

- Communication: video, voice, or text communication services, both traditional or spatial, that work with any engine or platform. The backbone for human communication within a virtual world ecosystem.
- Data Analytics: platforms that easily allow the tracking, management, and protection of usage data.
- Advertising: platforms that allow easy placement, tracking, and management of advertising content within a virtual world. These platforms are going to become more and more relevant with the growth of usage of multipurpose spatial ecosystems.
- Commerce: the evolution of in-game/app purchasing layers, offering to virtual world creators the ability to integrate transactions and order management systems inside their worlds. With virtual economies evolving further, this is going to become a fundamental key layer in the coming years.

6.5.2   Search Engines

In the new paradigm of information in space, traditional web searches will change skin. Both "what" to look for and "how" to look for it are likely to change. Already today, we use voice assistants for our research, assistants who will become more and more intelligent and will help us based on an intricate interweaving of variables flooded with data, rationalized, thanks to AI. By entering a store, the virtual assistant will be able to provide us with the guided path to our favorite products, having an infinite number of data available to guide us—not only the history of what we have done online but also of what we are looking at, what we have said, at our gestures, and one day, even at our neuronal responses. There will also be another type of research, much more "visual." Already today, thanks to applications such as Google Lens [20], AR makes it possible to obtain information relating to a physical object simply by pointing the camera at it. These applications will gradually become more relevant in a Spatial Web ecosystem, where we will increasingly need a visual search to make the objects of the world around us clickable. It is reasonable to expect today's camera-based AR applications embedded within social networking platforms (like Snapchat, Instagram, and Tik Tok) to increasingly add visual search capabilities.

6.5.3   Future Projections for Utility Platforms

Utility platforms are going to be more and more relevant in the future, especially on the following patterns:

1. Low-Code/No-Code Application Platforms and Connectors
   It is reasonable to expect the raising of new Low-Code or completely No-Code development platforms for 3D real-time applications, which will allow programmers and non-programmers to create pieces of software through graphical user interfaces and configuration, instead of traditional computer programming. These platforms will represent the key flexible ecosystem of the metaverse for two key purposes. The first is lowering barriers of entry for creators of new tools and applications, a fundamental step toward the democratization of spatial computing and virtual worlds. The second key purpose is having the new metaverse ecosystem grow toward a unique shared direction, enhancing software interoperability and counterbalancing the actual tendency of creating corporation-driven "walled gardens." New creation platforms shall be designed to act as hubs, enabling new capabilities to be exposed as microservices to any connected clients and applications. Today, NVIDIA Omniverse [5] has a similar approach, enabling universal interoperability across different applications and 3D ecosystem vendors, based on open standards and protocols. These platforms will embed plugins for different cloud-based services (see above) in order to facilitate in-app integrations and will offer a fully integrated content deploy pipeline, from Backend-as-a-service to Content Delivery Networks. Furthermore, to enhance interoperability, LCDP/NCDP platforms will also need a new set of connectors' (API) libraries, distributed as plugins and enabling applications to connect with each other.
2. Digital Twin Management
   Digital twins [21] are a fundamental brick of the new virtual ecosystem, allowing the living replica of physical objects to be persistently present and interactable within a virtual world, unlocking simulation and predictive capabilities, enhancing physical objects with intelligence layers, and allowing remote objects' control with a spatial/interactive interface. Digital Twin platforms include multiple layers such as IoT (defining communication standards with physical products), Data analytics (to add

intelligence and predictive capabilities), 3D spatial anchoring (the "AR Cloud" world), Network services (such as communication, etc.), and interaction (multiple applications, depending on the use case). Today, relevant digital twin management platforms already exist for major industrial assets and applications, as closed systems offered by software companies like PTC, SAP, and Siemens. With the expansion of the new virtual world-based ecosystems, any physical object is expected to have its digital twin accessible from AR or VR interfaces, and new open platforms are expected to evolve.

3. New Services

   With the evolution of new use cases, new services will evolve, mostly cloud based and very likely enabled by other remotely running technologies. Neural network-based services are going to become more and more evolved and distributed, like automatic content creation services, translation services, personalization services, and more. Other examples of new services are already visible today, like the appropriate behavior monitoring service that Facebook is developing within their Horizon world [22], or like the "voice-scanning" capabilities of Valorant Voice chat, which will ban the user in case of racist comments. Also, with the growth of multi-user virtual worlds, networking services will need to further evolve, giving the opportunity to create massive gatherings like virtual concerts or massive events. Blockchain-based services will also enable new opportunities like digital identity services, privacy, transactions, smart contracts, virtual currencies, and more.

6.6   Application Platforms

On top of all XR technology stacks, the application layer is composed of all experiences that the user of a headset can enjoy for personal or professional use. The experiences that a user can enjoy in AR or VR are varied, and they span through all possible software applications. More details about all possible fields of applications can be found in the other chapters of this book, while in here, the aim is just to give a brief overview of the various applications capabilities of the technology.

Today, the most common use case of AR/VR in the consumer space is entertainment [23]. VR is mostly used for gaming, while AR is predominantly used to apply modifications to camera images and videos, the so-called "filters." But other uses are starting to get traction in the XR community, such as fitness, with applications applying gamification to body movements like FitXR, and social networking, with social worlds such as VRChat or AltspaceVR. Also, AR has been implemented inside 2D mobile apps to improve their functionalities, like the try-on feature within Amazon or the AR directions within Google Maps.

The enterprise/commercial use is, on the other side, more consolidated. Some of the most common use cases of AR/VR technologies are:

- Remote 3D collaboration, to create and prototype 3D elements together with people from all over the world (e.g., Vive Sync, NVIDIA Omniverse, Spatial)
- Training, where VR has proved to be more effective than traditional training methods (e.g., STRIVR)
- Remote collaboration and assistance, with AR giving to experts the power of helping multiple field employees without leaving the office (e.g., Microsoft Dynamics 365)
- Healthcare, with multiple training or proctoring tools for doctors (e.g., Fundamental Surgery), or applications for neuroscience (e.g., Guided Meditation)
- Education, with experiences devoted to helping people in learning new concepts in an innovative and more engaging way (e.g., Rome Reborn)
- Art, one of the most receptive fields toward new technologies, with several applications

New use cases are constantly sprouting, AR/VR representing a pervasive technology applicable to pretty much every field of human activities. The more XR applications will grow, the more they won't just substitute their 2D software counterparts, but also several physical objects and activities. When virtual objects will be accessible with the same user experience and same quality, and serve for the same scope as their physical counterpart, they will very likely substitute them, as the history of digitization has proven during the last 50 years in many different fields, such as paper documents, music, and videos.

6.7   Future Research Agenda and Roadmap

6.7.1   Market Potential and Guiding Principles

Digitization, enhanced by new devices like personal and mobile computing, has dematerialized everything on its path, from paper to music, cameras, calendars, fax, and so on. XR holographic technologies, together with the metaverse, carry with them the intrinsic power to dematerialize almost every object that exists in the physical world. Every person, place, product, and process: we could call this impact the 4Ps of dematerialization. Today, this potential is limited by a poor user experience of software applications, related to the fact that most XR software platforms are still mainly accessed via 2D screens due to the limited availability of wearable devices. With their progressive mass distribution, helped by the advent of wearable consumer AR, we expect the whole ecosystem to become gradually more complex, embracing more and more applications coming from the consumer world. Since the metaverse represents a "soft copy" of the world enhanced with further virtual layers and intelligence, it's going to rapidly evolve in terms of complexity, progressively mimicking the complexity of the real world. This scenario is going to unlock a global market value that the consulting firm Pwc has assessed at 1.5Tn USD by 2030 [24]. Within this scenario, we would like to underline the following key principles in identifying the platforms to sustain with funding:

- Openness: the progressive complexity of the ecosystem is best embraced with a community-driven approach, allowing the creation of a fully interoperable ecosystem.
- Champions: while the US and China are paving the way with enormous investments in the field, there is a clear need for European champions within the key areas of application of technology.
- Accessibility, Scalability, and Feasibility

6.7.2   Future Research Agenda and Roadmap

We summarize here the suggested next steps for a European research agenda, focusing on the first layers of the platform ecosystem. As enabling platforms, the authors suggest focusing the efforts toward more stable and scalable infrastructures for (a) web-based real-time engines and frameworks, (b) AR Cloud, and (c) cloud rendering. Regarding content creation platforms, the authors suggest prioritizing the funding of tools to enhance

(a) automatic 3D content acquisition and optimization and (b) better content creation tools for casual and skilled creators. Within the human-centered platforms layer, the authors suggest focusing the research on (a) more powerful avatar creation and management tools, (b) a common ground for digital identity systems and conventions, and (c) further technology research in order to reach virtual beings that are indistinguishable from real ones yet following an ethical evolution. Among the utility platforms, the authors suggest a further development of (a) low-code/no-code application platforms and integration connectors with other systems, (b) open digital twin management platforms, and (c) new cloud-based services such as mass-gathering multiplayer or AI-powered services.

Overall, the authors suggest the roadmap prioritization: (1) web real-time engines, (2) AR-Cloud platforms, (3) low-code/no-code platforms, (4) virtual beings creation platforms, and (5) massive networking services.

References

1. Statista, Global mobile augmented reality (AR) users 2019-2024, 2021. https://www.statista.com/statistics/1098630/global-mobile-augmented-reality-ar-users/.
2. What Is The Magicverse (And Why)?, 2019. https://www.magicleap.com/en-us/news/op-ed/magicverse.
3. AR Will Spark the Next Big Tech Platform—Call It Mirrorworld, 2019. https://www.wired.com/story/mirrorworld-ar-next-big-tech-platform/.
4. ARKit and ARCore will not usher massive adoption of mobile AR, 2017. https://medium.com/super-ventures-blog/arkit-and-arcore-will-not-usher-massive-adoption-of-mobile-ar-da3d87f7e5ad.
5. NVIDIA Omniverse, 2020. https://developer.nvidia.com/nvidia-omniverse-platform.
6. I am Mica, 2019. https://www.magicleap.com/en-us/news/op-ed/i-am-mica.
7. Unity, XR Plugin Framework, 2021. https://docs.unity3d.com/Manual/XRPluginArchitecture.html.
8. Open AR Cloud, 2021. https://www.openarcloud.org/.
9. Measuring Head-Mounted Display's (HMD) Motion-To-Photon (MTP) Latency, 2021. https://www.optofidelity.com/blog/measuring-head-mounted-displays-hmd-motion-to-photon-mtp-latency.
10. Lidar is one of the iPhone and iPad's coolest tricks. Here's what else it can do, 2021. https://www.cnet.com/tech/mobile/lidar-is-one-of-the-iphone-ipad-coolest-tricks-its-only-getting-better/.
11. Threedy AI automatically converts 2D photos in 3D assets for AR!, 2020. https://skarredghost.com/2020/11/19/threedy-ai-from-picture-to-3d-model/.
12. Echo AR, 2021. https://www.echo3d.co/.

13. Facebook adds new avatars to Oculus VR: Here's how to get one, 2021. https://www.cnet.com/tech/computing/facebook-adds-new-avatars-to-oculus-vr-heres-how-to-get-one/.

14. MetaHuman Creator, 2021. https://www.unrealengine.com/en-US/digital-humans.

15. Facebook is building the future of connection with lifelike avatars, 2019. https://tech.fb.com/codec-avatars-facebook-reality-labs/.

16. Fable's virtual being Lucy takes a tour at virtual Sundance Film Festival, 2021. https://venturebeat.com/2021/02/05/fables-virtual-being-lucy-takes-a-tour-at-virtual-sundance-film-festival/.

17. Amazon Sumerian Hosts, 2020. https://docs.aws.amazon.com/sumerian/latest/userguide/assets-hosts.html.

18. Uncanny Valley, 2021. https://en.wikipedia.org/wiki/Uncanny_valley.

19. Massively multiplayer online role-playing game, 2021. https://en.wikipedia.org/wiki/Massively_multiplayer_online_role-playing_game.

20. Google Lens, 2019. https://lens.google/.

21. What is a digital Twin?, 2019. https://www.ibm.com/topics/what-is-a-digital-twin.

22. Facebook Horizon, 2019. https://www.oculus.com/facebook-horizon/.

23. 74 Virtual Reality Statistics You Must Know in 2021/2022: Adoption, Usage & Market Share, 2021. https://financesonline.com/virtual-reality-statistics/.

24. PWC, Seeing is Believing report, 2019, https://www.pwc.com/seeingisbelieving.

7

Human Perception Engineering

Evan G. Center[1*], Katherine Mimnaugh[1], Jukka Häkkinen[2]
and Steven M. Lavalle[1†]

*¹Center for Ubiquitous Computing, Faculty of Information Technology
and Electrical Engineering, University of Oulu, Oulu, Finland
²Department of Psychology and Logopedics, Faculty of Medicine,
University of Helsinki, Helsinki, Finland*

Abstract

In this chapter, we propose the foundations of a new field, perception engineering, to unify and guide XR research in human perception. The key idea is that designing, creating, implementing, and analyzing perceptual illusions themselves are the engineering focus, rather than devices. Perception engineering follows a dynamical systems approach to the human–XR device pairing by leveraging techniques from mathematical modeling, perceptual psychology, neuroscience, and robotics to better understand how the perceptual experience itself may be engineered. We then give attention to the current state and potential shortcomings of human perception and XR research, and set goals for the field to aspire toward best practices, inclusivity, and open-source modular technology.

Keywords: Human perception, predictive coding, dynamical systems, XR sickness, human subjects research, modular devices

7.1 Introduction

The notion that our visual system provides us with a truthful depiction of the world seems obvious at first glance. This intuition is inscribed in the saying "seeing is believing," and indeed, our visual systems transmit information in a faithful-enough manner that we may successfully navigate our

---

*Corresponding author: evan.center@oulu.fi
†Corresponding author: Steven.LaValle@oulu.fi

Mariano Alcañiz, Marco Sacco and Jolanda G. Tromp (eds.) Roadmapping Extended Reality: Fundamentals and Applications, (157–182) © 2022 Scrivener Publishing LLC

environments in most cases—but not in all cases. Have you ever had an interaction in traffic in which a vehicle seemingly "came out of nowhere?" Or how about the experience of spending half an hour looking for your

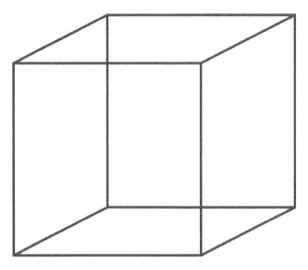

Figure 7.1 The Necker cube above has two equally probable three-dimensional (3D) interpretations, and as there is little additional information, the interpretation and consequently perception changes constantly. The illusion shows that the same information does not always lead to the same percept.

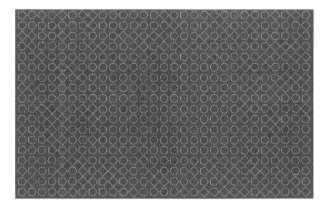

Figure 7.2 The reconstructive nature of vision is shown in uniformity illusion, in which the structures in the foveal vision determine the perception of peripheral patterns. The illusion can be perceived by holding fixation steady at the center of the image. Gradually, the central pattern fills the whole visual field [1].

Figure 7.3a What is portrayed in this image? If you are stumped, try looking at its rotated counterpart in Figure 7.3b on the next page.

keys that were in plain sight all along? Take also, for a different kind of example, the optical illusions presented in Figures 7.1–7.3.

These visual lapses and illusions should clarify that the process of seeing is not as simple as merely taking things in from the environment and producing exact copies of them in the head. Vision is a complex process whereby the light reflected from our environment impinges on our retinas in a configuration that is upside down and backwards relative to what we eventually perceive, is compressed by retinal ganglion cells, and is then sent along to the optic nerve to the brain where the signals are then reconstructed into something useful.

The reconstructive nature of visual processing is illustrated by the subjective experience of a rich and detailed visual experience. Actually, our brains do not maintain an image-like representation of the scene, but a sparse model that represents only the most relevant information. The examples of this representational sparseness are inattentional blindness and change blindness, in which we fail to notice significant changes in a scene [4].

Furthermore, evolutionary constraints determine human perception, namely, those features of the physical world that have not been relevant for our survival are not processed or perceived. Humans do not see magnetic fields or infrared radiation signaling temperature differences, but react automatically to sudden movement in the visual field and have a tendency to see faces in non-human surfaces.

Donald Hoffman has described visual perception as a biological interface to the world. According to Hoffman, the purpose of the visual system is not to build an accurate and detailed representation, but to quickly and efficiently solve adaptive problems when they arise [5, 6]. Perceptual processing utilizes statistical properties of the world to interpret the incoming sensory data. This is often characterized as Bayesian inference and

Figure 7.3b Another example of reconstruction is the Mooney face, in which the face is perceived with rounded patches of dark and light [2, 3]. The interpretation is based on assumptions about faces, as the more difficult perception of the inverted Mooney face shows.

is thought to be neurally realized as predictive coding [7]. Rather than explicitly relay some truth about the world, vision is tuned to discriminate expected utility.

On the one hand, this is great news for XR developers. Using presentations with stereoscopic disparity, among a slew of other tricks to provide monocular depth cues, XR devices can achieve powerfully convincing illusions that can provide users with helpful information or even transport them to different worlds. On the other hand, while our constructive visual processing makes illusions possible, it also poses its own unique challenges, and we still have a long way to go in terms of achieving optimal experiences throughout various XR avenues. Getting the perceptual experience right requires attention to detail. Furthermore, the prevalence of XR sickness remains a significant hurdle for more widespread adoption.

Advances in software and hardware continue at a rapid pace, yet we fail to see comparable advances in terms of the XR experience. We think that the reason for this disparity is clear: we must shift our focus from constructing the device and focus instead on constructing the perceptual experience itself. This shift will require drawing heavily not only from engineering, but also neuroscience and perceptual psychology. We propose a new research domain, *perception engineering*, to advance this cause. Only through a proper synthesis and expansion of this domain can we truly explore undiscovered territory in the XR space.

In the remainder of Section 7.1, we offer our view of what perception engineering entails. Then, in Section 7.2, we give an introduction to common methods in XR and human perception research and highlight issues we see as most critical in this area. Finally, in Section 7.3, we discuss new frontiers in XR and human perception. Here, we advocate for a renewed focus on the perceptual experience to be executed through perception engineering, advances in methodology, and the consideration of inclusion and individual differences.

Recommendations
1. Take advantage of theories from perceptual psychology and neuroscience to guide XR hardware and software development.
2. Prioritize use of best practices in psychology for XR research, including preregistration, a-priori power analyses, and effect size reporting.
3. Endorse the use of more representative samples, including striving for gender balance in research subjects, and request that demographic information is reported in publications.
4. Prioritize large-scale XR sickness projects, including subjective and objective methods development.
5. Advocate for inclusive development that makes XR more accessible for older adults and people with disabilities, and support the development of and research on XR systems for therapeutics and use for people with limited mobility.
6. Subsidize the development of an open-source modular XR research device.

7.1.1   A Perception Engineering Perspective

Previous research regarding XR and human perception has often taken a black-box approach to the human element of the system. Rather than attempt to model perceptual processes, the human element is treated as passive, independent, and opaque. Under the current implicit assumptions, inputs go in, responses come out, and changes are then made to the technology in light of the measured input–response pairing. The device is engineered, while the perceptual experience is merely seen as a byproduct.

This is a backwards way of viewing the problem. If what we really care about is the perceptual experience, then, the engineering of the device should be, at minimum, a byproduct of our desired perceptual experience. The perception engineering perspective seeks to take this idea even further by rejecting the notion that the perceptual experience is truly a black box and proposing that we model relevant components as a dynamical system.

7.1.1.1 A Convergence of Black Boxes and White Boxes

A daunting challenge has been that the brain and resulting human perception are largely treated as a "black box" that must be reverse-engineered through interactive trials and output measurements. In comparison, engineering systems are usually built from the ground up with known principles and primitives. This allows accurate mathematical modeling and simulation, thereby resulting in a "white box." For example, roboticists often talk about "perception" as a process that involves sensors, sensor fusion, and dynamical systems.

Although the brain itself remains somewhat of a black box, it is becoming more transparent. We have at our disposal an ever-growing body of neuroscience and perceptual psychology research from which to draw and inform our understanding of human perception. Borrowing from theories in these areas, we may test their hypotheses with our unique tools in the XR space and better model human perception in our own models. At the same time, we can draw from white-box models that arise in computer vision, robotics, and autonomous systems. Ultimately, the goal is to understand what it means to create perceptual illusions, from rigorous mathematical modeling to successful implementation and analysis. This will require a meeting in the middle between engineering principles and models from neuroscience and perceptual psychology.

As an example, one popular theory of brain function born out of this approach is predictive coding. Predictive coding, and more broadly, predictive processing, have gained massive traction over the last two decades and offer new ways of thinking about old XR problems. The predictive coding view of the brain states that rather than passively waiting for inputs, the brain forms active perceptual predictions about what it will encounter based on previous experience. These predictions are backpropagated from higher to lower regions in the processing hierarchy, and then input regions at the base of the hierarchy work primarily to send forward the prediction errors of initial predictions [8]. In this way, the brain operates as an efficient prediction machine that minimizes free energy, only spending extra processing power on surprising events, which then go on to optimize future predictions [9].

The predictive coding view has steadily accrued empirical support since its inception and has even begun to make an impact in clinical research settings [10]. A worthy target to progress in XR is to follow this kind of approach to improve our understanding of how to model and create perceptual illusions.

7.1.1.2   Towards Dynamical Systems-Based Models of Perceptual Illusions

Given the mounting evidence for this constructive view of perception, it no longer makes sense to conceive of humans and XR devices as passive and independent, but instead as active and *inter*active. In other words, the perceptual illusion can be engineered via a precise understanding of how a dynamical, predictive brain interacts with various aspects of an XR device, which is itself a dynamical, interactive white box system.

We can observe the benefits of taking on a more realistic dynamical systems level view by an analogy of the evolution seen within cognitive neuroscience over recent decades. Cognitive neuroscience in the 1990s was dominated by the advent of functional magnetic resonance imaging, a technology that can reveal brain activity with excellent spatial resolution, but suffers from relatively poor temporal resolution. These qualities of the technology seemingly led to a bias toward attaching labels to areas that showed selectivity toward certain functions while ignoring the temporal dynamics of networks within the system.

The research was nonetheless fruitful, in conjunction with neuropsychology, in terms of helping us to understand the macro and meso-scale brain regions that are necessary for producing specific behaviors and perceptual capabilities. However, the hyperfocus on brain regions potentially occluded what we now recognize to be one of the most integral aspects of brain function: that every region is connected to many other regions, and that a brain only functions effectively through cooperation within and among these various networks. By taking a systems neuroscience approach, we have seen significant progress in understanding complex dysfunction like that observed in schizophrenia, Parkinson's disease, depression, and anxiety [11, 12].

Similarly, perception engineering aspires to stop investigating only the individual building blocks and begins the work of understanding the dynamical interactive system of the XR–human perception pairing as a whole. This task will require multidisciplinary teams with research backgrounds in mathematics, engineering, computer science, neuroscience, and perceptual psychology.

7.1.1.3   Perception Engineering in Action: XR Sickness

There is abundant fertile ground for new discoveries in taking white box approaches to XR–human perception dynamical systems. Applying theories from neuroscience and perceptual psychology, and employing robotics and simulation techniques, can make the black box more transparent.

Take cybersickness (or, within the current context of XR systems, XR sickness) as an example. What if instead of taking for granted that aspects of the device cause cybersickness, we test the view that cybersickness arises as an interaction between the perceiver's perceptual predictions and certain aspects of the device? This view is taken in sensory rearrangement theories of cybersickness, in which the ordinary relations of the sensory inputs need to be rearranged and sickness is thought to accompany this adaptation [13, 14]. According to Welch and Mohler [15], there are at least five types of deficiencies that require sensory rearrangement: 1) intersensory conflicts, like sensory mismatches, 2) distortions of depth and distance, like when unnatural depth cues lead to depth compression, 3) distortion of form and size, like optical distortions, 4) delays of sensory feedback, and 5) sensory disarrangement (non-constant rearrangement requirements such as jitters; these are the most difficult to adapt to). If sickness is understood as a situation in which the system reacts to prediction errors, then experiencing sickness symptoms is not just a product of a badly designed device. The brain is also trying to adapt to a new situation in which the mapping between sensory and motor systems has changed.

The emphasis on prediction raises also the possibility of top–down modulation, such as expectations, as an important factor affecting the perception and experiences. Users interpret situations according to their previous knowledge that is applied to a specific situation. For example, the experience of cybersickness is affected by expectations [16], and can be tolerated with sufficient motivation or if other experiential benefits override the adverse experiences.

In practice, the predictive coding approach means that the research should treat sickness as a part of an interactive process in which task-related expectations and information needs shape the way users experience and perceive the technology-mediated environments. The technology is no longer just causing symptoms, but instead a part of a process in which symptoms occur.

7.1.1.4   Perception Engineering in Action: Pseudo-Haptics

Related to remedying XR sickness, methods to reduce sensory conflict by stimulating additional sensory modalities, such as providing pleasant odors [17] or including haptic feedback like airflow [18] and chair vibrations [19], have been tested. Already, the importance of incorporating an understanding of human perception into the design for better haptic feedback has been noted [20]. In all cases, the development and implementation of multimodal stimuli benefit from adopting a perception engineering approach.

An example of a way in which we can leverage our understanding of human perception in order to improve multisensory XR capabilities is by modulating one sensory experience through the manipulation of another sense. We can simply make slight modifications in software that trigger perceptual sensory illusions. An example of this is pseudo-haptic feedback, which is the use of visual cues to trigger haptic sensations. Earnst and Banks [21] proposed that maximum-likelihood estimation integration is used to determine how much either vision or haptic feedback dominates when there is conflicting or redundant sensory information in these domains below a certain threshold of discrepancy. When the conflicting information is too great, one sense is discounted, but otherwise, the sensory information is weighted by this integrator based on the predicted variance of the signal from each source, and then combined. Thus, by modifying visual feedback, illusory experiences of object qualities and interactions (like mass, texture, and friction) can be created [22], and have been successfully deployed in virtual reality (VR) to simulate different weights for virtual objects [23]. The elegance of this perception-constructing approach is that it does not require expensive equipment or complicated devices, and thus the time and costs in hardware development can be saved.

7.2   XR and Human Perception

The current XR research is held back by small, technology-dependent projects, in which human experience and perception are not the primary drivers. These small studies often produce results that are not cumulative, and thus more general theories of XR experience cannot be created. We suggest that a deep understanding of human XR experience requires large-scale projects that have technology-independent perception and experience-related goals.

7.2.1   Methods in XR and Human Perception Research

Early research in XR and human perception borrowed heavily from computer science and telecommunications, as well as experimental psychology in terms of experiment design and data analysis. The field has continued to adapt techniques from these areas as they each have evolved, with the more information-focused quality of experience techniques from telecommunications blending into a more human-focused concept of user experience used in industry, and with the addition of physiological recordings to existing psychophysics and questionnaire approaches from experimental psychology. Computer science has made a significant impact in terms of contributing simulation, machine learning, and computer vision tools.

Critically, because XR and human perception research methods have in large part been extracted from other fields and applied in contexts in which they may not always be appropriate, it is important that we pause and reevaluate how well they allow us to study the phenomena we wish to study. One example regarding XR sickness is touched on in the following section. An honorable goal would be to develop a set of fundamental methods that are most fitting to characterize human perception in this quickly evolving XR space.

7.2.2   XR Sickness

The most widely used techniques today remain subjective questionnaires, such as the Simulator Sickness Questionnaire (SSQ; [24]). Despite their popularity, the degree to which the SSQ, which was originally developed for military simulators, and other measures correctly map onto the psychological constructs they are attempting to measure is a topic of ongoing debate. The debate has prompted attempts to revise the questionnaires so that they would be more suitable for modern XR devices (e.g., [25] and [26]), or to supplement them with objective measures such as those given by computer vision and physiological recordings.

XR sickness research should also recognize the complexity of the phenomenon. In addition to the technical parameters, there are multiple other factors that affect adverse experiences. For example, physiological variables such as increased sickness susceptibility or subclinical visual problems, or psychological factors such as fears, preconceptions, or personality may affect the phenomenon. Furthermore, the positive experiences such as presence and immersion or emotions may modulate sickness. All of these factors have been investigated in earlier research, but the studies have mostly been small in size, so complex interactions between variables have not been well-characterized and generalizing beyond these studies is difficult. A large-scale study that could control for confounds and properly assess individual contributions from various factors is needed to put together the currently disparate pieces of the XR sickness puzzle.

One of these factors is XR content. Too often, experiences are attributed to technology when the real reason is the content. Content creation should combine the knowledge of perceptual processes and narrative rules to the creative possibilities enabled by the devices. Often, the content creators do have knowledge of best practices, but these are part of their creative toolbox and are not connected to the perceptual research. There is a good possibility for mutual learning here. Perceptual researchers should investigate the creative choices made by content creators as they may have useful perception-related ideas that could be translated into experimental research, and the content creators should be informed about the results of perceptual research that might have significant implications to the artistic choices they are making. In practice, cooperation between content creators from arts and film schools and perception scientists is needed. This would lead to benefits in both areas.

Cooperation should also lead to production of high-quality, freely available XR content that could be further used in research. Stimulus databases have had significant impact, for example, in emotion [27], and face perception research [28]. Creating this type of resource should also be the goal in XR research.

7.3   Future Research Agenda and Roadmap

Here, we shift the focus to more fundamental gaps that perception engineering researchers should consider. Although we refrain from hazarding predictions about the particulars of the field's development, we believe that rising to the following challenges will lead to advancements in our methods and understanding that will stand in contrast to the incremental progress previously seen.

7.3.1   Establishing Best Practices in XR and Human Perception Research

Psychological science has undergone a great deal of reform in response to a "replication crisis" over the course of the last decade. The crisis was spurred on in part by an incredible finding, namely, the discovery of extrasensory perception (ESP) in otherwise ordinary undergraduates [29], by a high-profile experimental psychologist. The manuscript withstood peer review and was published in a prestigious psychology journal, which left psychology researchers in a highly uncomfortable position: either accept that a concept as ludicrous as ESP actually exists, or recognize that the field's standard practices were so fundamentally flawed that researchers could arrive at a support for any idea, no matter how absurd.

This grim realization led to wide efforts to replicate findings new and old throughout the literature, and while some theories like the existence of ESP rested on a less solid foundation than others, the resulting level of support for the field as a whole did not inspire confidence. In a systematic set of replications of findings in psychology, only 36% of replications yielded statistically significant results compared to the 97% rate found in the original publications [30]. This poor replication rate surfaced in spite of the replication authors using well-powered samples and working with original authors and materials when available.

How could it be possible that the majority of research published in psychology was unreliable? The revelation was shocking to many but did not come as a surprise to those who had long criticized widely prevalent methodological and statistical practices in psychology (e.g., [31–33]). Sets of poor research practices collectively known as "p-hacking" [34] were one of the most obvious culprits for rampant false findings in the literature, and only through shining a spotlight on the danger of these practices and issuing concrete reforms has experimental psychology reestablished itself as a credible discipline.

Though psychology, and in particular the subfield of social psychology, received the most attention for such aforementioned questionable practices, p-hacking is no less widespread in many other fields. The effects of the replication crisis in psychology have rippled out to neuroscience [50, 51], and the topic is beginning to receive some recognition in XR as well [52]. XR research will fall prey to the same pitfalls as experimental psychology research unless we take to heart the lessons learned from the replication crisis. Here, we focus on power analysis and preregistration, two particularly helpful and easy-to-implement practices popularized by the best practices movement.

7.3.1.1   Power Analysis

How many coin flips would you need to tell whether a coin is fair? How many citizens' heights would you need to measure to tell whether Finns or Swedes are taller on average? Such questions speak to the issue of statistical power. Statistical power refers to the probability that you will detect a statistically significant effect given a particular statistical test, assuming that such an effect actually exists in the real world.

Power is determined by the effect's size (how much of an impact does the effect have?), the false positive rate (*alpha*; how often are we willing to accept an incidental positive result as real?), and our sample size (how many observations do we need?). While the false positive rate is conventionally fixed at .05, the effect size and sample size may vary. Researchers may only control the effect size to the extent that they choose to study effects that are larger or smaller, but have full control of sample sizes to the extent that they have sufficient funding, time, and populations of willing participants. The effect size-to-sample size relationship works out such that increasingly smaller effects require increasingly larger samples to find them; thus, while large effects may only require as few as 20 participants to reliably detect, smaller effects may require hundreds or even thousands of participants to reliably detect.

Why would we spend the resources needed to study small effects? Here, it is important to note the difference between statistical significance and practical significance. Imagine that we make a change to an HMD that results in an increase in presence ratings of 2%. Such a small change in presence ratings might not be of much practical significance in terms of a cost–benefit analysis for implementing the change. Imagine another scenario in which we make a change to an HMD that results in an increase in the probability of causing an epileptic seizure by 2%. This effect of equal magnitude to the previous example now carries much more practical significance given that a 2% increase here could mean inducing seizures in many individuals. This relatively small effect size could have a large real-world impact, and thus it would be important to spend the necessary resources to detect it and precisely estimate it.

Note that despite the differences in practical significance, either effect may or may not achieve statistical significance. Assuming that the effects are real, their likelihood of achieving statistical significance is a function of our sample size, and in turn, our power to detect them. This point should also underscore the importance of reporting estimated effect sizes along with p-values in order to help communicate an effect's practical significance rather than only whether it is statistically significant [53].

How large of a sample is large enough? Historically, studies in psychology have often used "rules of thumb" to guide sample sizes, defaulting to around 20 or 30 subjects per group. This sample range is observed in many XR studies as well. However, we now have the computational power to quickly perform power analysis in free-to-use software such as G*Power [54], which will give the precise sample size required to achieve a specified level of power for a given effect size. The results demonstrate that the old rules of thumb leave researchers woefully underpowered to detect most effects. When trying to detect a medium-sized effect (Cohen's $d = 0.5$), running 20 subjects per group in a two-group design renders only just over a 1 in 3 chance of detecting the effect (power = 34%), assuming the effect is actually there. In order to improve the odds of detecting the same effect to 4 out of 5 times (power = 80%; a common minimum benchmark used in power analysis), we would need to acquire 64 subjects per group, and would still miss this medium-sized effect 1 out of 5 times on average unless further increases to the sample were made. It should come as no surprise then that studies in psychology have been estimated to achieve only about 50% power on average [31, 55].

Most effects studied in psychology are thought to be of medium size or smaller (e.g., [56]; though note the authors' caution on how qualifiers like "medium" should be interpreted), which would imply that the same is likely to be true for much of the research in XR and human perception. Effect sizes become smaller when variability is high, and humans can be highly variable. Engineers are often used to getting precise measurements from their sensors, or in other scenarios, measurements that are imprecise, but imprecise in systematic ways. In perceptual psychology, we often instead use questionnaires or behavioral responses to tap into psychological constructs. This process does not afford the same precision as measurements of physical entities, and there is no guaranteed mapping between the measure and the construct; thus, power analysis becomes a critical tool for ensuring enough data are collected to observe effects. Yet, power analysis is often omitted from XR research procedures. In their review of the relationship between presence and cybersickness, Weech *et al.* [57] reported that only 3 of the 20 articles examined obtained at least 80% power to detect medium-sized effects, and only 1 of the 20 performed *a priori* power analysis, a procedure used to determine in advance how many subjects will be needed to detect an effect.

It is critical that *a priori* power analysis becomes standard in XR research because otherwise, researchers risk leaving their findings to chance. Perhaps counterintuitively, running large, comprehensive studies actually saves time and money. A high-powered study can precisely estimate an effect, whereas running many low- powered studies will often lead to mixed results and end up ultimately wasting more resources in trying to understand the effect in the long run. Of course, it is also possible to over-allocate time and resources to an area, yet here again, we can take advantage of power analysis to determine appropriate sample sizes for measuring a particular effect so that resources are not wasted by over-allocation either [50].

As noted, the estimated effect size will determine the required sample size, but how does one best estimate an effect size for an *a priori* power analysis?

There are several options here. One common route is to use the effect sizes reported in similar experiments in the literature. Though reported effect sizes are often overestimated due to a combination of low-powered studies that imprecisely estimate effects and publication bias (the tendency to not publish null results), they can still aid in determining a reasonable starting point for the power analysis. Similar experiments might not always exist in the literature, and thus another route is to run a pilot study in advance. Piloting is extremely beneficial for deciding the details of the methods and analysis, and is especially recommended when the resources are available and the experiment is the first of its kind. Another route is to use an effect size corresponding to the smallest effect that would still be theoretically interesting, or practically significant, and use this effect size to determine the required sample size.

7.3.1.2   Preregistration

We hope to have now made a convincing case for power analysis, but the reader might still be wondering how a leading experimental psychologist was able to publish evidence for ESP in a respected journal. To understand the answer to this question, we must turn to the thus far-little discussed third parameter in our power analysis equation: the false positive rate.

Inferential statistics allow scientists to, as the name would imply, make inferences. Unlike conclusions in logical deduction that necessarily follow from basic premises, the best we can do in regard to most scientific hypotheses is to infer, or in other words, to collect data that we may interpret as evidence favoring one alternative about the state of the world over another. Given that the nature of this type of reasoning is probabilistic rather than deterministic, errors will sometimes arise, and fields must decide how often certain types of errors are to be permitted. So far, in our discussion of power, we have focused on "type II" errors, or the potential to miss an effect when it is actually there. The other type of error we must consider concerns the false positive rate, or "type I" errors, in which we detect an effect when it is *not* actually there.

The idea of detecting something when it is not actually there might seem absurd at first glance, but type I errors are a natural consequence of inferential statistics. Consider that whenever we run a test to see whether a control group and a treatment group differ in an outcome variable, there is always some potential that the two groups will differ not because of the difference in treatment administered, but simply due to random chance, perhaps caused by some separate unknown influence or sampling bias. We can set our tolerance for accepting the anomalies arising due to chance as real effects in our statistics by setting the type I error rate, which is commonly fixed at 5% (*alpha* = .05). In other words, we accept as a field that 1 in every 20 effects reported in the literature is actually a false positive. That ratio might seem alarming, but the situation is even worse than it seems.

Imagine that we run a series of small studies. The data look promising at times, but no results are statistically significant. We keep making small tweaks to the study, until the 10th, or maybe the 20th, iteration. We finally arrive at a significant result that is then published. Consider another scenario. We instead run one large study instead of several small ones. We want to get the greatest value possible from the many hours that will be devoted to the project, so we collect a large amount of data on many different types of variables. After data collection is finished, we run 30 different statistical tests on all the dependent variables. Of the 30 tests, 2 are statistically significant. The 2 significant results are published, while the 28 nonsignificant results are not mentioned in the manuscript. In another study, we have fewer resources and want to manage them carefully, so we first run a handful of participants and run our analyses. There are no significant results yet, so we periodically add more subjects and rerun our analyses. Eventually, the result is significant, and this last test goes into the manuscript. For our final study, we are examining a correlation between two variables. Our resulting correlation is not quite statistically significant, but upon looking at the data, we see one point far away from the cluster of the others. It is clearly an outlier so we remove it, and now, the correlation is statistically significant and goes into the published literature.

We could go on, but at this point, the pattern should be clear. Our only protection against type 1 errors is our false positive rate fixed at 5%, but this rate was intended to apply to only one isolated test. In the first several examples, we are performing classic "p-hacking" by rolling the dice multiple times until we arrive at our desired result, and thus we are inflating our false positive rate well beyond the 5% level [49]. In the last example, we are making a choice about how to analyze the data after the results are known. These choices are what are known as "researcher degrees of freedom." The idea is that there are near-infinite ways to code and analyze any dataset, and going down this garden of forking paths where we let our biases or the data itself influence our decisions can lead to a drastic increase in our type 1 error rate [58]. Simmons *et al.* [34] demonstrated that using a combination of just three practices related to those above can push the type 1 error rate to a whopping 60%, meaning we would be more likely to report a false finding than not!

It is in this way that we can show evidence for ESP in undergrads [29], "chronological rejuvenation" (listening to a song by The Beatles made participants physically younger in age [34]), or even neural activity in a dead salmon [35]. While the latter two examples are parodies, the former and many others like it were not. To be clear, we do not intend to say that these are malicious actors trying to cheat the system in most cases; in fact, each of the practices in the scenarios described two paragraphs ago were common practices for many labs until the replication crisis brought these issues to light. The practices were inherited by naive researchers who likely did not fully grasp how such approaches could warp inferential statistics, and the fact that a researcher with no ill intent can so easily inflate the type 1 error rate of their study to such a degree is the most alarming aspect of this situation.

So how do we as a field address this issue? One very promising solution is preregistration [36]. A preregistered study is one in which all the details regarding how data will be collected and analyzed are documented and timestamped before the study is run. This process effectively narrows the researcher's degrees of freedom and prevents biases that could inflate type 1 errors from taking over. Related in spirit to preregistrations are registered reports [37]. In a registered report, the introduction and methods of a paper are written in advance and sent to a journal before the study is run. The journal then reviews the study proposal and accepts or rejects the study for publication based on its potential impact and methodological merits. If accepted, the study is run and the paper is published whether the results are statistically significant or not. This approach addresses not only inflation in type 1 error rates, but also publication bias, as the publication of the null result could still be of theoretical interest, and it could also prevent other labs from wasting resources on producing the same null result to the same problem.

Any disruption of the status quo tends to provoke backlash, and the campaign for preregistration was no exception. A common concern has been that requiring preregistration would discourage exploratory research. Proponents of preregistration respond that it does not actually discourage exploratory research, but instead only separates the exploratory from the confirmatory, preventing potentially spurious findings from being presented as confirmations of original hypotheses. Findings that were not predicted in the preregistration could still be published as exploratory results but would need a confirmatory follow-up experiment to provide more solid evidence. Another concern was that the process of preregistration is overly onerous, requiring researchers to know too many details in advance. This aspect can actually be seen as a strength rather than a weakness, as it requires researchers to think critically about the details of their project before they begin. A solid confirmatory study should have its details polished through piloting or previous similar experiments before resources are spent on data collection. Websites such as the Open Science Framework (https://osf.io/) provide architecture and templates to make the process of preregistration quite painless.

7.3.1.3   Supporting Best Practices

False positives are easy to obtain and difficult to overturn once published. Significant resources are wasted on underpowered studies that have little chance to detect real effects, and on extending research on effects that were false positives to begin with. While we cannot address every flaw and potential solution in XR methods here, power analysis and preregistration are two standards that could be easily implemented to significantly raise the quality of XR research and produce a more effective allocation of resources. We therefore advocate that preference should be given to projects that are willing to adopt these standards.

7.3.2   Individual Differences

There are some additional considerations regarding individual differences when addressing human perception in the design and research of XR technology. First, it is important to note the potential differences between genders; men have an average interpupillary distance (IPD) of about 64.7, and women have an average IPD of 62.3 [38]. A recent meta-analysis found that the number of female participants in VR research studies can impact the amount of VR sickness experienced after HMD use [39]. Though there have been conflicting findings as to whether men and women have different simulator sickness susceptibilities, there is evidence that a lack of proper IPD fit for women participants impacts these differences [40]. Therefore, proper gender balance in research studies is strongly merited, and the ability to properly adjust IPD may also be advised. Furthermore, Peck *et al.* [39] found that the number of female participants in VR research studies was associated with the number of female authors of VR manuscripts. Thus, it is important to encourage diverse research teams as well as more representative samples. Age, susceptibility to motion sickness, and gaming or VR use are also important individual characteristics to take into account [41].

Another important consideration is accessibility. The *World Report on Disability* from the World Health Organization estimated that about 15%

of the global population, or over 1 billion people, were living with a disability in 2010. This was a significant increase from an estimated prevalence of 10% of the world's population in 1970, so it is possible that the current numbers are even larger [42]. Furthermore, the 2006 United Nations *Convention on the Rights of Persons with Disabilities* enshrines the rights of people with disabilities as human rights, and outlines obligations for member states that ratify the treaty to address issues of accessibility and inclusion. Thus, the development of future XR technologies must also include the incorporation of recommendations and guidelines for accessibility that have been developed by organizations for people with disabilities, like the Disability Visibility Project (https://disabilityvisibilityproject. com/) and AbleGamers (https://ablegamers.org/), from the outset, and not as an afterthought [43, 44]. The World Wide Web Consortium (W3C) Web Accessibility Initiative (WAI) has published a comprehensive guide, the *XR Accessibility User Requirements* (Accessible Platform Architectures Working Group, [45]), that can be used to ensure that everyone can enjoy XR. Additionally, it should be considered that XR technologies can have enormous impacts on peoples' lives, like VR neurorehabilitation therapies that have been shown to restore some limb sensation and motor control for patients paralyzed from spinal cord injuries [46]. Therefore, opportunities to assist people with disabilities using XR, such as immersive telepresence [47] or XR therapeutics [48], merit further support for research and development.

7.3.3   Open-Source Modular Devices

An often-ignored, yet major, impediment to the growth of XR and human perception research is that the overwhelming majority of research is conducted using commercial products that can carry wildly different hardware parameters. Technology has advanced at such a rapid pace that today's cutting-edge devices make those from a decade ago look quaint. Even among current and upcoming devices, there is a gamut of consumer and corporate targets, with some devices retailing for less than €50, while others retail for thousands of euros. Such large gaps between price tags necessarily carry large gaps between the types of features users can expect to receive among these various devices, and these differences can in turn create confounds for researchers.

There are no scientific standards that dictate which device labs across the world use in their XR experiments. Instead, selections are made based on convenience and the availability of resources. While studying the same facet of XR and human perception, one lab might use the Oculus DK1, while another might use the Varjo XR3. When the two labs arrive at different conclusions on the topic they are trying to address, is the difference due to some discrepancy between their methods, some discrepancy between their contents, or a discrepancy between aspects of the two devices? Perhaps a mix of all three? Can we still trust results from 20 years ago that came from devices of that time period, or have our devices evolved so drastically over time that many of the problems associated with old devices are no longer relevant?

Consider a toy example in which we are trying to better understand motion sickness caused by motor vehicles. Pretend that there is a hypothesis in this field that the degree of motion sickness experienced is a function of how much food is in the stomach at the time of driving. Three labs around the world simultaneously begin studies to test this hypothesis, controlling how much their participants eat before starting them along their driving course, each lab without knowledge that the other two labs are busy addressing the same issue. Lab A has participants drive their course in a 1990 Toyota Camry and finds that an empty stomach is associated with greater motion sickness. Lab B has participants drive their course in a 2020 Lamborghini Aventador and finds that a full stomach is associated with greater motion sickness. Lab C has participants drive their course in a 2015 Mini Cooper and finds no relationship between stomach fullness and motion sickness.

Which lab's data should we believe? Despite attempting to study the same concept, the labs' tools for assessing the concept are so different that it can be difficult to draw conclusions. Compound this dilemma with underpowered studies and high false positive rates (see the section on best practices above) and we have truly gained nothing from this set of studies. This scenario demonstrates another case in which the field could be approaching things backwards; that is, we believe we are studying fundamental perception, when in fact, we are sometimes closer to studying *the devices themselves* instead. Our goal is to understand the construction of perceptual experiences, yet the obligatory reliance on commercial, rather than research-grade, tools obfuscates our path to understanding.

These devices are not usually made with researchers in mind, and why would they be? They are commercial products targeted to consumers, or in other cases, enterprise products targeted to businesses. How might we remedy this problem of associated potential confounds introduced to XR research? One solution would be the adoption of open-source modular devices. The name invokes two critical features: 1) open source, such that anyone can access the device free of property infringements and construct the device without requiring hefty financial resources, and 2) modular, such that researchers may mix and match device components and control for the impacts of various hardware features instead of being forced to work with the hardware features that were chosen by companies to target their particular user base. While related initiatives exist, such as holokit (https://holokit.io/) and CheApR (https://www.instructables.com/CheApR-Open-Source-Augmented-Reality-Smart-Glasses/), these are consumer-grade products that do not rise to the degree of quality that would be needed for scientific research. They also lack the modularity that would be key for understanding how different aspects of device hardware contribute to perception.

We believe that developing open-source modular devices is necessary if we are to ascend to our full potential as a scientific discipline. This initiative would require careful planning, dedicated personnel, and significant funding, but the payoff would be monumental in terms of the progress such an initiative could bring about. Developing open-source modular devices, along with the adoption of best practices, represents an opportunity to set a new, more solid foundation for XR research.

Funding

This work was supported by the HUMOR (3656/31/2019) project funded by Business Finland and by the PERCEPT (322637) project funded by the Academy of Finland.

References

1. Otten, M., Pinto, Y., Paffen, C.L., Seth, A.K., Kanai, R., The uniformity illusion: Central stimuli can determine peripheral perception. *Psychol. Sci.*, 28, 1, 56–68, 2017.

2. Mooney, C.M., Age in the development of closure ability in children. *Can. J. Psychol./Rev. Can. Psychol.*, 11, 4, 219, 1957.

3. Schwiedrzik, C.M., Melloni, L., Schurger, A., Mooney face stimuli for visual perception research. *PLoS One*, 13, 7, e0200106, 2018.

4. Simons, D.J. and Chabris, C.F., Gorillas in our midst: sustained inattentional blindness for dynamic events. *Perception*, 28, 9, 1059–1074, 1999.

5. Hoffman, D., *The case against reality: Why evolution hid the truth from our eyes*, WW Norton & Company, New York, New York, United States, 2019.

6. Hoffman, D.D., The interface theory of perception. *Curr. Dir. Psychol. Sci.*, 25, 3, 157–161, 2016.

7. Friston, K., The Free-Energy Principle: a Unified Brain Theory? *Nat. Rev. Neurosci.*, 11, 2, 127–38, 2010, https://doi.org/10.1038/nrn2787.
8. Rao, R.P. and Ballard, D.H., Predictive Coding in the Visual Cortex: a Functional Interpretation of Some Extra-Classical Receptive-Field Effects. *Nat. Neurosci.*, 2, 1, 79–87, 1999, https://doi.org/10.1038/4580.
9. Friston, K. and Kiebel, S., Predictive Coding under the Free-Energy Principle. *Philos. Trans. R. Soc. B: Biol. Sci.*, 364, 1521, 1211–21, 2009, https://doi.org/10.1098/rstb.2008.0300.
10. Smith, R., Badcock, P., Friston, K.J., Recent Advances in the Application of Predictive Coding and Active Inference Models within Clinical Neuroscience. *Psychiatry Clin. Neurosci.*, 75, 1, 3–13, 2020, https://doi.org/10.1111/pcn.13138.
11. Pläschke, R.N., Cieslik, E.C., Müller, V.I., Hoffstaedter, F., Plachti, A., Varikuti, D.P., Goosses, M. *et al.*, On the Integrity of Functional Brain Networks in Schizophrenia, Parkinson's Disease, and Advanced Age: Evidence from Connectivity-Based Single-Subject Classification. *Hum. Brain Mapp.*, 38, 12, 5845–58, 2017, https://doi.org/10.1002/hbm.23763.
12. Williams, L.M., Defining Biotypes for Depression and Anxiety Based on Large-Scale Circuit Dysfunction: a Theoretical Review of the Evidence and Future Directions for Clinical Translation. *Depress. Anxiety*, 34, 1, 9–24, 2016, https://doi.org/10.1002/da.22556.
13. Reason, J.T., Motion sickness adaptation: a neural mismatch model. *J. R. Soc. Med.*, 71, 11, 819–829, 1978.
14. Biocca, F.A. and Rolland, J.P., Virtual eyes can rearrange your body: Adaptation to visual displacement in see-through, head-mounted displays. *Presence*, 7, 3, 262–277, 1998.
15. Welch, R.B. and Mohler, B.J., Adapting to virtual environments, in: *Handbook of virtual environments: Design, implementation, and applications*, pp. 627–646, CRC Press, Boca Raton, Florida, United States, 2015.
16. Mao, A., Barnes, K., Sharpe, L., Geers, A.L., Helfer, S.G., Faasse, K., Colagiuri, B., Using Positive Attribute Framing to Attenuate Nocebo Side Effects: A Cybersickness Study. *Ann. Behav. Med.*, 55, 8, 769–778, 2021. In Press.
17. Keshavarz, B., Stelzmann, D., Paillard, A., Hecht, H., Visually induced motion sickness can be alleviated by pleasant odors. *Exp. Brain Res.*, 233, 5, 1353–1364, 2015, https://doi.org/10.1007/s00221-015-4209-9.
18. Paroz, A. and Potter, L.E., Impact of air flow and a hybrid locomotion system on cybersickness, 30th conference. *ACM Int. Conf. Proceeding Ser.*, 582–586, 2018, https://doi.org/10.1145/3292147.3292229.
19. D'Amour, S., Bos, J.E., Keshavarz, B., The efficacy of airflow and seat vibration on reducing visually induced motion sickness. *Exp. Brain Res.*, 235, 9, 2811–2820, 2017, https://doi.org/10.1007/s00221-017-5009-1.
20. Culbertson, H., Schorr, S.B., Okamura, A.M., Haptics: The Present and Future of Artificial Touch Sensation. *Annu. Rev. Control Rob. Auton. Syst.*, 1, 1, 385–409, 2018, https://doi.org/10.1146/annurev-control-060117-105043.

21. Ernst, M. and Banks, M., Humans integrate visual and haptic information in a statistically optimal fashion. *Nature*, 415, 429–433, 2002.

22. Lécuyer, A., Simulating haptic feedback using vision: A survey of research and applications of pseudo-haptic feedback. *Presence: Teleop. Virt. Environments*, 18, 1, 39–53, 2009, https://doi.org/10.1162/pres.18.1.39.

23. Weser, V. and Proffitt, D.R., Making the Visual Tangible: Substituting Lifting Speed Limits for Object Weight in VR. *PRESENCE: Virt. Augment. Real.*, 27, 1, 68–79, 2019, https://doi.org/10.1162/pres_a_00319.

24. Kennedy, R.S., Lane, N.E., Berbaum, K.S., Lilienthal, M.G., Simulator Sickness Questionnaire: An Enhanced Method for Quantifying Simulator Sickness. *Int. J. Aviat. Psychol.*, 3, 3, 203–20, 1993, https://doi.org/10.1207/s15327108ijap0303_3.

25. Sevinc, V. and Berkman, M.I., Psychometric evaluation of Simulator Sickness Questionnaire and its variants as a measure of cybersickness in consumer virtual environments. *Appl. Ergon.*, 82, 102958, 2020.

26. Hirzle, T., Cordts, M., Rukzio, E., Gugenheimer, J., Bulling, A., A Critical Assessment of the Use of SSQ as a Measure of General Discomfort in VR Head-Mounted Displays, in: *Proceedings of the 2021 CHI Conference on Human Factors in Computing Systems*, pp. 1–14, 2021, May.

27. Kurdi, B., Lozano, S., Banaji, M.R., Introducing the open affective standard-ized image set (OASIS). *Behav. Res. Methods*, 49, 2, 457–470, 2017.

28. Minear, M. and Park, D.C., A lifespan database of adult facial stimuli. *Behav. Res. Methods Instrum. Comput.*, 36, 4, 630–633, 2004.

29. Bem, D.J., Feeling the Future: Experimental Evidence for Anomalous Retroactive Influences on Cognition and Affect. *J. Pers. Soc. Psychol.*, 100, 3, 407–25, 2011, https://doi.org/10.1037/a0021524.

30. Open Science Collaboration, Nosek, B.A., Aarts, A.A., Anderson, C.J. *et al.*, Estimating the reproducibility of psychological science. *Science*, 349, 6251, 943–951, 2015, aac4716–aac4716. doi:10.1126/science.aac4716. hdl:10722/230596.

31. Cohen, J., The Statistical Power of Abnormal-Social Psychological Research: A Review. *J. Abnorm. Soc. Psychol.*, 65, 3, 145–53, 1962, https://doi.org/10.1037/h0045186.

32. Sedlmeier, P. and Gigerenzer, G., Do Studies of Statistical Power Have an Effect on the Power of Studies? *Psychol. Bull.*, 105, 2, 309–16, 1989, https://doi.org/10.1037/0033-2909.105.2.309.

33. Cohen, J., The Earth Is Round (p < .05). *Am. Psychol.*, 49, 12, 997–1003, 1994, https://doi.org/10.1037/0003-066x.49.12.997.

34. Simmons, J.P., Nelson, L.D., Simonsohn, U., False-Positive Psychology: Undisclosed Flexibility in Data Collection and Analysis Allows Presenting Anything as Significant. *Psychol. Sci.*, 22, 11, 1359–66, 2011, https://doi.org/10.1177/0956797611417632.

35. Bennett, C.M., Miller, M.B., Wolford, G.L., Neural Correlates of Interspecies Perspective Taking in the Post-Mortem Atlantic Salmon: an Argument for Multiple Comparisons Correction. *NeuroImage*, 47(Suppl 1), S125, 2009.

36. Nosek, B. A., Ebersole, C. R., DeHaven, A. C., & Mellor, D. T., The preregistration revolution. Proceedings of the National Academy of Sciences of the United States of America, 115, 11, 2600–2606, 2018. https://doi.org/10.1073/pnas.1708274114

37. Nosek, B.A. and Lakens, D., Registered Reports. *Soc. Psychol.*, 45, 3, 137–41, 2014, https://doi.org/10.1027/1864-9335/a000192.

38. Dodgson, N.A., Variation and extrema of human interpupillary distance, in: *Stereoscopic Displays and Virtual Reality Systems XI*, vol. 5291, pp. 36–46, 2004, https://doi.org/10.1117/12.529999.

39. Peck, T.C., Sockol, L.E., Hancock, S.M., Mind the Gap: The Underrepresentation of Female Participants and Authors in Virtual Reality Research. *IEEE Trans. Visual. Comput. Graphics*, 26, 5, 1945–1954, 2020, https://doi.org/10.1109/TVCG.2020.2973498.

40. Stanney, K., Fidopiastis, C., Foster, L., Virtual Reality Is Sexist: But It Does Not Have to Be. *Front. Rob. AI*, 7, 1–19, January, 2020, https://doi.org/10.3389/frobt.2020.00004.

41. Saredakis, D., Szpak, A., Birckhead, B., Keage, H.A.D., Rizzo, A., Loetscher, T., Factors associated with virtual reality sickness in head-mounted displays: A systematic review and meta-analysis. *Front. Hum. Neurosci.*, 14, 1–17, March, 2020, https://doi.org/10.3389/fnhum.2020.00096.

42. World Health Organization and World Bank. *World report on disability.* Geneva, Switzerland: World Health Organization, 2011. Retrieved from www.who.int/about/licensing/copyright_form/en/index.html%0Ahttp://www.larchetoronto.org/wordpress/wp-content/uploads/2012/01/launch-of-World-Report-on-Disability-Jan-27-121.pdf.

43. Formaker-Olivas, B., *Why VR/AR Developers Should Prioritize Accessibility in UX/UI Design*, The Academy of International Extended Reality, London, United Kingdom, 2019, Retrieved from https://aixr.org/insights/why-vr-ar-developers-should-prioritize-accessibility-in-ux-ui-design/.

44. Phillips, K.U., *Virtual Reality Has an Accessibility Problem*, Springer Nature, London, United Kingdom 2020, Retrieved from https://blogs.scientificamerican.com/voices/virtual-reality-has-an-accessibility-problem/.

45. Accessible Platform Architectures Working Group, *XR Accessibility User Requirements. W3C First Public Working Draft*, 2020, Retrieved from https://www.w3.org/TR/2020/WD-xaur-20200213/.

46. Donati, A.R.C., Shokur, S., Morya, E., Campos, D.S.F., Moioli, R.C., Gitti, C.M., Nicolelis, M.A.L., Long-Term Training with a Brain-Machine Interface-Based Gait Protocol Induces Partial Neurological Recovery in Paraplegic Patients. *Sci. Rep.*, 6, April, 1–16, 2016, https://doi.org/10.1038/srep30383.

47. Zhang, G., Hansen, J.P., Minakata, K., Hand- and gaze-control of telepresence robots, in: *Proceedings of the 11th ACM Symposium on Eye Tracking Research & Applications*, pp. 1–8, ACM, New York, NY, USA, 2019, https://doi.org/10.1145/3317956.3318149.

48. Hilty, D.M., Randhawa, K., Maheu, M.M., McKean, A.J.S., Pantera, R., Mishkind, M.C., Rizzo, A., A Review of Telepresence, Virtual Reality, and Augmented Reality Applied to Clinical Care. *J. Technol. Behav. Sci.*, 5, 2, 178–205, 2020, https://doi.org/10.1007/s41347-020-00126-x.

49. Bakker, M., van Dijk, A., Wicherts, J.M., The Rules of the Game Called Psychological Science. *Perspect. Psychol. Sci.*, 7, 6, 543–54, 2012, https://doi.org/10.1177/1745691612459060.

50. Button, K.S., Ioannidis, J.P., Mokrysz, C., Nosek, B.A., Flint, J., Robinson, E.S., Munafò, M.R., Power Failure: Why Small Sample Size Undermines the Reliability of Neuroscience. *Nat. Rev. Neurosci.*, 14, 5, 365–76, 2013, https://doi.org/10.1038/nrn3475.

51. Poldrack, R., Baker, C., Durnez, J. et al., Scanning the horizon: towards transparent and reproducible neuroimaging research. *Nat Rev Neurosci.*, 18, 115–126, 2017. https://doi.org/10.1038/nrn.2016.167

52. Edward Swan, J., The Replication Crisis in Empirical Science: Implications for Human Subject Research in Mixed Reality. *2018 IEEE International Symposium on Mixed and Augmented Reality Adjunct (ISMAR-Adjunct)*, 2018, https://doi.org/10.1109/ismar-adjunct.2018.00019.

53. Sullivan, G.M. and Feinn, R., Using Effect Size—or Why the P Value Is Not Enough. *J. Grad. Med. Educ.*, 4, 3, 279–82, 2012, https://doi.org/10.4300/jgme-d-12-00156.1.

54. Faul, F., Erdfelder, E., Lang, A.-G., Buchner, A., G*Power 3: A Flexible Statistical Power Analysis Program for the Social, Behavioral, and Biomedical Sciences. *Behav. Res. Methods*, 39, 2, 175–91, 2007, https://doi.org/10.3758/bf03193146.

55. Fraley, R.C. and Vazire, S., The N-Pact Factor: Evaluating the Quality of Empirical Journals with Respect to Sample Size and Statistical Power. *PLoS One*, 9, 10, 1–12, 2014, https://doi.org/10.1371/journal.pone.0109019.

56. Schäfer, T. and Schwarz, M.A., The Meaningfulness of Effect Sizes in Psychological Research: Differences Between Sub-Disciplines and the Impact of Potential Biases. *Front. Psychol.*, 10, 1–13, 2019, https://doi.org/10.3389/fpsyg.2019.00813.

57. Weech, S., Kenny, S., Barnett-Cowan, M., Presence and Cybersickness in Virtual Reality Are Negatively Related: A Review. *Front. Psychol.*, 10, 1–19, 2019, https://doi.org/10.3389/fpsyg.2019.00158.

58. Gelman, A. and Loken, E., The garden of forking paths: Why multiple comparisons can be a problem even when there is no "fishing expectation" or "p-hacking" and the research hypothesis was posited ahead of time, Columbia University, 348, 2013. Retrieved from http://www.stat.columbia.edu/~gelman/research/unpublished/p_hacking.pdf.

8

Extended Reality and Artificial Intelligence: Synergic Approaches in Real World Applications

Maria di Summa[1]*, Vito Reno[1], Pierluigi Dibari[1], Gaetano Pernisco[1], Marco Sacco[2] and Ettore Stella[1]

[1]Institute of Intelligent Industrial Technologies and Systems for Advanced Manufacturing National Research Council of Italy, Via Amendola, Bari, Italy
[2]Institute of Intelligent Industrial Technologies and Systems for Advanced Manufacturing National Research Council of Italy, Via Previati 1/E, Lecco, Italy

Abstract

Today extended reality focuses on itself a big attention by industrial and research communities. Many investments will be devoted to these technologies in the next years. Therefore, this technology has to give new and performant answers. On the other hand, deep learning algorithms are having a notable impact in many fields with interesting results. A challenging proposal is to merge extended reality and artificial intelligence in order to build a synergic collaboration between technologies to support and preserve a human-centric vision.

Keywords: Extended reality, virtual reality, artificial intelligence, deep learning, Industry 4.0

8.1 Introduction

In the Fourth Industrial Revolution era, the eXtended Reality (XR) continues to be, in its various forms and declinations, one of the technologies that focuses on itself an unchanged interest of the research and industrial worlds.

Corresponding author: maria.disumma@stiima.cnr.it

Mariano Alcañiz, Marco Sacco and Jolanda G. Tromp (eds.) Roadmapping Extended Reality: Fundamentals and Applications, (183–192) © 2022 Scrivener Publishing LLC

Virtual Reality (VR), Augmented Reality (AR), and XR, however, are now facing a crucial step in their evolution. In fact, technological development has reached a significant level of improvement. The bottleneck is today represented by two key points:

a)   the need for a widespread diffusion of these technologies, even within small industrial entities,

b)   the need for integration between the various technologies that allows us to offer more comprehensive services, while maintaining intact the centrality of the human being.

It is precisely in this panorama that the combination of Artificial Intelligence (AI) and XR represents the necessary step to overcome the impasse. The synergistic collaboration of these two technologies contains the answer for both of the above problems. In fact, the use of automatic systems that are able to analyze data and provide additional information together with innovative visualization techniques represent a performing support tool for the operator who remains central in carrying out his/her task. These two technologies lend themselves to be integrated into a smart system that combines the strength of the machine in analyzing huge amounts of data with the typically human ability to perform complex decision-making tasks, explaining the decision-making process itself.

AI is the ability of the machine to emulate the human brain in performing complex reasoning tasks. It presents itself as an extremely generic concept that can be expressed in many ways. In particular, one of the possible approaches in performing automatic reasoning is the use of deep learning algorithms. For decades, AI has been a key technology in the development of all leading sectors of the economic development of modern society, ranging from construction to Industry 4.0, from medical systems to safety, generally speaking. The fluctuating trend of interest on the part of the scientific community in this technology has often depended on the technological limits that have stood in the way of achieving the goal. Fortunately, today, this technology has reached a turning point, thanks to the development of new approaches and in particular, those related to machine learning with a particular focus on deep learning. In the field of services, the ability to interpret large amounts of data by these algorithms represents an undisputed benefit; furthermore, the capability to automate many processes is an effective way to increase in performance and to have cost reduction. Predictive maintenance and quality control are just some of the possible applications of AI.

With particular reference to deep learning algorithms and models, they are mainly based on the artificial imitation of a network of neurons in a human brain and are referred to as Convolutional Neural Networks (CNNs). Deep learning algorithms are composed of various levels of cascading neurons, each of which has the output of the previous level as its input, that need to be properly trained on specific datasets to be effectively used in practical applications. Deep learning algorithms can be supervised or unsupervised. You have supervised algorithms when the reference model was previously built knowing the goal perfectly, using appropriately labeled data (i.e., giving the model the desired correspondence between inputs and outputs). In supervised learning, a portion of data is used to train the machine to achieve a certain goal, while the remaining part is used for testing and validation purposes.

Unsupervised learning, on the other hand, works without a previous learning base. It does not need labeled data, but the algorithm makes its own decisions, sorts the variables, establishes its rules, and creates its model as it analyzes the data progressively. The two main techniques that an unsupervised learning algorithm implements are clustering and dimensionality reduction: the first is used to assign categories (or labels) to the input data, while the second is useful to obtain a compact and meaningful representation of the input by reducing and combining all the variables that are fed to the model.

Deep learning algorithms enable the machine to autonomously classify data and structure them hierarchically. This allows the system to solve complex problems and gradually improve performance in an iterative learning process similar to that of the human mind.

On the other hand, AR is a technology that allows enriching the reality perceived by the human eye. AR increases the information content of the perceived reality of the user with additional digital objects and provides the user who uses it not only with a cognitive aid, but also with decision-support, if digital objects are the result of an elaboration/processing of data and not a simple visualization.

The rest of the contribution is structured as follows: Section 8.2 reports a literature review and some insights about the effective application of XR and AI in practical use cases; and Section 8.3 gives some realistic hypotheses about the future direction of research applications in this field, as well as a roadmap for the development of research activities and projects.

8.2   XR and Artificial Intelligence

Deep learning and AR technologies are used together for many purposes in a wide variety of applications. The fusion of these two technologies offers interesting perspectives because, thanks to XR, the centrality of the human being remains a fundamental element even in this new industrial revolution (the so-called Industry 4.0). On the other hand, AI makes it possible to increase human functionality, thanks to the contribution of the machine. Therefore, the synergy of these two technologies represents an undoubted benefit. The literature shows that the scientific community is moving in the direction of putting man and machine in cooperation to improve human performance. To support this claim, the following section comprises evidences and working examples of applications in different domains in the last few years.

In many strategic sectors such as construction, human expertise is still a critical element as stated in Karaaslan *et al.* [1]; for this reason, it is essential to support the operators and even enhance their contribution while they are performing specific tasks related to their work.

Another area where the synergistic use of AR and AI represents a crucial turning point is represented by the hands-free interaction of the human being with the robot. The applications of these human–machine interactions range from the health sector to manufacturing that uses manipulating robots. In fact, as an example, if we think of a disabled person who does not have the use of hands, he/she could still interact with an automatic wheelchair using AR as described in Park *et al.* [2]. Industries are noticing good opportunities on AR and mobile robots to increase their productivity. In the manufacturing sector, to reduce costs and improve performance, the traditional manual methods for identifying defects in assembly operations are being replaced with human–machine integrated intelligent systems as defined by Wang *et al.* [3]. Furthermore, to facilitate the use of AR applications, a good calibration between the real environment and AR device represents the first step. An example that deals with dynamic environments, particularly challenging in the presence of mobile robots, is reported in Kästner *et al.* [4], where the authors propose a method to perform the calibration-leveraging object detection using a depth sensor and exploiting a neural network, working directly on three-dimensional data such as raw point clouds.

Some of the most typical problems of the use of AR in the industrial field are represented by visual mismatching, incorrect occlusions, and some difficulties to estimate depth from AR images. A hybrid system that uses deep learning techniques as demonstrated by Kim *et al.* [5] represents a possible solution to these problems and allows increasingly widespread AR. In this work, the authors define an approach to fix the issues related to the estimation of image depth, which can lead to visual mismatching and incorrect occlusions in the case of failure, without using AR markers or depth cameras. Deep learning tools are adopted to recognize physical facilities in the scene and predict their depth map. After that, a three-dimensional (3D) point cloud of each recognized object is derived to provide a better visualization of the environment.

In Park *et al.* [6], instead, the authors propose a deep-learning-based AR method that is able to map the environment, avoiding the use of artificial markers but leveraging only Red Green Blue Depth (RGB-D) data. This approach performs an instance segmentation to the snapshot-based RGB-D data using a CNN model. Then, it uses an iterative closest points algorithm to align a virtual model to the real object and synchronize the virtual information. In another of his works, the same author focuses more on task assistance, i.e., helping users to perform their tasks by providing additional and useful information. In particular, Park *et al.* [7] gives the possibility to observe physical objects through an AR support and create 3D replicas of them, in order to share information or improve collaboration with other users.

However, there are many other more practical examples in the manufacturing field. For instance, Wang *et al.* [8] describes a deep learning strategy for damage detection in real time. The user can wear its AR smart glasses, and identify damaged areas in a region of interest around him/her. Additionally, it allows to assess the severity of cracks and corroded zones.

In the context of Industry 4.0, another very popular trend is to integrate collaborative robotics with mixed reality; a further step forward is to combine these two technologies with AI [9]. This allows to automate and make industrial processes even more efficient while leaving the centrality of man unaltered. Another interesting example is related to robot teleoperation. Zhou *et al.* [10] propose an effective interface to help human operators in manipulating remote robotic systems. The images captured by the robot are segmented by adopting deep learning models. The resulting information is used to reconstruct the robot's surrounding environment in a new virtual scenario, which is faster and easier to handle. This should help the operator in gaining situational awareness about the robot.

Another sector in which the combination of XR and AI has already been investigated for years is that of simulators for training operators in the most varied sectors. In the medical field, for example, these two technologies are becoming increasingly indispensable in training operators in the execution of complex tasks such as regional anesthesia [11]. Also, it is possible to exploit these technologies to support dermatologists in early diagnosis of skin cancer-reducing errors, the time to get a response, and consequently, the patient's concern. An innovative work by Francese *et al.* [12] proposes an approach leveraging a CNN to classify skin lesions and show additional information in real time directly on a mobile device. Another example in the same field is proposed in Orciuoli *et al.* [13] and regards the development of a system mainly based on a mobile application to support operators dealing with bedsores. The application developed in Orciuoli *et al.* [13] is based on AR supported by deep learning to measure, classify, and trace the evolution of single bedsores. Furthermore, it offers support to the operator to make decisions about the treatment to execute without substituting human thinking.

Finally, Tanzi *et al.* [14] propose a system to assist surgeons during *in-vivo* robot-assisted radical prostatectomy procedures. A CNN is employed to perform a semantic segmentation of endoscopic images leading to the creation of a 3D model of the patient's organ shown in the augmented scenario, providing helpful information for the doctor.

In last years, the safety field is also rapidly changing and improving by the use of these technologies. One of the proposals in this field is an application to exploit them to help users in critical situations and activities, such as fire extinguishing. Firefighting is a critical activity in which multiple actions occur at the same time, and for the operator, it is essential to always make the right decision and to safely operate in a dangerous environment. With this goal, Bhattarai *et al.* [15] developed an embedded system that can capture images from RGB and thermal and depth cameras fitted on the firefighter's personal protective equipment and analyze these data using a deep learning model. The system returns augmented images to the firefighter's visor, highlighting relevant elements such as doors and windows that cannot be visible to the naked eye.

In the same context, AR systems are strongly adopted also for the operators' training, as they provide cheaper, safer, and potentially unlimited solutions with respect to traditional ones. Heirman *et al.* [16] present an XR technology for firefighters' training. Not only does it grant protection from many real risks, but it also allows the development of scenarios too expensive or dangerous to simulate in the real world. In this case, deep learning techniques are applied to achieve realistic fire propagation, considering the material of the objects involved in the simulated environment. As regards driving safety, a system to support drivers in poor visibility conditions is proposed by Limmer *et al.* [17]. In particular, the framework developed is able to predict the road course by exploiting a CNN, properly trained on a large number of road images taken at nighttime or in adverse weather conditions. After that, the information coming from the deep learning model is combined with radar sensor and map data, before being effectively shown to the user in the AR navigation system.

Eventually, out of the fields just analyzed and reported beforehand, there are many other examples of particular applications. A combination of deep learning and AR technologies is adopted to support customers in large retail stores is shown in Cruz *et al.* [18], with the aim of helping them moving inside the store. To find a specific product, customers can take a photo of the area where they are located and send it through their smartphone to the system. Then, the system exploits a previously trained deep learning model, which is able to recognize the different areas of the store. After spotting the customer, AR techniques can be applied to provide useful additional information. Likewise, many other experiences can be easily enriched by adopting these kinds of solutions. Khan *et al.* [19] try to enhance users' museum experience at the Taxila Museum in Pakistan. They developed a smartphone application that is able to recognize artefacts in real time, through a CNN. As usual, supportive multimedia information is provided to the user through the same smartphone. By considering the users' feedback, the adopted strategy improved their experience. In a similar context, an alternative approach to assess the user's experience that uses a deep learning model to predict the visual attention in VR is reported in Li *et al.* [20]. The developed system has been designed primarily for VR museums, but it can be easily extended to a wide range of other environments. In particular, it works by evaluating the user's eye movements and the virtual object coordinates in real time. As for the previous applications, this allows to get a better awareness of the user experience and consequently to enhance it.

If on the one hand, today, we are witnessing an epochal technological revolution, on the other hand, an increasing interest is reserved for the environment. In this sense, the set of the technologies presented in this chapter can represent an effective and efficient support tool in safeguarding the environment. In fact, thanks to mixed reality and deep learning algorithms, it is possible to build synergic solutions that are able to handle dynamic occlusions and perform, for example, landscape index estimation for both existing and designed landscape assessment [21].

8.3   Future Research Agenda and Roadmap

Today, we are witnessing a real explosion of virtual and AR applications, mainly due to market pressure. In a report by Klecha & Co., there is the talk of an increase in investments in VR and AR for 2023 equal to 121 billion dollars. In this context, these technologies must be ready to provide solid answers to the companies that will make the investments to improve the industrial processes implementing a new business. The role of AI in XR becomes fundamental in order to transform AR applications in something more than tools for simply viewing virtual objects on real backgrounds, while keeping a user-centered approach.

The utopian design of creating AI-driven digital humans for XR worlds finally seems to have reached a turning point. Today, thanks to the development of AI and XR, we finally have all the tools necessary to design complex digital systems that safeguard the centrality of the human being as highlighted in Wienrich and Latoschik [22]. Thanks to the support of these technologies, humans will be able to perform complex tasks that require specific cognitive skills and the machines will be able to deal with heavy, repetitive and unrewarding tasks.

In the medium term, the research aspects related to the integration of these two technologies are represented by the resolution of precision problems in the positioning of virtual objects, the calculation of distances of virtual objects within real images, using virtual images to increase the dimensionality of dataset and understand how to, virtually, visualize the results of data processing.

In the long term, however, the most ambitious objectives will be:

a) to achieve an increasingly harmonious coexistence of humans and machines through an increasingly stronger integration between the two technologies

b) to extend the use of these tools to diversified industrial environments by analyzing from time to time, depending on the context, how the processing and presentation of data must take place

c) to increase the systems' performance in terms of data processing of current devices for their effective and efficient use in virtual environments

References

1. Karaaslan, E., Bagci, U., Catbas, F.N., Artificial Intelligence Assisted Infrastructure Assessment using Mixed Reality Systems. *Transp. Res. Rec.*, 2673, 12, 413–424, 2019.
2. Park, K.-B., Choi, S.H., Lee, J.Y., Ghasemi, Y., Mohammed, M., Jeong, H., Hands-Free Human–Robot Interaction Using Multimodal Gestures and

Deep Learning in Wearable Mixed Reality. *IEEE Access*, 9, 55448–55464, 2021.

3. Wang, S., Guo, R., Wang, H., Ma, Y., Zong, Z., Manufacture Assembly Fault Detection Method based on Deep Learning and Mixed Reality. *2018 IEEE International Conference on Information and Automation (ICIA)*, pp. 808–813, 2018.

4. Kästner, L., Frasineanu, V.C., Lambrecht, J., A 3D-Deep-Learning-based Augmented Reality Calibration Method for Robotic Environments using Depth Sensor Data. *2020 IEEE International Conference on Robotics and Automation (ICRA)*, vol. 8, pp. 1135–1141, 2020.

5. Kim, M., Choi, S.H., Park, K.-B., Lee, J.Y., A Hybrid Approach to Industrial Augmented Reality Using Deep Learning-Based Facility Segmentation and Depth Prediction. *Sensors*, 21, 1, 307, 2021.

6. Park, K.-B., Choi, S.H., Kim, M., Lee, J.Y., Deep learning-based mobile augmented reality for task assistance using 3D spatial mapping and snapshot-based RGB-D data. *Comput. Ind. Eng.*, 146, 106585, 2020.

7. Park, K.-B., Kim, M., Choi, S.H., Lee, J.Y., Deep learning-based smart task assistance in wearable augmented reality. *Rob. Comput.-Integr. Manuf.*, 63, 101887, 2020.

8. Wang, S., Zargar, S.A., Yuan, F.-G., Augmented reality for enhanced visual inspection through knowledge-based deep learning. *Struct. Health Monit.*, 20, 1, 426–442, 2021.

9. Židek, K., Piteľ, J., Balog, M., Hošovský, A., Hladký, V., Lazorík, P., Iakovets, A., Demčák, J., CNN Training Using 3D Virtual Models for Assisted Assembly with Mixed Reality and Collaborative Robots. *Appl. Sci.*, 11, 9, 4269, 2021.

10. Zhou, T., Zhu, Q., Du, J., Intuitive robot teleoperation for civil engineering operations with virtual reality and deep learning scene reconstruction. *Adv. Eng. Inf.*, 46, 101170, 2020.

11. McKendrick, M., Yang, S., McLeod, G.A., The use of artificial intelligence and robotics in regional anaesthesia. *Anaesthesia*, 76, S1, 171–181, 2021.

12. Francese, R., Frasca, M., Risi, M., Tortora, G., A mobile augmented reality application for supporting real-time skin lesion analysis based on deep learning. *J. Real-Time Image Process.*, 18, 4, 1247–1259, 2021.

13. Orciuoli, F., Orciuoli, F.J., Peduto, A., A Mobile Clinical DSS based on Augmented Reality and Deep Learning for the home cares of patients afflicted by bedsores. *Proc. Comput. Sci.*, 175, 181–188, 2020.

14. Tanzi, L., Piazzolla, P., Porpiglia, F., Vezzetti, E., Real-time deep learning semantic segmentation during intra-operative surgery for 3D augmented reality assistance. *Int. J. CARS*, 16, 9, 1435–1445, 2021.

15. Bhattarai, M., Jensen-Curtis, A.R., Martínez-Ramón, M., An embedded deep learning system for augmented reality in firefighting applications. *2020 19th IEEE International Conference on Machine Learning and Applications (ICMLA)*, pp. 1224–1230, 2020.

16. Heirman, J., Selleri, S., De Vleeschauwer, T., Hamesse, C., Bellemans, M., Schoofs, E., Haelterman, R., Exploring the possibilities of Extended Reality in the world of firefighting. *2020 IEEE International Conference on Artificial Intelligence and Virtual Reality (AIVR)*, pp. 266–273, 2020.

17. Limmer, M., Forster, J., Baudach, D., Schüle, F., Schweiger, R., Lensch, H.P.A., Robust Deep-Learning-Based Road-Prediction for Augmented Reality Navigation Systems at Night. *2016 IEEE 19th International Conference on Intelligent Transportation Systems (ITSC)*, pp. 1888–1895, 2016.

18. Cruz, E., Orts-Escolano, S., Gomez-Donoso, F., Rizo, C., Rangel, J.C., Mora, H., Cazorla, M., An augmented reality application for improving shopping experience in large retail stores. *Virtual Real.*, 23, 3, 281–291, 2019.

19. Khan, M.A., Israr, S., S Almogren, A., Din, I.U., Almogren, A., Rodrigues, J.J.P.C., Using augmented reality and deep learning to enhance Taxila Museum experience. *J. Real-Time Image Process.*, 18, 2, 321–332, 2021.

20. Li, X., Shan, Y., Chen, W. *et al.* Predicting user visual attention in virtual reality with a deep learning model. *Virtual Reality*, 25, 1123–1136, 2021. https://doi.org/10.1007/s10055-021-00512-7

21. Kido, D., Fukuda, T., Yabuki, N., Assessing future landscapes using enhanced mixed reality with semantic segmentation by deep learning. *Adv. Eng. Inf.*, 48, 101281, 2021.

22. Wienrich, C. and Latoschik, M.E., eXtended Artificial Intelligence: New Prospects of Human-AI Interaction Research. *Front. Virtual Real.*, 2, 94, 2021.

9

Extended Reality & The Backbone: Towards a 3D Mirrorworld

Jolanda G. Tromp[1,2]

¹Center for Visualization & Simulation (CVS), Duy Tan University, Da Nang, Viet Nam
²3D-DIANA, University of Malaga, Malaga, Spain

Abstract

Extended reality (XR) technologies are rapidly morphing together with Industry 4.0 cyberphysical twins, and multi-user games and game-engine developers' software, into a concept called the metaverse, enabled by the advancements of a breadth of graphics technology, including game engines, augmented reality (AR) wearables, real-world scans, and virtual reality (VR). The future XR metaverse runs on top of the internet backbone, similar to the world wide web, and connects and decentralizes AR and VR spaces and experiences. Whether this will be an open immersive network for entertainment, education, enterprise collaboration, group-gaming, and social gatherings, or a one-world walled garden, the XR metaverse will have to be built collaboratively by many developers and organizations, because it is to huge to be built by one organization alone. It has to be built in coordination, in order to make things interoperable, and the only way to achieve this is through collaboration and openness to create a shared innovation ecosystem. Open standards and open source are essential elements of the future of XR, enabling the future XR metaverse, which is so huge, and the implications of widespread adoption are so influential that we must create it together in cross-disciplinary, international collaboration and stay vigilant to mitigate the inherent risks to privacy and security.

Keywords: Extended reality, backbone, Industry 4.0, metaverse, open standards, open source

Email: jolanda.tromp@duytan.edu.vn

Mariano Alcañiz, Marco Sacco and Jolanda G. Tromp (eds.) Roadmapping Extended Reality: Fundamentals and Applications, (193–228) © 2022 Scrivener Publishing LLC

9.1   Introduction

The desire for visual storytelling, creating knowledge compendiums, and mirror worlds is as old as humankind. Advances in computing technologies are now making it possible to create real-time interactive eXtended reality (XR) shared user experiences, via computer-generated three-dimensional (3D) representations of the real world and all kinds of augmented reality (AR) or virtual reality (VR), mirror world (MW) simulations, in combination with artificial intelligence (AI), machine learning (ML), the blockchain and the 5G-enabled Internet of Things (IoT) facilitating 3D mixed reality (MR) spatial computing-enabled future scenarios of use. While the actual use-cases that will be enabled by the convergence of these technologies are still being explored, there is a substantial underlying data-economy that attracts the global tech giants to fight for monopoly and monopsony power. There is a potential for governments and companies to put data revenue growth before moral and ethical issues, turning the public resource Internet into a walled garden sensitive to surveillance, censorship, data manipulation, and security breaches. This raises urgent social and political questions that are reviewed here. The critical uncertainties of the key XR technologies are reviewed, and the implications for the success of XR are discussed in Section 9.2. The subsequent sections present a number of solutions: decentralization, Section 9.3; interoperability and the XR backbone, Section 9.4, open source and open standards, Section 9.5, which are summarized in the final section: future research and roadmap, Section 9.6.

9.1.1   Spatial Computing Paradigm Shift

The next few years are going to see many developments in terms of how we interact with computers. Firstly, the manner of access to the internet and virtual world is fragmenting, and no longer restricted to a personal computer on a desk or an expensive, cabled, cumbersome head-mounted display [1, 2]. User interfaces are shifting to wearables with speech control, projection on surfaces in the real world, removing the final friction of handheld and laptop computing, creating a hands-free mobility, rather than the current small-screen full-focus, full-attention-demanding devices that isolate the user's attention to the digital realm at the expense of their awareness of the physical realm. VR facilitates an immersive experience, allowing users to create and share digital experiences in an immersive world in real time. AR facilitates users to see the real world merged with computer-generated overlays of digital assets and animations, and learn from, interact with, and share the information in collaboration with other remote or co-located users in the physical world [3]. This allows many different use-cases, many of which have been unexplored, or undiscovered, and many of which are expected to affect business models, content types, and user experiences, which will emerge in many different settings, such as large scale, small scale, indoor, outdoor, wearable, handheld, embedded, hyper-personalized, hyper-localized, and globalized [4]. This will give rise to a huge diversification of hardware and software, and specialist developers.

Secondly, virtual 3D spaces allow us to organize and visualize information in new and more natural ways. Like the Microsoft Windows metaphor, using office space analogies to help users interact with digital data in the analogy of desktop, folders, and files, for storing documents in nested two dimensional (2D) or two and a half dimensional (2.5D) hierarchies, the 3D interaction paradigm extends this metaphor to allow us to interact with data similar to the physical world at large, with data landscapes, objects, layers, and macro and micro viewing. This extended physical space metaphor is expected to significantly reduce the mental effort involved in today's user experience of managing complex data sets, beyond locating a document in a folder on a drive. For long-distance collaboration and exploring 3D digital designs, we want shared viewing and communicating about 3D digital assets, in 3D shared spaces, and view real-time updates of the products and processes that produce the data, which is made possible by the 5G-enabled smart IoT, and the big data analysis enabled visualizations [5], and together, these are facilitating the future of mobile 3D spatial computing.

9.1.2   Historical Background of the XR Concept

We are now at a point in time where the basic technologies to make this complex concept a reality are coming of age and are converging. However, this 3D interaction paradigm is not new in terms of conceptualization [6–9]. A few notable early ideas are reviewed below.

In 1934, Otlet, a Belgian bibliographer and entrepreneur, conceived of a plan for a global network of "electric telescopes" that would allow anyone in the world access to a vast library of books, articles, photographs, audio recordings and films, wireless networks, speech recognition, and social network-like features that would allow individuals to "participate, applaud, give ovations, sing in the chorus," and described a mechanism for transmitting taste and smell [10]. Otlet imagined all these endeavors converging into a global knowledge network that he dubbed the Mundaneum, his vision of a utopian network: "Everything in the universe, and everything of man, would be registered at a distance as it was produced. In this way a moving image of the world will be established, a true mirror of his memory. From a distance, everyone will be able to read text, enlarged and limited to the desired subject, projected on an individual screen. In this way, everyone from his armchair will be able to contemplate the whole of creation, in whole or in certain parts" [11]. This is potentially the earliest description of the XR -enabled metaverse.

In 1935, Weinbaum presented what is considered the first fictional model for VR in his short story Pygmalion's Spectacles: a pair of goggles that enabled "a movie that gives one sight and sound [...] taste, smell, and touch. [...] You are in the story, you speak to the shadows (characters) and they reply, and instead of being on a screen, the story is all about you, and you are in it" [11]. This is potentially the earliest conception of MR or AR glasses.

In 1945, Bush conceived the Memex, an idea for an encyclopedia of the future having a mesh of associative trails running through it, akin to hyperlinks, stored in a memex system, a form of memory augmentation involving a microfilm-based "device in which an individual stores all his books, records, and communications, and which is mechanized so that it may be consulted with exceeding speed and flexibility. It is an enlarged intimate supplement to his memory" that could emulate the way the brain links data by association rather than by indexes and traditional, hierarchical storage paradigms, and be easily accessed as "a future device for individual use ... a sort of mechanized private file and library" in the shape of a desk [11]. The memex was also intended as a tool to study the brain itself. The concept of the memex inspired Nelson in the development of the early hypertext systems in 1965, which in turn inspired Berners–Lee to conceive of the World Wide Web in 1998.

In 1995, Microsoft released Bob, a custom version of Windows that was aimed at making it easier for new users to get around their computer by making it look like a "house" with "rooms," but in subsequent iterations of the Microsoft Windows Operating System (MS Windows OS), only the "virtual assistants" in MS Office, Clippy, a cartoon paperclip that pops up with hints and tips, and the MS Windows XP's little guide dog, was used.

Fast forward to the 21st century, Facebook launched a virtual-reality meeting service, Horizon Workrooms, where people gather remotely, wearing headsets and meeting as if they were physically there in an online virtual meeting space, with hand-tracking to allow them a precise pointer to write in the virtual space, to facilitate collaboration. Facebook announced recently that in five years, they would be a "metaverse company," declaring it the "successor to the mobile internet." They also recently announced international tests with prototype AR glasses, and launched Ray-Ban Stories, their first "smart glasses" featuring two cameras, a microphone, speaker, and voice assistant. Today, they announced that Meta is the new name for Facebook, and Horizon Worlds is the new name for Facebook Horizon and that they are removing support for Unity-based worlds, encouraging creators building with that game engine to seek release on the Oculus Store. Facebook lost a bid on Unity, one of a few world-leading real-time 2D and 3D development platforms, which instead went public on the stock market in late 2020. Meanwhile in 2017, Microsoft bought the social VR company and platform AltspaceVR, recently used as a pandemic solution for the internationally famous yearly Burning Man festival, generating a lot of international attention, and MS is currently heavily investing in "enterprise metaverse" solutions. NVIDIA launched Omniverse in 2021, a powerful, multiGraphics Processing Unit (multi-GPU), real-time simulation and collaboration platform for 3D production pipelines in collaboration with Pixar, based on Pixar's Universal Scene Description software. The 3D interface allows for a much more visual, spatial information storage and visualization space, the advantages of which are largely unexplored.

The Metaverse [12, 13] has currently become the popular concept and term for the notion of the 3D internet. The term was made popular by Stephenson [14] and went more mainstream recently via the 2018 Ready Player One movie, based on the book by Cline [15] with the 3D computer-generated virtual world called Oasis and the popularization of cryptocurrency trading, further discussed below. The conceptions of an XR-enabled metaverse came forth from the Cyberpunk Sci-Fi genre made popular in 1983 by Gibson [16] who called his computer-generated virtual world Cyberspace, a term that has since become the popular nickname for the internet. In Gibson's books, Cyberspace is a concept describing a widespread interconnected digital technology: "A consensual hallucination experienced daily by billions of legitimate operators, in every nation, by children being taught mathematical concepts... A graphic representation of data abstracted from the banks of every computer in the human system. Unthinkable complexity. Lines of light ranged in the nonspace of the mind, clusters and constellations of data. Like city lights, receding" [16]. Cyberpunk plots typically center on conflict among AIs, hackers, and megacorporations, set in a near-future dystopian Earth-based scenario.

9.1.3   Virtualization Drivers

Based on the current convergence of new technologies [17–21], users and smart machines are going to be increasingly more connected in a future 3D cyberspace of XR- enabled virtual or augmented world, based on spatial computing technologies, generating a network of 3D metaverses, a metaverse of metaverses, and a smart 3D world wide web. A virtualization of the real social world, educational institutes, and the workplace is already happening, and the COVID-19 pandemic has accelerated this pre-existing trend, which may well continue in case further infectious disease control measures are needed. This points at the compelling health and safety need to create long-term remote schooling and work solutions. In addition to this compelling health and safety use-case of long-distance collaboration mediated by XR, there are several compelling business-innovation, eco-innovation, and social-innovation imperatives and incentives for the creation of this interconnected series of virtual worlds, which are reviewed below.

The breakthrough value of the future XR metaverse lies in the ability to visualize and interact with real-time data from integrated smart IoT-enabled digital assets in various use-cases, in real time throughout our daily personal and production chain practices, and viewing them together with the associated data, these practices produce in 3D computer-generated contextual simulations. For instance, big data about cities are projected onto 3D digital replicas of those cityscapes at the source of the data; big data about the body are visualized on the virtual or real body on the location on the body of the source of the data. Changes in the data, fictional or factual, can be visualized in real time, and the user is provided with a dashboard to monitor and control the multitude of interacting data-producing devices. The XR space provides the context, the basic space within which multiple users can view, drive, control, and optimize the physical processes, not only for the virtual representations, but also for the physical item. For instance, the remote control of a robot or camera drone. This spatial mapping concept has been popularized under diverse terms such as spatial computing, cyber-physics twins, mirrorworlds, mechatronics, and Industry 4.0. The integration, visualization, and data-informed predictions can facilitate faster customization and responsiveness to breakdowns and data-informed predictions to drive management decisions. The digital transformation of manufacturing/production and related industries enables value creation data analytics that can help improve processes' products and the means of production, when machines get networked and have the IoT-enabled intelligence to 'communicate', creating new ways of production, value creation, and real-time optimization [22, 23], with potentially exponential improvements.

The benefits of economies of scale that made centralized production in remote locations away from the actual market profitable, have come to the end, and the resulting global supply chains as we have known them, have also come to the end due to the global need to reduce the CO_2 pollution associated with the industry and society we had before the pandemic and global sustainability crisis [31, 32]. Centralized production and long-distance global supply-chains have also demonstrated severe shortcomings during the COVID-19 pandemic, where the risk of having a production site that is geographically distant from its market increased, from logistics costs, supply chain disruption, increased potential exposure, and the transmission of the virus cross-borders, etc. Production units are forecast to become smaller and versatile, making multiplication efficient, which magnifies the need for new tools to do efficient simulation and visualization, ensuring rapid expansions for a range of products and the associated production units [33]. This type of agile production environment needs rapid 3D group visualization and prototyping tools, with flexible access for multiple users, all along the supply-chain, interacting together with the digital representations, with real-time capabilities. Using XR, a new global virtual production chain is enabled, which can significantly reduce the need to use the old-style CO_2-polluting supply-chain model. The opportunities of virtual supply chain substitutes are largely unexplored.

Generative design is a new AI & ML-driven rapid design iteration and optimization process supervised by a human designer, and additive manufacturing is a rapid physical prototyping technique using 3D printing. These will most likely have widespread impact on the future of manufacturing and the global supply-chain models. With XR, there is no need for prototypes to be built physically: in a virtual environment, different configurations can be tested and explored by physically and geographically dispersed production teams and the buyers of the products. AR and VR enables buyers and mechanics to preview the new designs on location and analyze fit and efficiency before any physical model has been produced, transported into place, or traveling to the production showroom, saving vast amounts of resources, and contributing to a reduction in CO_2 related to the old way of design and procurement.

Finally, the current design-brief that design engineers are tasked with, is to maximize carry-over ratios from one project to the other, and this does not apply to generative-designed additive-manufactured parts. Generative design and additive manufacturing have the potential to be more cost-effective. This is especially relevant, considering the trend for personalized customization that is becoming in high demand, creating the need for rapid, realistic, and real-time visualization tools that function flexibly and are remotely accessible and editable in multi-user 3D digital collaboration-enabled spaces, a function envisioned for the future XR-enabled Metaverse.

There are clearly a great number of virtualization drivers, and there is clearly a great advantage on many levels and great potential on many levels for XR technologies, and many unexplored use-cases. Additionally, when XR technology solutions are being used, users' demand will start to influence design ideas and new ways of using XR-enabled technology solutions will become apparent. To enable these solutions, there are a number of critical uncertainties that have to be addressed first. These uncertainties will influence the potential for success of XR solutions. The next section will give a breakdown of the key XR technologies and the critical uncertainties involved.

9.2   Critical Uncertainties for the Future of XR

There are four key XR-enabled Metaverse technology components: Virtual Reality, Augmented Reality, Mirrorworlds, and the User and Usage Data and Cloud processing, Smart *et al.* [9], see Figure 9.1. These key components have associated critical uncertainties that will affect the success of XR. There are two key continua that influence the way in which the XR enabled-Metaverse technologies are developing: 1) the spectrum ranging from augmentations to simulations, and 2) the spectrum ranging from intimate (identity focused) to external (world focused), see Figure 9.1 [9]. The continua augmentation–simulation,

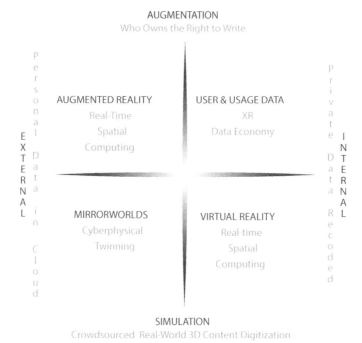

Figure 9.1 XR metaverse roadmap diagram (adapted from Smart *et al.*, 2007).

and intimate–external represent a spectrum of critical uncertainties, because exactly how things are evolving is a process that has just started.

Smart *et al.* [9] make a useful distinction between the different technologies that are part of the future Metaverse vision in their extensive report based on a cross-industry public foresight project with $100K funding, the "Metaverse Roadmap." This research was conducted in 2007 and many anticipated changes have taken place, and these are reviewed below (updated in terms of adding latest technology developments SLAM and cloud data processing). However, with the advances in XR technology and the mainstream adoption that is taking place, adequate solutions for the critical uncertainties for XR success have now become urgent.

The open issues are discussed below by looking at how these critical uncertainties affect the four key XR metaverse components in the current 2021 technology convergence. The four key XR metaverse components and the critical uncertainties are discussed below in terms of the latest technology developments and what the implications are for further development and the future XR metaverse.

9.2.1   VR and AR: Real-Time Spatial Computing

XR technologies rely on real-time engines, and spatial computing technology, to enable the ability to associate location in space [24], using: 1) SLAM (Simultaneously Locating and Mapping) technologies, to track a user's body and surrounding objects in space as it moves and reorients via cameras and sensors, and 2) the "AR cloud," the concept of a networked database with locative metadata and a store of 3D animations, delegating a lot of data processing to the cloud, in order to keep the form factor of the XR device as light and small as possible. SLAM advances since 2007 (the year of the report by Smart *et al.* [9]), are notable: 360° photogrammetry, videogrammetry, and LiDAR (light or laser imaging detection and ranging) technologies have started to be used to create texturing for simulations based in real-world 360° physically based capturing and rendering, which can greatly speed up the creation of 3D computer graphics for the building of mirrorworlds. Additionally, since 2007, there have been significant advances in cloud computing technologies and IoT technologies. Cloud computing has started facilitating the increasingly more voluminous user-generated data and machine-generated data, to be processed and stored in the cloud, i.e., servers on the internet, and the form factor of XR equipment is becoming lighter and smaller because a lot of data processing is relegated to the cloud rather than restricted to the device itself. Virtual environments need awareness of the real world to help the user to avoid bumping into real-world objects, and AR needs a much deeper awareness and connection to the objects in the real world. The data privacy and security that the VR and AR systems collect are poorly regulated due to the novelty of the technology, leading to all kinds of potentially dystopian scenarios for the future of XR, further discussed below.

9.2.2   Mirrorworlds: Cyberphysical Twinning

Mirrorsworlds or cyberphysical twin systems combine VR and AR technologies with IoT, AI, and ML, to show and control how to connect the operational technologies with the information technologies. Connecting smart objects and being able to visualize and interact with them from a distance, enable new kinds of use-cases for human–machine collaboration, machine–machine interaction, and machine–real world object manipulation, unlocking the synchronization and optimization of work processes and worksites. This facilitates humans to move from procedural tasks to knowledge tasks and allows humans to do what they still do better than AI-enabled robots: creative problem- solving. Automated warehouse operations are cutting-edge examples of these technologies.

Building the bridge between the physical and the digital world is a complex multifaceted and multidisciplinary challenge [25, 26]. The overarching challenge is to digitize every centimeter of the world, semantically attribute it, and make it open, easy, and accessible. A digital scan of the real world needs to happen and will happen as part of the XR metaverse. It is a massive challenge and needs a lot of pilot solutions with real world data and the ability to process that data and stream it over the internet. If we can digitize the world at scale, the cost of content creation will go down significantly because of the reusability factor.

9.2.3   User and Usage Data: The New XR Data Economy

Digital user behaviors are creating unique patterns of activity, and hyper-personal digital data, allowing data analysts to observe user-choices, and further optimize their processes and products and influence user engagement. More usage means more data. More data mean more knowledge on how to improve the algorithms for personalized information selection; improvements to the design; and improvements to the attractiveness of the product, service, or sales offerings. Via the accretion of that data, behavioral patterns can be analyzed, making that data potentially as valuable as oil or gold, creating a data economy, and prompting huge investments in Customer eXperience (CX) measurements with XR Head-Mounted

Display (HMD) with biosensor technologies. Firms build profiles out of this surveillance data and use it to create a feedback loop that is designed to increase user engagement, and make people come back as much as possible, for as long as possible. These ever-more personalized data patterns are the commodity sought after by vendors, data analysts, marketeers, governments, and hackers, and already the carelessness or disregard of the privacy of that data has been creating security breaches, data hijackings, and broad concerns about potentially dystopian futures.

Clearly, the XR metaverse is an economy, not just a brokering space for games. Actually, it is an economy of economies of economies and a shift away from the way we work and organize ourselves and our societies so far [48]:

- **The global data economy:** This is an opportunity to track historic data in a way we have never been able to track and analyze it before.
- **The societal data economy:** Early adopters are creating training data through their activities, not just for current system optimizations, but also for future systems and for optimizing everything from climate change, to how we do things and live and use resources.
- **The personal data economy:** The metaverse will allow people to operate online to sell goods and create digital wares.

Rapid advances in the e-commerce blockchain and cryptocurrency technologies are allowing developers to monetize their creations, and trade and sell them inside, outside, and between different virtual worlds and in the real world. XR development skills training is in high demand, and more affordable training that is open to anyone, is essential to fulfil the demand for skilled XR operators and developers [53–57]. Content consumers are often fascinated with the opportunity to create their own 3D content and see it as an opportunity to learn a new trade.

A recent development in the cryptocurrency field is the non-fungible token (NFT), initially developed to sell unique art items, and rapidly expanding to include digital art and items to be used by digital avatars in digital space. This enables developers of digital items for digital spaces, to create and trade, uniquely owned user experiences and interactions, facilitating a new online economy, and the transfer of digital goods across digital worlds. It is to be expected that users, once they have purchased a digital asset, want to take that with them from one virtual world to another, rather than having to purchase a similar item in each of these worlds, leading to the need for a cloud-based backbone, interoperability, and standardization, meaning in this case, to be able to seamlessly travel from one virtual world to another, with the same virtual assets. For example, Dolce & Gabbana recently announced a new collection of fashion items that can be purchased as NFTs and worn by digital avatars. The NFT has the potential to empower the end-user, because it enables them to own their own data and monetize them.

During the early days of the information superhighway developments, it did not take long for the media and telecommunications giants to understand that user interactions leave a digital trail, and that the users' interest in and valuation of a product or service can be assessed and grown because of the collection and analysis of the data from a user's interaction with it, and started the aim to control this pervasive data network. The notion of a 3D internet-based XR metaverse where user behavior can be recorded, in response to the recent upsurge of emerging technologies to make it possible, is again attracting the media and telecommunication giants, businesses, investors, private developers and traders, governments, cyber-security, and standards organizations. While in this report of 2017, it was noted as "an emerging concern for once the market for XR products would grow, to implement policy measures regarding privacy and ethics of XR data collection" [52], we have now reached that point in time where there is a need for urgent public discussions about the implications and additional global and local regulations. These types of public and legal acceptance and trust-facilitating measures are influential in forming and shaping the XR backbone over time.

9.2.4   Augmentation: The Right to Write

The augmentation of the real world is leading to large questions regarding AR annotations on our physical space: who is allowed to map augmentations on a private property? Who decides or controls what augmented annotations go where and why? Limiting the power of data collecting and space mapping tech companies, and surveillance capitalism [27], is vital and will depend on the currently emerging global discussions, disagreements, and emergent regulations over the years to come.

According to Pesce and Parisi [28] the fathers of the Virtual Reality Markup Language (VRML), we need urgent arbitration for the emerging AR Right to Write. "Who has the right to speak for a volume of space? When AR is deployed more broadly, the systems will be able to annotate space at scale. There are already commercial approaches to the Right to Write. There are three systems already in place and probably already more than that by now. They take that right and place it entirely inside a commercial context. Microsoft systems has developed a spatial language Azure Spatial Anchors, and that is built into all their Hololens products, which allows you to store your spatial language either privately or publicly inside the device. Google has its ARCore Cloud Anchors that provides the same service for the ARCore augmented reality platform inside it. Apple has its own AR Kit Location Anchors. Each of these private systems has their own private interface to space and the location of metadata in space. None of these systems respects the boundaries of each other, and none of these systems are inherently designed to respect the privacy or the boundaries of the property in which they are locating metadata. It is time to develop regulations and guidelines build into the basic design of these systems" [28].

Pesce [29] proposed a Mixed Reality Service[1], a position statement submitted to the W3C Workshop on the Web and Virtual Reality[2], which is a way of being to permission a space. It acts as an analogue to DNS. DNS converts names into numbers, while MRS converts locations or coordinates into Universal Resource Identifiers, which can present a list of ownerships and permissions, which can then be used by any software to render the locative metadata or to either present or forbid the presentation, or to publish or forbid the publishing of the locative metadata inside of a space. It is possible to conceive these systems, but we are going to need them at scale by the time there are millions or tens of millions or hundreds of millions of spectacle-type AR devices operating around the world, which could be the case by 2030 or, at the latest, 2035 [29]. Pesce predicts that we have a limited amount of time to get all the work done, get these systems out, get them tested, and have them deployed at scale.

9.2.5   Simulation: Crowdsourcing Real World 3D Digital Content

Capturing the world in realistic detail is a massive job and not something that one person, or team, or company can do alone. In recognition of this, Epic Games is working on making the underlaying technologies accessible, not just the asset library, to give anyone the autonomy to easily digitize anything, whether that is a professional photographer with high-end equipment or an enthusiast with a smartphone camera, so that anyone should have the ability to bring anything scanned in the real world, into the digital world at good quality that is indistinguishable from reality [46].

Epic Games started developing the hardware, software, and team necessary to scan photorealistic 3D content and make it accessible for everyone in the form of a public digital library of ready-made assets, 10 years ago on a mission to scan the world. The output from capturing the real world

---

[1]https://medium.com/ghvr/mixed-reality-service-ce469783fd68
[2]https://www.w3.org/2016/06/vr-workshop/slides/mixed-reality-service.pdf

are the building blocks needed to build any other digital scene, using any game engine and sets of these scans, to compose an interactive real-time environment or, in the case of virtual production, using the same scans with gITF technology, merging the physical and scanned sets, physically immersing creators in the digital world. Currently, they have a team of 200 collaborators, spread across the globe, building this library and scan production technology, and capturing everything from complete biomes to urban environments, processed into individual assets.

Scanning the world key challenges to resolve, according to Bergsman [46]:

1. High-quality scanning for the smartphone.
2. Scan processing needs to be automated in the cloud.
3. Final content standardized in terms of quality, texture density, adding categorization information, unified delivery systems, etc.
4. The creation of digital worlds using the scan library should be easier than building with Lego blocks, using swarming technology and procedural placement systems.
5. Develop a comprehensive scanning field guide and news series to help educate the next generation of adventurers and learn how they can take part.

Cesium is working toward bridging the gap between the digital and physical world, seamlessly merging both, using the concept of 3D tiles, a spatial index for subdividing and tiling massive global-scale 3D content, which enables creating semantically annotated, rich digital representations, to replicate every detail down to the millimeter [26]. They aim to facilitate the adoption of 3D tiles and gITF for the XR metaverse, for all engines and platforms, via various open networks, investing heavily into powerful open-source runtime engines and libraries to enable all developers and platforms to integrate 3D tiles and make 3D tiles the best and easiest way to bring scalable real-world 3D content to all platforms. They also give developers access to the content pipelines that enable creators to process data into 3D tiles, while adding to the state of VR, tiling optimization, and compression to take full advantage of what the data is and how to stream it optimized for the devices of the future, making rich metaverse experiences with real-world location and data as frictionless as possible. Their aim is to enable everybody through advancing open 3D standards, open-source runtime engines and libraries, and content pipelines for open 3D formats, supporting and building an active ecosystem of education, collaboration, and community.

The most impactful challenges in terms of a digital scan of the world are summarized as follows [26]:

1. Capturing the real world: photogrammetry at global scale, and open and accessible 3D data
2. Content pipelines: pipelines for 3D and semantics using AI and ML, game-like visual quality and performance, easy and accessible creator tools
3. Runtime and engines: compression algorithms and interoperability, building the ecosystem with 3D tiles and gITF

Early in 2021, Facebook bought Scape Technologies, an AR startup whose aim was to create a 3D map of the whole world. The game developer Niantic just bought the AR maps startup 6D.ai, and it is building a dynamic 3D map of the world to enable new kinds of planet-scale AR experiences. Niantic uses crowd-sourced data collection designs, involving the users and their devices in creating scans of their surroundings. There is value in the ability to create a real-time dynamic spatial index, continuously updated and amplified by users, allowing 3D maps to recognize when things have changed and update themselves automatically. In 2012, they launched Ingress, where players had to upload photos of locations of interest, which became portals within the game, and those geolocations were later used for their AR game Pokémon Go and other games. For their latest game, Harry Potter: Wizards Unite, users' devices are collecting 3D location scans every 5 sec. The 3D scans make it easier for 3D developers to make shared experiences and environmental augmentations that can persist even if the user who generated them has left from the scene. Additionally, there is great value in the data collected from the users' behavior in space and over time, because these spatial behavioral data can function as a training data for AI/ML to learn to detect intimate individual behavioral patterns [30].

9.2.6 Intimate Technologies: Private Biodata Recording and Processing

Intimate technologies are focused inward, aimed at the individual user or object. VR and AR technologies are increasingly combined with eye-tracking, opening new areas of application in which visual perception and related cognitive processes can be studied and gaze detection is already used to fine-tune the user experience feedback loop. Eye tracking allows the device to record the direction of the eye gaze for each eye, blinking patterns, positional eye information, eye status, and pupil properties such as dilation, unique iris characteristics, and facial attributes such as wrinkles, skin color, and facial expressions, thus not only measuring the user's view direction and precise location and object that the user is gazing at, but also potentially providing unique user information such as personality traits, mental health, skills and abilities, sleepiness, drug consumption, age, ethnic background, physical health, gender, and mental workload[3].

In addition to the eye-tracking, HMDs can have EEG and galvanic skin response sensors built into the headset and collect even more detailed brain and body activities. While this information can be used for XR cognitive and physical rehabilitation, and brain–computer interfaces (BCIs), the concern remains that huge amounts of biometric data from the user are being streamed from the camera and sensors facing inward in the HMD can be collected, meaning that private data that uniquely identify the user can be stored and analyzed automatically, outside of the users' direct access or control. At the very minimum, the users of the HMD biodata-collecting devices should be duly notified of the recording activities and how to control the data-streaming and permissions, and a public debate of the privacy issues is necessary [35, 36].

9.2.7   External Technologies: Personal Data in the Cloud

External technologies are focused outward, aimed at the world at large, the implications of which are further discussed. The outwards-facing surveillance sensors that are built into VR and AR HMDs, map our homes, workspaces, and cities, and the inward-facing surveillance sensors in the HMDs, and sousveillance bio-data collecting personal devices and smart IoT-driven objects in the environment, capture our private data. Together, these technologies are creating an omnidirectional panopticon of deeply networked personal data collection facilitation unlike anything we have created before, capturing data that are potentially directly streamed into the device manufacturer's service cloud, without user control. Regulations are urgently needed to decide who owns that data; why should it leave the user's device? [34].

9.3   XR and Decentralization: Blockchain Infrastructure

A 3D global XR metaverse needs to be modular, so that all developers can plug in their creations, facilitating the natural growth of a large metaverse of metaverses that can intercommunicate to evolve [37]. To achieve this modular metaverse, it needs to be based on open standards, so that we can all share, create, interact, and work together to create and interact in these virtual worlds, similar to how the world wide web evolved. What we

---

[3]https://xrsi.org/definition/biometrically-inferred-data-bid

have learned from developing the web is that decentralized technology is fundamental to this, and that at the same time, having hubs is important, because it allows these different hubs unlimited scalability, plugging into the fabric we currently know as the web. For instance, we do not go to one place to consume videos, the news, and social media; we go to several different places that act as a hub [37].

Decentralization will allow the XR metaverse to consist of multiple interconnected worlds, some of them controlled by companies, and some built by the users, some highly detailed, glossy, and polished, some experimental and consisting of rough prototypes, and all accessible in a similar way to how we access a Universal Resource Locator (URL) or Internet Protocol (IP) address, rather than one proprietary metaverse, with one look, one economy, and one set of rules, controlled by one tech giant [28]. If not decentralized, the final user experience could become one place in a "walled garden," where a single company benefits, especially if they sell their own proprietary software and hardware as an exclusive way to enter these virtual space, with one identity and shape, and one set of rules, giving the company a lot of power to shape the online experiences and information exposure of their users [28].

There are several decentralizing forces emerging through advances in the fields of the smart IoT combined with 5G technology, which can now pass through 20 GB per second, allowing operational technologies to communicate with information technologies, and the blockchain facilitating a secure way for individuals to deal directly with each other, without an intermediary like a government, bank, or other third party.

A modular XR metaverse is essential to rapid evolution, with elements that plug in and become part of the experience [37]. In terms of graphics, we currently have Unreal Engine, Unity, Open Source 3D Engine (O3DE), Omniverse, etc. In terms of distributed cloud computing services, which host some of the AI, we currently have AWS, Azure, and GCP. In terms of advertising and social networks, we currently have Applovin, Adcolony, Facebook, and Snapchat. And in terms of innovative gameplay and scientific simulations, we currently have game studios, digital twin developments, and scientific research.

XR developers in different industries are currently already using amazing tools, suited to their workflows, which should not be replaced. Instead, things should be additive, taking things that work well, and enhancing them by connecting them together through open standards. Once that connection exists, that opens new opportunities to add new things, utilizing the NVIDIA rendering and physics power, adding them to the existing tools and workflows people already have [38].

In the early 1990s, the term information superhighway became popular to describe the emerging internet, the digital backbone that was expected to become the communication channel for commerce, collaboration, and entertainment. The internet that evolved developed into an open and proprietary network of networks, and the emerging world wide web functions as a decentralizing technology, allowing any company or institution to profile itself and its wares, and eventually enabling citizens to add their voice and ideas to a globalized conversation and commerce platform, consisting of a limitless number of places, purposes, and products, accessible via all kinds of browsers, apps and devices, virtual shopfronts, and themed member groups. These technologies provide the backbone of the information superhighway that we know now, also popularly referred to as cyberspace, enabling an infinite ever-changing marketplace, sharing, and experiencing information and items in the virtual and real world, accessible as a parallel digital world of information and social connections.

Similar to the early visions of the information superhighway, early visions of a 3D internet version started emerging, and as early as 1994, the first version of VRML was developed, the 3D modeling language that builds on top of Hypertext Markup Language (HTML), the world wide web modeling language. It was inspired by the text-based virtual social networked adventure games of the 1990s, called Multi User Dungeons (MUDs) and Multi User Dungeons Object Oriented (MOOs) [39], which anyone could start if they had access to a server connected to the internet and open it to anyone with the IP address to enter it, made popular by a myriad of international users and different themed versions, each with their own internal regulations and economies, distributed across the internet backbone.

From the beginning of the web and HTML 1.0, we have been adding many standards, including WebGL, reaching HTML 5, which make it possible for different browsers to display content in the same way and enable all the different apps we have in 2021 [38]. WebGL allows us to include lightweight 3D representations in the 2D web. However, for the future XR Metaverse, it is not sufficient to put 3D into the 2D web; we need a full 3D web and embed the 2D web inside it, and to be able to build this, we need new standards [38]. For instance, there is a big difference between the documents we have in the 2D web, versus the 3D web, and the data sets and data sizes are much larger. We need an incremental core, a backbone engine that can communicate the differences and the things that change in the 3D world, unlike the 2D web, where you can simply reload the webpage. This new backbone is not a single proprietary killer-app, owned by one company, but a series of backbone technologies, evolving into a new paradigm for global computing [40]. See LAMINA1 by Neal Stephenson*.

---

*https://discord.gg/lamina1

9.4 XR and the Backbone: Enabling Critical Functionalities

The critical functionalities to support the growth of XR to a global scale are: interoperability functionality and standards, and a more precise taxonomy. The XR-enabled metaverse, 3D-pervasive world-scale virtual mirror spaces and augmentations of real spaces, will have many use-cases, some proprietary and some open, some unique, some overlapping, with people, objects, services, businesses, and events, taking place in multiple, interconnected virtual and augmented spaces. From a technological point of view, we are still developing the hardware and software to run systems at scale, meaning that virtual spaces will continue to have a hardware/software-dictated capped amount of active users at one time in one virtual space. We need a lot of virtual spaces, with different functions, connected and part of a bigger virtual world, and all these nested virtual spaces are accessible via nodes on the internet. We want our avatar to be aware of the different worlds and receive updates from all those spaces and worlds, and we want to take our avatar, our tools and inventory with us when we teleport from one world to another.

While the functionalities and purposes of different virtual worlds and AR apps will differ depending on the goal of the applications, there are four critical design constants, at the experiential and functional level in common for all users: the social (people), semantic (objects), architectural (spaces), and time–space changes of the actors (people and objects), for which interoperability is essential [42]. Everything that exists on these levels is affected by time passing and spatial changes of/in itself, avatars, objects, and data-changing state or behavior, moving in space, in a world that is constantly updating for each user that is sharing the scene and influencing it [41]. These critical backbone functionalities are reviewed in the following sections.

9.4.1 Social Level: XR Metaverse Populated by Users and Digital Agents

The XR metaverse is populated by users, and AI-driven virtual agents. Users and agents can take on any number of different virtual representations, or avatars, not necessarily humanoid, and they can interact with each other via virtual body animations that can be controlled by the user or the AI that drives the agent. Users want a dashboard where they can define their own look and behaviors based on computer-animated behavioral sequences, and they may want to define the character, look, and behaviors of autonomously animated virtual agents. Users can interact with them or employ them for any number of tasks. For instance, an agent could represent them or their company at virtual meetings, using a script of commonly asked questions and responses and signal the user if unscripted actions are needed. Virtual worlds can run a huge amount of these autonomously animated digital humanoids simultaneously, and users want to create personalized interactions and experiences for each one individually or as a group. Due to the effort and potential costs involved in defining these characters and their behaviors, users need them to be interoperable across different virtual worlds. This means that they need to be able to take their virtual body and virtual agents from one virtual world to another, and maintain continuity across these different worlds, so that the same knowledge and behaviors are available in these different worlds, and these different entities need to be able to stay interconnected, potentially in a peer-to-peer way, for instance, while they act as digital assistants on your behalf across different virtual worlds [43].

Autonomous humans have to be interoperable on different platforms and aware of both 2D and 3D content, run on all platforms, have standardized behavior formats, be able to adapt to different languages and culturally appropriate styles of interaction, have different and configurable personalities, have the digital characters connect with different devices, transverse different digital worlds while maintaining continuity, interconnect in a potentially peer-to-peer way, have personal digital assistant functionality, create and populate the XR metaverse at scale with autonomous virtual agents [43].

Using AI, ML, and 3D simulations of the digital agent and virtual world, huge advances are being made in increasing the autonomous intelligence of future agents. For instance, BabyX was developed by Soul Machines [44], a fully autonomous virtual human that can learn and have behaviors like a real person, starting with a clean slate, like how a baby learns, based on a biological approach of learning about the world, using digital intelligence. The animation is driven from the inside out, in the same way that our brain animates us, and BabyX's behaviors and decisions are made internally to drive what it does [43]. Users need rules and regulations for conduct and privacy, awareness, and the ability to design and adapt our own virtual representations and those of the digital agents that we own or interact with.

9.4.2   Objects Level: XR Metaverse Objects and Semantic Infrastructure

3D real and virtual objects need associated attributes and behaviors that are portable between different virtual worlds and can adapt to those different worlds and communicate with other. Developers are trying to figure out how to bring an object purchased in one virtual world to another world so that it can be used there too, as well as how to make objects from virtual worlds interconnect and overlap with functional IoT-enabled and non-functional objects in the real world, and how they and the users could be enabled to interact with the real-world objects from the virtual world, or at the very least avoid crashing into objects in the real world that surround the user's physical body [45]. To build that awareness, we need interoperability for the 3D assets in terms of attributes and behaviors, so that not only the 3D asset is reproduced in other virtual worlds, but the attributes and behaviors are also inherited and functional in these other virtual worlds.

Additionally, mixing and overlapping the real world and the virtual world requires dealing with all kinds of IoT sensor input from objects in the real world, which is sent to the virtual world and vice versa. Developers want to make content that can make sense of these data in a virtual world, that allows the virtual world and virtual users to be aware of and react to it, so that content becomes feedback and send information that needs to come back into the real world, and vice versa. Currently, there is no common way to define attributes and behaviors on top of these assets and the infrastructure to make it possible is still being researched and developed [45]. It will pose huge computing challenges to bring IoT services to the masses, at the level and ubiquity of the current world wide web, considering that the future Internet of Everything is expected to be 50–100 times bigger than the current Internet, and the users and environments interacted on/with by dynamic IoT services evolve constantly. The internet of smart things is the enabling the pillar of digitizing everything, because "Things" are embedded in the systems, with the capability of collecting data, and passing data on, and being controlled by users. The ability to visualize the IoT services, in the situation they are collected from and that adapts and controls them, in a virtual or augmented world setting, provides the context to the services, and this contextualization plays a significant role in enhancing the user experience of these MR, on-demand, real-time, personalized experiences, which has not been fully explored yet.

9.4.3 Architectural Level: XR Metaverse Spaces

Users navigate and assign functions to spaces, both in the real world and the virtual world, and need the ability to locate information in space. The XR metaverse consists of multiple virtual worlds, where each virtual world is made of one or more interconnected spaces, some open and available to anyone and some private closed spaces, and other spaces may constantly change as they are pre-visualization and design testing spaces for all kinds of industrial and manufacturing prototypes and these spaces are experimental and simple in terms of decorations, while other spaces and worlds are glossy and highly detailed in terms of architectural design and décor. Some are going to be realistic and mirror the real world spaces, other spaces are going to be fantasy based, or depict futuristic scenarios that do not have a counterpart in the real world. The current challenge is to allow users to be developers, and facilitate developers to create spaces rapidly and collaboratively, and define interoperability so that spaces can be reused and recycled between virtual worlds, and so that a space or structure created or purchased in one virtual world, can be uploaded to another world and used there too.

Currently, there is an interoperability challenge for architects and industrial designers who want to use their 3D Building Information Modeling (BIM) or Computer-Aided Design (CAD) models in VR or AR, in terms of model complexity incompatibilities. There are market-ready systems that can import BIM and CAD software 3D modeling data and automatically convert it to 3D models that can be displayed in AR or VR applications. However, the associated functionality or animation of the 3D models for AR or VR is not something that is automatically added, nor something that an industry 3D architecture or industrial modeler would typically know or develop as part of their current education or skill set. The BIM or CAD model is much more complex than a typical XR model for a multi-user interactive experience would be, because it can. However, the complexity of the 3D model makes it more difficult for the real-time engine to render everything. Reducing the complexity of the 3D models is a skilled, manual and time-consuming process because the interoperability between the BIM, CAD and XR real-time engines is currently still very limited in customization.

Additionally, the XR real-time engine would need to provide the proprietary control that is strongly essential to the competitive environment in which these cross-disciplinary industries operate. These challenges are caused partly by the fact that XR development is not a mainstream skill in industry yet, and there is a lack of XR experts who are knowledgeable about the interoperability issues involved in these processes, further exacerbated by the variety of traditional and newly emerging software platforms, with most existing 3D data modeling software platforms not designed for interactivity or visualization aesthetics in a platform different from the one the models were created with. This means that the production pipeline for industry models in XR is more complex than necessary and interoperability standards are not only essential, but also complex to create due to the cross-disciplinary nature of the interoperability between industry and the XR real-time engines that exist today.

9.4.4   Space–Time Continuum: Dynamically Changing and Configurable Infrastructure

There is huge potential for new use-cases where digital twins and human doppelgänger avatars exist in the parallel metaverse and behave according to your instructions, but learning faster than you personally ever could, from the interaction data, your preferences, and its own behavioral data analyses. Digital agents would be able to access the information about the surrounding world, and digest it to optimize a user's choices and opportunities. To be able to visualize, simulate, monitor, or access virtual, real, or MR IoT-enabled devices and other user and usage data, using a VR- or AR-based control dashboard, we can record, analyze, understand, and regulate information access, and manage the permissions, security, and privacy regulations to control our data sharing. A huge impact on the way we work and organize our time has been predicted, in ways that are subject to the natural evolution of user demand and creativity.

A few functionalities that will become very useful are being in two places at once [4], with a digital agent that represents you; teleporting between virtual worlds, when your digital agent alerts you if you are needed there; moving in time, not only is it possible to move back in time, moving into the past and reviewing past occurrences in much more detail than the human mind is typically able to recall, but we can also move forward in time, moving into all kinds of hypothetical future scenarios via virtual simulations, while physically remaining in the same place and time [4] and dynamically viewing a changing data landscape as you browse or work in collaboration with remote colleagues via the 3D-enabled internet [47].

According to Perey [4], an important aspect is reality capture and how we can put reality in a very distributed hyperlocal concept and edge computing service. Location is the critical glue for the XR metaverse, because the need to link to geospatial location is fundamental for the functioning of personalized services [4]. Individual experiences will be unique to that person, at that place and point in time and reproduced from their perspective. One of the things that will be important to resolve is individual-user-controlled, real-time continuous contextual search throughout multiple virtual worlds and in stored past virtual events [4].

Richter [48] studies historic datasets for In-Q-Tel, a non-profit venture capital firm and think-tank, which started 20 years ago, initially by the central intelligence agency (CIA) of the USA, and now represents all kinds of different US intelligence agencies and their allies, and all of whom invest in future technologies, not just for their current national security mission, but also for the future of security at large, and international security. Her research informs the think-tank division, who is trying to figure out what comes next and where to invest in future technologies, to encourage it and shape it.

In-Q-Tel are working on how digitization and visualization of space and time, is shifting how we know what we know about the world, on the intersection between the metaverse, smart interactive environments, smart city spaces, smart houses, and how it is changing our physical world, our physical form, our personalities, and our workforce, turning into data economies, where everything about you is known, by tracking all of your different digital personalities, your environment, and your digital interactions. This kind of surveillance is unlike anything we have seen before [48].

One of the most important observations is that there is the beginning of the development of two types of metaverses in terms of ubiquitous surveillance policies and privacy management: a totalitarian one and a democratic one [48]. According to Richter's [48] research, Australia is leading the democratic campaign in terms of early regulation and early policy for getting data sets to talk to each other, for getting data privacy pieces in place, which is going to be important for the future metaverse, and they are setting a useful template for the rest of the world doing development in this area.

9.5   XR Open Sharing and Interoperability

The role of openness for the future XR metaverse developments is that it benefits the corporate and community interests, where each organization improves the XR metaverse experience through their focused disciplines, allowing the implementation to speak for itself, and enabling uncontested Blue Ocean projects to thrive and appear from anywhere [37]. Openness benefits the metaverse through an open and decentralized community, allowing the XR metaverse to grow and stabilize with an open and sustainable ecosystem.

Open sharing has the greatest speed of growth and innovation to create interoperability [37]. Through the evolution of people communicating and working together, there are unlimited resources, because anyone can join at anytime from anywhere, unlike single companies that have organizational restrictions on sharing to protect their IP rights, which can slow down the speed of growth. Without open standards as a common model to build on, we will have a problem of interoperability and moving things between different virtual worlds [37].

There are a number of different types of interoperability needed for the XR industry to move forward:

1. Between virtual worlds and the objects and avatars traversing between them
2. Between different software development platforms that are part of the XR development pipeline
3. Between different standards that regulate different technology parts of the XR hardware designs and software protocols

Bringing together so many advances in technologies at this scale, with decentralized control, is going to take an unprecedented level of interoperability between different platforms and products [49]. Interoperability standards have always been the foundation on which the ecosystems are build out to pervasive scale. Interoperability standards define precise communication though a specification that enables multiple conformant implementations [49]. We need a strong foundation of cooperative standards, from many standards agencies, because there is no other way to make sure that the [XR] metaverse is going to be truly global and pervasive [49].

9.5.1   Open Source and Open Standards

Open source and open standards are the starting point for openness, which prevents vendor lock-in, so that anyone can contribute, creating sustainable ecosystems, which are an important thing, because the XR metaverse is a business opportunity, which needs to have sustainable ecosystems embedded for it to function. There is a difference between open source and open standards that is not always understood, and both are powerful drivers that move the XR industry forward [49]:

- Open source is about implementation and freely sharing code with execution rights, made by anyone, anywhere, or with licensing terms, so that whatever people put in, it can be free and open to the community, and easily shared. With a decentralized community collaborating, and different organizations and types of backgrounds of expertise and development needs, the potential for growth and diversity is at its best. They tend to use open standards because they try to avoid reinventing the wheel if possible. Open source is a very powerful way to drive industry forward.

- Open standards is about the specification, creating a standard that is freely available, to adopt and implement standards that people can use, and the focus is on portability and interoperability. Common technological standards are essential for widespread adoption [49]. Standardization is what enables the interoperability of platforms and services across virtual worlds. Open standards drive industry cooperation.

Standards are developed by standards developing organizations (SDOs), enabling industry cooperation and academic inclusive participation on open-source projects, or with well-defined multi-company governance and intellectual property frameworks [49]. There are many standards organizations, each with a specific area of expertise. Truly, open standards are not controlled by any one company; they are created through meetings and and an exchange of ideas and experiences of the developers. Open standards boards consist of a foundation of stakeholders focused on clarifying the standards, and maintaining quality and creating new features, because these come out of the needs of the customers and end-users [49]:

- Open source is concerned with creating shared implementations by many different contributors, and this works best when there is no competitive advantage in implementation. Industry consensus is needed to share implementation resources, and it needs rapid updates, which can create forks and fragmentation, so it needs governance to reach a clear shared model. Open- source projects enable multiple contributors to cooperate to build shared implementations, which can produce engines and applications that could often not be built by one company alone.

- Open standards are conceived through a shared specification writing process, and the specifications are developed through many consecutive implementation rounds, and this works best when there is a competitive advantage in implementation innovation. Industry needs multiple implementations and a stable design target. It can take time to generate consensus on a new version for a standard, because conformance testing is a vital aspect of it.

Open standards are not the only source that drives industry cooperation. Actually, they are a part of a larger flywheel effect, which is crucial to the innovation ecosystem and process. This innovation ecosystem flywheel and why it is important, is described below.

9.5.2 The XR Innovation Ecosystem Flywheel

Open standards provide the broad connective tissue for foundational rich products, and open-source projects help the community and industry to thrive and innovate. Open source and open standards are complementary and almost always leverage each other forward, creating the flywheel for innovation in the XR ecosystem. The XR innovation ecosystem flywheel is a critical part of the growth of the future XR metaverse functionalities. It consists of the technical developers' community, businesses, and profitable products [49]. According to Trevett, president of the open standards group Khronos, an open, non-profit, member-driven consortium of 170 organizations developing, publishing, and maintaining royalty-free interoperability standards for 3D graphics, VR, AR, parallel computation, vision acceleration, and machine learning: "The developers' community has real needs for new functionalities, and they build the technologies along with the other companies involved. Those then turn into products, which in turn open new markets, which then allows more involvement from the different developer communities and groups that become involved in the open development. From a business perspective you have projects that come out of this, and these can turn into products, and ultimately into profits, creating the balance for the flywheel between community and commerce. These projects need this ecosystem, supporting the openly developed technology into commercial products and solutions, allowing the companies to make profit and re-invest into the projects and back into the technical community, which keeps the flywheel going" [49].

Standardization is not always the answer to every problem. Proprietary technology and open standards have a complex and interdependent relationship [49]. Proprietary products are much more effective at driving rapid innovation and evolution of new techniques and technologies, and successful innovative products can remain dominant in the hands of a smart market leader and retain long-term advantage. Effective standardization only emerges when there is a recognized wider need for proven and well-understood technology and industry is ready and motivated to reduce fragmentation [49]. At this point, business interests are better served by cooperation than competition, according to Trevett: "Areas of emerging consensus are beachhead standardization opportunities" [49].

In the long term view, an open standard that is not controlled by or dependent on any one single company can be the thread of continuity needed for sustained progress of the industry [49]. Multi-company governance for open standards is essential, but standards should not be created too soon, and when they are, they should satisfy the wider need for all technologies involved. There are already many XR metaverse components that are understood and for which standardization is underway. Standards move the industry forward and free competitive energy to develop new ways to innovate and create value [49, 50].

9.6   Future Research Agenda and Roadmap

Together, these technological advances represent a paradigm shift in our current style of computing, with a lot of potential, and many technical, ethical, and security concerns. This kind of fundamental shift in technological abilities and advances is asking for carefully researched new design paradigms [58], and essential global security and privacy regulations. A technology backbone consists of the hardware, software, rules, and regulations based on shared values, and agreements about standards to achieve it, with an economic aspect to drive its demand, development, and maintenance. There are three core areas for research to accelerate XR metaverse development [51]: 1) scaling distributed graphics systems, 2) natural language processing, including content moderation, and 3) making the 3D content creation pipeline more efficient to empower content creators. No single project or product can solve all the technological, legal, and sociological issues involved in developing the XR metaverse, and previous experience with developing the web that provides the common foundation for a diversity of embedded platforms, experiences, and services, has shown that it needs to be developed as a decentralized model. In a similar way as the web has evolved, the XR metaverse will evolve and transform through a mix of ideas, experimentation, commercial successes and failures, and innovations that will compete and synergize, with the market naturally selecting those products that attract customers and users and move the industry forward. These proven solutions will organically emerge and become widely adopted, providing the foundation for the next round of innovation [49]. There are significant opportunities for all companies contributing to XR metaverse solutions.

In the immediate future, we need:

1. We need restrictions on who is annotating space and why they are annotating it: who would have permission to annotate it? Who would be able to see it? We must build that into the basic design of these systems.

2. XR systems are streaming huge amounts of data from the outside and inside world and huge amounts of biometric data from the user, a omnidirectional panopticon, meaning that XR technologies are a new class of surveillance devices, unlike any other device ever conceived in any technology so far, and we need urgent regulations.

3. Whoever is building the HMDs will be streaming into their service cloud, and regulations are needed about freedom and privacy in terms of who owns that data, and who controls if any of that data leave my device, further debate and regulations are needed in terms of how permission is controlled for data exchanged on immediate moment-by-moment basis.

4. Currently, developers are having a hard time building the XR metaverse because they must integrate a lot of connectivity between sensor data, assets, world, and personal contextual information with the virtual simulation, and they have to think about what a shared experience looks like in the real world versus the virtual world, because in the current development infrastructure, there are no ways to enable that yet.

5. We need interoperability and openness because there is an infinite number of use-cases, and lots of different form factors.

In the near and medium-term future, these are the urgent and important challenges:

1. We need to develop systems with the smallest eco and CO_2 footprint.
2. We need an incremental core, an engine that can communicate the differences and the things that change in the 3D world, unlike the 2D web, where you can simply reload the webpage.
3. XR developer tools should be additive, taking things that work well, and enhancing them by connecting them together through open standards.
4. Fostering openness for the future XR metaverse developments to allow Blue Ocean projects to thrive and appear from anywhere, allowing the metaverse to grow and stabilize with an open and sustainable ecosystem.
5. World-aware computing needed: Developers must deal with the fragmentation of the computer because content will be partially running on the smartphone, wearable devices, some in the cloud and some on the laptop, and they will need a way to put all this together. It is the job of the toolmakers to help developers do all this in a way that makes sense and accessible.
6. World-aware authoring needed: anyone that wants to use a digital item can modify that item, and not just with the computer, mouse, and keyboard, if we want something that is intended to augment and interact with the world.
7. Explore the potentials of the 3D Interaction paradigm shift for User Experience and User Interface (UXUI) and how we can improve the way we interact with computers in general.
8. The agility of XR app development is very suitable for rapid prototyping of solutions for the 17 global Sustainable Development Goals (SDGs), and more can be done to investigate the opportunities to optimize both on a global level and a local, city, province, country, as well as personal level, using XR.
9. We need to rapidly increase the available amount of trained, skilled developers, and operators for XR-enabled application and systems building and operating, including maintenance and training robots with ML, and we need to start training these developers and operators for the future.
10. We need to develop systems that are accessible for all, and inclusive of diversity.

Acknowledgments

The information in this chapter is based on the latest developments in the XR field, which are currently moving very rapidly. In particular: XR4ALL Webinar - XR landscape in Central and Eastern Europe, January 2021; Facebook: The Future of XR in Europe, April 2021; XR4All Congress, April 2021; VRAR Association Global Summit: Enabling The Workforce of the Future with Knowledge Networks, June 2021; State of XR & Learning: Report Launch party, June 2021, XR4ALL-Contribution to XR Landscape and Research Agenda in the wiki, July 2021; Moving Towards a Massive Use of XR in EU Industrial Processes, August 2021; Building the Open Metaverse, SIGGRAPH, August 2021 and specifically Neil Trevett, The Khronos Group; Rev Lebaredian, NVIDIA; Royal O'Brien, Linux Foundation; Vladimir Vukicevic, Unity; Teddy Bergsman, Epic Games; Shehzan Mohammed, Cesium; Mark Sagar, Soul Machines; Morgan McGuire, Roblox; Samantha G. Wolfe, PitchFWD/New York University; Ash M. Richter, In-Q-Tel; Christine Perey, Perey Research & Consulting; Nadine Alameh, Open Geospatial Consortium; and AR Dilemmas, SIGGRAPH, August 2021, Mark Pesce, University of Sydney, and VR/AR Global Summit - Fall 2021 European Edition, VR/AR Association, September 2021.

The research and writing of this text was partially financed by a research grant from Universidad de Málaga for Dr. Tromp as visiting researcher from State University of New York in Oswego (SUNY), NY, USA, at the DIANA Research Group, University of Malaga and the Spanish National Project SAVLab (Grant No. PID2019-107854GB-I00 / AEI / 10.13039/501100011033), Malaga, Spain.

References

1. Qualcomm, *The Mobile Future of eXtended Reality (XR)*, Qualcomm Technologies, Inc., USA, 2020. https://www.qualcomm.com/media/documents/files/the-mobile-future-ofextended- reality-xr.pdf, AWE-USA presentation

2. Schreer, O., Pelivan, I., Kauff, P., Schäfer, R., Hilsmann, A., Chojecki, P., Koch, Th., Wiegratz, R., Royan, J., Deschanel, M., Murienne, A., Launay, L., Verly, J., *D4.1: Revised Landscape Report, final report "eXtended Reality for All" project*, XR4ALL Consortium, Germany, 2020.

3. Ran, X., Slocum, C., Gorlatova, M., Chen, J., ShareAR: Communication-Efficient Multi-User Mobile Augmented Reality. *HotNets '19: Proceedings of the 18th ACM Workshop on Hot Topics in Networks*, November 2019, pp. 109–116, 2019, https://doi.org/10.1145/3365609.3365867.

4. Perry, Ch., Perey Consulting, Building the Open Metaverse, BOF. *SIGGRAPH 2021*, August 2021, 2021.

5. Olshannikova, E., Ometov, A., Koucheryavy, Y., Olsson, Th., Visualizing Big Data with augmented and virtual reality: challenges and research agenda. *J. Big Data*, 2, 22, 2015, DOI 10.1186/s40537-015-0031-2.

6. Gelernter, D., *Mirror Worlds: The Day Software Puts the Universe In a Shoebox... How it Will Happen and What It Will Mean*, Oxford University Press, New York, USA, 1992.

7. Negroponte, N., *Being Digital*, Vintage Books, Random House, NY, USA, 1995.

8. Laurel, B., *Computers as Theatre*, 2nd edition, Addison-Wesley, USA, 2014.

9. Smart, J., Cascio, J., Paffendorf, J., Bridges, C., Hummel, J., Hursthouse, J., Moss, R., *Metaverse Roadmap: Pathways to the 3D Web, a cross-industry public foresight project*, Acceleration Studies Foundation, USA, 2007, accelerating.org; retrieved from: metaverseroadmap.org.

10. Wright, A., *Cataloging the World: Paul Otlet and the birth of the Information Age*, Oxford University Press, Oxford, UK, 2014.

11. Otlet, P., *Monde*, Editions Mundaneum, Brussels, 1888, Retrieved 6 April 2020.

12. Ball, M., *The Metaverse: What It Is, Where to Find it, Who Will Build It, and Fortnite*, USA, 2020, retrieved from: http://matthewball.vc.

13. Ball, M., *The Metaverse Primer*, USA 2021, retrieved from: http://matthewball.vc.

14. Stephenson, N., *Snow Crash*, Bantam Books, USA, 1992.

15. Cline, E.C., *Ready Player One*, Crown Publishing Group, USA, 2011.

16. Gibson, W., *Neuromancer*, Ace, USA, 1984.

17. Schwab, K., The Fourth Industrial Revolution. *World Economic Forum (WEF)*, 2016.

18. Capgemini, *Augmented and Virtual Reality in Operations: A guide to investments*, Capgemini research search report, global. 2019, https://www.capgemini.com/wp-content/uploads/2018/09/AR-VR-in-Operations1.pdf.

19. Hadwick, A., *VRX XR Industry Insight report 2019-2020*, vr-intelligence, USA, 2019, https://s3.amazonaws.com/media.mediapost.com/uploads/VRXindustryreport.pdf.

20. Accenture, *Waking Up To A New Reality: Building a responsible future for immersive technologies, G20*, Young Entrepreneurs Alliance (YEA), 2020, https://www.accenture.com/_acnmedia/Accenture/Redesign-Assets/DotCom/Documents/Global/1/Accenture-G20-YEA-report.pdf.

21. XR association, *A New Reality in Immersive Technology (XR): Insights and Industry Trends*, XR Association, Washington, USA, 2021.

22. Malakuti, S., Schlake, J., Ganz, Ch., Petersen, H., Digital Twin: An Enabler for New Business Models. *Conference: Automation 2019, Project: BaSys4.0*, July 2019, 2019.

23. Doolani, S., Wessels, C., Kanal, V., Sevastopoulos, Ch., Jaiswal, A., Nambiappan, H., Makedon, F., A Review of Extended Reality (XR) Technologies for Manufacturing Training. *J. Technol.*, 8, 77, 2020.

24. Greenwold, S., *Spatial Computing*, MIT, USA, 2003, Retrieved from: https://acg.media.mit.edu/people/simong/thesis/SpatialComputing.pdf.

25. Coltekin, A., Lochhead, I., Madden, M., Christophe, S., Devaux, A., Pettit, Ch., Lock, O., Shukia, S., Herman, L., Stachon, Z., Kubicek, P., Snopkova, D., Bernardes, S., Hedley, N., Extended Reality in Spatial Sciences: A Review of Research Challenges and Future Directions. *ISPRS Int. J. Geoinf.*, 9, 439, 2020, doi: 10.3390/ijgi9070439, https://www.mdpi.com/2220-9964/9/7/439/pdf.

26. Mohammed, S., Building the Open Metaverse, BOF. *SIGGRAPH 2021*, August 2021, Cesium, 2021.

27. Zuboff, S., Big other: Surveillance Capitalism and the Prospects of an Information Civilization. *J. Inf. Technol.*, 30, 1, 75–89, 2015, https://doi.org/10.1057/jit.2015.5.

28. Pesce, M., AR Dilemmas. *Keynote speech at SIGGRAPH 2021*, August 2021, 2021.

29. Pesce, M., Mixed Reality Service. *Position statement submitted to the W3C Workshop on the Web and Virtual Reality*, 23 September 2016, 1995, https://mixedrealitysystem.org/spec/MRS_Draft_2_September_2016.pdf.

30. Webb, A., *The Big Nine: How Tech Titans & Their Thinking Machines Could Warp Humanity*, PublicAffairs, USA, 2019.

31. NEXT-NET, Next Horizons for European Supply Chains. *Strategic Research and Innovation Agenda, Horizon 2020, NEXT-NET Consortium*, European Commission, 2019.

32. Schwab, K. and Zahidi, S., The Global Competitiveness Report: How Countries are performing on the Road to Recovery, special edition 2020. *World Economic Forum*, 2020.

33. Simões, B., Creus, C., del Puy Carretero, M., Guinea Ochaíta, A., Streamlining XR Technology Into Industrial Training and Maintenance Processes, in: *The 25th International Conference on 3D Web Technology (Web3D '20)*, November 9–13, 2020, Virtual Event, Republic of Korea. ACM, New York, NY, USA, 7 Pages, 2020, https://doi.org/10.1145/3424616.3424711.

34. Pesce, M., *Augmented Reality: Unboxing Tech's Next Big Thing*, Wiley, USA, 2020.

35. Tromp, J., Le, C., Le, B., Le, D.-N., Massively Multi-user Online Social Virtual Reality Systems: Ethical Issues and Risks for Long-Term Use, in: *Social Networks Science: Design, Implementation, Security, and Challenges*, 06/2018, pp. 131–149, 2018, ISBN: 978-3-319-90058-2, DOI:10.1007/978-3-319-90059-9_7.

36. Hall, S. and Takahashi, R., *Augmented and virtual reality: The promise and peril of immersive technologies*, McKinsey report, USA, 2017, https://www.mckinsey.com/industries/technology-media-and-telecommunications/

our-insights/augmented-and-virtual-reality-the-promise-and-peril-of-immersive-technologies.

37. O'Brian, R., Linux Foundation, Building the Open Metaverse, BOF. *SIGGRAPH 2021*, August 2021, 2021.

38. Lebarian, R., Nvidia, Building the Open Metaverse, BOF. *SIGGRAPH 2021*, August 2021, 2021.

39. Bartle, R., *Designing Virtual Worlds*, New Riders, USA, 2003.

40. Greenhalgh, C.M., Bullock, A., Tromp, J., Benford, S.D., Evaluating the Network and Usability Characteristics of Virtual Reality Conferencing, in: *Telepresence. BT Telecommunications Series*, vol. 16, P.J. Sheppard and G.R. Walker (Eds.), Springer, Boston, MA, 1999, https://doi.org/10.1007/978-1-4615-5291-8_9.

41. Tromp, J.G., *Systematic Usability Design and Evaluation for Collaborative Virtual Environments*, PhD. Thesis, Mechanical, Materials and Manufacturing Engineering and Management, University of Nottingham, UK, 2001.

42. Tromp, J.G., Steed, A., Wilson, J.R., Systematic Usability Evaluation and Design Issues for Collaborative Virtual Environments. *Presence Teleop. Virt. Environments* 06/2003, 12, 3, 241–267, 2003, DOI:10.1162/105474603765879512.

43. Sagar, M., Soulmachines, Building the Open Metaverse, BOF. *SIGGRAPH 2021*, August 2021, 2021.

44. Soul Machines, *Overview of Our Digital Brain: How the Soul Machines Digital Brain is autonomously animating Digital People*, Soul Machines, USA, 2021, ebook retrieved from: https://www.soulmachines.com/.

45. Vukicevic, V., Unity, Building the Open Metaverse, BOF. *SIGGRAPH 2021*, August 2021, 2021.

46. Bergsman, T., Epic Games, Building the Open Metaverse, BOF. *SIGGRAPH 2021*, August 2021, 2021.

47. Dieberger, A. and Tromp, J., 3D Hypertext- The Information City Project: a Virtual Reality User Interface for Navigation in Information Spaces, in: *The User Experience Review, Apple Computer*, vol. 11, Jan/Feb, Erickson, T. (Ed.), pp. 2–9, 01/1995.

48. Richter, A., In-Q-Tel, Building the Open Metaverse, BOF. *SIGGRAPH 2021*, August 2021, 2021.

49. Trevitt, N., The Khronos Group, Building the Open Metaverse, BOF. *SIGGRAPH 2021*, August 2021.

50. Lundy, M., Gottret, M.V., Ashby, J., Learning alliances: An approach for building multistakeholder innovation systems. *ILAC Brief*, 8, 4, 2005, https://hdl.handle.net/10568/70181.

51. McGuire, M., Roblox, Building the Open Metaverse, BOF. *SIGGRAPH 2021*, August 2021, 2021.

52. Bezegova, E., Ledgard, M.A., Molemaker, R., Oberc, B.P., Vigkos, A., *Virtual Reality and its Potential For Europe*, ECORYS, Belgium, 2017, https://xra.org/wp-content/uploads/2020/07/rs-vr-potential-europe-01.pdf.

53. Davies, A., Fidler, D., Gorbis, M., *Future Work Skills 2020*, Institute for the Future for the university of Phoenix Research Institute, USA, 2011. www.iftf. org.

54. Fernandez-Matias, E., *Automation, digitisation and platforms: Implications for work and employment, The employment impact of the automation of services (170901)*, Eurofound, Luxembourg, 2018, *Automation, digitisation and platforms: Implications for work and employment*, Publications Office of the European Union, Luxembourg, https://www.eurofound.europa.eu/sites/default/files/ef_publication/field_ef_document/ef18002en.pdf.

55. Peruffo, E., Rodriguez Contreras, R., Mandl, I., Bisello, M., *Game-changing technologies: Transforming production and employment in Europe*, Eurofound Office of the European Union, Luxembourg, 2020.

56. Lee, M.J.W., Georgieva, M., Alexander, B., Craig, E., Richter, J., *State of XR & Immersive Learning Outlook Report 2021*, Immersive Learning Research Network, Walnut, CA, 2021, ISBN: 978-1-7348995-1-1.

57. Ziker, C., Truman, B., Dodds, H., Cross Reality (XR): Challenges and Opportunities Across the Spectrum, in: *Innovative Environments in STEM Higher Education*, Ryoo and Winkelmann (Eds.), Springerbriefs in Statistics, Springer Nature Switzerland AG, 2021.

58. Ratenou, *Ratenau Manifesto: Set 10 design requirements for tomorrow's digital society now*, Rathenau Institute, Den Hague, the Netherlands, 2021, https://www.rathenau.nl/sites/default/files/2020-10/Rathenau_Manifesto_set_10_design_requirements_tomorrows_digital_society_now_Rathenau_Instituut.pdf.

10

Human Factors and Ergonomics

Marta Mondellini[1], Vera Colombo[1,2], Sara Arlati[1],
Glyn Lawson[3]* and Sue Cobb[3]

[1]*Institute of Intelligent Industrial Systems and Technologies for Advanced Manufacturing (STIIMA), Italian National Research Council (CNR), Lecco, Italy*
[2]*Department of Electronics, Information and Bioengineering, Politecnico di Milano, Milan, Italy*
[3]*Human Factors Research Group, University of Nottingham, Nottingham, UK*

Abstract

Technological advances, lower cost, and greater availability of extended reality (XR) have led to more widespread applications and uptake of these technologies. Simulated environments can be used to study, measure, and influence human behavior in a variety of situations, and there are many examples of application in education, training, and rehabilitation, among others. However, the quality of the user experience and effectiveness of these applications are influenced by a variety of factors including the design of, and interaction with, the technology. This chapter presents an overview of human factors/ergonomics (HF/E) issues associated with XR with reference to user experience models defined in early virtual reality research. Using case examples that show how multisensory and multimodal interaction techniques can enhance the realism and efficacy of the user experience, and how XR technology can be used to deliver engaging and effective rehabilitation programs for older users, the importance of HF/E considerations are highlighted. Recommendations for future research include: the need for deeper understanding regarding optimum design of simulation content and multimodal user interaction; cost/benefit analysis taking into account user characteristics and the context of use; a provision of guidelines to aid technology producers during the design process for development of new XR applications; and standardized protocols for the evaluation of user experiences.

Keywords: Human factors, ergonomics, multisensory interaction, multimodal interaction, human–computer interface

Corresponding author: Glyn.Lawson@nottingham.ac.uk

Mariano Alcañiz, Marco Sacco and Jolanda G. Tromp (eds.) Roadmapping Extended Reality: Fundamentals and Applications, (229–256) © 2022 Scrivener Publishing LLC

10.1   Introduction

Recent advances in integrated multimedia systems have made virtual reality (VR) and other technologies [augmented reality (AR)/mixed reality (MR)/extended reality (XR)—hereafter referred to as XR] accessible to a wider consumer market. The lower cost and availability of XR consumer devices have contributed to an increased interest in the application of XR in diverse fields of application including engineering, medicine, education, industry, and entertainment [1]. In 2020, 5 million high-end XR head-mounted displays (HMDs) were sold, with forecasted sales rising to 43.5 million by 2025 [2]. Advances in XR technologies have resolved some of the problems identified in early VR systems [3, 4]. For example, faster computing power reduces system response time, providing smoother interaction and improving the user experience (UX) [5, 6]. However, wider diversification of application use has also generated new issues of concern. For example, more complex virtual environments introduce a higher level of optic flow that increases the speed of the perceived motion and, as a consequence, the level of sensory conflict, potentially increasing the risk of undesirable symptoms of motion sickness [7, 8]. To ensure safe, efficient, and effective use of XR applications, it remains essential to consider human factors (HF) issues when designing applications using XR technologies [9, 10].

Differences between types of XR technology should be also considered, and it should be noted that much of the HF research in the literature refers to VR technology. VR systems comprise a variety of component parts including software (3D digital environment) and hardware (display technologies such as projected screens and HMDs, physical interaction devices) that may be configured in different ways according to the requirements for a given use case application. Therefore, some of the factors and associated UX effects that have been identified during the use of VR, may be extended also to AR and MR (e.g., the aspects concerning the design of the virtual content). Factors more related to the physical characteristics of XR devices may require specific considerations; VR, AR, and MR offer different ways of interaction, visualization modalities and different levels of immersion.

Disregarding the specific configuration of technology, in most cases, the aim of XR is to facilitate humans in performing a task. Consequently, the capabilities and limitations of the target user, and considerations related to the context of use, also play a key role for the effectiveness of XR environments.

Thus, the analysis of HF/E of XR has an impact on producers of technology and may suggest new strategies and outline which directions are worth investing in. Not only should producers of technology consider HF/E to improve the success of their products, but also potential secondary users, or application facilitators (e.g., clinical personnel in the field of rehabilitation, workers in the manufacturing field, teachers and educators for training and learning applications, etc.). Selection of the optimal technology platform (e.g., VR/AR/MR), visualization device (e.g., HMD vs. semi-immersive projected screen), and interaction device (e.g., voice vs. gesture control), is an important aspect in designing applications that can be effective for a given purpose. A key point, which will be discussed in the final section of this chapter, is the design phase that should consider all of these aspects, including target users, in the process of choosing the optimal XR system, virtual content, and scenario of use.

10.2   XR and Human Factors

10.2.1   Framework of HF Issues

Since the 1990s, researchers have investigated HF issues of VR, AR, MR, and more recently, XR. Initial reviews identified a range of factors that may influence UX and suitability of applications using these technologies, such as cybersickness, user and task characteristics, and the type of feedback provided to users [3, 11, 12]. HF research advocated examination of three main aspects of technology use: human performance efficiency, health and safety concerns (e.g., discomfort, harm or injury), and social implications [10]. A variety of effects that could arise during and/or after a VR experience were identified, including: symptoms of simulator sickness, physical ergonomics effects, changes in physiological state, performance changes, and participant experience. These were collectively referred to as virtual reality-induced symptoms and effects (VRISE), and could include positive as well as negative effects [11].

As VR systems developed, combined with increasing awareness of UX and the aftereffects of use, an international team of 25 leading experts in VR and HF met in the late 1990s to discuss the state of the art in factors affecting the UXs of VR [13]. The outcome of this panel discussion identified key issues of concern including sensory discordance experienced by technology use and established a research agenda which called for standardization in the methods used for measurement of VR aftereffects and a greater understanding of presence and its influence on UX. Considerable research focus has subsequently been conducted to establish consistency in definition and evaluation of presence [14–16]. Initial frameworks highlighted the influence of VR system and VE design, individual characteristics of the user and the methods of UX evaluation on research studies investigating VRISE, and identified a need for guidelines for VR/VE design and application use, including duration of simulation exposure, considerations regarding how the system is integrated with other tasks in the context of use, and training for users [9]. Following examination of HF issues in a number of case examples of VR use, Sharples *et al.* noted how technology improvements had resolved previous HF issues related to VR system and VE design [6]. For example, the advent of remote tracking technologies and more compact systems (e.g., a battery, computer console and wires worn on the back of the user), helped in reducing the restriction of user movement and safety hazards of tripping over wires. However, while increased available computing power reduced the impact of frame rate and latency on user interaction, extending the requirements for user interaction in collaborative VR systems, made possible by increased computing power and reduced cost of visualization display systems, highlighted a new set of HF issues related to multiuser interaction and the effects of passive visualization and subsequent increase in risk of symptoms. A need for standardization in guidelines for, and evaluation of, VR usability and interaction was called for [6]. Meanwhile, researchers at the University of Virginia Tech presented a taxonomy of methods for evaluation of VEs [17] and advocated a usability engineering approach to ensure user-centered design and evaluation of user interaction methods designed for VR [18] and AR applications [19]. This approach established requirements for interaction design, progressively informed using detailed task analysis, expert review and application of heuristic guidelines and formative and summative user evaluation of interface and interaction design options.

Whilst these frameworks differed in regard to the specific focus and level of detail presented, with some listing different types of symptoms that users could experience, and others identifying variations in technical characteristics, at a general level, they all recognized that UX was influenced by a combination of factors related to: the technology used (e.g., hardware elements including computer system and visual display) and method of user interaction; content of the VE (e.g., visual complexity and quality of graphics) and interface design; the user task and context of use; and individual user characteristics (including susceptibility to motion sickness and other symptoms). A simplified representation is shown in Figure 10.1.

In their development of a simplified framework diagram, Nichols and Patel [9] emphasized the interrelationship between these factors, suggesting that the UX could be influenced positively, and negatively, by improvements to one or more of the design elements:

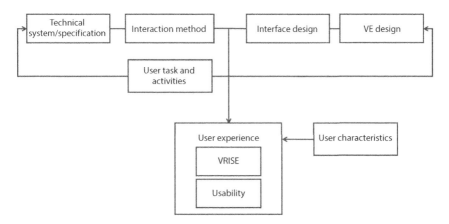

Figure 10.1 Factors influencing UX of interaction with VR (adapted from models presented in [3, 9–11, 18, 19].

"For example, a more photorealistic environment may increase the sense of presence experienced by the participant, but may also increase the extent of sensory conflict between the visual and vestibular system, and thus increase symptoms. Similarly, the experience of sickness could distract the participant from the VE, and thus reduce their sense of presence."

It should also be considered that often UX is detected through self-report questionnaires at the end of the experience. In addition to the limits of subjective measures [20], questionnaires sometimes investigate the experience as a whole, as in the case of the User Experience Questionnaire [21], and are sometimes designed to investigate specific variables, such as the sense of presence or acceptability. This can make it difficult to compare UX outcomes between studies and between XR systems; tools designed for cross-media use, such as The International Test Commission–Sense of Presence Inventory (ITC-SOPI) [22], are increasingly popular in research.

In addition to the UX effects of using VR, Behr *et al.* highlighted ethical implications related to the use of VR [23]. They identified four major potential risks that need to be considered: motion sickness, information overload (i.e. the information provided should not exceed the user's ability to process it because excessive or too-complex stimuli may cause frustration), intensification of the experience and re-entry into the real world (during which emotional, cognitive, or behavioral disturbances may occur). Including these factors in XR research studies is fundamental in order to ensure that all ethical issues are properly addressed [23].

10.2.2   Where Are We Now?

Much of the research conducted since 2000 has focused on separate aspects of XR technology development, and evaluation of usability, utility, and effectiveness of its use in specific application domains. Considerable discussion has taken place regarding the definition of the concept of 'presence' and how to evaluate it. Much of the research has examined the relationship between presence and UX. Factors affecting the usability and user acceptance of XR technology have also been explored [6]. The following paragraphs present a brief overview of research on these topics.

10.2.2.1   *Presence*

Despite the discussion regarding different definitions and dimensions, the concept of presence is universally described as the feeling of leaving the physical location, and of being transported to a VE [24].

An open question is which immersion-related factors influence presence. Cummings and Bailenson [5] identified a medium effect of the overall immersion features on perceived presence, with particular reference to place illusion (PI).

Image quality is not essential to construct a spatial model of self-location [5, 14]. Instead, most users are able to exploit low-fidelity cues to reconstruct the scenario they are supposed to represent. On the other hand, to increase plausibility (Psi), good tracking level, stereoscopy, and field of view are necessary. In particular, the tracking level is fundamental to interact with, and exert control over, the environment; stereoscopy and field of view intervene to assess the distance of 3D objects placed in the users' surroundings, and to facilitate the perception of the virtual space as a real one, respectively.

Cybersickness also appears to have an influence on presence. In 2019, Weech *et al.* [24] reviewed the literature investigating whether a correlation between presence and cybersickness exists, and if it would be possible to manipulate it with a single approach. A negative correlation between presence and sickness is more plausible, possibly mediated by factors such as vection, navigation control, and display factors. The relationship is therefore not straightforward; more immersion is linked not only to a higher weighting of perceptual cues and spatial presence but also to an enhanced chance to violate user's expectations, thus causing cybersickness. Nonetheless, it has been shown that people experiencing more presence also suffer less from cybersickness; therefore, it could be possible that a sense of presence suppresses cybersickness, by shifting attention away from sensory mismatch and other potential cybersickness-promoting factors [25, 26]. Vice versa, it could be sickness that distracts the user from feeling present [3, 11, 27, 28].

Finally, subjective characteristics also seem to play a role in the arousal of sickness (e.g., gender, age, VR experience), and these factors could have an impact on the perception of presence too [24, 29].

10.2.2.2 Usability

Designing usable and effective XR environments represents a challenge for scientists, developers, and HF experts. Indeed, traditional usability principles do not apply specifically to unique XR characteristics, such as wayfinding (i.e., the ability to maintain the knowledge of one's position and orientation while moving in a virtual/augmented space [30]) or object selection and manipulation). Moreover, user-specific factors must be considered, such as presence, comfort, and side-effects. Stanney *et al.* [31] provide guidance for designers with their framework to assess usability specifically in VEs (though the dissertation can be extended to all XR technologies) via a multicriteria assessment. In particular, the Multi-criteria Assessment for Usability in Virtual Environments (MAUVE) addressed the following limitations of standard usability assessment tools: (i) point-and-click interactions that were not representative of XR technologies interactions; (ii) insufficient consideration of the quality of system outputs (in terms of visual, haptic, and auditory feedback); (iii) variations in application of assessment of presence and cybersickness; (iv) performance measures, such as time and accuracy, do not characterize what happens in XR environments; and (v) no consideration for multiuser interaction.

With the emerging need for wider consideration of all XR technologies, i.e., the real–mixed–virtual continuum defined by Milgram *et al.* (1994) [32], the issue of determining the usability of human–computer interfaces (HCIs) has become more complicated. Ergonomics knowledge concerning MR systems, for instance, is still lacking, and the rapid evolution of technology makes it difficult to reach consensus regarding the efficiency, effectiveness and user satisfaction of these applications in several fields [33]. Despite the extensive body of research knowledge related to the design and usability of VR and AR technologies, some of which may be applicable for the evaluation of XR technologies, a few concerns still remain [33]. The design of the testing procedure, including considerations for the environment in which it takes place and methods of data collection may be problematic when the task includes interactions between the real and the virtual world. For example, planning the usability testing of a collaborative MR environment demonstrates how difficult these procedures may be.

The physical environment must be appropriately set up; when moving from the assessment of a PC-based software to the evaluation of an XR application in which the user can move, talk, and walk around, the surroundings become important. Possible obstacles (e.g., cables, indoor furniture) must be removed, and larger spaces are required. These elements introduce much variability, making the assessment environment less controlled, and the data extraction more difficult [17, 33].

In addition, there may be issues related to the assessment procedure; when performing a usability assessment of XR, it is important to keep in mind that only a few people are familiar with such a technology. Nowadays, it is almost impossible to distinguish experts from novices (and compare their responses as happens in standard HCI assessment), and to design experiments in which the "intuitive" performance is analyzed [33]. Rather, it is necessary to instruct all users before starting the test, possibly introducing a bias in the evaluation [33].

It is possibly because of these reasons—and to ease the evaluation of newer technologies—that recent research has focused on the heuristic evaluation of usability, examined in conjunction with technology acceptance [34], UX [35], presence [36], cybersickness [37], physical and mental workload [38].

10.2.2.3   Technology Acceptance

The individual adoption and use is a pivotal point to take into consideration when designing and developing new technology systems and applications. The technology acceptance model (TAM) [39] and its subsequent extensions [40, 41], are the most popular framework used to understand users' acceptance of XR technology [42]. Although the latest version of TAM [41] takes into account multiple factors including social influence and individual characteristics, established technology acceptance theories may be insufficient to apply directly to XR technology. Several authors have proposed extensions and additions to the TAM framework to better explain the users' intentions for the real use of XR technologies.

Sledgianowski and Kulyiwat [43] added the variable "critical mass" (the amount of users that, once reached, ensures that the product is quickly used by the whole community) to TAM, showing that it seems to influence the use of social networks; this factor predicts also perceived usefulness (PU) and perceived ease of use (PEOU) [44], and the use of AR technology [45].

In AR and VR systems [45], users are drawn to the perceived playfulness and trustworthiness derived from the application [46, 47]. Venkatesh and Speier [48] studied positive and negative moods and their relation to acceptance, and concluded that mood can influence both the intrinsic motivation and the intention to use a technology; in particular, positive mood had a short-term impact on intrinsic motivation and intention to use, whereas negative mood had a long-term impact on them. Huang *et al.* [47] extended the model to incorporate hedonic elements, namely, emotional involvement, positive emotions, and flow experience, to evaluate the navigation experience in 3D environments in tourism. They concluded that perceived ease of use and perceived usefulness had positive and significant impacts on enjoyment during the 3D experience and on emotional involvement mental and users' state of flow [47, 48].

In their recent work, Sagnier *et al.* [49] tested the application of TAM to study the acceptance of VR, proposing an extended model that included some specific variables related to the UX, VR, and user characteristics. They found that the pragmatic quality of the system—the component that helps the user achieve goals and contributes to a positive UX—has a positive effect on the perceived ease of use, while the hedonic quality-stimulation, the component that satisfies some users' need, was significantly correlated with perceived usefulness. Cybersickness had a significant negative effect on intention to use VR, but presence was not significantly correlated with the intention to use. Finally, personal innovativeness, namely, the personal willingness to try out any new information technology, had a significant effect on perceived usefulness but not on the perceived ease of use and intention to use. This finding is consistent with other studies, where the "openness to experience" personality trait [50] corresponds to users who are more aware of the functional benefits of IT, which affects their intent to use [51].

Chuah [42] organized several factors that influence the adoption of XR technology into themes based on their similarity. This categorization includes in the concept of acceptability many of the factors studied individually, such as the sense of presence and cybersickness, and takes into consideration numerous studies. Some examples are reported below. Zsila *et al.* [52] pointed out that people play AR games (e.g., Pokémon Go) to reduce boredom (hedonic benefit, associated with multisensory, fantastic, and emotional aspects of the UX) and other scholars underlined that users prefer technologies that make them look original and wealthy and that are aesthetically beautiful [53], as well as technologies that offer the feeling of physical well-being, thanks to satisfaction with the design [51]. A high sense of presence, a media-specific factor in Chuah's categorization [42], correlates with positive attitudinal and users' behavioral outcomes in some studies [54], but this relationship is not confirmed [49]. Other studies have shown a negative correlation between the acceptability of the technology and the perception of risk due to use; above all, cybersickness is an important factor that decreases the adoption of technologies, such as VR glasses [55]. Users' behavior is guided also by their need to be accepted by others, especially in situations where technology is visibly used around other people [56], as in the case of wearable XR technology.

10.2.3   Where Are We Going?

In the following sections, recent case studies of research conducted by the authors are used to: i) identify considerations that need to be taken into account when developing new applications of multisensory XR systems and ii) demonstrate a user-centered design approach to design of an XR application for the rehabilitation of older adults.

10.2.3.1   *Case Example 1: Multisensory Interaction*

To date, most research in XR has focused on areas related to visual perception. This is understandable, as most XR technologies are primarily visualization technologies, although commercial systems are usually also offered with some form of audio provision. However, for many of the experiences created in XR environments, additional senses, such as smell (olfaction), touch (haptic/tactile) or heat (thermoception), would play an important role in the real-world equivalent. Consider for example, the use of XR for researching human behavior in a building fire evacuation. While an audio-visual system could represent the sight of the flames and smoke in the building, and the sound of the fire and the alarm, it would not afford the sense of heat (from the fire itself, or from touching a door leading to a burning room) or smell of smoke/burning artefacts. Similarly, when using XR as part of a development process for a product that the user will be required to touch, hold, and otherwise interact with physically (most products!), it is easy to realize that an evaluation based on visual feedback alone would omit key aspects relating to the comfort, fit, and overall pleasure of using the product.

Thus, multisensory XR has the potential to offer VEs that are more representative of those of the real world than audio-visual XR. However, greater immersion comes at a cost. An obvious cost is that of the technology—there will likely be a monetary value associated with buying the kit to enable a multimodal experience. A further cost is associated with the development effort required to implement the multimodal technology into a usable VE. In comparison to audio-visual technologies, technologies that stimulate the additional senses are not as advanced or as widely available, although as XR technologies proliferate the consumer market, we are seeing greater availability of devices that have been developed to cater for the other senses. There is still likely to be development work to integrate the audio-visual and additional modality technologies. The development work should involve not only making the simulation technologies function appropriately in response to events in the VE but also optimizing the multimodal experience for the user. Importantly, consideration should be given to ensuring the safety of the technology.

Returning to the building fire example given above, Lawson *et al.* [57] developed a multimodal fire evacuation simulator to explore the impact of adding simulated heat and smell to an audio-visual experience of a building fire. In this case, heat was provided via three 2 kW infrared patio heaters, with a bespoke heat modulation system, in which fins opened and closed to adjust the heat users experienced as their distance to the source of the heat (the fire) changed in the VE. The smell of smoke was provided via an off-the-shelf scent diffuser, and a pre-manufactured smoke fragrance. The heat and smell were triggered by scripts such that as the participant approached the fire in the virtual world, the fins would open and the scent diffuser would activate, thus providing the heat and smell (for more details, see Nilsson *et al.* [58]). Experimental work showed that the multimodal experience resulted in differences in behavior and subjective responses when compared to the audio-visual experience. In general, there was evidence to suggest that the multimodal experience was treated more like a real building fire than the audio-visual experience [59]. However, a follow-up study did not provide an evidence for multimodality over an audio-visual VE when the simulator was tested as a training tool [57].

This case study serves to highlight several important points. Firstly, the development effort was considerable in order to produce a working prototype. Many months' work was required to link the heat and smell devices to the virtual world, ensure that a timely delivery of the heat was provided to the participant, develop appropriate triggers for the scent diffuser, and develop measures to control the risks associated with heat and smell delivery, etc. Related to this development effort, it is worth considering both whether multimodality is needed and justified for a particular application, and what evidence is available to support its use. For the fire simulator, the application clearly indicates the potential benefits of multimodality in that heat and smell are important elements of a fire event, and previous work had given theoretical and practical reasons to believe that multimodality would enhance the experience (e.g., [60–62]). Despite this strong foundation, we still found no evidence to support the use of multimodality on the basis of our fire simulator training study. Thus, it is appropriate to approach multimodal simulation cautiously and consider the evidence to support its use.

In another project, we aimed to address well-known issues with depth perception in VEs [63] through the use of worn vibro-tactile devices, which would activate when the wearer touches an object in the virtual world [64]. In one of the conditions, we found that accuracy on a reaching task improved when users were told to prioritize haptic feedback over visual; this serves to highlight that more work is needed to understand how the senses interact in XR. Moreover, we found some evidence to suggest that certain participants' task performance benefited far more from the haptic feedback than other participants. This requires further investigation, but links to the question about whether the investment costs are justifiable— they may be for a proportion of the population, but perhaps not needed for all users.

In conclusion, multimodal XR is an exciting area of development, and has the potential to enhance our experiences in virtual worlds. However, its use requires consideration, in particular with regards to the costs of the technology and the necessary development effort. Moreover, multimodality should be justified on the basis of scientific evidence, rather than excitement about a new technology!

10.2.3.2   Case Example 2: Rehabilitation—Older Adults

Rehabilitation is one of the fields in which XR technologies have been most employed [65, 66]. In fact, XR allows users to train in an ecological, controllable, and safe environment, and offers feedback in real time, thus promoting an error-free learning environment, in which better clinical outcomes could be achieved [67]. Moreover, XR has been proven to enhance the motivation to exercise, and thus to promote better compliance to the proposed treatment, also when unsupervised (e.g., in a home-based setting) [68].

In spite of these advantages, and the widespread use of XR in rehabilitation, there are some issues related to HF that researchers and developers need to take into account when designing a new XR-based rehabilitative program, especially when dealing with the most recent technologies. For instance, immersive virtual reality (IVR) has the potential to fully immerse the user in a computer-generated world: this has been shown to have a positive effect on presence, and thus on motivation and possibly also on the quality of the performances [24, 69]. On the other hand, the use of HMDs may cause cybersickness, and provoke musculoskeletal disorders due to the weight of the headset, or repetitive strain [53]. It is important to note that, in the context of rehabilitation, users may include vulnerable populations, and thus the requirements normally set for healthy people may not be sufficient. For example, controllers may be too heavy to lift for patients with muscle weakness, or remembering how to handle interactions may be not immediate for people with cognitive deficits [70].

As guidance for a possible pathway to follow when designing an IVR-based rehabilitative intervention, we present a case example detailing the process applied in the development of an IVR application dedicated to older adults with mild cognitive impairment (MCI). In particular, the starting scenario foresees a 2D VR-based validated system, composed of a cycle-ergometer and a projected touch screen. Such a system allows older adults to perform 20 minutes of aerobic activity, while navigating in a virtual park, and 20 minutes of cognitive training to be performed in a virtual supermarket [71]. In the attempt of making the two scenarios (i.e., the park and the supermarket) more immersive, and thus able to elicit presence, motivation, and better clinical outcomes, the path presented in Table 10.1 was followed.

As can be seen in Table 10.1, only the last two steps are related to the clinical effectiveness of the proposed applications. All of the previous phases are devoted to assess and eliminate any potential HF issues in order to reach the clinical trial phase with an application that is safe, ergonomically acceptable, and—above all—more enjoyable and capable of eliciting presence than the corresponding 2D versions. In case of failure, i.e., some outcomes are not acceptable to proceed forward, the (re)design of the application should be performed again, to correct errors according to the needs that study participants have highlighted.

Using the above pathway, our case example developed two IVR applications: a CAVE-based park, which also included a cognitive task to enhance user's control, and an HMD-based supermarket in which locomotion occurred naturally. Both were evaluated positively in terms of usability and the acceptance of technology by target users [79, 80]. In our experience, the preliminary testing stages were essential as young adults complained of cybersickness during the trial that required cycling with the HMD [81]— and thus, the IVR technology had to be replaced. Vice versa, the experience with the HMD was enjoyable and free from side effects in the case of the supermarket [82]; however, the usability test was important, because it made it clear that interactions had to be reviewed.

Table 10.1 Process applied in design of immersive VR-based applications dedicated to physical and cognitive training [73].

Phase	What to do	Specifications
(Re)design for immersion	Consider the characteristics of the VE and define specific requirements, considering existing literature and known safety guidelines with the aim of reducing the likelihood of cybersickness.	1) *Park* (i.e., a navigational scenario): • Avoid bends and brakes, and situations inducing sensory mismatch [7] • Prefer (Cave Automatic Virtual Environment) CAVE-based systems to HMDs, since they are less occlusive of the real world mode; in the latter case, focus on HMDs with good visual (resolution, frame rate) quality [5, 11] • Consider adding elements enhancing user control over the environment or sense of agency (e.g., possibility to turn) [24, 28]; • Limit the whole exposure to 20–30 minutes at maximum [72, 73]. 2) *Supermarket* (i.e., a non-navigational scenario): • Avoid teleportation, and prefer natural walking for navigation [74] • Prefer HMDs with high visual (resolution, frame rate) quality [5, 11] • Consider adding elements enhancing user control over the environment or sense of agency (e.g., interactions with virtual objects) [28] • Design a simple and intuitive interaction method [31] • Limit the whole exposure to 20–30 minutes at maximum [72, 73]
Lab test	Revise the application for bugs and malfunctions; make first preliminary tests.	• Trial of the application many times in a lab setting; the participation of colleagues that have not participated in the development is encouraged.

(Continued)

Table 10.1 Process applied in design of immersive VR-based applications dedicated to physical and cognitive training [73]. (*Continued*)

Phase	What to do	Specifications

Usability test #1	Design a trial to assess usability and side-effects on a sample of **non-vulnerable individuals**.	• Sample size: n ≥ 5 (healthy young adults) [75];
		• Outcomes:
		  ○ Usability (e.g., Multiguideline Accessibility and Usability Validation Enviroment MAUVE; System Usability Scale, SUS [76]);
		  ○ Cybersickness (especially in the case of navigational environments, e.g., Simulator Sickness Questionnaire SSQ [77]);
		  ○ Sense of presence (e.g., ITC-SOPI [22])
		  ○ other UX-related variables (e.g., flow [78]).

Usability test #2	Design a trial to assess usability, side-effects and acceptance of technology (when applicable) on a sample of **target users**.	• Sample size: n ≥ 5 (older adults with MCI);
		• Outcomes:
		  ○ Usability (e.g., SUS)
		  ○ Cybersickness (especially in the case of navigational environments, e.g., SSQ)
		  ○ Acceptance of technology (e.g., TAM3 [41])
		  ○ Other variables of interest (e.g., cognitive and physical ergonomics, perceived effort), also via think-aloud protocols

Pilot trial	Design a feasibility study with a representative sample trial to assess the feasibility of the intervention.	• Sample size: n ≥ 5 for each group (older adults with MCI); • Outcomes: ○ Clinical outcomes of interest (i.e., cognitive outcomes)

(*Continued*)

Table 10.1 Process applied in design of immersive VR-based applications dedicated to physical and cognitive training [73]. (*Continued*)

Phase	What to do	Specifications
Randomized controlled trial	Design a randomized clinical trial according to evidence-based medicine principles.	• Sample size: large enough to obtain statistical power (older adults with MCI). • Outcomes: ○ Clinical outcomes of interest (i.e., cognitive outcomes)

A further step forward can be made—following an assessment of clinical effectiveness—to implement the same type of interventions in the home. In this case, requirements related to usability, acceptance, and safety must be stricter, because the clinician or researcher will not be available to supervise the training to: (1) ensure that the gaming area is clear (e.g., the user is far enough from windows or stairs; pets do not cross over while the person is immersed and walking) and (2) intervene in case of errors (e.g., crash of the application) or adverse events (e.g., falls, occurrence of sickness). Thus, proper training of care-givers is not negligible.

10.3   Future Research Agenda and Roadmap

In spite of advances in hardware and software technologies, it is evident that issues related to HF/E in XR still exist [29, 83, 84]. Stanney *et al.* [84] suggest that cybersickness represents a problem that could jeopardize the promise of XR. There is a need, therefore, for the HF/XR research community to help technology developers by providing a clear guidance on HF principles to inform XR design (i.e., to include a consideration of user tasks and context of use), and to establish standardized tools and protocols for the evaluation of the design suitability and UX of XR applications.

10.3.1   Design Methods

In HF and HCI research, it is well known that a user-centered design approach, in which the end-user is considered within the design process, is essential to ensure effective design [72]. This theme has been repeatedly underlined in the development of new technologies [85–87]. Moreover, the application of HF during the early stages of development not only improves the efficiency and productivity of technology as well as human performance [12, 88, 89]; it also reduces costs due to design errors and avoids outcomes that do not satisfy end users [90–92].

Several methodologies have been created in order to guide developers in introducing HF/E in the early stages of design, including user-centered design and participatory design [93], heuristic evaluation [94], user analysis [95], and scenario-based design [96]. Unfortunately, methods to understand user's needs and requirements are often not applied when designing and developing XR applications [92]. Saghafian *et al.* [87] interviewed application developers in AR, MR, or VR (designers, developers, chief executives, and the research director) to find out how HF are applied within the design process. It emerged that most of those who participate in the application development are not familiar with HF principles, even if they apply them in design; moreover, the perception of HF among technology developers is commonly limited to usability. There is therefore a need for further developments of tools that offer guidance for designers, including recommendations (e.g., MAUVE [31]) or best practices inferred from experimental activities [97].

The developers interviewed by Saghafian [87] commented that HFs are not applied enough in their field, due to several issues including: increasing the diversity of end user characteristics (e.g., age, interests, needs), rapid evolution of technologies, and the lack of a standardized HF protocol for XR applications design and evaluation [87]. Furthermore, a wider access to authoring tools enabling people who have no specialist training in HCI to create XR applications presents a greater need for design guidance and support for developers [98]. With the increasing application of XR technology in new areas, it is important that representative end users are involved in the design-development process and that their requirements are adequately considered. For example, with population aging, it is necessary to take into account that, with physical and cognitive decline (also physiological), some of the "traditional" interaction methods may not be appropriate [83]. Conversely, the COVID-19 pandemic highlighted the need for investing in new methods to provide continuous education to children when they are not physically present in schools [99]. XR technologies offer potential for the development of engaging learning environments that children could use at home. However, limited research has been conducted to explore the UXs of young people. Future work in HF/E is thus needed to define new safety recommendations and guidelines for increasingly diverse applications of XR, including those used by vulnerable populations.

10.3.2   Technology Improvements

Besides better design and evaluation of the UX, improving XR technology also offers benefits in terms of enhancing the sense of presence, usability, and technology acceptance, and reducing cybersickness. This is especially true in the case of VR environments; it seems to be less common in AR or MR applications [100], but studies aimed at evaluating longer exposure to these technologies are still lacking [84]. Technological aspects that affect HF/E in HMDs include the weight of the device, and the range of adjustment of interpupillary distance (IPD). It has been suggested that the poor IPD fit of early HMDs for users of smaller stature is a more likely explanation for reported gender differences in the experience of cybersickness symptoms than an increased susceptibility of females to cybersickness per se [84]. It is therefore important to design new devices to be accessible to as many users as possible, considering also their anatomical characteristics (e.g., for children).

Moreover, improvements are required for all those devices aimed at rendering force, haptic or tactile feedback. Current haptic devices are encumbered, and may cause an inadequate physical load to the user's hand or arms. Similarly, consideration is needed in the design of platforms and other systems developed to provide vestibular cues: the presence of a moving platform may indeed be of help in reducing cybersickness, but the UX research on this topic is still sparse [67].

Consideration must also be given to the design of new interaction technologies: up to now, device-free gestures are under development, but they lack tactile feedback; the presence of interaction devices, instead, may be uncomfortable, make the application difficult to interact with [82], and cause unnatural user's behaviors [101, 102]. Finally, other interaction modalities, e.g., via biofeedback or voice, should be improved and evaluated in well-designed usability studies.

10.3.3   Short- to Mid-Term, Areas of Interest

1. Further work should be conducted to understand the cost/benefit analysis of multimodal experiences across a range of application areas and activities (design, communication, research, etc.) within the XR. This work is likely to evolve as the costs of technology changes, but in general, more work is needed to understand when multimodal experiences would be most beneficial.

2. An interesting line of work is to explore the ways in which the senses operate together in multimodal XR. Relatedly, researchers have for a time been interested in what level of fidelity is required in multisensory XR [60]. This, and further challenges about how the senses interact in multimodal environments, needs further investigation.

3. As indicated above, further work is needed to understand how to best deliver and implement multimodal VEs. This relates to the cost/benefit analysis, but the development of guidelines for how to design and implement multimodal XR in research, consumer, industrial, and other applications would be useful.

10.3.4   Longer-Term Research Opportunities

1. Establish a better understanding as to why certain people benefit more from multimodal experiences than others, including how individual characteristics affect these experiences, and in what ways. Further work could identify the mechanisms to identify these differences, and recommend configurations that will optimize users' experiences.

2. Define tools allowing for the investigation of the variables of interest (e.g., presence, cybersickness) during the experience in XR, with the aim of capturing user feedback at specific moments, without interrupting the flow of experience, or causing a break in presence.

3. Improve not only the theoretical models of cybersickness and aftereffects (as suggested by Stanney *et al.* [84]) but also presence, usability, and acceptance models, in order to better address applications and XR system design.

4. Define new tools aimed at investigating the UX in collaborative/social environments.

Recently published research articles and review papers represent an evident effort in creating a framework that includes all the variables that influence the adoption of new technologies. Nonetheless, there is currently no univocal framework that considers all the variables studied to date. In an attempt to summarize the main considerations provided in this work, an updated version of the framework diagram reported in Figure 10.1 is proposed, as represented in Figure 10.2.

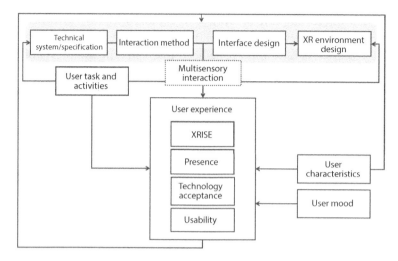

Figure 10.2 Revised HF/E framework of factors influencing UX of interaction with XR.

The UX now includes the symptoms and effects, referred to as XRISE (eXtended reality-induced symptoms and effects), sense of presence, and technology acceptance and usability. These have been identified as the main categories that contribute to the UX. According to the different models depicted in Section 10.2.2, each category may be further expanded including more specific variables, e.g., Perceived Usability (PU) and Perceived Ease Of Use (PEOU), in the case of technology acceptance, or considering the mentioned variables as multidimensional rather than one dimensional. For example, the sense of presence is considered both one dimensional (e.g., [49, 55]) and multidimensional [42]. As stated above, following a user-centered approach is recommended and, therefore, the user characteristics should also have an impact on specifications of the XR application: on the choice of technology and interaction method as well as on the design of the interface and the VE content. The user characteristics (e.g., age, gender, digital literacy) are predefined factors that influence the UX; an unpredictable factor that also has an impact on UX is the mood of the user in the moment that they enter the XR experience. This variable has been added to the updated diagram to fill a current gap; i.e., in Chuah's work [42], the most complete model, the user's mood, is not fully considered, except for positive feelings such as enjoyment.

Acknowledgments

The work reported in Section 10.2.3.1 was supported by the Institution of Occupational Safety and Health through its research fund, and by the

Engineering and Physical Science Research Council (EP/N00549X/1). The work reported in Section 2.3.2 was supported by the Italian Ministry of Health within the Young Researcher Project GR-2013-02356043: "A comprehensive preventive program for dementia tailored on the neuropsychological profile of persons with Mild Cognitive Impairment: cognitive stimulation, physical intervention and healthy nutrition, a randomized controlled trial," and within the project PE-2013-02355948 "High-end and Low-End Virtual Reality Systems for the Rehabilitation of Frailty in the Elderly."

References

1. Slater, M. and Sanchez-Vives, M.V., Enhancing our lives with immersive virtual reality. *Front. Robot. AI*, 3, 74, DEC, 2016.
2. Vailshery, S.L., *AR/VR headset shipments worldwide 2020-2025 | Statista*, Statista, New York, 2021.
3. Wilson, J.R., Effects of participating in virtual environments: A review of current knowledge. *Saf. Sci.*, 23, 1, 39–51, 1996.
4. Newby, G.B., Virtual reality: Scientific and technological challenges. *Libr. Inf. Sci. Res.*, 18, 3, 278–280, 1996.
5. Cummings, J.J. and Bailenson, J.N., How Immersive Is Enough? A Meta-Analysis of the Effect of Immersive Technology on User Presence. *Media Psychol.*, 19, 2, 272–309, 2016.
6. Sharples, S., Stedmon, A.W., D'Cruz, M., Patel, H., Cobb, S., Yates, T., Saikayasit, R., Wilson, J.R., Human Factors of Virtual Reality - Where are We Now? *Meet. Divers. Ergon.*, 173–186, 2007.
7. Sharples, S., Cobb, S., Moody, A., Wilson, J.R., Virtual reality induced symptoms and effects (VRISE): Comparison of head mounted display (HMD), desktop and projection display systems. *Displays*, 29, 2, 58–69, 2008.
8. Chang, E., Kim, H.T., Yoo, B., Virtual Reality Sickness: A Review of Causes and Measurements. *Int. J. Hum. Comput. Interact.*, 36, 17, 1658–1682, 2020.
9. Nichols, S. and Patel, H., Health and safety implications of virtual reality: A review of empirical evidence. *Appl. Ergon.*, 33, 3, 251–271, 2002.
10. Stanney, K.M., Mourant, R.R., Kennedy, R.S., Human factors issues in virtual environments: A review of the literature. *Presence Teleoperators Virtual Environ.*, 7, 4, 327–351, 1998.
11. Cobb, S.V., Nichols, S., Ramsey, A., Wilson, J.R., Virtual Reality-Induced Symptoms and Effects (VRISE). *Presence Teleoperators Virtual Environ.*, 8, 2, 169–186, 1999.
12. Stanney, K., Realizing the full potential of virtual reality: human factors issues that could stand in the way. *Proc. - Virtual Real. Annu. Int. Symp.*, 1995.

13. Stanney, K. and Salvendy, G., Aftereffects and Sense of Presence in Virtual Environments: Formulation of a Research and Development Agenda. *Int. J. Hum. Comput. Interact.*, 10, 2, 135–178, 1998.

14. Wirth, W. *et al.*, A process model of the formation of spatial presence experiences. *Media Psychol.*, 9, 3, 493–525, 2007.

15. Slater, M., Place illusion and plausibility can lead to realistic behaviour in immersive virtual environments. *Philos. Trans. R. Soc. B Biol. Sci.*, 364, 1535, 3549–3557, 2009.

16. Biocca, F., Harms, C., Burgoon, J.K., Toward a More Robust Theory and Measure of Social Presence: Review and Suggested Criteria. *Presence Teleoperators Virtual Environ.*, 12, 5, 456–480, 2003.

17. Bowman, D.A., Gabbard, J.L., Hix, D., A survey of usability evaluation in virtual environments: Classification and comparison of methods. *Presence Teleoperators Virtual Environ.*, 11, 4, 404–424, 2002.

18. Gabbard, J.L., Hix, D., Swan, J.E., User-centered design and evaluation of virtual environments. *IEEE Comput. Graph. Appl.*, 19, 6, 51–59, 1999.

19. Swan, J.E. and Gabbard, J.L., Usability engineering for augmented reality: employing user-based studies to inform design. *IEEE Trans. Vis. Comput. Graph.*, 14, 3, 513–525, 2008.

20. O'Brien, H.L. and Lebow, M., Mixed-methods approach to measuring user experience in online news interactions. *J. Am. Soc. Inf. Sci. Technol.*, 64, 8, 1543–1556, 2013.

21. Laugwitz, B., Held, T., Schrepp, M., Construction and evaluation of a user experience questionnaire. *Lect. Notes Comput. Sci. (including Subser. Lect. Notes Artif. Intell. Lect. Notes Bioinformatics)*, 5298 LNCS, 63–76, 2008.

22. Lessiter, J., Freeman, J., Keogh, E., Davidoff, J., A cross-media presence questionnaire: The ITC-sense of presence inventory. *Presence Teleoperators Virtual Environ.*, 10, 3, 282–297, 2001.

23. Behr, K.M., Nosper, A., Klimmt, C., Hartmann, T., Some practical considerations of ethical issues in VR research. *Presence Teleoperators Virtual Environ.*, 14, 6, 668–676, 2005.

24. Weech, S., Kenny, S., Barnett-Cowan, M., Presence and cybersickness in virtual reality are negatively related: A review. *Front. Psychol.*, 10, 158, FEB, 2019.

25. Cooper, N., Milella, F., Cant, I., Pinto, C., White, M.D., Meyer, G.F., The Effects of Multisensory Cues on the Sense of Presence and Task Performance in a Virtual Reality Environment. *EuroVR 2015*, October, 2015.

26. Busscher, B., de Vliegher, D., Ling, Y., Brinkman, W.P., Physiological measures and self-report to evaluate neutral virtual reality worlds. *J. Cyber Ther. Rehabil.*, 4, 1, 15–25, 2011.

27. Usoh, M., Catena, E., Arman, S., Slater, M., Using presence questionnaires in reality. *Presence Teleoperators Virtual Environ.*, 9, 5, 497–503, 2000.

28. Witmer, B.G. and Singer, M.J., Measuring presence in virtual environments: A presence questionnaire. *Presence Teleoperators Virtual Environ.*, 7, 3, 225–240, 1998.

29. Saredakis, D., Szpak, A., Birckhead, B., Keage, H.A.D., Rizzo, A., Loetscher, T., Factors associated with virtual reality sickness in head-mounted displays: A systematic review and meta-analysis. *Front. Hum. Neurosci.*, 14, 96, 2020.

30. Darken, R.P. and Sibert, J.L., Wayfinding strategies and behaviors in large virtual worlds, in: *Conference on Human Factors in Computing Systems - Proceedings*, pp. 142–149, 1996.

31. Stanney, K.M., Mollaghasemi, M., Reeves, L., Breaux, R., Graeber, D.A., Usability engineering of virtual environments (VEs): Identifying multiple criteria that drive effective VE system design. *Int. J. Hum. Comput. Stud.*, 58, 4, 447-481, 2003.

32. Milgram, P., Takemura, H., Utsumi, A., Kishino, F., Telemanipulator and Telepresence Technologies II. *Proc. SPIE - Int. Soc. Opt. Eng.*, 2590, 2351, pp. 282–292, 1995.

33. Bach, C. and Scapin, D.L., Obstacles and Perspectives for Evaluating Mixed Reality Systems Usability. *Comput. Des. User Interfaces*, 2004.

34. Tuena, C., Pedroli, E., Trimarchi, P.D., Gallucci, A., Chiappini, M., Goulene, K., Gaggioli, A., Riva, G., Lattanzio, F., Giunco, F., Stramba-Badiale, M., Usability issues of clinical and research applications of virtual reality in older people: A systematic review. *Front. Hum. Neurosci.*, 14, Article 93, April, 2020.

35. Tan, H., Sun, J., Wenjia, W., Zhu, C., User Experience & Usability of Driving: A Bibliometric Analysis of 2000-2019. *Int. J. Hum. Comput. Interact.*, 37, 4, 297–307, 2021.

36. Schnack, A., Wright, M.J., Holdershaw, J.L., Immersive virtual reality technology in a three-dimensional virtual simulated store: Investigating telepresence and usability. *Food Res. Int.*, 117, 40–49, 2019.

37. Somrak, A., Pogačnik, M., Guna, J., Suitability and comparison of questionnaires assessing virtual reality-induced symptoms and effects and user experience in virtual environments. *Sensors (Switzerland)*, 21, 4, 1–24, 2021.

38. Pruitt, J., Marques, M., Singer, H., Blatchford, A., HP Windows Mixed Reality vs Meta 2: Investigating Differences in Workload and Usability for a Ball-sorting Task. *Pegasus Rev. UCF Undergrad. Res. J.*, 13, 1, 06, 2021.

39. Davis, F.D., Perceived usefulness, perceived ease of use, and user acceptance of information technology. *MIS Q. Manage. Inf. Syst.*, 13, 3, 319–339, 1989.

40. Viswanath, V. and Davis, F.D., A Theoretical Extension of the Technology Acceptance Model: Four Longitudinal Field Studies. *Manage. Sci.*, 46, 2, 186–204, May 2014, 2000.

41. Venkatesh, V. and Bala, H., Technology acceptance model 3 and a research agenda on interventions. *Decis. Sci.*, 39, 2, 273–315, 2008.

42. Chuah, S., Wearable XR-Technology: Literature Review, Conceptual Framework and Future Research Directions. *Int. J. Technol. Mark.*, 13, 4, 205–259, 2019.

43. Sledgianowski, D. and Kulviwat, S., Using social network sites: The effects of playfulness, critical mass and trust in a hedonic context. *J. Comput. Inf. Syst.*, 49, 4, 74–83, 2009.

44. Glass, R. and Li, S., Social influence and instant messaging adoption. *J. Comput. Inf. Syst.*, 51, 2, 24–30, 2010.

45. Makki, T.W., DeCook, J.R., Kadylak, T., Lee, O.J.Y., The Social Value of Snapchat: An Exploration of Affiliation Motivation, the Technology Acceptance Model, and Relational Maintenance in Snapchat Use. *Int. J. Hum. Comput. Interact.*, 34, 5, 410–420, 2018.

46. Domina, T., Lee, S.E., MacGillivray, M., Understanding factors affecting consumer intention to shop in a virtual world. *J. Retail. Consum. Serv.*, 19, 6, 613–620, 2012.

47. Huang, Y.C., Backman, S.J., Backman, K.F., Moore, D.W., Exploring user acceptance of 3D virtual worlds in travel and tourism marketing. *Tour. Manage.*, 36, 490–501, 2013.

48. Venkatesh, V. and Speier, C., Computer technology training in the workplace: A longitudinal investigation of the effect of mood. *Organ. Behav. Hum. Decis. Process.*, 79, 1, 1–28, 1999.

49. Sagnier, C., Loup-Escande, E., Lourdeaux, D., Thouvenin, I., Valléry, G., User Acceptance of Virtual Reality: An Extended Technology Acceptance Model. *Int. J. Hum. Comput. Interact.*, 36, 11, 993–1007, 2020.

50. Crant, J.M., Devaraj, S., Easley, R.F., How does personality matter? Relating the five-factor model to technology acceptance and use. *Inf. Syst. Res.*, 19, 1, 93–105, 635–647, 2008.

51. Rauschnabel, P.A., Brem, A., Ivens, B.S., Who will buy smart glasses? Empirical results of two pre-market-entry studies on the role of personality in individual awareness and intended adoption of Google Glass wearables. *Comput. Hum. Behav.*, 49, 2015.

52. Zsila, Á., Orosz, G., Bőthe, B., Tóth-Király, I., Király, O., Griffiths, M., Demetrovics, Z., An empirical study on the motivations underlying augmented reality games: The case of Pokémon Go during and after Pokémon fever. *Pers. Individ. Differ.*, 133, 56–66, 2018.

53. Jung, Y., Kim, S., Choi, B., Consumer valuation of the wearables: The case of smartwatches. *Comput. Hum. Behav.*, 63, 899–905, 2016.

54. Schuemie, M.J., Van der Straaten, P., Krijn, M., Van der Mast, C.A.P.G., Research on presence in virtual reality: A survey. *Cyberpsychol. Behav.*, 4, 2, 183–201, 2001.

55. Herz, M. and Rauschnabel, P.A., Understanding the diffusion of virtual reality glasses: The role of media, fashion and technology. *Technol. Forecast. Soc. Change*, 138, 228–242, 2019.

56. Hein, D.W.E. and Rauschnabel, P.A., Augmented Reality Smart Glasses and Knowledge Management: A Conceptual Framework for Enterprise Social Networks. *Enterp. Soc. Netw.*, 83–109, 2016.

57. Lawson, G., Shaw, E., Roper, T., Nilsson, T., Bajorunaite, L., Batool, A., *Immersive virtual worlds: Multi-sensory virtual environments for health and safety training*, IOSH, London, 2019.

58. Nilsson, T., Shaw, E., Cobb, S.V.G., Miller, D., Roper, T., Lawson, G., Meng-Ko, H., Khan, J., Multisensory virtual environment for fire evacuation training, in: *Extended Abstracts of the 2019 CHI Conference on Human Factors in Computing Systems*, 2019.

59. Shaw, E., Roper, T., Nilsson, T., Lawson, G., Cobb, S.V.G., Miller, D., The heat is on: Exploring user behaviour in a multisensory virtual environment for fire evacuation. *Conf. Hum. Factors Comput. Syst. – Proc.*, 2019.

60. Chalmers, A. and Ferko, A., Levels of realism: From virtual reality to real virtuality. *Proc. - SCCG 2008 24th Spring Conf. Comput. Graph.*, 2010.

61. Kinateder, M., Ronchi, E., Nilsson, D., Kobes, M., Müller, M., Pauli, P., Mühlberger, A., Virtual reality for fire evacuation research. *2014 Fed. Conf. Comput. Sci. Inf. Syst. FedCSIS 2014*, 2014-Janua, 2014.

62. Smith, S.P. and Trenholme, D., Rapid prototyping a virtual fire drill environment using computer game technology. *Fire Saf. J.*, 44, 4, 559–569, 2009.

63. Renner, R.S., Velichkovsky, B.M., Helmert, J.R., The perception of egocentric distances in virtual environments - A review. *ACM Comput. Surv.*, 46, 2, 1–40, 2013.

64. Lawson, G., Roper, T., Abdullah, C., Multimodal 'sensory illusions' for improving spatial awareness in virtual environments. *ACM Int. Conf. Proceeding Ser.*, 06-08-Sept, 2016.

65. Rose, T., Nam, C.S., Chen, K.B., Immersion of virtual reality for rehabilitation - Review. *Appl. Ergon.*, 69, 153–161, 2018.

66. Gorman, C. and Gustafsson, L., The use of augmented reality for rehabilitation after stroke: a narrative review. *Disabil. Rehabil. Assist. Technol.*, 14, 1–9, 2020.

67. Rizzo, A. and Kim, G.J., A SWOT analysis of the field of virtual reality rehabilitation and therapy. *Presence Teleoperators Virtual Environ.*, 14, 2, 119–146, 2005.

68. Standen, P.J., Threapleton, K., Connell, L., Richardson, A., Brown, D.J., Battersby, S., Sutton, C.J., Platts, F., Patients' use of a home-based virtual reality system to provide rehabilitation of the upper limb following stroke. *Phys. Ther.*, 95, 3, 350–359, 2015.

69. Riva, G., Waterworth, J.A., Waterworth, E.L., The layers of presence: A bio-cultural approach to understanding presence in natural and mediated environments. *Cyberpsychol. Behav.*, 7, 4, 402–416, 2004.

70. Coldham, G. and Cook, D.M., VR usability from elderly cohorts: Preparatory challenges in overcoming technology rejection, in: *2017 National Information Technology Conference (NITC)*, pp. 131–135, 2017.

71. Mrakic-Sposta, S., Di Santo, S.G., Franchini, F., Arlati, S., Zangiacomi, A., Greci, L., Moretti, S., Jesuthasan, N., Marzorati, M., Rizzo, G., others, Effects of combined physical and cognitive virtual reality-based training on

cognitive impairment and oxidative stress in MCI patients: A pilot study. *Front. Aging Neurosci.*, 10, 282, 2018.

72. Hakkinen, J., Vuori, T., Paakka, M., *Postural stability and sickness symptoms after HMD use*, November 2002, 2005.

73. Oculus, *Health and safety warnings.* https://www.oculus.com/legal/health-and-safety-warnings/

74. Mayor, J., Raya, L., Sanchez, A., A comparative study of virtual reality methods of interaction and locomotion based on presence, cybersickness and usability. *IEEE Trans. Emerg. Top. Comput.*, 9, 1542–1553, 2019.

75. Faulkner, L., Beyond the five-user assumption: Benefits of increased sample sizes in usability testing. *Behav. Res. Methods Instrum. Comput.*, 35, 3, 379–383, 2003.

76. Brooke, J., A 'quick and dirty' usability scale, in: *Usability evaluation in industry*, pp. 189–194, 1996.

77. Kennedy, R.S., Lane, N.E., Berbaum, K.S., Lilienthal, M.G., Simulator sickness questionnaire: An enhanced method for quantifying simulator sickness. *Int. J. Aviat. Psychol.*, 3, 3, 203–220, 1993.

78. Csikszentmihalyi, M., *Finding flow: The psychology of engagement with everyday life*, Basic Books, New York, 1997.

79. Pedroli, E. *et al.*, Characteristics, usability, and users experience of a system combining cognitive and physical therapy in a virtual environment: Positive bike. *Sensors (Switzerland)*, 18, 7, 2343, 2018.

80. Arlati, S., Di Santo, S.G., Franchini, F., Mondellini, M., Filiputti, B., Luchi, M., Ratto, F., Ferrigno, G., Sacco, M., Greci, L., Acceptance and usability of immersive virtual reality in older adults with objective and subjective cognitive decline. *J. Alzheimer's Dis.*, [In press], 80, 1025–1038, 2021.

81. Mondellini, M., Arlati, S., Greci, L., Ferrigno, G., Sacco, M., Sense of presence and cybersickness while cycling in virtual environments: Their contribution to subjective experience. *Lect. Notes Comput. Sci. (including Subser. Lect. Notes Artif. Intell. Lect. Notes Bioinformatics)*, 10850 LNCS, 3–20, 2018.

82. Mondellini, M., Arlati, S., Pizzagalli, S., Greci, L., Sacco, M., Ferrigno, G., Sacco, M., Assessment of the usability of an immersive virtual supermarket for the cognitive rehabilitation of elderly patients: A pilot study on young adults, in: *2018 IEEE 6th International Conference on Serious Games and Applications for Health (SeGAH)*, pp. 1–8, 2018.

83. Kim, Y.M., Rhiu, I., Yun, M.H., A Systematic Review of a Virtual Reality System from the Perspective of User Experience. *Int. J. Hum. Comput. Interact.*, 36, 10, 893–910, 2020.

84. Stanney, K., Lawson, B.D., Rokers, B., Dennison, M., Fidopiastis, C., Stoffregen, T., Weech, S., Fulvio, J.M., Identifying Causes of and Solutions for Cybersickness in Immersive Technology: Reformulation of a Research and Development Agenda. *Int. J. Hum. Comput. Interact.*, 36, 19, 1783–1803, 2020.

85. Lewis, C.H. and Griffin, M.J., Human factors consideration in clinical applications of virtual reality. *Stud. Health Technol. Inform.*, 44, 35–56, 1997.

86. Paes, D. and Irizarry, J., A usability study of an immersive virtual reality platform for building design review: Considerations on human factors and user interface. *Constr. Res. Congr. 2018 Constr. Inf. Technol. - Sel. Pap. from Constr. Res. Congr. 2018*, 2018-April, Front Psychol. 2021; 12: 634352. 2018.

87. Saghafian, M., Sitompul, T.A., Laumann, K., Sundnes, K., Lindell, R., Application of Human Factors in the Development Process of Immersive Visual Technologies: Challenges and Future Improvements. 12, 2021.

88. Fernando Capretz, L., Bringing the human factor to software engineering. *IEEE Software*, 31, 2, 102–104, 2014.

89. Calp, M.H. and Akcayol, M.A., The importance of human-computer interaction in the development process of software projects. *Glob. J. Inf. Technol.*, 2015.

90. Redström, J., Towards user design? on the shift from object to user as the subject of design. *Des. Stud.*, 27, 2, 123–139, 2006.

91. Houssin, R. and Coulibaly, A., An approach to solve contradiction problems for the safety integration in innovative design process. *Comput. Ind.*, 62, 4, 398–406, 2011.

92. Sætren, G.B., Hogenboom, S., Laumann, K., A study of a technological development process: Human factors—the forgotten factors? *Cogn. Technol. Work*, 18, 3, 595–611, 2016.

93. Harte, R., Glynn, L., Rodríguez-Molinero, A., Baker, P.M., Scharf, T., Quinlan, L.R., ÓLaighin, G., A Human-Centered Design Methodology to Enhance the Usability, Human Factors, and User Experience of Connected Health Systems: A Three-Phase Methodology. *JMIR Hum. Factors*, 4, 1, 2017.

94. Nielsen, J. and Molich, R., Heuristic evaluation of user interfaces, in: *Conference on Human Factors in Computing Systems - Proceedings*, pp. 249–256, 1990.

95. Dillon, A. and Watson, C., User analysis in HCI - The historical lessons from individual differences research. *Int. J. Hum. Comput. Stud.*, 45, 6, 619–637, 1996.

96. Carroll, J.M. and Haynes, S.R., Scenario-based design, in: *Handb. Human-Machine Interact. A Human-Centered Des. Approach*, 2011.

97. Gabbard, J.L. and Hix, D., Usability Engineering of Virtual Environments, in: *Handb. Virtual Environ*, 2014.

98. Ashtari, N., Bunt, A., McGrenere, J., Nebeling, M., Chilana, P.K., Creating Augmented and Virtual Reality Applications: Current Practices, Challenges, and Opportunities. *Conf. Hum. Factors Comput. Syst. – Proc.*, 2020.

99. Timovski, R., Koceska, N., Koceski, S., Review: The use of Augmented and Virtual Reality in Education, 2020. https://eprints.ugd.edu.mk/27294/

100. Sun, X., Houssin, R., Renaud, J., Gardoni, M., A review of methodologies for integrating human factors and ergonomics in engineering design. *Int. J. Prod. Res.*, 57, 15–16, 2019.

101. Furmanek, M.P., Schettino, L.F., Yarossi, M., Kirkman, S., Adamovich, S.V., Tunik, E., Coordination of reach-to-grasp in physical and haptic-free virtual environments. *J. Neuroeng. Rehabil.*, 16, 1, 1–14, 2019.

102. Collins BSc, J., Hoermann PhD, S., Regenbrecht Dr Ing, H., Comparing a finger dexterity assessment in virtual, video-mediated, and unmediated reality. *Int. J. Child Health Hum. Dev.*, 9, 3, 333–342, 2016.

11

XR and Neurorehabilitation

Sara Arlati[1]* and Davide Borghetti[2]

[1]*Institute of Intelligent Industrial Systems and Technologies for Advanced Manufacturing (STIIMA), Italian National Research Council (CNR), Lecco, Italy*
[2]*Dia.Ri. srls, Accredited Healthcare Facility for Neuropsychological Rehabilitation, Terricciola (PI), Italy*

Abstract

Neurological disorders represent the major cause of disability worldwide. Since years, XR has been used to support the administration of motor and cognitive rehabilitation programs, on the basis of the hypothesis that it was able to increase the motivation to train, and thus the compliance to the treatment and the performances of the patients. Nowadays, the first evidence from well-structured studies and literature reviews seems to confirm this hypothesis, reporting positive outcomes, especially when XR is used in conjunction with other treatments. Moreover, patients' motivation appears to be positively influenced, and so it is for their general attitude toward technology, even in the case of patients with no previous experience with XR. On the other hand, the large heterogeneity of the investigated programs—in terms of technology, immersion, proposed task, duration, frequency, and intensity—makes it impossible to draw definitive conclusions in terms of defining the optimal pathology-specific (or symptom-specific) treatment. This makes the use of XR in standard care still remote, and allowed highlighting a series of open challenges that still exist in the field. In the future, answering these challenges will provide patients with safe, tailored, and adaptable rehabilitation programs that can be carried out at home, and healthcare systems with the means to implement effectively and extensively the paradigm of continuity of care, thus reducing the societal and economic burden related to the management of neurological disorders.

Keywords: XR, neurological disorders, rehabilitation, cognitive training, physical exercise, continuity of care

Corresponding author: Sara.Arlati@stiima.cnr.it

Mariano Alcañiz, Marco Sacco and Jolanda G. Tromp (eds.) Roadmapping Extended Reality: Fundamentals and Applications, (257–282) © 2022 Scrivener Publishing LLC

11.1   Introduction

The term *neurological disorders* covers a diverse set of conditions resulting from injury or impairments of the nervous system. Such disorders represent the major cause of disability and are the second cause of death worldwide [1]. Also, at a social level, this set of pathologies represent an important challenge: in 2006, the World Health Organization (WHO) estimated that neurological conditions constitute over 6% of the global burden of diseases [2]. In spite of the increasing attention on non-communicable diseases and the effort of the scientific and medical communities, in 2017, the United Nations (UN) General Assembly stated that the reduction in the burden of these disorders has been insufficient to achieve the UN sustainable development goal targets by 2030 [1].

Neurological disorders include different conditions that generally cause the person to experience—either at the acute or chronic level—motor, cognitive, and/or sensory impairments. The presence of disabilities is also often connected to the reduced autonomy in the activities of daily living (ADLs), and thus to a lower quality of life (QoL).

For what concerns the management of neurological disorders, treatments could be diverse, and are clearly dependent on the etiology of the disease and on its symptoms. For some neurological disorders, non-pharmacological interventions—based on the repetition of skill-oriented motor or cognitive tasks—could be implemented to improve clinical outcomes, and also to recover specific functions.

In these cases, eXtended Reality (XR) technologies have been emerging as promising solutions for administering innovative treatments. Indeed, XR has the advantage of recreating ecological scenarios, allowing the patients to (re)train in a safe and controlled environment, and also to better associate the executed task to real life, thus enhancing the transfer of the acquired capabilities to ADLs.

Moreover, XR technologies allow for the generation of real-time feedback that could improve patient's awareness, thus allowing the implementation of unsupervised programs that could be exploited also at home [3].

Finally, XR could contribute in making the rehabilitative session more engaging and motivating, promoting higher adherence and, consequently, better recovery. The increase of sense of presence (SoP), generally associated to technologies able to provide high immersion, is a key element in this process of engagement of the user. SoP, in fact, represents the psychological feeling of being "there" in a computer-generated environment [4], and has been proved to enhance the experience of a virtual world, making it more motivating, and possibly eliciting better performances [5].

Because of this reason, the advent of good-quality and relatively affordable virtual reality (VR) devices has paved the way for the implementation of immersive scenarios dedicated to motor and cognitive rehabilitation.

In spite of the advantages, it has to be remembered that the use of immersive technologies, especially if they are occlusive of real world, may cause cyber-sickness, i.e., a series of subjective symptoms arising because of the XR-induced sensory mismatch [6]. Safety concerns as balance issues, due to the increase of body sway [7], during immersion, or risk of trips have to be considered too. Also, at a psychological level, there may be some side-effects, especially when dealing with emotional contents [8]; in all these cases, both the beginning of the immersion and aftereffects due to "return to reality" may induce disorientation in the XR user [9], especially if he/she suffers from a cognitive disability.

In the following paragraphs, the current state of the art regarding the use of XR in rehabilitation is presented. Open challenges—also related to the above-mentioned side-effects—and points of strength are then pointed out and discussed.

11.2   XR and Neurorehabilitation

According to the WHO [2], the 10 most spread diseases affecting the nervous systems are (from higher to lower prevalence): migraine and headache disorders, neurological injuries (among which spinal cord injury (SCI) and traumatic brain injury (TBI), stroke, epilepsy, Alzheimer's disease and other dementias, neuro-infections, Parkinson's disease (PD), and multiple sclerosis (MS)). Besides these primary pathologies, another important issue—that may have a detrimental effect on the autonomy and the QoL of patients in the context of neurological disorders—is pain. Thus, this issue will be considered too.

As already mentioned, for some of these diseases, no rehabilitative treatment is neither possible nor necessary, because of the intrinsic characteristics of the disease: e.g., neuroinfections as the viral encephalitis, poliomyelitis, or tuberculosis first require the treatment of the primary cause of disease. The same applies to pathologies deriving from malnutrition. For some others, as headaches and epilepsy, the treatment with drugs is the most widespread and effective. Also, in the latter cases, proposing the patient with images that flash quickly has to be avoided not to induce seizures or symptoms.

For the remaining neurological disorders, the implementation of an XR-based non-pharmacological intervention may be not only effective but also preferred because it is free from drug-related side-effects.

For instance, drugs inhibiting acetylcholinesterase (i.e., galantamine) have been employed to manage the symptoms of dementia. However, they have been proved to increase the death rate, and their use has to be strictly regulated to adequately balance risks and benefits. This fact has raised a question in terms of ethical issues, that—with non-pharmacological interventions—can be avoided or, at least, limited.

11.2.1   XR and Neurological Injuries

The most common neurological injury is TBI. It is a disruption in the normal function of the brain, usually resulting from a violent blow or jolt to the head, or penetrating head injury. The severity of a TBI depends on the extent of the damage to the brain, ranging from a brief change in mental state to significant and lasting functional impairments, related to cognition, vision, mobility, and mental health [10]. TBI contributes to worldwide death and disability more than any other traumatic insult, with 69 million individuals sustaining a TBI each year [11].

In spite of the only recent attention toward cognitive and physical rehabilitation in TBI, rehabilitation has been proven to have great impact on the QoL of TBI patients. XR technologies have been used successfully as a therapeutic intervention.

Regarding physical rehabilitation, VR is the most frequently used XR technology, and its main application regards gait and balance deficits. Mostly, commercially available systems have been used to conduct systematic studies; Motek CAREN and GRAIL systems, and Nintendo Wii Fit are some (semi-immersive and expensive, and non-immersive and affordable, respectively) examples for what concerns standing balance [12]; pressure-sensitive mats with piezoresistive sensors are an example of sensor devices aimed at retraining seated balance and trunk control [13, 14]. Most of these training programs had positive outcomes improving balance and general motor functions; nonetheless, they have been mostly implemented in case studies or small randomized controlled trials (RCTs) [12, 15]. Benefits in upper limbs' motion were recorded with programs targeting such body parts: improvements were also proven to be effectively transferred to real life [16], as it was for ADL training [17]. VR has also been used effectively—in a single-case study—to improve vestibular issues, such as dizziness and unbalance caused by a head trauma [18]. In spite of this successful experience, particular attention has to be paid on cyber-sickness, as it could represent an issue in the TBI population [12]. The administration of VR-based interventions should be made cautiously, especially in the acute stage, during which patients may be more sensitive.

Regarding cognitive training, both non-immersive and immersive VR have been used and validated in several trials. Deficits from mild to severe were addressed by focusing on memory, attention, executive functions, behavioral control, and the regulation of mood, with weak evidence of improvements in all these cognitive domains [19, 20].

The use of AR and MR for TBI rehabilitation is possibly more limited than for other neurological disorders. An AR application was presented by Chang *et al.* in 2018: its aim was to train autobiographical memory [21]. All the six participants who took part in the study reported improvements in memory and well-being, but once again, it was just a pilot study. AR employment has finally given promising outcomes in shoulder rehabilitation giving the patients a biofeedback on activated muscles [22], and in vocational rehabilitation, demonstrating its capability to make patients acquire new skills [23].

Another common neurological injury is SCI, i.e., a traumatic injury resulting from the fracture, dislocation, crushing, or compression of the spine. It can also result from a wound that penetrates and cuts the spinal cord, or from non-traumatic events such as arthritis, cancer, inflammation, and severe disk degeneration. SCI can result in either a complete or a partial damage of the spinal cord major functions (e.g., motor, sensory, autonomic, and reflex) [24]. A recent review [25] has pointed out that VR, either immersive or non-immersive, could be effective in improving motor, balance, and aerobic capacities in people with SCI and in reducing pain (see also § 2.6). No particular side-effects have been recorded, also in the case of immersive technology, but some cases of musculoskeletal pain, fatigue, and the inability to keep concentration were reported [26, 27]. Contrary to TBI, systems that were most frequently employed for SCI rehabilitation were non-commercial; this is possibly due to the need of designing systems specifically dedicated to patients with SCI, and thus with (often) severe functional sensorimotor limitations [25].

The cases of application of AR/MR for sensorimotor rehabilitation after SCI are very limited [28]. Besides the application presented before for shoulder retraining [22], which has been positively administered also to patients with SCI, no other attempt to use AR/MR has been found (sometimes, improper terms to define the technology have been used [29]), with the exception of a few systems dedicated to train wheelchair-maneuvering abilities [30, 31].

11.2.2 XR and Stroke

Stroke is one of the major causes of death and disability in industrialized countries [2]. Stroke occurs when a part of the brain experiences an interruption of blood supply, thus preventing the tissue to get oxygen and nutrients. The interruption of the blood flow could be due to an ischemia, i.e., a focal occlusion of a cerebral vessel, or a hemorrhage, i.e., the escape of blood from an injured vessel [2].

In recent years, stroke mortality has greatly decreased. On the other hand, people living with neurological impairments resulting from a stroke and lacking autonomy in ADLs has dramatically increased [32]. Indeed, recent trends have highlighted an increase in the incidence of stroke among young people, especially as a consequence of trauma [33, 34]. In spite of the better general health status characterizing young adults (more plasticity, lack of comorbidities), the consequences related to occurrence of stroke in young age are substantial and long lasting, because of the long survival after the event [33].

Stroke can result both in cognitive and sensorimotor deficits; both may however be recovered. Long-lasting, challenging, intensive, and skill-oriented training has indeed been proven effective in promoting the recovery of functions by stimulating neuroplasticity [35].

Cognitive interventions for stroke patients are described in §2.3; clinical studies focusing on dementia often consider mixed samples with patients with neurodegenerative dementia (Alzheimer's disease, PD, and Lewy body dementia) or with cognitive issues resulting from a stroke.

With regards to sensorimotor rehabilitation, much data is currently available; this fact is reflected also by the high number of systematic reviews and meta-analyses on the topic [36–39]. Depending on the area of investigation, these reviews concluded that VR could be effective in improving lower [40] and upper limb functions [37, 40], reducing disability [40–42], and increasing QoL [37, 41], either alone or in conjunction with other types of training (i.e., VR training was sometimes administered to increase the training time). Immersive VR—experienced via HMDs—has revealed potentially more effective than non-immersive VR in trials that compared their use [43]. Especially in the context of limb rehabilitation, the use of actuated devices, coupled to VR scenarios, to assist or support patients' movements, is quite common; literature contains examples of the use of end-effector devices [44], and exoskeletons for upper limb [45, 46], and hand function recovery [47]. Exoskeletons to assist walking are also present [48], but less common due to their higher complexity. In addition to actuated devices, sensors to track patients' movements are also fundamental to render an appropriate feedback, considering that often, post-stroke patients lack an awareness of their body posture [49] (e.g., Microsoft Kinect, Nintendo Wii balance board, data-gloves, wearable devices).

The use of AR to provide rehabilitative treatments to post-stroke patients is, as for other pathologies, more limited. In addition, many works made use of inappropriate terms, mistaking AR for VR [50]. There have been attempts to use this technology to retrain both upper limbs and lower limbs' functions. In the first case, augmented exercises foresaw the implementation of the mirror therapy paradigm, or proposed contextualized exercises (e.g., drag and drop, memory game) [50]. In the second case, HMD-based AR was used to implement feedback during functional electric stimulation (FES)-assisted movements, or to propose obstacles to avoid while walking on a treadmill [50]. All these studies were, however, preliminary: most of them reported positive outcomes in terms of usability, users' engagement and meaningfulness [51, 52]. However, some drawbacks were present, e.g., the occurrence of fatigue and discomfort because of the prolonged sitting [53], the occurrence of dizziness [54], and negative experiences due to technological malfunctions, in particular related with tracking [55, 56].

11.2.3   XR and Dementia

Dementia is a pathological condition, generally chronic or progressive, caused by a disease of the brain. It manifests with the impairment of intellectual functions, and with the gradual deterioration of mental and (later) physical functions, leading to disability and ultimately death [57]. As already mentioned, though there exists the chance of treating dementia with a pharmacological therapy, researchers are focusing their efforts on non-pharmacological interventions.

Additionally, in the case of progressive pathologies as Alzheimer's Disease or vascular dementia, it seems possible to try and intervene in the prodromal stage to slow down the progression of dementia, and mitigate its symptoms by acting on modifiable risk factors [58]. Among the most effective interventions, there are the provision of physical activity [59], cognitive training [60], and a healthy diet and lifestyle guidelines [61].

Recently, several VR-based interventions have been investigated to improve clinical outcomes and the QoL of people with dementia [62]. Generally, VR technologies have been used to support the administration of the above-mentioned interventions, in order to make them adaptive to each patient's needs, and more engaging [63]. Regarding physical exercise, VR has been used to accompany balance, flexibility, and aerobic exercise, providing a contextual scenario and real-time feedback to patients [64]. It has often been used in conjunction with other devices such as sensor-based platforms (e.g., Wii Fit Balance Board [65]), markerless tracking devices (e.g., Microsoft Kinect [66]), or fitness equipment (e.g., cycle-ergometer [63]). In spite of a high heterogeneity of the studies, promising outcomes have emerged: exergames seem to improve psychomotor parameters more than standard care [67]. Results have also showed that exergames could be effective in improving psychometric, daily functioning, and psychiatric (e.g., apathy) outcomes [64, 66]. Another important outcome was that all patients enrolled in the studies reported high levels of motivation: their adherence was consequently satisfying.

For what concerns the administration of cognitive training, VR has also been employed extensively, often in the form of computerized cognitive training [68]. A few RCTs have been carried out too, providing evidence that such treatments could be effective both at cognitive and emotional levels [69].

Recently, researchers have started investigating the possibility of employing immersive VR to administer cognitive interventions to people with MCI or dementia [70]. Recent reviews have shown that this technology could be used effectively to treat cognitive deficits in older adults [70, 71], though some concerns remain in terms of the safety and arousal of cyber-sickness. Up to date, most studies have involved applications that do not require participants to walk and to actively interact with virtual objects—though preliminary studies have shown their feasibility and acceptance [72]. Safety concerns, especially in terms of balance (i.e., the risk of falls), should, however, be kept in mind, in particular for patients with mild or severe dementia [72].

Regarding AR and MR in dementia treatment, applications are less common. Most of the existing applications are focused on providing assistance in daily life [73], often through annotations, rather than on the training of cognitive or motor functions. Preliminary studies have, however, demonstrated the feasibility of AR/MR-based interventions too [74, 75].

11.2.4 XR and Parkinson's Disease

PD is a neurological progressive syndrome characterized by motor and non-motor symptoms. Among the first, there are bradykinesia, rest tremor, rigidity, and postural disturbances. Non-motor symptoms are the freezing of gait, speech and swallowing difficulties, disturbance of sleep, and dementia [2].

Gait and balance are generally impaired since the first phases; PD indeed affects the motor learning process, and forces the patient to compensate by using alternative neural circuits, generally involving attentions, sensory stimuli, and vision [76]. In such a condition, environmental complexity, dual-task load, and distraction represent situations of high risk: indeed, falls in PD patients are two-to-three times more frequent than in age-matched samples [77].

A multidisciplinary approach is currently encouraged for the management of PD; in particular, physiotherapy has been recognized as an additional effective treatment to be added to well-established pharmacological therapy and surgical interventions [78]. Moreover, once again, the implementation of a sustained and prolonged program throughout time plays a key role [79]. That is why XR technologies can be of benefit also in this case.

A recent Cochrane review showed that VR-based intervention could induce benefits on the step and stride length and improvements in balance, gait, ADL, QoL, and cognitive functions [80]. As for MS, most of the applications used in RCTs were commercially available applications exploiting sensors and systems, e.g., Nintendo Wii, Microsoft Kinect, Motek CAREN, and the KSD dancing system [80, 81].

Some attempts have been made also using immersive VR and AR. In the first cases, studies were focused on the recovery of upper limb functions and improvement of gait parameters—by proposing obstacle avoidance tasks [82], distracting elements [83], and floor cues to avoid the freezing of gait on a treadmill [84]. Whenever assessed, cyber-sickness did not emerge as an issue [83].

Regarding AR, its use to support PD patients began in the late 90s [85, 86]. Most of the applications presented in literature are devoted to generate floor cues to reduce the freezing of gait, and improve speed and cadence [87], also by providing dance exercises [88, 89]. Studies that exploited wearable devices also reported that benefits do occur with AR-supported training, and that are generally also retained when the augmented cues are removed [87, 90]. However, more studies are needed, as evidence is still mixed [91].

11.2.5   XR and Multiple Sclerosis

MS is a progressive inflammatory disease in which the immune system attacks a nerve's myelin, causing communication issues between the brain and the peripherical nervous system; eventually, nerves could be permanently damaged or deteriorated by sclerotic plaques. Around 3 million people in the world are affected by MS, but a lot of cases may not have been diagnosed [2]. The pathology onset occurs between 20 and 50 years old, and currently, there is no cure. Nonetheless, a series of interventions could improve some symptoms, reduce the recovery time after an attack, and help in managing the pathology throughout life.

XR technologies have emerged in the rehabilitation of MS because of two main reasons: first, motor skill exercises are proposed in a repetitive and insistent pattern; second, standard care requires the patients to reach rehabilitation centers, and to be supervised by the clinical personnel who has to assess the quality of the exercise. However, this may not be efficient, especially considering that people with MS often present mobility issue and are no longer ambulatory 20 years after onset.

Studies have shown that VR-based interventions could be effective in improving arm functions, balance and gait parameters [92, 93]. Also, VR could contribute to reduce the perceived effort [93], and to optimize sensory information processing, by enabling anticipatory postural control [94]. Using avatars also seemed a potential benefit, as it may strengthen the use-dependent plastic changes in higher sensory-motor areas belonging to the mirror neuron system [95].

Most of the applications foresaw the use of a commercially available platform for (tele)rehabilitation (e.g., Khymeia system or Motek CAREN), or games to be performed with additional sensors (e.g., Microsoft Kinect or Nintendo Balance Board). In a few cases, VR was associated with a robotic device, or an FES system [93].

Nonetheless, most of the studies had small sample sizes, and reported issues related to fatigue, high-physical requirements, sensory loss, and spasticity; therefore, outcomes should be interpreted cautiously.

In 2020, an RCT first investigated the effects of an immersive VR treatment on balance, mobility, and fatigue in patients with MS. The group using immersive VR obtained benefits that were comparable to the control group, who received standard balance training, besides closed-eyes balance, which improved more, and single-leg balance, which improved less. The authors hypothesized that these outcomes may be the results of an enhanced training of somatosensory stimuli integration occurring in immersive VR, and a lack of real world awareness that make movements in VR more cautious [96]. Another recent RCT evaluated the effectiveness of a gait training program, performed on a treadmill, and supported by immersive VR [97]. In this case, gait and obstacle negotiation parameters improved, making the authors conclude that immersive VR is feasible and useful for people with MS and moderate disabilities.

In spite of the benefits that AR/MR could introduce in the rehabilitation of people with MS (e.g., it would not occlude the real world, thus reducing the risk of unwanted or unnatural behaviors [96]), applications [98, 99] are very limited. As in the case of dementia, however, a few successful trials using HoloLens to measure gait parameters have been done [100, 101], thus opening the possibility of using this tool with rehabilitative purposes as well.

11.2.6   XR and Pain

In the context of neurological disorders, pain can be categorized as *neuropathic*—whenever its cause can be attributed to a damage or a disease of the neural pathways transmitting the painful stimuli, either at a central or peripheral level—or *nociceptive* —when it is a neurological disease that indirectly causes the secondary activation of pain pathways [2].

XR technologies have found their way in the treatment of pain, because pharmacological treatments are often only of partial benefit, especially in the case of neuropathic pain, whose origin is currently still debated [102]. XR has been proven to act on pain because of two different mechanisms: distraction, i.e., the diversion from the nociceptive stimulus, and neuroplasticity, i.e., the long-term reorganization of neuronal structure, also for what concerns the transmission of the painful stimuli [103].

Regarding neuropathic pain, applications described in literature are mainly focused on neuroplasticity, rather than distraction [104]. In particular, most of them are aimed at recreating an appropriate body imagery, e.g., by simulating virtual walking for patients with spinal cord injury, or visualizing and stimulating via a tactile feedback the missing/impaired body part in both patients with spine lesions or amputations (i.e., suffering from the so-called phantom limb pain) [103, 105, 106]. These applications exploiting either (immersive) VR and AR often included sensors dedicated to the recreation of the impaired body part movements; some examples were: MoCap sensors (i.e., inertial, marker-less commercial sensors, and data-gloves [107, 108]) to capture the movements of the non-impaired limb according to the mirror therapy paradigm [109], and location sensors [110] or surface please replace with electromyography electrodes [106, 111] to be placed on the stomp to compute the movements on the basis of the residual muscular activity.

A first attempt to use MR has been done too [112]. However, the results of its use are available only on healthy participants. For what concerns other technologies, preliminary outcomes appear promising, both at short and long term [26, 103]. Nonetheless, strong clinical evidence is still lacking due to the shortness of RCTs, and to the great differences existing among the various tested systems. XR applications' design would be better informed by a series of best practices, which, at the moment, have not been established yet [104].

Regarding the treatment of musculoskeletal pain, XR-based treatments either exploited the same paradigms used to treat neuropathic pain—i.e., promoting a diverse body image (e.g., changing artificially the degree of neck rotation in patients with chronic neck pain [113] or increasing the range of motion of the arm with spasticity [114])—or proposed a physical training to try to act on the primary source of pain [115].

Also, in the case of musculoskeletal pain, distraction did not emerge as the primary mechanism to treat pain. Successful attempts to implement distractive contexts are instead present when dealing with acute pain (e.g., in specific and limited-in-time situations [116, 117]).

11.3   Future Research Agenda and Roadmap

This chapter presents the state of the art with regard to the use of XR technologies in the rehabilitation of neurological disorders. Not all existing neurological disorders have been included in this chapter for the reasons of brevity. However, the treatment of pathologies that are different from the above-mentioned ones—such as cerebral palsy, amyotrophic lateral sclerosis, brain tumors—may be assimilated to the presented XR-supported training programs, especially when symptoms are similar, and with the same progression.

What emerges from this analysis is that XR represents a promising tool to address the challenges presented by several neurological disorders, both in terms of motor/physical rehabilitation and of cognitive training.

Recently, the advent of more affordable and portable XR devices—with also good visual and audio quality—(e.g., HTC Vive and Oculus headsets, or Microsoft HoloLens and Meta 2) has also paved the way for a more pervasive use of immersive virtual and augmented scenarios for rehabilitative purposes.

However, differences exist among XR devices, and this has an influence on their application to the rehabilitative field. Non-immersive VR or semi-immersive VR are more frequently employed than fully immersive VR; AR use is still very limited, with the exception of specific interventions (e.g., showing cues to avoid freezing in PD), possibly because devices have not reached complete technological maturity yet. Microsoft HoloLens—which could be considered among the most up-to-date devices—has a limited field of view, and interactions are difficult to be handled by a patient with motor disabilities or phonation problems, in the case of gesture and voice commands, respectively.

This calls for a continuous improvement of devices—especially those dedicated to AR and MR—which not only should improve in terms of visual and audio quality but also in order to make the interaction more intuitive as possible. Challenges related to human factors and ergonomics increase with the immersion of the device, and, in general, with the complexity of the proposed system. When using headsets, the weight of the device, the potential risk of trips and falls, the presence of a cable, and (especially) the arousal of cybersickness are all aspects that cannot be neglected [118]. Thus, the process of chasing more *presence*, in order to stimulate motivation and program compliance, has to be long, and performed step by step in order to consider all these aspects (see also Chapter 10 on human factors and ergonomics).

There is an open field for research in terms not only of devices, but also of XR applications and the context of use. Many of the evidence-based studies present in literature make use of commercially available systems (e.g., Motek GRAIL and CAREN, Nintendo Wii, Microsoft Kinect exergames) and their in-app games. This, from the one hand, eases the attainability and excludes the risk of bugs, but, on the other hand, partially limits the potentiality of XR to be tailored on specific patients' needs. In fact, a specific training program can be rather obtained with *ad-hoc* designed applications, which are present in the literature, but in a minor amount.

A further step forward in the customization of training can be done by adding artificial intelligence (AI) to XR application. AI, in all its forms, seems promising to provide customization (i.e., via rule-based algorithms as in sematic-based reasoning) and also adaptation (i.e., via machine learning) of the training on the basis of the current patient performances. Besides the clinical effectiveness of patient-specific training, the implementation of these paradigms is important also to foster patients' adherence. A program that adequately challenges the ability of each individual is in fact essential to engage the patient creating a sort of *flow* [119], and exclude the risk of boredom, and thus of drop-outs.

The need of measuring specific variables of interest, e.g., cyber-sickness, presence, flow, or engagement also raises a question in the context of XR and rehabilitation. Up to now, the standard procedure foresees the collection of data via the administration of a questionnaire right at the end of the XR experience. However, this method may not capture all the feelings experienced while being immersed in XR; in addition, answers may be biased, as questions may be difficult to comprehend and interpret—in particular, for patients—as often taken from different contexts (e.g., the technology acceptance questionnaire [120] has been designed for the use of a computer in a work-related scenario; the simulator sickness question-naire in the context of the use of driving simulators [121]).

Psychological implications related to the use of XR have to be further explored, not only in terms of user experience but also for what concerns pos-sible emotional implications. Indeed, the emotional component of an XR expe-rience may be elicited by proposing the patient his/her memories, or places, people, and sounds, which could help in reliving specific situations. Such a recall function might act on memory rehearsal, and consequently influence compliance, mood, isolation, and social behaviors. Therefore, deepening the knowledge regarding these factors can be either pivotal to enhance the effec-tiveness of the proposed neurological intervention, or detrimental, if used in an inappropriate way. Ethical concerns must, therefore, be kept in mind.

In general, we can conclude that there are still some open challenges that both the medical and the technological research have to face in order to make XR become part of standard care in neurorehabilitation. A Strengths, Weaknesses, Opportunities, and Threats (SWOT) analysis showing the current XR status (updated from the work of Rizzo *et al.* [122]) is depicted in Table 11.1.

As it can be noticed from Table 11.1, challenges are not only related to technological and human–computer interaction factors, but also to clini-cal and methodological aspects. Though for many of the above-mentioned pathologies, different RCTs and several literature reviews have been per-formed, still there is the need to identify which treatment could be the optimal one to address a specific impairment. The heterogeneity of the interventions, in terms of XR technology, administered motor or cogni-tive exercise, and frequency and duration of the training program, does not allow to draw any conclusions regarding the optimum for each pathol-ogy and severity of symptoms. This calls for larger RCTs involving a large group of patients, and, when applicable, to sub-groups analyses to assess the benefits for each category of patients involved.

Another point deals with the knowledge of the clinical personnel. To promote the actual spreading of XR technologies in the clinical practice, in fact, it is essential that the people using it are informed about potentialities, available instruments, and possible drawbacks. This and other key steps that are necessary to proceed forward for the implementation of XR-based rehabilitative programs are depicted in Table 11.2.

The fulfillment of all the objectives presented in Table 11.2 will lead to the design of tailored interventions, designed on each specific patient, both in terms of content and of employed technology, with undoubted benefits in terms of patients' well-being and clinical outcomes.

Table 11.1 SWOT analysis of XR technologies for neurorehabilitation; black dots present technology-related topics, whereas white squares indicate clinical issues.

Strengths	Weaknesses
• enhanced ecological validity; • control of stimuli and difficulties; • real-time performance feedback; • safe training environment; • high engagement and motivation, and thus better compliance; • flexibility and customization of training; • low-cost and good quality XR devices; □ first promising evidence of effectiveness.	• interaction methods; • physical and cognitive ergonomics; • data privacy, management, and analysis; • cyber-sickness and aftereffects; • methodology of assessment of subjective variables related to user experience; □ lack of large RCTs; □ heterogeneity of evaluated XR applications.
Opportunities	Threats
• new devices and more intuitive interaction systems; • ad-hoc developed XR applications; • add-on of artificial intelligence for customization and adaptation; • home-based treatment and telerehabilitation; • enhancing effects by the exploitation of emotional contents.	• training of operators; • ethical issues; • development of applications for long-term use; • scarce familiarity/acceptance with/of new technologies; • comorbidities of patients (pain, vision–auditory issues, etc.); • use of emotional contents in an inappropriate way; □ lack of chances to perform long-term trials.

Moreover, such an achievement will lead to the implementation of more robust national healthcare systems, which will be able to respond to the growing needs of their citizens with neurological disorders, by implementing effectively the paradigm of the continuity of care, even in unexpected situations (e.g., the COVID-19 pandemic). Finally, providing long-term support to patients in their homes will also have a positive effect at the economic level; indeed, the societal and economic burden related to the management of chronic pathologies has rapidly increased in the last years, because of longer life expectancy, also among patients. It is thus time for researchers, clinicians, and XR companies to invest in XR technologies for neurorehabilitation, especially to try and face the challenges of the still less-investigated pathologies.

Table 11.2 Short-term and long-term perspectives for the use of XR in neurorehabilitation.

Topic	Short-term perspectives	Long-term perspectives
XR devices	• improve visual and audio quality of XR devices; • improve interaction modalities, especially for AR/MR; • develop safe and intuitive XR systems to be used for home-based unsupervised rehabilitation;	• improve haptics in XR devices; • improve interaction in social and collaborative environments; • design immersive devices that limit at most the occurrence of cyber-sickness while promoting presence (e.g., design devices that could be used also from patients with headache, epilepsy);
XR applications	• design and develop ad-hoc application to answer a specific category of patients' needs; • integrate AI in XR environment to customize and adapt the training according to each single user's needs; • invest on social and collaborative XR environments for rehabilitation;	• develop authoring tools that clinical personnel can use autonomously to design patient-oriented training programs;
Continuity of care	• promote telerehabilitation via safe XR application;	• promote the building of infrastructures to support the continuity of care in all areas (internet connection, privacy and safety of personal data);

(Continued)

Table 11.2 Short-term and long-term perspectives for the use of XR in neurorehabilitation. (*Continued*)

Topic	Short-term perspectives	Long-term perspectives
Studies/trials	• ease the process of ethical clearance (whenever possible, without violating ethical principles); • perform long RCTs with adequate sample sizes, to assess whether motivation is maintained throughout the training program;	
Clinical personnel	• Inform clinical personnel regarding the potential of XR technologies.	• train clinical personnel to use the XR system and to support patients in doing so, also with specific educational programs (e.g., hybrid programs involving medical and technological competences).

References

1. Feigin, V.L. *et al.*, Global, regional, and national burden of neurological disorders, 1990–2016: a systematic analysis for the Global Burden of Disease Study 2016. *Lancet Neurol.*, 18, 5, 2019.
2. World Health Organization, *Neurological Disorders: Public Health Challenges*, WHO Press, Geneva, Switzerland, 2006.
3. Schiza, E., Matsangidou, M., Neokleous, K., Pattichis, C.S., Virtual Reality Applications for Neurological Disease: A Review. *Front. Robot. AI*, 6, 100, 2019.
4. Witmer, B.G. and Singer, M.J., Measuring presence in virtual environments: A presence questionnaire. *Presence Teleoperators Virtual Environ.*, 7, 3, 225–240, 1998.
5. Coelho, C., Tichon, J., Hine, T.J., Wallis, G., Riva, G., Media presence and inner presence: The sense of presence in virtual reality technologies, in: *Emerging Communication: Studies in New Technologies and Practices in Communication*, pp. 25–45, IOS Press, Amsterdam, 2012.

6. Weech, S., Kenny, S., Barnett-Cowan, M., Presence and cybersickness in virtual reality are negatively related: a review. *Front. Psychol.*, 10, 158, 2019.

7. Hakkinen, J., Vuori, T., Paakka, M., *Postural stability and sickness symptoms after HMD use*, November 2002, 2005.

8. Diemer, J., Alpers, G.W., Peperkorn, H.M., Shiban, Y., Mühlberger, A., The impact of perception and presence on emotional reactions: A review of research in virtual reality. *Front. Psychol.*, 6, 26, JAN, 2015.

9. Kenwright, B., Virtual Reality: Ethical Challenges and Dangers [Opinion]. *IEEE Technol. Soc. Mag.*, 37, 4, 20-25, 2018.

10. Werner, C. and Engelhard, K., Pathophysiology of traumatic brain injury. *Br. J. Anaesth.*, 99, 1, 4–9, 2007.

11. Dewan, M.C., Rattani, A., Gupta, S., Baticulon, R.E., Hung, Y.-C., Punchak, M., Agrawal, A., Adeleye, A.O., Shrime, M.G., Rubiano, A.M., Estimating the global incidence of traumatic brain injury. *J. Neurosurg.*, 130, 4, 1–18, 2019.

12. Aida, J., Chau, B., Dunn, J., Immersive virtual reality in traumatic brain injury rehabilitation: A literature review. *NeuroRehabilitation*, 42, 4, 441–448, 2018.

13. Betker, A.L., Desai, A., Nett, C., Kapadia, N., Szturm, T., Game-based exercises for dynamic short-sitting balance rehabilitation of people with chronic spinal cord and traumatic brain injuries. *Phys. Ther.*, 87, 10, 441-448, 2007.

14. Betker, A.L., Szturm, T., Moussavi, Z.K., Nett, C., Video Game-Based Exercises for Balance Rehabilitation: A Single-Subject Design. *Arch. Phys. Med. Rehabil.*, 87, 8, 1389-1398, 2006.

15. Pietrzak, E., Pullman, S., McGuire, A., Using Virtual Reality and Videogames for Traumatic Brain Injury Rehabilitation: A Structured Literature Review. *Games Health J.*, 3, 4, 202–214, 2014.

16. Holden, M.K., Dettwiler, A., Dyar, T., Niemann, G., Bizzi, E., Retraining movement in patients with acquired brain injury using a virtual environment. *Stud. Health Technol. Inform.*, 81, 202–214, 2001.

17. Yip, B.C.B. and Man, D.W.K., Virtual reality (VR)-based community living skills training for people with acquired brain injury: A pilot study. *Brain Inj.*, 23, 13–14, 192–198, 2009.

18. Gottshall, K.R. and Sessoms, P.H., Improvements in dizziness and imbalance results from using a multi disciplinary and multi sensory approach to vestibular physical therapy - A case study. *Front. Syst. Neurosci.*, 9, 106, August, 2015.

19. Zanier, E.R., Zoerle, T., Di Lernia, D., Riva, G., Virtual reality for traumatic brain injury. *Front. Neurol.*, 9, 345, May, 2018.

20. Alashram, A.R., Annino, G., Padua, E., Romagnoli, C., Mercuri, N.B., Cognitive rehabilitation post traumatic brain injury: A systematic review for emerging use of virtual reality technology. *J. Clin. Neurosci.*, 66, 209–219, 2019.

21. Chang, C., Hinze, A., Bowen, J., Gilbert, L., Starkey, N., Mymemory: A mobile memory assistant for people with traumatic brain injury. *Int. J. Hum. Comput. Stud.*, 117, 4–19, 2018.

22. Aung, Y.M. and Al-Jumaily, A., Augmented reality-based RehaBio system for shoulder rehabilitation. *Int. J. Mechatron. Autom.*, 4, 1, 52–62, 2014.

23. Chang, Y.J., Kang, Y.S., Huang, P.C., An augmented reality (AR)-based vocational task prompting system for people with cognitive impairments. *Res. Dev. Disabil.*, 34, 10, 3049–3056, 2013.

24. Dumont, R.J., Okonkwo, D.O., Verma, S., John Hurlbert, R., Boulos, P.T., Ellegala, D.B., Dumont, A.S., Acute Spinal Cord Injury, Part I: Pathophysiologic Mechanisms. *Clin. Neuropharmacol.*, 24, 5, 254–264, 2001.

25. De Araújo, A.V.L., Neiva, J.F.D.O., Monteiro, C.B.D.M., Magalhães, F.H., Efficacy of Virtual Reality Rehabilitation after Spinal Cord Injury: A Systematic Review. *BioMed. Res. Int.*, 2019, 184–192, 2019.

26. Villiger, M., Bohli, D., Kiper, D., Pyk, P., Spillmann, J., Meilick, B., Curt, A., Hepp-Reymond, M.C., Hotz-Boendermaker, S., Eng, K., Virtual reality-augmented neurorehabilitation improves motor function and reduces neuropathic pain in patients with incomplete spinal cord injury. *Neurorehabil. Neural Repair*, 27, 8, 675–683, 2013.

27. Roosink, M., Robitaille, N., Jackson, P.L., Bouyer, L.J., Mercier, C., Interactive virtual feedback improves gait motor imagery after spinal cord injury: An exploratory study. *Restor. Neurol. Neurosci.*, 34, 2, 227–235, 2016.

28. de Miguel-Rubio, A., Dolores Rubio, M., Alba-Rueda, A., Salazar, A., Moral-Munoz, J.A., Lucena-Anton, D., Virtual reality systems for upper limb motor function recovery in patients with spinal cord injury: Systematic review and meta-analysis. *JMIR mHealth uHealth*, 8, 12, e22537, 2020.

29. Heyn, P., Baumgardner, C., McLachlan, L., Bodine, C., Mixed-reality exercise effects on participation of individuals with spinal cord injuries and developmental disabilities: A pilot study. *Top. Spinal Cord Inj. Rehabil.*, 20, 4, 338–345, 2014.

30. Caetano, D., Valentini, C., Mattioli, F., Camargos, P., Sá, T., Cardoso, A., Lamounier, E., Naves, E., The Augmented Reality Telerehabilitation System for Powered Wheelchair User's Training, *J. Commun. Inform. Syst.* 35, 1, 51–60, 2020.

31. Maule, L., Fornaser, A., Tomasin, P., Tavernini, M., Minotto, G., Da Lio, M., De Cecco, M., Augmented robotics for electronic wheelchair to enhance mobility in domestic environment. *Lect. Notes Comput. Sci. (including Subser. Lect. Notes Artif. Intell. Lect. Notes Bioinformatics)*, 10325 LNCS, 21–32, 2017.

32. Baumann, M., Lurbe-Puerto, K., Alzahouri, K., Aïach, P., Increased residual disability among poststroke survivors and the repercussions for the lives of informal caregivers. *Top. Stroke Rehabil.*, 18, 2, 162–171, 2011.

33. Ekker, M.S., Verhoeven, J.I., Vaartjes, I., Van Nieuwenhuizen, K.M., Klijn, C.J.M., De Leeuw, F.E., Stroke incidence in young adults according to age, subtype, sex, and time trends. *Neurology*, 92, 21, e2444-e2454, 2019.

34. Mueller, J., The causes of stroke in the young. *J. Emerg. Med.*, 4, 5, 137–143, 1986.

35. Kleim, J.A. and Jones, T.A., Principles of experience-dependent neural plasticity: Implications for rehabilitation after brain damage. *J. Speech Lang. Hear. Res.*, 51, 1, S225-S239, 2008.

36. Mekbib, D.B., Han, J., Zhang, L., Fang, S., Jiang, H., Zhu, J., Roe, A.W., Xu, D., Virtual reality therapy for upper limb rehabilitation in patients with stroke: a meta-analysis of randomized clinical trials. *Brain Inj.*, 34, 4, 456–465, 2020.

37. Domínguez-Téllez, P., Moral-Muñoz, J.A., Salazar, A., Casado-Fernández, E., Lucena-Antón, D., Game-Based Virtual Reality Interventions to Improve Upper Limb Motor Function and Quality of Life after Stroke: Systematic Review and Meta-analysis. *Games Health J.*, 9, 1, 1–10, 2020.

38. Laver, K.E., Lange, B., George, S., Deutsch, J.E., Saposnik, G., Crotty, M., Virtual reality for stroke rehabilitation. *Cochrane Database Syst. Rev.*, 11, 1–164, 2017.

39. Laver, K.E., George, S., Thomas, S., Deutsch, J.E., Crotty, M., Virtual reality for stroke rehabilitation. *Cochrane Database Syst. Rev.*, 2, 1–100, 2015.

40. Lee, H.S., Park, Y.J., Park, S.W., The effects of virtual reality training on function in chronic stroke patients: A systematic review and meta-analysis. *BioMed. Res. Int.*, 2019, 7595639, 2019.

41. Aramaki, A.L., Sampaio, R.F., Reis, A.C.S., Cavalcanti, A., Dutra, F.C.M.S., Virtual reality in the rehabilitation of patients with stroke: an integrative review. *Arq. Neuropsiquiatr.*, 77, 4, 268–278, 2019.

42. Kim, W.-S., Cho, S., Ku, J., Kim, Y., Lee, K., Hwang, H.-J., Paik, N.-J., Clinical Application of Virtual Reality for Upper Limb Motor Rehabilitation in Stroke: Review of Technologies and Clinical Evidence. *J. Clin. Med.*, 9, 10, 3369, 2020.

43. Palacios-Navarro, G. and Hogan, N., Head-mounted display-based therapies for adults post-stroke: A systematic review and meta-analysis. *Sensors (Switzerland)*, 21, 4, 1111, 2021.

44. Lledó, L.D., Díez, J.A., Bertomeu-Motos, A., Ezquerro, S., Badesa, F.J., Sabater-Navarro, J.M., García-Aracil, N., A comparative analysis of 2D and 3D tasks for virtual reality therapies based on robotic-assisted neurorehabilitation for post-stroke patients. *Front. Aging Neurosci.*, 8, 205, Aug, 2016.

45. Housman, S.J., Scott, K.M., Reinkensmeyer, D.J., A randomized controlled trial of gravity-supported, computer-enhanced arm exercise for individuals with severe hemiparesis. *Neurorehabil. Neural Repair*, 23, 5, 505–514, 2009.

46. Taveggia, G., Borboni, A., Salvi, L., Mule, C., Fogliaresi, S., Villafane, J.H., Casale, R., Efficacy of robot-assisted rehabilitation for the functional recovery of the upper limb in post-stroke patients: a randomized controlled study. *Eur. J. Phys. Rehabil. Med.*, 52, 6, 767–773, 2016.

47. Singh, N., Evidence of Neuroplasticity: A Robotic Hand Exoskeleton Study for Post-Stroke Rehabilitation. *J. Neuroeng. Rehabil.*, 18, 1, 1–15, 2021.

48. Vinoj, P.G., Jacob, S., Menon, V.G., Rajesh, S., Khosravi, M.R., Brain-controlled adaptive lower limb exoskeleton for rehabilitation of post-stroke paralyzed. *IEEE Access*, 7, 132628–132648, 2019.

49. Mottura, S., Fontana, L., Arlati, S., Zangiacomi, A., Redaelli, C., Sacco, M., A virtual reality system for strengthening awareness and participation in rehabilitation for post-stroke patients. *J. Multimodal User Interfaces*, 9, 4, 341–351, 2015.

50. Gorman, C. and Gustafsson, L., The use of augmented reality for rehabilitation after stroke: a narrative review. *Disabil. Rehabil. Assist. Technol.*, 1–9, 2020.

51. Correa-Agudelo, E., Ferrin, C., Velez, P., Gomez, J.D., Computer imagery and neurological rehabilitation: On the use of augmented reality in sensorimotor training to step up naturally occurring cortical reorganization in patients following stroke. *Stud. Health Technol. Inform.*, 220, 71–76, 2016.

52. Hoermann, S., Ferreira dos Santos, L., Morkisch, N., Jettkowski, K., Sillis, M., Devan, H., Kanagasabai, P.S., Schmidt, H., Krüger, J., Dohle, C., Regenbrecht, H., Hale, L., Cutfield, N.J., Computerised mirror therapy with Augmented Reflection Technology for early stroke rehabilitation: clinical feasibility and integration as an adjunct therapy. *Disabil. Rehabil.*, 39, 15, 1503–1514, 2017.

53. Pinches, J. and Hoermann, S., Automated instructions and real time feedback for upper limb computerized mirror therapy with augmented reflection technology. *J. Altern. Med. Res.*, 10, 1, 37–46, 2018.

54. Park, Y.-H., Lee, C., Lee, B.-H., Clinical usefulness of the virtual reality-based postural control training on the gait ability in patients with stroke. *J. Exerc. Rehabil.*, 9, 5, 489–494, 2013.

55. Collins BSc, J., Hoermann PhD, S., Regenbrecht Dr Ing, H., Comparing a finger dexterity assessment in virtual, video-mediated, and unmediated reality. *Int. J. Child Health Hum. Dev.*, 9, 3, 333–341, 2016.

56. King, M., Hale, L., Pekkari, A., Persson, M., Gregorsson, M., Nilsson, M., An affordable, computerised, table-based exercise system for stroke survivors. *Disabil. Rehabil. Assist. Technol.*, 5, 4, 288–293, 2010.

57. Dementia A NICE–SCIE Guideline on supporting people with dementia and their carers in health and social care, British Psychological Society, Leicester, UK, 2016.

58. Gauthier, S., Reisberg, B., Zaudig, M., Petersen, R.C., Ritchie, K., Broich, K., Belleville, S., Brodaty, H., Bennett, D., Chertkow, H., others, Mild cognitive impairment. *Lancet*, 367, 9518, 1262–1270, 2006.

59. Heyn, P., Abreu, B.C., Ottenbacher, K.J., The effects of exercise training on elderly persons with cognitive impairment and dementia: A meta-analysis. *Arch. Phys. Med. Rehabil.*, 85, 10, 1694–1704, 2004.

60. Huntley, J.D., Gould, R.L., Liu, K., Smith, M., Howard, R.J., Do cognitive interventions improve general cognition in dementia? A meta-analysis and meta-regression. *BMJ Open*, 5, 4, e005247, 2015.

61. Loef, M. and Walach, H., Midlife obesity and dementia: Meta-analysis and adjusted forecast of dementia prevalence in the United States and China. *Obesity*, 21, 1, E51–E55. 2013.

62. Sobral, M. and Pestana, M.H., Virtual reality and dementia: A bibliometric analysis. *Eur. J. Psychiatry*, 34, 3, 120–131, 2020.
63. Mrakic-Sposta, S., Di Santo, S.G., Franchini, F., Arlati, S., Zangiacomi, A., Greci, L., Moretti, S., Jesuthasan, N., Marzorati, M., Rizzo, G., others, Effects of combined physical and cognitive virtual reality-based training on cognitive impairment and oxidative stress in MCI patients: A pilot study. *Front. Aging Neurosci.*, 10, 1–11, 2018.
64. Zhao, Y., Feng, H., Wu, X., Du, Y., Yang, X., Hu, M., Ning, H., Liao, L., Chen, H., Zhao, Y., Effectiveness of exergaming in improving cognitive and physical function in people with mild cognitive impairment or dementia: Systematic review. *JMIR Serious Games*, 8, 2, e16841, 2020.
65. Padala, K.P., Padala, P.R., Malloy, T.R., Geske, J.A., Dubbert, P.M., Dennis, R.A., Garner, K.K., Bopp, M.M., Burke, W.J., Sullivan, D.H., Wii-fit for improving gait and balance in an assisted living facility: a pilot study. *J. Aging Res.*, 2012, 597573, 2012.
66. Amjad, I., Toor, H., Niazi, I.K., Pervaiz, S., Jochumsen, M., Shafique, M., Haavik, H., Ahmed, T., Xbox 360 Kinect Cognitive Games Improve Slowness, Complexity of EEG, and Cognitive Functions in Subjects with Mild Cognitive Impairment: A Randomized Control Trial. *Games Health J.*, 8, 2, 144–152, 2019.
67. Karssemeijer, E.G., Aaronson, J.A., Bossers, W.J., Donders, R., Rikkert, M.G.O., Kessels, R.P., The quest for synergy between physical exercise and cognitive stimulation via exergaming in people with dementia: a randomized controlled trial. *Alzheimers. Res. Ther.*, 11, 1, 3, 2019.
68. García-Betances, R.I., Arredondo Waldmeyer, M.T., Fico, G., Cabrera-Umpiérrez, M.F., A succinct overview of virtual reality technology use in Alzheimer's disease. *Front. Aging Neurosci.*, 7, 1–8, 2015.
69. Kim, O., Pang, Y., Kim, J.H., The effectiveness of virtual reality for people with mild cognitive impairment or dementia: A meta-analysis. *BMC Psychiatry*, 19, 1, 219, 2019.
70. Clay, F., Howett, D., FitzGerald, J., Fletcher, P., Chan, D., Price, A., Use of Immersive Virtual Reality in the Assessment and Treatment of Alzheimer's Disease: A Systematic Review. *J. Alzheimer's Dis.*, 75, 1, 23–43, 2020.
71. Strong, J., Immersive Virtual Reality and Persons with Dementia: A Literature Review. *J. Gerontol. Soc. Work*, 63, 3, 2020.
72. Arlati, S., Di Santo, S.G., Franchini, F., Mondellini, M., Filiputti, B., Luchi, M., Ratto, F., Ferrigno, G., Sacco, M., Greci, L., Acceptance and usability of immersive virtual reality in older adults with objective and subjective cognitive decline. *J. Alzheimer's Dis.*, 80, 3, 209–226, 2021.
73. Blattgerste, J., Renner, P., Pfeiffer, T., Augmented reality action assistance and learning for cognitively impaired people - A systematic literature review. *ACM Int. Conf. Proceeding Ser.*, 2019.
74. Ferreira, L.D.A., Cavaco, S., Bermúdez, S., Feasibility Study of an Augmented Reality System for People With Dementia, proceeding: In: *ICAT-EGVE*

2018 - *International Conference on Artificial Reality and Telexistence and Eurographics Symposium on Virtual Environments;* Bruder, Gerd and Yoshimoto, Shunsuke and Cobb, Sue, The Eurographics Association, pp. 141–148, 2018.

75. Astell, A.J., Fels, D., Desai, S., People with dementia experiencing presence in mixed reality technologies. *Alzheimer's Dement.*, 16, S7, 2020.

76. Stuart, S., Lord, S., Hill, E., Rochester, L., Gait in Parkinson's disease: A visuo-cognitive challenge. *Neurosci. Biobehav. Rev.*, 62, 76–88, 2016.

77. Pickering, R.M., Grimbergen, Y.A.M., Rigney, U., Ashburn, A., Mazibrada, G., Wood, B., Gray, P., Kerr, G., Bloem, B.R., A meta-analysis of six prospective studies of falling in Parkinson's disease. *Mov. Disord.*, 22, 13, 1892–9000, 2007.

78. Fox, S.H., Katzenschlager, R., Lim, S.Y., Ravina, B., Seppi, K., Coelho, M., Poewe, W., Rascol, O., Goetz, C.G., The movement disorder society evidence-based medicine review update: Treatments for the motor symptoms of Parkinson's disease. *Mov. Disord.*, 26, SUPPL. 3, S2–S41 2011.

79. Tomlinson, C.L., Herd, C.P., Clarke, C.E., Meek, C., Patel, S., Stowe, R., Deane, K.H.O., Shah, L., Sackley, C.M., Wheatley, K., Ives, N., Physiotherapy for parkinson's disease: A comparison of techniques. *Cochrane Database Syst. Rev.*, 2014, 6, 1–119, 2014.

80. Dockx, K., Van den Bergh, V., Bekkers, E.M.J., Ginis, P., Rochester, L., Hausdorff, J.M., Mirelman, A., Nieuwboer, A., Virtual reality for rehabilitation in Parkinson's disease. *Cochrane Database Syst. Rev.*, 2013, 10, 1–52, 2013.

81. Lei, C., Sunzi, K., Dai, F., Liu, X., Wang, Y., Zhang, B., He, L., Ju, M., Effects of virtual reality rehabilitation training on gait and balance in patients with Parkinson's disease: A systematic review. *PLoS One*, 14, 11, e0224819, 2019.

82. Finley, J.M., Gotsis, M., Lympouridis, V., Jain, S., Kim, A., Fisher, B.E., Design and Development of a Virtual Reality-Based Mobility Training Game for People With Parkinson's Disease. *Front. Neurol.*, 11, 1-13, 2021.

83. Kim, A., Darakjian, N., Finley, J.M., Walking in fully immersive virtual environments: an evaluation of potential adverse effects in older adults and individuals with Parkinson's disease. *J. Neuroeng. Rehabil.*, 14, 1, 16, 2017.

84. Lheureux, A., Lebleu, J., Frisque, C., Sion, C., Stoquart, G., Warlop, T., Detrembleur, C., Lejeune, T., Immersive Virtual Reality to Restore Natural Long-Range Autocorrelations in Parkinson's Disease Patients' Gait During Treadmill Walking. *Front. Physiol.*, 11, 572063, 2020.

85. Weghorst, S., Augmented Reality and Parkinson's Disease. *Commun. ACM*, 40, 8, 47–48, 1997.

86. Riess, T. and Weghorst, S., Augmented reality in the treatment of Parkinson's disease. *Proc. Med. Meets Virtual Real. III, San Diego*, p. 18, 1995.

87. Janssen, S., De Ruyter Van Steveninck, J., Salim, H.S., Bloem, B.R., Heida, T., Van Wezel, R.J.A., The Beneficial Effects of Conventional Visual Cues

Are Retained When Augmented Reality Glasses Are Worn. *Parkinsons Dis.*, 2020, 4104712, 2020.

88. Tunur, T., DeBlois, A., Yates-Horton, E., Rickford, K., Columna, L.A., Augmented reality-based dance intervention for individuals with Parkinson's disease: A pilot study. *Disabil. Health J.*, 13, 2, 100848, 2020.

89. Abbasi, J., Augmented reality takes Parkinson disease dance therapy out of the classroom. *JAMA - J. Am. Med. Assoc.*, 317, 4, 346–348, 2017.

90. Wang, Y.W., Chen, C.H., Lin, Y.C., Balance Rehabilitation System for Parkinson's Disease Patients based on Augmented Reality. *2nd IEEE Eurasia Conf. IOT, Commun. Eng. 2020, ECICE 2020*, 2020.

91. Janssen, S., de Ruyter van Steveninck, J., Salim, H.S., Cockx, H.M., Bloem, B.R., Heida, T., van Wezel, R.J.A., The Effects of Augmented Reality Visual Cues on Turning in Place in Parkinson's Disease Patients With Freezing of Gait. *Front. Neurol.*, 11, 195, 2020.

92. Massetti, T., Trevizan, I.L., Arab, C., Favero, F.M., Ribeiro-Papa, D.C., De Mello Monteiro, C.B., Virtual reality in multiple sclerosis - A systematic review. *Mult. Scler. Relat. Disord.*, 8, 107–112, 2016.

93. Maggio, M.G., Russo, M., Cuzzola, M.F., Destro, M., La Rosa, G., Molonia, F., Bramanti, P., Lombardi, G., De Luca, R., Calabrò, R.S., Virtual reality in multiple sclerosis rehabilitation: A review on cognitive and motor outcomes. *J. Clin. Neurosci.*, 65, 106–111, 2019.

94. Ortiz-Gutiérrez, R., Cano-de-la-Cuerda, R., Galán-del-Río, F., Alguacil-Diego, I.M., Palacios-Ceña, D., Miangolarra-Page, J.C., A telerehabilitation program improves postural control in multiple sclerosis patients: A Spanish preliminary study. *Int. J. Environ. Res. Public Health*, 10, 11, 5697–5710, 2013.

95. Calabrò, R.S., Naro, A., Russo, M., Leo, A., De Luca, R., Balletta, T., Buda, A., La Rosa, G., Bramanti, A., Bramanti, P., The role of virtual reality in improving motor performance as revealed by EEG: a randomized clinical trial. *J. Neuroeng. Rehabil.*, 14, 1, 1–16, 2017.

96. Ozkul, C., Guclu-Gunduz, A., Yazici, G., Atalay Guzel, N., Irkec, C., Effect of immersive virtual reality on balance, mobility, and fatigue in patients with multiple sclerosis: A single-blinded randomized controlled trial. *Eur. J. Integr. Med.*, 35, 101092, 2020.

97. Peruzzi, A., Cereatti, A., Della Croce, U., Mirelman, A., Effects of a virtual reality and treadmill training on gait of subjects with multiple sclerosis: A pilot study. *Mult. Scler. Relat. Disord.*, 5, 91–96, 2016.

98. Baram, Y. and Miller, A., Glide-symmetric locomotion reinforcement in patients with multiple sclerosis by visual feedback. *Disabil. Rehabil. Assist. Technol.*, 5, 5, 323–326, 2010.

99. Ferdous, S.M.S., Improve accessibility of virtual and augmented reality for people with balance impairments. *Proc. - IEEE Virtual Real.*, 2017.

100. Koop, M.M., Rosenfeldt, A.B., Johnston, J.D., Streicher, M.C., Qu, J., Alberts, J.L., The HoloLens Augmented Reality System Provides Valid Measures of

Gait Performance in Healthy Adults. *IEEE Trans. Hum.-Mach. Syst.*, 50, 6, 584–592, 2020.

101. Guinet, A.L., Bouyer, G., Otmane, S., Desailly, E., Validity of hololens augmented reality head mounted display for measuring gait parameters in healthy adults and children with cerebral palsy. *Sensors*, 21, 8, 2697, 2021.

102. Cole, J., Virtual and augmented reality, phantom experience, and prosthetics. in: *Psychoprosthetics*, P..Gallagher, D. Desmond, M. Maclachlan (eds.), Springer Verlag, London, 141–153, 2008.

103. Austin, P.D. and Siddall, P.J., Virtual reality for the treatment of neuropathic pain in people with spinal cord injuries: A scoping review. *J. Spinal Cord Med.*, 44, 1, 8–18, 2021.

104. Trost, Z., France, C., Anam, M., Shum, C., Virtual reality approaches to pain: toward a state of the science. *Pain*, 162, 2, 325–331, 2021.

105. Wittkopf, P.G., Lloyd, D.M., Johnson, M.I., Managing limb pain using virtual reality: a systematic review of clinical and experimental studies. *Disabil. Rehabil.*, 41, 26, 3103–3137, 2019.

106. Ortiz-Catalan, M., Sander, N., Kristoffersen, M.B., Håkansson, B., Brånemark, R., Treatment of phantom limb pain (PLP) based on augmented reality and gaming controlled by myoelectric pattern recognition: A case study of a chronic PLP patient. *Front. Neurosci.*, 8, 1–7, 2014.

107. Sano, Y., Ichinose, A., Wake, N., Osumi, M., Sumitani, M., Kumagaya, S.I., Kuniyoshi, Y., Reliability of phantom pain relief in neurorehabilitation using a multimodal virtual reality system. *Proc. Annu. Int. Conf. IEEE Eng. Med. Biol. Soc. EMBS*, 2015-Novem, 2015.

108. Desmond, D.M., Og'Neill, K., De Paor, A., McDarby, G., MacLachlan, M., Augmenting the reality of phantom limbs: Three case studies using an augmented mirror box procedure. *J. Prosthet. Orthot.*, 18, 3, 74–79, 2006.

109. Rothgangel, A. and Bekrater-Bodmann, R., Mirror therapy versus augmented/virtual reality applications: towards a tailored mechanism-based treatment for phantom limb pain. *Pain Manage.*, 9, 2, 151–159, 2019.

110. Mousavi, A., Kalganova, T., Sandner-Kiesling, A., Flor, H., Cole, J., Noroozi, S., Zhang, J.J., Gilhooly, M., Gilbert, D., Heiner, M., Phantom Limb Syndrome: An exploratory attempt to propose a VIrtual Personalised Solution to a Painful Problem, in: *EMBC'10: 32nd Annual International Conference of the IEEE Engineering in Medicine and Biology Society. IEEE & EMB Engineering in Medicine and Biology Society*, 2010.

111. Lendaro, E., Mastinu, E., Håkansson, B., Ortiz-Catalan, M., Real-time classification of non-weight bearing lower-limb movements using EMG to facilitate phantom motor execution: Engineering and case study application on phantom limb pain. *Front. Neurol.*, 8, 470, Sep, 2017.

112. Bahirat, K., Raval, G., Chung, Y.Y., Desai, K., Riegler, M., Annaswamy, T., Prabhakaran, B., Using Mr. MAPp for lower limb phantom pain management. *MM 2019 - Proc. 27th ACM Int. Conf. Multimed.*, 2019.

113. Harvie, D.S., Broecker, M., Smith, R.T., Meulders, A., Madden, V.J., Moseley, G.L., Bogus Visual Feedback Alters Onset of Movement-Evoked Pain in People With Neck Pain. *Psychol. Sci.*, 26, 4, 1071–1075, 2015.

114. Feintuch, U., Tuchner, M., Lorber-Haddad, A., Meiner, Z., Shiri, S., VirHab - A virtual reality system for treatment of chronic pain and disability. *2009 Virtual Rehabil. Int. Conf. VR 2009*, 2009.

115. Sarig Bahat, H., Takasaki, H., Chen, X., Bet-Or, Y., Treleaven, J., Cervical kinematic training with and without interactive VR training for chronic neck pain - a randomized clinical trial. *Man. Ther.*, 20, 1, 68–78, 2015.

116. Guo, C., Deng, H., Yang, J., Effect of virtual reality distraction on pain among patients with hand injury undergoing dressing change. *J. Clin. Nurs.*, 24, 1–2, 115–120, 2015.

117. Scapin, S., Echevarría-Guanilo, M.E., Fuculo Junior, P.R.B., Tomazoni, A., Gonçalves, N., Virtual Reality As Complementary Treatment in Pain Relief in Burnt Children. *Texto Contexto - Enferm.*, 29, e20180277, 2020.

118. Stanney, K., Lawson, B.D., Rokers, B., Dennison, M., Fidopiastis, C., Stoffregen, T., Weech, S., Fulvio, J.M., Identifying Causes of and Solutions for Cybersickness in Immersive Technology: Reformulation of a Research and Development Agenda. *Int. J. Hum. Comput. Interact.*, 36, 19, 1783–1803, 2020.

119. Csikszentmihalyi, M., *Finding flow: The psychology of engagement with everyday life*, Basic Books, New York, 1997.

120. Venkatesh, V. and Bala, H., Technology acceptance model 3 and a research agenda on interventions. *Decis. Sci.*, 39, 2, 273–315, 2008.

121. Stanney, K.M., Kennedy, R.S., Drexler, J.M., Cybersickness is not simulator sickness, in: *Proceedings of the Human Factors and Ergonomics Society annual meeting*, pp. 1138–1142, 1997.

122. Rizzo, A. and Kim, G.J.J., A SWOT analysis of the field of virtual reality rehabilitation and therapy. *Presence Teleoperators Virtual Environ.*, 14, 2, 119–146, 2005.

Use of XR's Technologies for Consumer Behavior Analysis

Cristina Gil-Lopez, Jaime Guixeres*, Javier Marín-Morales and Mariano Alcañiz

Instituto de Investigación e Innovación en Bioingeniería,
Universitat Politècnica de València, Valencia, Spain

Abstract

Marketing scholars and practitioners see extended reality (XR0 as a new tool for both producing optimal consumer experiences and studying consumer behavior aspects. This chapter will explore the use of XR technologies for consumer behavior research. It analyzes XR as a very promising tool to examine various customer behavioral patterns in dynamic, complex, and realistic situations that will enhance our knowledge of new models of buyer–product and buyer–seller relationships. First, it will provide an updated definition of the consumer shopping experience mediated by highly immersive virtual technology. Moreover, it will discuss how the experience of virtual reality affects human emotions. Finally, it will propose a framework that will allow the creation of controlled laboratory situations to study the factors that affect the acceptability of new products and retail spaces and the influence that the different elements that surround consumers have on their decisions.

Keywords: Consumer behavior, consumer neuroscience, digital marketing, extended realities, virtual experience in marketing, consumer behavior metrics

12.1 Introduction

The massive development of extended reality (XR) technologies has brought shopping activities and consumer experience into a new conceptualization. One of the main reasons for this accelerated growth is their potential use as very promising technological tools capable to produce

Corresponding author: jguixeres@i3b.upv.es

Mariano Alcañiz, Marco Sacco and Jolanda G. Tromp (eds.) Roadmapping Extended Reality: Fundamentals and Applications, (283–308) © 2022 Scrivener Publishing LLC

satisfying shopping experiences resembling those experienced in physical stores [1]. A growing body of knowledge is proposing XR as critical digital technologies that will lead to new marketing opportunities. XR technologies will enable the development of a new purchase channel based on virtual stores in which to interact with products and sellers.

On the other hand, XR can also be considered as an experimentation tool to analyze the influence of the different components of products, stores, and sellers on the customer retail experience.

This chapter propose XR as a very promising tool to examine various customer behavioral patterns in dynamic, complex, and realistic situations that will enhance our knowledge of new models of buyer–product and buyer–seller relationships. XR will allow the creation of controlled laboratory situations to study the factors that affect the acceptability of new products and retail spaces and the influence that the different elements that surround consumers have on their decisions. By doing so, it is expected to achieve a more comprehensive analysis of specific affective and cognitive responses experienced by customers when visiting a retail context and the different behaviors that are provoked by these responses.

To this end, it is necessary to consider a new conceptualization of the definition of consumer experience in XR technologies contexts. The general theoretical framework that conceptualizes customer experience in the retail context is detailed in Section 12.2.

In Section 12.3, a general framework for the use of XR technologies for consumer behavior research is proposed.

12.2   The Concept of Virtual Consumer Experience

With the boost of XR technologies, consumers' shopping experience are expected to be enriched in many ways. Therefore, current consumer research is keen to investigate the relationships between buyers and products/sellers in diverse virtual environments considering all aspects of the consumer behavior. Based on the scope that the use of digital technology already has in shopping activities, we highlight the importance of interactivity between buyers and suppliers, as a critical mediator of satisfactory consumer experiences, which is today generating a large amount of research in this area.

12.2.1   Definition of Consumer Experience in Marketing Research

In the last decade, the term **consumer experience** has become increasingly popular in different business segments, especially in retail. It is defined as the result of the interaction between a consumer and the different selling channels of an organization [2]. Given the proven impact that a satisfactory purchase experience has on brand acceptance (e.g., [3]), bringing an effective interaction with products and sellers has become an strategic priority for most marketers.

The general theoretical framework that conceptualizes customer experience is originally based on the stimuli–organism–response model (S-O-R; [4–7]). The S-O-R model argues that environmental variables (stimuli) influence affective and cognitive processes in shoppers' minds (organism), triggering psychophysiological responses that origin several types of behavioral outcomes: (1) sensory (senses), (2) emotional (feeling), (3) cognitive (thinking), (4) physical (actions), and (5) social interaction (relate) experiences [8]. From this idea, emerges the relational norms ruling the different types of relationships between sellers and customers. Thus, consumer experience originates from two typologies of relations:

    1) The customer–product relationship [9].
    2) The customer–seller relationship [10].

Both types of relations provide consumers with a more complete knowledge of products through the flow of direct and indirect experiences. Whereas direct experiences derived from physical interactions of the consumer with products, indirect experience arise from various sources that include advertising, environmental components, and digital media. With the emergence of XR technologies allowing a fully immersive experience in highly realistic environments, new products affordances are proposed, thus changing dramatically the conceptualization of consumer experience [11].

12.2.2 Towards a New Conceptualization of Consumer Experience in Virtual Reality Contexts

In understanding the effects of virtual technology in the consumption experience, many research currently focuses on how consumers interact within the virtual environments during ongoing shopping activities. In VR environments, the shoppers can browse a store in real time, being completely immersed in the experience from virtually anywhere. This results in better consumer learning compared with online shopping or more traditional forms of purchase experience [11]. Researchers agree that virtual technology brings the experience of presence, known as the sense of "being there" [12–15]. As suggested by Daugherty *et al.*, "*A virtual experience is a simulation of a real or physical experience, which occurs within a computer-mediated environment, and has been constructed to be located between direct (i.e., product trial) and indirect (i.e., traditional advertising) experience along the spectrum of consumer learning*" [15].

The capability of XR technologies to create new shopping experiences is conceptualized as virtual commerce, or v-commerce, which, in the future, will redefine—if not replace—the current online shopping landscape [1, 16, 17]. Several advantages of in-store VR sales have been already identified by marketers, especially in retailing contexts [18–20]. Among them, a realistic **interactivity** remains critical in virtual shopping practices [21] since it allows the buyer to co-participate, act, and learn while improving the feedback from the retailer. Such exchange has been highlighted as a very pleasant and enjoyable shopping experience from the buyer's perception, thus facilitating an effective two-way communication [22].

Importantly, this redefinition of consumer experience will directly impact the consumer relationship with marketers, possibly leading to new ways of buyer–seller communication. Evidence shows that these relationships are beyond what the marketing literature has traditionally characterized as a mutual exchange orientation[1], which, at some point, limits the role of the consumer [9, 23]. In a virtual shopping context, consumers can adopt different roles, being potentially more active at all stages of the shopping process. This virtual relationship paradigm has the potential to completely change the way retailers interact with consumers, prompting them to continuously adapt their communication strategies to the particular needs of different types of consumers [1].

From a **consumer perspective**, the application of virtual technology in shopping purchase practices creates new ways of shopping experiences that were never seen before. Firstly, VR enables a more **personal shopping experience** (i.e., personalization) that could advance to higher degree of interactivity with sellers and other buyers. We found in the literature several examples of personalized VR-AR experiences, with furniture [24, 25], cosmetics [18] and fashion clothes [26] as selling products potentially susceptible of being optimized through the use of XR technology.

Secondly, customers are more willing to browse and try new products when the **logistical limitations are removed**. This translates into shopping

---

[1]The purpose of traditional marketing exchanges with consumers is the creation of interpersonal long-term relationships through continuous and mutually adaptive relationships. Using such relational communication, the companies position themselves successfully in the business landscape.

experiences that are not limited by time or physical location, resulting in a truly immersive experience with minimal effort (e.g., teleportation; [27, 28]). Third, the **"try-before-you-buy"** advantage found in VR purchases provides consumers with high-fidelity solutions or hidden drawbacks of the offered products [29], which they might not otherwise see in traditional stores or available online shopping channels. Finally, the function of an anthropomorphic virtual shopping assistant in form of a sales-avatar supports the **social virtual metaphor** eliciting a more human-like shopping experience [30, 31].

A key aspect widely studied in the literature refers to how the experience of **virtual reality (VR) impacts human emotions**. As shown in some studies, three-dimensional (3D) technology affects the emotional states of consumers, which, to some extent, influence purchase intention and customer satisfaction [32–35]. From a consumer behavior framework, the purchase experience is shaped by a combination of implicit behavior reactions—such as neurophysiological activity and emotional responses—[36–38] and selling environmental factors such as atmospheric elements [39–41]. Several academic studies show that VR expands emotional and hedonic components of the shopping process offering a unique experience with a high mimicry of the real world [42–44]. For example, when it comes to affecting the emotions of consumers, most retailers concentrate their efforts on creating an attractive store environment that includes all the sensory components capable of directing their attention and provoking pleasant experiences to consumers (e.g., [45, 46]). For this reason, understanding the multiple ways humans direct their attention and engage with products while navigating v-commerce spaces is critical to guiding retailers/market experts in the design of effective virtual shopping spaces.

With such a multisensorial enrichment and personalization capability offered by current XR technologies, consumers involved in virtual shopping activities are following the steps to build new marketing relationships with sellers [1, 47]. For instance, by investing more time and effort in recreating the experience with different versions of the product, consumers can learn to better satisfy their preferences, thus adopting a more active role during the shopping journey. In the words of Allimamy *et al.*, using VR technology may increase the interaction between customer and seller since it reduces the perceived risks of buying a particular product while increasing trust and the co-creating the role of customers [48]. Therefore, to get a profound understanding of revolutionary changes that are about to come in the purchasing sector, clear models redefining consumer experience according to this virtualization expansion need to be devised.

12.3   A Framework for the Use of XR in Consumer Behavior Research

12.3.1   Using XR in Marketing

In the past, the XR was very restrictive due to the price of the hardware, the specific technical skills required, and human efforts needed to work with the devices and develop the environments [49]. However, the XRs are becoming more popular due to the performance improvements in the latest generation of commercial HMDs in terms of resolution, the field of view, immersion levels, and the fall in their price [50]. It has boosted the application of XR in many areas that analyzes human behavior, and specifically in marketing and consumer behavior research. The increase of this interest is shown in Figure 12.1, which presents the number of papers published applying XR to consumers. In particular, the Scopus database was queried using the following search string TITLE-ABS-KEY ("virtual reality" OR "augmented reality" OR "extended reality") AND TITLE-ABS-KEY ("consumer" OR "marketing" OR "retail") AND DOCTYPE (ar OR re). The number of papers has been increased to 278% in the last 5 years, from 2016 to 2020.

Hence, we are starting to realize the huge potential that XRs have to enhance our understanding of shopper behavior, allowing us to control, isolate, and manipulate a vast number of complex variables, and analyze their influence in the behavior of the consumers. XRs can become a commonplace tool in marketing research; however, there is not a common

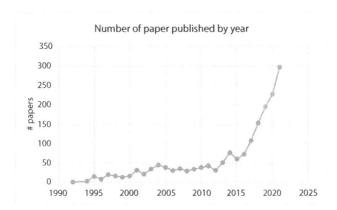

Figure 12.1 Evolution of the number of papers published each year on the topic of XR and consumer or marketing or retail. The total number of papers to be published in 2021 has been extrapolated using data up to June 09, 2021.

framework to develop these experiments. Moreover, further research is needed to understand the validity of XRs, that is, the capacity to evoke a response from the user in a simulated environment similar to one that might be evoked by a physical environment [51]. In addition, it is critical to understand how intrinsic XR features, as the navigation metaphor, influence the reality perceived by the consumer and his or her behavior.

12.3.2   XR Environment Characterization

Regarding the characterization of the extended reality environment (XRE), it can be divided considering the purpose, technical specifications, and XR quality measures. The purpose defines the aim of the experiment for what the XRE has been created, and the technical specifications describe the technology used, the interface devices used, and the interaction techniques designed. The XR quality measurement analyzes the user's experience of the simulation (see Figure 12.2).

12.3.2.1   Purpose

Concerning the purpose, the previous research performed using XR in consumer behavior research can be classified into three main groups. The first one is for the virtual presentation of physical products. It can be used as a new communication channel between the brands and the consumers for existing products [52], or as a tool to analyze the consumer's reactions in order and test future products that are in the conceptualization or design phase, providing valuable information in the decision-making process [53]. The second purpose is to use XRE to analyze new store design concepts. It allows designers to test future shops or retail stores before

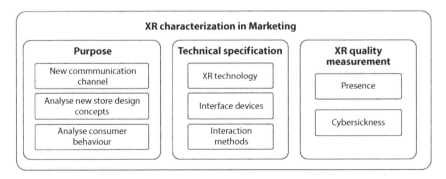

Figure 12.2 Taxonomy of XR characterization in marketing.

their construction [54] and also to test particular product displays or retail stores' layout [55]. Finally, the last purpose is to study in detail the behavior of a consumer during a stage of shopper journey. Previous research analyzes the use of XRE to predict consumer behavior in physical stores by means of the analysis of the consumer in the virtual simulation of the store [56]. Other researchers analyze how different changes in the XR can modulate the shopper experience in terms of enjoyment, consumer learning, engagement, or purchase intention [57]. Finally, XR is also used to analyze shopper characteristics as impulsivity traits [58].

12.3.2.2   Technical Specification

Concerning the technical specifications, they can be divided into three types: technology, interface devices, and interaction techniques.

12.3.2.2.1   XR Technology

A specific XR technology needs to be selected to be used: VR, augmented virtuality, or augmented reality (AR). Each of them has pros and cons, depending of the purpose of the experiment. For example, in order to simulate a whole new store, VR is an economical tool to design, providing a high presence. On the other hand, if the purpose is to test three alternatives of a new furniture in a real fashion shop, AR can offer a better approach since the design will be analyzed, considering the real context in which it needs to be analyzed.

12.3.2.2.2   Interface Devices

The interface devices are the hardware and software components that present information to the subjects and collect their interaction. They are the communication channel between the XR and the subjects, and can be divided into the output and the input interface. The input interface includes the devices that present the information to the subjects. The hardware is composed of the display interfaces, which send the information to the human perceptual system. The majority of them use visual and auditory stimuli, but in recent research, it was found that they also use haptic [59], olfactory [60], and taste stimuli [61]. However, there are still problems to achieve high fidelity in portable haptic, olfactory, and taste devices. On the other hand, the fidelity of the audiovisual stimuli in XR has been vastly improved in recent years, improving the sense of presence, immersion [62], and engagement [63]. The XR studies need to present a detailed description of the interface device used, based on previous work that provides classification for XR, for example, Krevelen and Poelman for AR [64], and Hale and Stanney for VR [65].

On the other hand, the output interface includes the set of devices that allow the user to communicate with the XRE. It includes not only devices such as a joystick, which is the most popular output device in commercial HMD, but also other human–computer interfaces as voice recognition, natural body movements, or biomarkers. The interface used need to be carefully selected and reported in XR research, since the device can affect the user experience [66] and performance [67]. A detailed classification of the output interfaces is presented in LaViola *et al.* [68].

12.3.2.2.3   Interaction Methods

Interaction techniques are the software method used to allow the user to interact with the XRE using the output interface. It includes techniques for selecting/manipulating objects, traveling, wayfinding, and controlling the system [68]. The method used affects several features of the experience and behavior of the users. In particular, they can modulate the presence [69], cognitive load [70], and human performance. A detailed classification of the methods is presented in LaViola *et al.* [68].

12.3.2.3   XR Experience Quality Measures

In the experiment that analyzes the consumer behavior using XR, the scientific success depends on providing a convincing sense of reality where the subjects tend to respond realistically to situations and the event simulated. It is called "response as if real," and it is highly recommended to assess it using two measures: presence and cybersickness.

12.3.2.3.1   Presence

Presence is a metric applicable to any XR experience, understood as the perceptual illusion of non-mediation and a sense of "being there" [71]. A high degree of presence creates in the user the sensation of physical presence and the illusion of interacting and reacting as if (s)he was in the real world [72]. It can be measured using either subjective and objective measures. Subjective measures include self-report questionnaires during or after the XR experience, the most common being the Presence Questionnaire [73]; the Immersive Tendencies Questionnaire [73]; and the SUS scale [74]. Despite the limitations of self-report assessment, they are the most common approach due to the fact that they easily provide valuable information. In addition to those questionnaires, objective measures are based on correlations of presence with psychophysiological signals, such as heart rate variability (HR), electrodermal activity (EDA), or task performance [75]. A detailed classification of the presence measures is presented in Skarbez *et al.* [76]. Even though presence is a key measure of the XR experience, it is still limited to the number of experiments that uses presence measures in XR research.

12.3.2.3.2   Cybersickness

The main adverse effects during an XR experiment that highly affects to the experience is cybersickness. It is defined as the constellation of symptoms of discomfort and malaise produced by VR exposure [65]. It can reduce the skill of the subjects as it takes competence [77] and can produce an early termination of the experiment. Therefore, the measure of cybersickness is another key measure of the XR experience. As presence, it can be measured using subjective and objective methods. The most common are the Simulator Sickness Questionnaire [78] and Fast Motion Sickness Scale [79]. A detailed classification of the cybersickness measures is presented in Gavgani *et al.* [80].

12.3.3   Consumer Behavior in XR

12.3.3.1   *General Framework*

The sources to measure the consumer behavior in an XR can be divided into the behavioral sensors integrated in the XR device, and the physiological sensors that need external devices to be registered. The present framework can be applied to any XRE (Figure 12.3), but it is optimized for VR environments since the commercial HMD nowadays offers many integrated sensors as head tracking, eye tracking, or microphone for voice analysis.

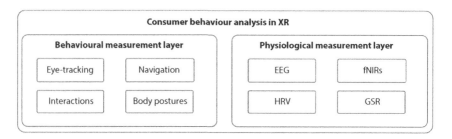

Figure 12.3 Taxonomy of consumer behavioral measurement layer in XR.

12.3.3.2   General Considerations

12.3.3.2.1   Pre-Training Familiarization Environment

The success of an XR experiment depends on if the behavior of the subject is as close as possible to reality. To this extent, a crucial aspect which all studies should be started is the phase that we call familiarization. At this stage, the user is immersed in a very aseptic scenario that allows him to become familiar with the way of interacting, navigating, and using the XR and the sensors.

12.3.3.2.2   Minimum Frame Rate

The signals collected need to accomplish a minimum frame rate to be considered as a valid measurement. It is especially important to control the frequency of the eye-tracking devices integrated in HMD, which are usually connected with the motor graphic engine and, therefore, are dependent to the complexity of the environment and the GPU performance. In other words, if the VR environment it is very complex the frame rate of the eye-tracking in the VR can decrease. In order to apply fixation identification algorithms, it is important to have a sampling rate greater than 50Hz being ideal to reach 100 Hz [81].

12.3.3.2.3   Establish a Baseline to Normalize

Some features that can be calculated from the XR experience, especially those related to physiological responses, need a baseline to be normalized. As examples, the EDA conductance which measure stress is important to be normalized using a neutral stimulus due to the inter-subjects differences in the magnitude of conductance. It can also be applied to other features as velocity of movements in navigation. It is important to note that the pre-training familiarization scenario cannot be used as a neutral environment for baseline, since it can be affected by the "wow" effects that affects the first minutes during an XR experience [82].

12.3.3.2.4   Segmenting Space Into Areas of Interest

During the XR experience, several metrics need to be calculated considering when the shopper is inside a specific zone on the physical space or interacting or looking at a specific area at the shelf level. To this extent, the space needs to be segmented in two-dimensional (2D) areas of interest (AOIs), which need to be designed for each XRE and purpose. For example, Masoud *et al.* (2021) [58] divided the floor plan of the VR Store in several AOIs considering the distance to the shelves: adjacent, near, and far. In addition, to analyze the 3D movements of head and hands, it is necessary to define 3D zones of interest (ZOIs).

12.3.4 Behavior Measurement Layer

12.3.4.1 Eye Tracking

Eye tracking is based on recognizing the position of the gaze through the analysis of the orientation of the pupils based on general metrics (see Table 12.1) and specific AOIs (Table 12.2). Nowadays, many commercial HMDs as HTC Vive Eye include an integrated eye-tracking device. It works with infrared emitters and sensors. It has a 110 degrees field of view and lenses with a resolution of 1440 × 1600 pixels per eye (2880 × 1600 pixels

Table 12.1 General eye-tracking metrics.

Metrics	Description
Number of fixations	Number of fixations detected
Mean time per fixation	Average time of every fixation
Number of saccades	Number of Saccades detected by the algorithm where a saccade is the rapid movement between fixations
Mean dispersion of the saccade	Mean dispersion of taking in account all the saccades detected
Sum of dispersion of the saccade	Sum in total of every dispersion for all the saccades. Saccade total amplitude
Number of short saccades	Number of saccades that the amplitude is over a threshold. Usually, above 4.6° is consider as a short saccade.
Number of long saccades	Number of saccades that the amplitude is below a threshold. Usually, below 4.6° is consider as a long saccade.
Long vs. short ratio	Relation between long saccades and short saccades. Higher number represent explorative dynamics, and lower represents focal dynamics.
Total distance vertical and horizontal	The distance in the horizontal and vertical axis is measured

Table 12.2 AOI related eye-tracking metrics.

Metrics	Description
Number of AOIs looked	Total number of AOIs looked
Number of visits to an AOI	Number of visits to an AOI. A visit is defined as a set of consecutive fixations on a AOI
Number of revisits to an AOI	Number of revisits to an AOI. It will be the number of visits minus one
Time to first visit	Time to first visit to an AOI
Mean Time AOI	Mean time looking at the same AOI
Mean Time AOI (%)	Percentage of the time spend to look at a particular AOI divide by the total time
Sequence	Position of the AOI in a temporal sequence ordered by the time that has been looked first

combined). The gaze data was collected at a variable sampling rate of 60–70 Hz using runtime software integrated into unity. From gaze raw data, a dispersion algorithm was implemented in order to extract fixations and saccades. The algorithm used for the classification is the dispersion-threshold identification (I-DT) using a distance-dispersion thresholds between 1 and 1.6° and time windows between 0.25 and 0.4, with 1° and 0.25 s being the optimum [81]. Every duration and centroid are computed for each fixation. After that, the rest of the metrics for eye tracking are computed using this information. Although currently, the implementation of eye-tracking in AR devices is still limited, some researchers are starting to integrate gaze recognition systems in devices as Hololens 2 [83].

In addition to these quantitative metrics, heatmaps are a valuable tool to be used as a descriptive picture of the gaze pattern [84].

12.3.4.2 Navigation

The movement of the subject's head can be recorded in VR settings by using the location tracking and gyroscope sensors of HMD. This movement in 2D environment, i.e., without considering height is referred to as navigation raw data. The following metrics (Table 12.3) can be calculated based on this position among time, in combination with a spatial segmentation of the environment using zenithal AOIs.

Table 12.3 Navigation metrics.

Metrics	Description
Number of Visits to an AOI	Number of times that an AOI has been visited by the subject.
Time Spent in an AOI	Time spent by the subject in each AOI
Mean of Velocity in each AOI	Average velocity of travel in each AOI
Mean of Acceleration in AOIs	Average acceleration of movement in each AOI
Total Distance of AOIs	Total distance that the subject travels in each AOI
Time of First Visit of AOIs	Time taken by the subject to reach an AOI from the beginning of the experiment of the task
Total Time of Navigation	Time spent traveling the entire space
Number of Stops	Total number of stops made in the session. A stop is defined as a segment of time where the movement of the subjects are below a specific threshold, which need to be defined considering the tracking system
Average Duration of Stops	Average time of stops made in the session
Percentage of Short Stops	Short stop are defined as the stop with less than 10 s
Total Distance Traveled	Total distance that the subject travels during the experiment

In the analysis of is also possible to represent zenithal heatmaps to show the patterns of the movements of the subjects among the VR space.

12.3.4.3 Interaction

In VR environments, the users interact with the environment using different devices, as a joystick, the interaction with several objects can be recorded and analyzed. In the consumer behavior research experiment usually is recorded several metrics (Table 12.4) related to the number of products picked, dropped, and purchased.

Table 12.4 Interaction metrics.

Metrics	Description
Number of objects picked & dropped	Total number of objects picked and dropped in each task
Number of objects bought	Total number of objects bought in each task
Total price	Accumulated price of the objects bought for each task
Decision after interaction	Decision taken after the interaction (e.g., buy—yes/no)

12.3.4.4 Body Gestures

The raw body data consist of the movement of the user in three dimensions. As an example, the position of the hand can be recorded based on the interaction devices used as joysticks. It supposes a valuable source of information since in many consumer environments, the subjects interact with product using hands. A several set of metrics (Table 12.5) can be

Table 12.5 Body posture metrics.

Metrics	Description
Visiting time in ZOI	Time spent in each ZOI
Total movements	Total distance that the hand moves in a session
Total movements in ZOIs	Total distance that the hand moves in each ZOI
Number of visits	Number of times that the hands visits an ZOI
Time of first visit of ZOIs	Time taken by the hand to reach first ZOI
Average velocity of movements	Average velocity of hand's movements
Average velocity of movements in ZOIs	Average velocity of hand's movements in each ZOI
Average accelerations of movements	Average accelerations of hand's movements
Average accelerations of movements in ZOIs	Average accelerations of hand's movements in each ZOI

calculated based on the 3D dynamics of the subjects during an XR experience. The metrics are similar to the navigation features, but they are calculated considering the ZOIs, which are defined as 3D AOIs.

12.3.5   Physiological Measurement Layer

The following sensors can be integrated in XR research using external devices in order to collect the physiological responses of the consumers. Each of them assesses the physiological dynamics of the autonomic and central nervous system.

12.3.5.1   *Electroencephalography*

The electroencephalography (EEG) is defined as electrical activity of an alternating type recorded from a scalp's surface after being picked up by metal electrodes and conductive media. It is presented as a measure of the central nervous system. EEG may capture the electric potentials of the brain synchronized to specific events, as well as changes in baseline neural oscillations [85]. EEG presents several advantages for the decision-making research, due to the high temporal resolution and reduced cost, including the use of wearable devices. Those devices can be used in the combination of XR devices as VR HMD. The advantages of using EEG for decision-making research include the measure of ongoing cortical activity with a high temporal resolution and reduced costs, maybe using wearable monitoring devices [86]. It allows to perform a quantitative assessment of cortical responses to cognitive/emotional events, and the decoding of cognitive states through biomarkers derived from brain signals. Bazzani *et al.* (2020) presents a systematic review of the use of EEG in marketing research [87]. Moreover, preliminary studies are starting to use EEG in consumer behavior research based on XRE [88].

12.3.5.2   *Functional Near-Infrared Spectroscopy*

Functional near-infrared spectroscopy (fNIRS) is a non-invasive technique that allows for measuring changes in tissue hemodynamics and oxygenation in the human head [89]. Since fNIRS is sensitive to microvascular hemodynamics in the cortex, this technique has been widely used to detect brain functional activation [90]. Because of this, connectivity analysis can be performed to decode connectivity patterns observed under various psychophysiological activities, such as attention. Some research used fNIRs to analyze consumer-related metrics [91], but their implementation in XRE is still limited.

12.3.5.3   Heart Rate Variability

Beside the central nervous system activity, the autonomic nervous system activity is a valuable source of information to measure the unconscious physiological dynamics during a decision-making task. In particular, the sympathetic nervous system and the parasympathetic nervous system play a fundamental role in the cardiovascular control, regulating emotion-related changes such as blood pressure, respiration, and heart rate. One of the physiological dynamics that the autonomic nervous system modulates is the beat-to-beat variability series, also known as heart rate variability (HRV) [92]. It can be associated with cognitive states sustaining unconscious decision-making. Several previous research use HRV to assess emotional states in XRE [93], but their applications for consumer behavior research are still limited.

12.3.5.4   Electrodermal Activity

Electrodermal activity (EDA) is another measure of the autonomic nervous system dynamics. It refers to change in the electrical properties of the skin that are directly related to the eccrine sweat gland activity. The variation of the EDA can be represented by a two-compartment pharmacokinetic model in which the sweat concentration is assumed to change only by diffusion. The EDA signal results from the sum of two components: the tonic component that represent the slow-varying changes, and the phase component that represents the fast variation related to an external stimulus. EDA is also often used to assess emotional states in VR research [94], and is widely used in consumer neuroscience studies [95].

12.4   Future Research Agenda and Roadmap

Traditionally, most human decision-making theories have been based on a human mind's model, which assumes that humans can deliberate and verbalize accurately their attitudes, emotions, and behaviors. Therefore, most theoretical constructions have been based on explicit measures such as questionnaires and interviews and think -aloud techniques. However, most decisions are made unconsciously. Thoughts and feelings shape decisions as well as interactions between humans. Advances in neuroscience have revealed that most of the brain processes that regulate our emotions, attitudes, and decisions are beyond our consciousness [96]. Implicit processes (brain functions that occur automatically and out of conscious control and awareness) have a considerable influence in relevant psychological constructs and human neurocognitive mechanisms, such as consumer decisions [97]. There is a wide range of techniques that allow capturing and modeling implicit processes. These techniques are based on non-invasive monitoring including functional magnetic resonance imaging [98], fNIRS [99], eye tracking [100], electroencephalography (EEG) [101], as well as other more peripheral physiological correlates linked to the so-called central autonomic network, such as EDR [102], prosody from speech, respiration dynamics, cardiac HRV [103] and cardio-respiratory coupling. What all these techniques have in common is that they all seek to provide an estimate of the construct of interest without having to directly request the participant for a verbal report. Its main attraction is that these indirect estimates are likely to be free from worries of social desirability. For all these techniques, data gathering usually takes place, observing the participants' behavior in a real scenario or through experiments in laboratory settings. In both cases, experiments are characterized by a low ecological validity: in real situations because it is not possible to control completely the stimuli involved in the experience, while in a laboratory, subjects are confronted with controlled stimuli that do not include other variables that are present in real-life situations.

XR technologies are today the most technologically advanced tools for the generation of artificial realities. XR merges real with virtual worlds to generate environments where physical and digital objects coexist and interact in real time. XR recreates real-life situations with high sensory fidelity, while controlling both the situations and stimuli that influence human behavior through the real-time measurement of human reactions to such stimuli. When humans use XR, they experience a sense of presence [104] that allows them to interact and behave into the virtual environment as if they acted, behaved, and interacted in real life. It has been shown that the neural mechanisms that humans have in virtual environments are very similar to the mechanisms that originate in real life [105]. Studies have already demonstrated the usefulness of XR application to several domains of the social cognitive neurosciences [106]. However, up to date, XR has not been used together with business methodologies with the aim to apply it for consumer behavior purposes as a way of enhancing the stimuli control and the ecological validity of implicit measures.

The proposed approach defines a perfect scheme to generate controlled environments that can be used to observe human behavior. Different aspects can be analyzed from a neuroscience perspective, including perception, the control of movement, learning, memory, and emotional aspects. Accounting for such a multidimensional complex representation will substantially increase the reliability of the metrics obtained in previous studies [107]. However, reversely to available algorithms that usually rely on basic statistics and simple inference to process single measurements' data [108], it is necessary for the development of advanced data processing techniques based on artificial intelligence and machine learning to combine them into novel multidomain decision-making. In this way, functional measures from brain and autonomic nervous system dynamics will be passed up to the artificial intelligence core to properly merge them, while selecting the best candidate biomarkers for decision-making modeling. The processing platform can integrate users' individual differences, psychometrics, and behavioral patterns while interacting with virtual situations using XR.

The multisensorial nature of immersive consumer experience provided by XR technologies is revolutionizing shopping practices, resulting in a prominent impact in today's business landscape. Within the framework of marketing science, the proposed definition of consumer experience in virtual shopping scenarios highlights the increasing role of users in generating more meaningful experiences. Therefore, the identification of key factors capable of generating satisfactory shopping experiences in virtual retail trading will lead to a change in the relationships between a customer and a seller/product. As society becomes even more digitized, a new conceptualization of consumer experience in virtual environments becomes necessary. Further investigation on this topic needs to be addressed in future research to understand the phenomena of v-commerce in relation to consumers' preferences and new types of product affordances.

References

1. Alcañiz, M., Guixeres, J., Bigné, E., Virtual reality in marketing: a framework, review and research agenda. *Front. Psychol.*, 10, 1530, 2019.
2. Becker, L. and Jaakkola, E., Customer experience: fundamental premises and implications for research. *J. Acad. Market. Sci.*, 48, 630, 2020.
3. Hubert, M., Blut, M., Brock, C., Backhaus, C., Eberhardt, T., Acceptance of Smartphone-Based Mobile Shopping: Mobile Benefits, Customer Characteristics, Perceived Risks, and the Impact of Application Context. *Psychol. Market.*, 34, 175–194, 2017.
4. Changa, H.J., Eckmanb, M., Yanb, R.N., Application of the stimulus-organism-response model to the retail environment: The role of hedonic

motivation in impulse buying behavior. *Int. Rev. Retail. Distrib. Consum. Res.*, 21, 233–249, 2011.

5. Fiore, A.M. and Kim, J., An integrative framework capturing experiential and utilitarian shopping experience. *Int. J. Retail Distrib. Manage.*, 35, 421–442, 2007.

6. Vieira, V.A., Stimuli-organism-response framework: A meta-analytic review in the store environment. *J. Bus. Res.*, 66, 1420–1426, 2013.

7. Jacoby, J., Stimulus-Organism-Response Reconsidered: An Evolutionary Step in Modeling (Consumer) Behavior. *J. Consum. Psychol.*, 12, 51–57, 2002.

8. Schmitt, B., Experiential Marketing. *J. Mark. Manage.*, 15, 53–67, 1999.

9. Mathwick, C., Understanding the online consumer: A typology of online relational norms and behavior. *J. Interact. Mark.*, 16, 40–55, 2002.

10. Bagozzi, R.P. and Verbeke, W.J.M.I., Biomarketing: An emerging paradigm linking neuroscience, endocrinology, and genetics to buyer-seller behavior, in: *Routledge Companion to Future of Marketing*, pp. 107–133, Routledge, Abingdon, 2014.

11. Li, H., Daugherty, T., Biocca, F., The Role of Virtual Experience in Consumer Learning. *J. Consum. Psychol.*, 13, 395–407, 2003.

12. Baños, R.M., Botella, C., Garcia-Palacios, A., Villa, H., Perpiña, C., Alcañiz, M., Presence and reality judgment, in Virtual environments: A unitary construct? *Cyberpsychol. Behav.*, 3, 3, 327–335, 2000.

13. Lee, K.M., Presence, explicated. *Commun. Theory*, 14, 27–50, 2004.

14. Mestre, D.R., On the usefulness of the concept of presence, in: Virtual reality applications. *Eng. Real. Virtual Real*, SPIE, Bellingham, p. 93920, 2015.

15. Daugherty, T., Li, H., Biocca, F., Consumer learning and the effects of virtual experience relative to indirect and direct product experience. *Psychol. Market.*, 25, 568–586, 2008.

16. de Regt, A. and Barnes, S.J., V-Commerce, in: *Retail: Nature and Potential Impact*, pp. 17–25, Springer, Cham, 2019.

17. El Boudali, A., Mantelet, F., Aoussat, A., Berthomier, J., Leray, F., A State of Art on Kansei-Engineered Virtual Shops: A Study on the Possibilities of V-Commerce, in: *Advances in Intelligent Systems and Computing*, pp. 11–19, Springer Verlag, Berlin, 2018.

18. Bonetti, F., Warnaby, G., Quinn, L., Augmented Reality and Virtual Reality, in: *Physical and Online Retailing: A Review, Synthesis and Research Agenda*, pp. 119–132, Springer, Cham, 2018.

19. Bulearca, M. and Tamarjan, D., Augmented Reality: A Sustainable Marketing Tool? *GBMR*, 2, 2, 237–252, 2010.

20. Bug, P. and Bernd, M., The Future of Fashion Films, in: *Augmented Reality and Virtual Reality*, pp. 281–301, Springer, Singapore, 2020.

21. Merrilees, B., Interactive brand experience pathways to customer-brand engagement and value co-creation. *J. Prod. Brand Manage.*, 25, 402–408, 2016.

22. Park, M. and Yoo, J., Effects of perceived interactivity of augmented reality on consumer responses: A mental imagery perspective. *J. Retail. Consum. Serv.*, 52, 52, 101912, 2020.

23. Lefaix-Durand, A. and Kozak, R., Integrating transactional and relational exchange into the study of exchange orientation in customer relationships. *J. Mark. Manage.*, 25, 9, 1003–1025, 2009.

24. Lee, I.J., Applying virtual reality for learning woodworking in the vocational training of batch wood furniture production. *Interact. Learn. Environ.*, 1–19, 2020.

25. Phan, V.T. and Choo, S.Y., Interior Design in Augmented Reality Environment. *Int. J. Comput. Appl.*, 5, 16–21, 2010.

26. Park, M., Im, H., Kim, D.Y., Feasibility and user experience of virtual reality fashion stores. *Fash. Text.*, 5, 1–17, 2018.

27. Farah, M.F., Ramadan, Z.B., Harb, D.H., The examination of virtual reality at the intersection of consumer experience, shopping journey and physical retailing. *J. Retail. Consum. Serv.*, 48, 136–143, 2019.

28. Schnack, A., Wright, M.J., Holdershaw, J.L., Does the locomotion technique matter in an immersive virtual store environment? – Comparing motion-tracked walking and instant teleportation. *J. Retail. Consum. Serv.*, 58, 102266, 2021.

29. Smink, A.R., Frowijn, S., van Reijmersdal, E.A., van Noort, G., Neijens, P.C., Try online before you buy: How does shopping with augmented reality affect brand responses and personal data disclosure. *Electron. Commer. Res. Appl.*, 35, 2019.

30. Hoppe, M., Rossmy, B., Neumann, D.P., Streuber, S., Schmidt, A., MacHulla, T.K., A Human Touch: Social Touch Increases the Perceived Human-likeness of Agents in Virtual Reality, in: *Conf. Hum. Factors Comput. Syst. - Proc*, Association for Computing Machinery, New York, 2020.

31. Moon, J.H., Kim, E., Choi, S.M., Sung, Y., Keep the Social in Social Media: The Role of Social Interaction in Avatar-Based Virtual Shopping. *J. Interact. Advert.*, 13, 1, 14–26, 2013.

32. Domina, T., Lee, S.E., MacGillivray, M., Understanding factors affecting consumer intention to shop in a virtual world. *J. Retail. Consum. Serv.*, 19, 613–620, 2012.

33. Gabisch, J.A., Virtual world brand experience and its impact on real world purchasing behavior. *J. Brand Manage.*, 19, 18–32, 2011.

34. Lau, K.W. and Lee, P.Y., Shopping in virtual reality: a study on consumers' shopping experience in a stereoscopic virtual reality. *Virtual Real.*, 23, 255–268, 2019.

35. Pizzi, G., Scarpi, D., Pichierri, M., Vannucci, V., Virtual reality, real reactions?: Comparing consumers' perceptions and shopping orientation across physical and virtual-reality retail stores. *Comput. Hum. Behav.*, 29, 96, 1–12, 2019.

36. de Wijk, R.A. and Noldus, L.P.J.J., Implicit and explicit measures of food emotions, in: *Emotion Measurement*, pp. 169–196, Elsevier, Amsterdam, 2021.

37. Verhulst, N., Vermeir, I., Slabbinck, H., Larivière, B., Mauri, M., Russo, V., A neurophysiological exploration of the dynamic nature of emotions during the customer experience. *J. Retail. Consum. Serv.*, 57, 102217, 2020.

38. Yoo, S.C., Peña, J.F., Drumwright, M.E., Virtual shopping and unconscious persuasion: The priming effects of avatar age and consumers' age discrimination on purchasing and prosocial behaviors. *Comput. Hum. Behav.*, 48, 62–71, 2015.

39. Sherman, E., Mathur, A., Smith, R.B., Store Environment and Consumer Purchase Behavior: Mediating Role of Consumer Emotions. *Psychology & Marketing*, 14, 361–378, 1997.

40. Grewal, D., Roggeveen, A.L., Nordfält, J., The Future of Retailing. *J. Retail.*, 93, 1, 1–6, 2017.

41. Kim, J.H., Kim, M., Kandampully, J., Buying environment characteristics in the context of e-service. *Eur. J. Mark.*, 43, 1188–1204, 2009.

42. Herz, M. and Rauschnabel, P.A., Understanding the diffusion of virtual reality glasses: The role of media, fashion and technology. *Technol. Forecast. Soc Change*, 138, 228–242, 2019.

43. Kim, M.J., Lee, C.K., Jung, T., Exploring Consumer Behavior in Virtual Reality Tourism Using an Extended Stimulus-Organism-Response Model. *J. Travel Res.*, 69–89, 59, 1, 2020.

44. Flavián, C., Ibáñez-Sánchez, S., Orús, C., The impact of virtual, augmented and mixed reality technologies on the customer experience. *J. Bus. Res.*, 100, 547–560, 2019.

45. Baek, E., Choo, H.J., Lee, S.H. (Mark), Using warmth as the visual design of a store: Intimacy, relational needs, and approach intentions. *J. Bus. Res.*, 88, 91–101, 2018.

46. Orth, U.R. and Wirtz, J., Consumer Processing of Interior Service Environments: The Interplay Among Visual Complexity, Processing Fluency, and Attractiveness. *J. Serv. Res.*, 17, 296–309, 2014.

47. Al-Imamy, S., *The effect of co-creation through exposure to augmented reality on customer perceived risk, perceived trust and purchase intent*, University of Otago, North Dunedin, 2018.

48. Javaheri, H., Mirzaei, M., Lukowicz, P., How far can Wearable Augmented Reality Influence Customer Shopping Behavior. *EAI International Conference on Mobile and Ubiquitous Systems: Computing, Networking and Services*, pp. 464–469, 2020.

49. Cipresso, P., Chicchi, I.A., Alcañiz, M., Riva, G., The Past, Present, and Future of Virtual and Augmented Reality Research: A network and cluster analysis of the literature. *Front. Psychol.*, 9, 2086, 2018.

50. Marin-Morales, J., Llinares, C., Guixeres, J., Alcañiz, M., Emotion Recognition in Immersive Virtual Reality: From Statistics to Affective Computing. *Sensors*, 20, 5163, 2020.

51. Rohrmann, B. and Bishop, I.D., Subjective responses to computer simulations of urban environments. *J. Environ. Psychol.*, 22, 319–331, 2002.

52. Brody, A.B. and Gottsman, E.J., Pocket BargainFinder: a handheld device for augmented commerce, in: *Int. Symp. Handheld*, Springer, Berlin, pp. 44–51, 1999.

53. Jaeger, S.R. and Porcherot, C., Consumption context in consumer research: Methodological perspectives. *Curr. Opin. Food Sci.*, 15, 30–37, 2017.

54. van Herpen, E., van den Broek, E., van Trijp, H.C.M., Yu, T., Can a virtual supermarket bring realism into the lab? Comparing shopping behavior using virtual and pictorial store representations to behavior in a physical store. *Appetite*, 107, 196–207, 2016.

55. Meißner, M., Pfeiffer, J., Pfeiffer, T., Oppewal, H., Combining virtual reality and mobile eye tracking to provide a naturalistic experimental environment for shopper research. *J. Bus. Res.*, 100, 445–458, 2019.

56. Burke, R.R., Virtual reality for marketing research, in: *Innovative Research Methodologies in Management*, pp. 63–82, Palgrave Macmillan, Cham, 2018.

57. Bigné, E., Llinares, C., Torrecilla, C., Elapsed time on first buying triggers brand choices within a category: A virtual reality-based study. *J. Bus. Res.*, 69, 1423–1427, 2016.

58. Moghaddasi, M., Martin-Morales, J., Khatri, J., Guixeres, J., Chicchi Giglioli, I.A., Alcañiz, M., Recognition of Customers' Impulsivity from Behavioral Patterns in Virtual Reality. *Appl. Sci.*, 11, 4399, 2021.

59. Xia, P., New advances for haptic rendering: state of the art. *Vis. Comput.*, 34, 271–287, 2018.

60. Ischer, M., Baron, N., Mermoud, C., Cayeux, I., Porcherot, C., Sander, D., Delplanque, S., How incorporation of scents could enhance immersive virtual experiences. *Front. Psychol.*, 5, 736, 2014.

61. Ranasinghe, N., Nakatsu, R., Nii, H., Gopalakrishnakone, P., Tongue mounted interface for digitally actuating the sense of taste, in: *16th Int. Symp*, IEEE, Piscataway, pp. 80–87, 2012.

62. Slater, M., Immersion and the illusion of presence in virtual reality. *Br. J. Psychol.*, 109, 431–433, 2018.

63. Buttussi, F. and Chittaro, L., Effects of different types of virtual reality display on presence and learning in a safety training scenario. *IEEE Trans. Vis. Comput. Graph.*, 24, 1063–1076, 2017.

64. Van Krevelen, D.W.F. and Poelman, R., A survey of augmented reality technologies, applications and limitations. *IJVR*, 9, 1–20, 2010.

65. Hale, K.S. and Stanney, K.M. (eds.), *Handbook of virtual environments: Design, implementation, and applications*, CRC Press, 2014. https://doi.org/10.1201/b17360.

66. Jerald, J., Human-centered design for immersive interactions, in: *IEEE Virtual Reality*, pp. 431–432, IEEE, Piscataway, 2017.

67. Kim, H. and Choi, Y., Performance comparison of user interface devices for controlling mining software in virtual reality environments. *Appl. Sci.*, 9, 2584, 2019.

68. LaViola, J.J., Kruijff, E., McMahan, R., Bowman, D.A., Poupyrev, I., *3D user interfaces: theory and practice*, Addison-Wesley Professional, 2017.

69. Seibert, J. and Shafer, D.M., Control mapping in virtual reality: effects on spatial presence and controller naturalness. *Virtual Real.*, 22, 79–88, 2018.

70. Varma, V. and Nathan-Roberts, D., Gestural interaction with three-dimensional interfaces; current research and recommendations, in: *Proc. Hum. Factors Ergon. Soc. Annu. Meet*, Sage CA, Los Angeles, pp. 537–541, 2017.

71. Slater, M. and Wilbur, S., A Framework for Immersive Virtual Environments (FIVE): Speculations on the Role of Presence in Virtual Environments. *Presence Teleop. Virt.*, 6, 603, 1997.

72. Heeter, C., Being There: The Subjective Experience of Presence. *Presence Teleop. Virt.*, 1, 262, 1992.

73. Witmer, B.G. and Singer, M.J., Measuring presence in virtual environments: A presence questionnaire. *Presence*, 7, 225, 1998.

74. Usoh, M., Catena, E., Arman, S., Slater, M., Using Presence Questionnaires in Reality. *Presence Teleop. Virt.*, 9, 497, 2000.

75. Roncadin, C., Guger, S., Archibald, J., Barnes, M., Dennis, M., Working memory after mild, moderate, or severe childhood closed head injury. *Dev. Neuropsychol.*, 25, 21, 2004.

76. Skarbez, R., Brooks Jr., F.P., Whitton, M.C., A survey of presence and related concepts. *ACM Comput. Surv.*, 50, 1, 2017.

77. Nalivaiko, E., Davis, S.L., Blackmore, K.L., Vakulin, A., Nesbitt, K.V., Cybersickness provoked by head-mounted display affects cutaneous vascular tone, heart rate and reaction time. *Physiol. Behav.*, 151, 583, 2015.

78. Kennedy, R.S., Drexler, J.M., Compton, D.E., Stanney, K.M., Lanham, D.S., Harm, D.L., Configural Scoring of Simulator Sickness, Cybersickness and Space Adaptation Syndrome: Similarities and Differences, in: *Virtual Adaptive Environments: Applications, Implications, and Human Performance Issues*, p. 247, 2003.

79. Keshavarz, B. and Hecht, H., Validating an efficient method to quantify motion sickness. *Hum. Factors*, 53, 415, 2011.

80. Mazloumi Gavgani, A., Walker, F.R., Hodgson, D.M., Nalivaiko, E., A comparative study of cybersickness during exposure to virtual reality and "classic" motion sickness: are they different? *J. Appl. Physiol.*, 125, 1670, 2018.

81. Llanes-Jurado, J., Mar\'\in-Morales, J., Guixeres, J., Alcañiz, M., Development and calibration of an eye-tracking fixation identification algorithm for immersive virtual reality. *Sensors*, 20, 4956, 2020.

82. Marín-Morales, J., Higuera-Trujillo, J.L., De-Juan-Ripoll, C., Llinares, C., Guixeres, J., Iñarra, S., Alcañiz, M., Navigation Comparison between a Real and a Virtual Museum: Time-dependent Differences using a Head Mounted Display. *Interact. Comput.*, 31, 208, 2019.

83. Kapp, S., Barz, M., Mukhametov, S., Sonntag, D., Kuhn, J., ARETT: Augmented Reality Eye Tracking Toolkit for Head Mounted Displays. *Sensors*, 21, 2234, 2021.

84. Maurus, M., Hammer, J.H., Beyerer, J., Realistic heatmap visualization for interactive analysis of 3D gaze data, in: *Proc. Symp. Eye Track. Res. Appl*, p. 295, 2014.

85. Teplan, M., others, Fundamentals of EEG measurement. *Meas. Sci. Rev.*, 2, 1, 2002.

86. Marin-Morales, J., Higuera-Trujillo, J.L., Llinares, C., Guixeres, J., Alcaniz, M., Valenza, G., Real vs. Immersive Virtual Emotional Museum Experience: a Heart Rate Variability Analysis during a Free Exploration Task. *11th Conf. Eur. Study Gr. Cardiovasc. Oscil. Comput. Model. Physiol. New Challenges Oppor*, pp. 12–13, 2020.

87. Bazzani, A., Ravaioli, S., Faraguna, U., Turchetti, G., Is EEG Suitable for Marketing Research? A Systematic Review. *Front. Neurosci.*, 14, 1343, 2020.

88. Horvat, M., Dobrinić, M., Novosel, M., Jerčić, P., Assessing emotional responses induced in virtual reality using a consumer EEG headset: A preliminary report, in: *41st Int. Conv. Inf. Commun. Technol. Electron. Microelectron*, IEEE, Piscataway, pp. 1006–1010, 2018.

89. Pfeifer MD, L.R. and Scholkmann, F., Signal Processing in Functional Near-Infrared Spectroscopy (fNIRS): Methodological Differences Lead to Different Statistical Results. *Front. Hum. Neurosci.*, 11, 641, 2018.

90. Tachtsidis, I. and Papaioannou, A., Investigation of Frontal Lobe Activation with fNIRS and Systemic Changes During Video Gaming. *Adv. Exp. Med. Biol.*, 789, 89, 2013.

91. Krampe, C., Gier, N.R., Kenning, P., The application of mobile fNIRS in marketing research—Detecting the "First-Choice-Brand" effect. *Front. Hum. Neurosci.*, 12, 433, 2018.

92. van Ravenswaaij-Arts, C.M.A., Kollee, L.A.A., Hopman, J.C.W., Stoelinga, G.B.A., van Geijn, H.P., Heart rate variability. *Ann. Intern. Med.*, 118, 436, 1993.

93. Marín-Morales, J., Higuera-Trujillo, J.L., Greco, A., Guixeres, J., Llinares, C., Scilingo, E.P., Alcañiz, M., Valenza, G., Affective computing in virtual reality: emotion recognition from brain and heartbeat dynamics using wearable sensors. *Sci. Rep.*, 8, 1, 2018.

94. Granato, M., Gadia, D., Maggiorini, D., Ripamonti, L.A., An empirical study of players' emotions in VR racing games based on a dataset of physiological data. *Multimed. Tools Appl.*, 79, 33657, 2020.

95. Lajante, M., Droulers, O., Dondaine, T., Amarantini, D., Opening the "black box" of electrodermal activity in consumer neuroscience research. *J. Neurosci. Psychol. Econ.*, 5, 238, 2012.

96. Nosek, B.A., Hawkins, C.B., Frazier, R.S., Implicit social cognition: From measures to mechanisms. *Trends Cogn. Sci.*, 15, 4, 2011.

97. Bagozzi, R.P. and Verbeke, W.J., An emerging paradigm linking neuroscience, endocrinology, and genetics to buyer–seller behavior, in: *The Routledge Companion to the Future of Marketing*, p. 107, 2014.

98. Cunningham, W.A., Raye, C.L., Johnson, M.K., Implicit and explicit evaluation: fMRI correlates of valence, emotional intensity, and control in the processing of attitudes. *J. Cogn. Neurosci.*, 16, 10, 2004.

99. Kopton, I.M. and Kenning, P., Near-infrared spectroscopy (NIRS) as a new tool for neuroeconomic research. *Front. Hum. Neurosci.*, 8, 6, 549, 2014.

100. Amodio, D.M., Harmon-Jones, E., Devine, P.G., Individual differences in the activation and control of affective race bias as assessed by startle eyeblink response and self-report. *J. Pers. Soc Psychol.*, 84, 4, 738, 2003.

101. Rodríguez, A., Rey, B., Clemente, M., Wrzesien, M., Alcañiz, M., Assessing brain activations associated with emotional regulation during virtual reality mood induction procedures. *Expert Syst. Appl.*, 42, 3, 2015.

102. Sequeira, H., Hot, P., Silvert, L., Delplanque, S., Electrical autonomic correlates of emotion. *Int. J. Psychophysiol.*, 71, 1, 50–6, 2009.

103. Lane, R.D., Neural substrates of implicit and explicit emotional processes: a unifying framework for psychosomatic medicine. *Psychosom. Med.*, 70, 2, 214–231, 2008.

104. Slater, M., Place illusion and plausibility can lead to realistic behaviour in immersive virtual environments. *Philos. Trans. R. Soc Lond. B, Biol. Sci.*, 364, 1535, 3549–3557, 2009.

105. Alcañiz, M., Rey, B., Tembl, J., Parkhutik, V.A., neuroscience approach to virtual reality experience using transcranial Doppler monitoring. *Presence*, 18, 2, 97–111, 2009.

106. Parsons, T.D., Virtual reality for enhanced ecological validity and experimental control in the clinical, affective and social neurosciences. *Front. Hum. Neurosci.*, 9, 9, 660, 2015.

107. Alcañiz, M., Parra, E., Chicchi Giglioli, I.A., Virtual reality as an emerging methodology for leadership assessment and training. *Front. Psychol.*, 9, 1658, 2018.

108. Marín Morales, J., Torrecilla-Moreno, C., Guixeres-Provinciale, J., Llinares-Millán, C., Methodological bases for a new platform for the measurement of human behaviour in virtual environments. *DYNA-Ingeniería e Industria*, 92, 1, 2017.

XR for Industrial Training & Maintenance

Luca Greci

Institute of Intelligent Industrial Technologies and Systems for Advanced Manufacturing - STIIMA, Italian National Research Council, Milano (MI), Italy

Abstract

With the introduction of Industry 4.0, traditional industrial manufacturing and processes are turning into "digital practices." Products and procedures are becoming increasingly intricate due to the exponential rise of industrial internet of things (IIoT) technologies, which have been introduced to improve and support processes and control systems. Workers will need new skills to address challenges that technology alone cannot answer because of this complexity. In the context of Industry 4.0, extended reality (XR) appears to be a promising solution for training and maintenance operations. Several studies have demonstrated the benefits of using XR for assembly, training, and maintenance tasks. However, they have all been described as specific use cases or devices. Before XR becomes widely used, the industry must overcome two-dimensional and three-dimensional data standardization challenges, authoring tools, new interfaces, a semantic understanding of real-world objects, tasks to perform, hardware solutions, user acceptance, and performance analysis.

Keywords: Smart glasses, XR, maintenance, training, Industry 4.0, user acceptance

13.1 Introduction

Industrial training has always played a key role in ensuring the efficiency of industrial activities such as assembly and maintenance.

Training is the process of learning the necessary skills, abilities, and knowledge for a specific job or activity [1]. Employees' abilities can be

Email: Luca.Greci@stiima.cnr.it

Mariano Alcañiz, Marco Sacco and Jolanda G. Tromp (eds.) Roadmapping Extended Reality: Fundamentals and Applications, (309–320) © 2022 Scrivener Publishing LLC

shaped, and their performance can be improved through training [2]. Employees can acquire confidence in their capabilities and increase their performances due to the training, thus reducing absenteeism and turnover. Employees could learn how to use corporate goods in a suitable, safe, and cost-effective manner through training, reducing accidents and equipment damage, and trial-and-error learning. Employees also require less supervision and have higher competence, efficiency, and production, which results in less time, money, and resources spent.

Traditional manufacturing and industrial procedures are turning into "digital practices" [3] due to the Industry 4.0 paradigm. Through the internet, every object, machine, assembly line, and entire factory are "smart" and unified into a network, allowing interaction with other devices and humans. The network enables the "smart objects" (SOs) to generate and share information. The more data the SOs collect, the smarter they become; in turn, this leads to more efficient and productive factories, where less is wasted.

Industry 4.0 encompasses the entire product life cycle, including design, assembly, use, and maintenance. Industry 4.0 also requires a cultural shift in handling and interpreting the large volumes of data generated by SOs to achieve operational excellence through better decision-making and how to use technology to accelerate growth [4, 5]. The Fourth Industrial Revolution has begun [6], and factories and processes will be automated soon, with machines equipped with self-monitoring capabilities [7]. Via technologies such as big data, industrial internet of things (IIoT), artificial intelligence (AI), augmented reality (AR), and virtual reality (VR), SOs will be context-aware and communicate between themselves and humans co-workers. As a result, processes are smoother and free up workers for other activities [8]. The way workers operate will be drastically changed as a result of this revolution. Different skills will be required with the next generation of workers: jobs that require hard skills will be replaced by others requiring soft skills, such as leadership, adaptability, cognitive abilities, and problem-solving skills. A novel training strategy that can proactively expand the knowledge base of resources [2] is critical to develop these skills. Training programs must be scalable, tailored, and flexible in educating workers with Industry 4.0-compliant soft and hard skills.

Extended reality (XR) technologies, such as VR, AR, and mixed reality (MR), have emerged as promising solutions for developing such novel training programs. Through XR, it is possible to design location-aware applications to interact with SOs and processes via cloud computing strategies enabled by AI and the internet of things (IoT) [9]. Indeed, XR has the advantage of supporting workers in learning how to operate on a new machine or task and assisting technicians in performing complicated maintenance tasks. XR training guides workers step by step through a task by displaying spatially positioned virtual cues superimposed over physical machinery (AR/ MR) or three-dimensional (3D) models of machinery (VR). The hints are usually displayed in infographics, texts, or videos and are provided in real-time retrieving information from the SO network or the cloud [10].

Furthermore, AR and MR during the current pandemic situation have demonstrated the value of XR technologies to provide remote support and assistance.

13.2   XR and Industrial Training and Maintenance

The introduction of the Industry 4.0 paradigm is causing a total transformation in the industrial ecosystem, demanding the recruitment of a new generation of workers with capabilities other than those necessary on a traditional shop floor.

Traditional training is expensive due to the cost of training materials and employees and the usage of machinery and equipment, and it frequently causes a production halt.

Furthermore, it focuses on memorizing steps appropriate for physically demanding or routine tasks, rather than preparing people for new roles and responsibilities and helping them manage the changes in work patterns and procedures, as required by Industry 4.0.

Instead, thanks to the use of XR technologies, big data, IIoT, and artificial intelligence (AI) in the "smart factory," employees will have access to the most up-to-date and correct information in context, when and where they need it most.

Indeed, by using XR-based training and maintenance applications, workers will be able to: view and interpret data coming from the "smart factory," collaborate remotely with a senior technician to solve an unknown problem, and finally test knowledge and skills in performing assembly and maintenance activities, including machines that are not physically available.

In the following sections, the state of the art of XR technologies in industrial training and maintenance is presented and discussed.

13.2.1   XR and Training

The exponential growth of IIoT technologies to improve and support processes and control systems requires a new generation of workers with digital and soft skills who can handle the errors that machines are incapable of managing. Several studies have been carried out to determine the advantages of adopting XR technologies in manufacturing training. Compared to traditional training methods (text based, videos, face to face), virtual training emerges as the most effective technique in the majority of the cases.

For product development [11], learning, training [2], ergonomics [12], and layout planning, VR has proven to be a safe and cost-effective tool. Furthermore, it enables personnel to be trained in extremely hazardous locations or in situations that are impossible to replicate in the real world.

V-learning (VL) allows users to practice whenever and wherever they want. Employees can practice as needed, work safely, and receive real-time performance feedback and ratings. VL has shown to be an excellent way to reduce training time while keeping business operations running smoothly.

Doolani *et al.* [2] found that VR-based training was preferable to traditional training techniques in terms of the user's understanding, satisfaction, the number of errors, and completion time.

VR can also aid in the acquisition of soft skills. V-learners were 275% more confident in applying the skills learned after training, 4× faster to train than in the classroom, more focused than their non-e-learning peers, and, lastly, 3.75× more emotionally linked to content than classroom learners, according to Report [13].

As for VR, several studies have been done to assess the usage of AR technology in manufacturing, assembly, and maintenance tasks. Doolani *et al.* [2] and Gavish *et al.* [14] have demonstrated that using AR minimizes the number of errors while increasing the training transfer abilities.

Unlike VR, where the user is fully immersed in a digital environment, AR allows the user to see the real world: such feature can help with training and learning in situations where real-world interactions and environmental awareness are essential, such as on the shop-floor.

In comparison to VR, AR and MR may provide workers with real-time context-awareness and a step-by-step tutorial on the shop floor without diverting their attention away from the workpiece [15]. Work instructions must evolve from simple, static documentation prepared with little-to-no concern for the user experience to adaptable workforce multipliers tailored ergonomically to improve performance independent of the user's skill level. By switching from document-based work instructions to AR, manufacturing companies will obtain faster throughput and lower rework and have fewer quality issues.

AR can also keep track of the task progress, provide feedback, give recommendations, and perform quality control. Finally, AR can be used to save relevant information provided by employees who formerly performed a specific activity, such as problems and suggestions for how to complete a task.

13.2.2   XR and Maintenance

Maintenance is one of the most common services in the industry, as it guarantees that physical assets operate correctly and continuously. Even before Industry 4.0, it was a knowledge-intensive task. Nowadays, a single asset may require dozens of maintenance procedures or entail hundreds of components and complex steps; thus, keeping track of each operation is impracticable, if not impossible. Furthermore, the equipment has longer life cycles, and the decentralization of industrial networks has resulted in the geographical distribution of equipment that needs to be maintained. Given that ensuring safety and availability at a low cost is a difficult achievement, it is evident that the maintenance industry has to face significant challenges that necessitate a new approach [16].

The application of XR technologies, such as MR and AR, for shop floor maintenance has yielded positive results in the ease of use, task efficiency, and reduced accident risk, demonstrating that this technology can improve maintenance operations [17].

The benefits of employing XR technologies for maintenance activities are evident. Workers will always have the most up-to-date information and will not have to relearn when data get old or when new equipment or products are added to a factory, saving time and enhancing productivity. Furthermore, they can have real-time context-aware information and suggestions from the expert team.

Unfortunately, all this research is focused on specific use cases and applies to a single machine or piece of equipment; thus, the resulting solution does not apply to large infrastructures with several machine subsystems and equipment to maintain.

Hardware, software (e.g., authoring tools), data collecting and management, interfaces, and semantic comprehension of the physical environment are all areas where XR technologies for shop floor maintenance need to be investigated further [16, 18].

While XR is still immature for usage on the field [19], using AR for remote maintenance has been proven feasible during the COVID-19 pandemic.

Today, commercial remote maintenance apps (e.g., TeamViewer, PTC Vuforia Chalk) are available, but these solutions are limited to a specific device or ecosystem. In any case, in 2020, AR was removed from Gartner's

Hype Cycle as it is no longer considered an emerging technology and ready to move from pilot to enterprise productivity [20].

The evolution of computer vision techniques, from tracking specific images to SLAM (simultaneous localization and mapping), has allowed AR applications to run on devices like PCs and smartphones and bringing head-mounted AR platforms on the market, such as Microsoft's HoloLens and Magic Leap's display [18].

Remote maintenance uses XR technologies to share and record the real-world environment and augment it with expert knowledge. Specialists share their knowledge, videos, and technical data with maintainers via digital annotations, guiding them through the procedures step by step.

AR maintenance applications can record expert users doing operations, which technicians using AR can access and use on-site. Creating step-by-step instruction libraries allows companies to retain knowledge and improve the skills of new employees after older staff leave, increasing productivity and safety while lowering equipment downtime and improving first-time fix rates.

13.2.3   XR Issues

XR technologies seem effective in addressing the new challenges of Industry 4.0: training new workers skills and helping employees cope with the increasing complexity of products and processes [21, 22].

However, the promising results of XR are always referred to as specific use cases or devices. At the same time, "smart factories" require an XR industrial training and maintenance system that is scalable, customizable, flexible, and standardizable.

The added value of XR training has been demonstrated in situations where hazards or costs make traditional training infeasible. The better performance results after XR training compared to conventional training are still under investigation due to the lack of long-term studies, the heterogeneity of the training tasks, and the variability of the populations studied, as reported in Doolani *et al.*, Kaplan *et al.*, and Aromaa *et al.*

The acceptance and effectiveness of XR technologies depend on three main factors: individual differences, task designation, and technologies [23].

The use of XR training systems has higher performance for untrained workers than for experts [25]. For an experienced worker, the time to complete the task is longer with digital information than without. They reported that they are distracted by the XR instructions because they already know how to perform the job [26]. Using XR is thus advantageous for inexperienced workers until they know how to perform the activity; after that, XR can slow down the time it takes to accomplish the task, just as it does for specialists.

Fast-Berglund *et al.* [27] claim that utilizing remote instruction XR to complete an assembly work takes longer than using face-to-face instructions, especially for the first assembly.

Moreover, the transition from XR to reality was not smooth as the completion time increased. On the other hand, the assembly quality was better with XR (100%) than with face-to-face instructions (89%). Most participants, regardless of age, were delighted with the technology and found it easy to use. Therefore, XR seems to be more suitable for specialized and time-consuming tasks, such as complex assembly, operations with many tasks/long cycle time, and advanced maintenance [27].

Another aspect to consider is what happens when users become dependent on XR features and become unavailable or when the technology fails [15].

In Wolfartsberger *et al.*, Funk *et al.*, and Siltanen and Heinonen, some issues (comfort, field of view, registration) related to the use of smart glasses when performing training or maintenance activities are reported.

Smart glasses, even those with an explicit industrial focus, are not suitable for outdoor use in harsh weather conditions. In addition, the protective equipment worn by workers (e.g., gloves) makes interaction with touch screen-based devices and gesture recognition difficult. Finally, the use of voice commands is problematic due to background noise or language barriers.

To use smart glasses, users need to spend time learning how to interact with them. Small monocular displays are unsuitable for reading large amounts of data and require changing focus from the work area to the display to see the information. Large devices are not suitable for use in the field due to weight and dimensions that limit the user's field of view.

Headaches, problems focusing on instructions, visual fatigue, and concentration performance have been reported after prolonged use of such devices.

Overcoming challenges in data (preparation, formats, visualization), the authoring tool, innovative interfaces, a semantic understanding of real-world objects [18], tasks to be performed, hardware solutions, user acceptance, and performance analysis will allow releasing an XR industrial training and maintenance system scalable, adaptable, flexible, and standardizable.

13.3   Future Research Agenda and Roadmap

This chapter presents the current state of the art on the use of XR technologies in industrial training and maintenance. This investigation reveals that XR is a viable tool for dealing with the issues presented by Industry 4.0, both in terms of training and maintenance. Still, several issues must be addressed before the manufacturing industry adopts XR applications. There is an open field for research about devices, XR applications, interfaces, user acceptance, and data standardization (Table 13.1).

Defining a standard exchange format for two-dimensional and 3D data can expand the applicability of the XR system. Data standardization will allow devices to receive instructions on performing a task and reporting

Table 13.1 Outlook for future developments of the topic and applications.

Research topics and applications	Years to mainstream adoption			
	Less than 2 years	2 to 5 years	5 to 10 years	More than 10 years
Data standardization	x			
User interface		x		
User interaction			x	
User acceptance		x		
Authoring tool		x		
Task designation	x			
Smart glasses			x	
Artificial intelligence			x	
Semantic understanding of real world				x
Performance analysis	x			

task completion or errors to the computerized maintenance management system, improving maintenance planning, organization, and management. Furthermore, it avoids wasted time and errors in translating data between different tools and devices, making it easier to compare data from different sources.

In addition, the lack of an industry standard for user interface design and user interaction for XR devices makes content creation complex and non-intuitive, only for IT experts. The development of user interface design guidelines and usability criteria for XR context [25] and authoring tools for non-technical designers and end-users will assist the enterprise in adopting XR.

Extending the field of view, making the glass wearable, and improving voice-based interaction in loud situations are all topics that need to be investigated further for mass adoption of smart glasses in the industrial business, according to Siltanen and Heinonen [28].

In addition to the technological issues, user acceptance, organizational structure, and employee training are also relevant [29]. User involvement before and during the implementation phase of the XR system can increase the acceptance of the new workday and improve the system's efficacy.

In skilled workers, using XR was found to experience a slowdown in task completion time and an increase in perceived cognitive load because the information provided was appropriate to the context but not to the user's expertise.

Presenting information matched to the user's abilities prevents the system from pacing the task, lengthening the completion time, or providing unnecessary and distracting information. It allows increasing motivation in tedious activities [30].

Similarly, task definition (physical or cognitive) may influence the benefit from XR training, but it is not yet clear how, and thus further research should be conducted [23].

Finally, transferring the use of XR from specific use cases to generic situations is essential to develop strategies that allow XR to understand the real world by becoming user aware and context aware. Artificial intelligence (AI) such as deep learning, ontology, and expert systems to adapt to broader scene variations, and user preferences can enhance XR methods. AI can change XR applications from controlled objects and environments to generic objects and unconstrained working environments [31], allowing XR applications to be used extensively in the whole manufacturing industry.

References

1. Falola, H.O., Osibanjo, A.O., Ojo, S., II, Effectiveness of training and development on employees' performance and organisation competitiveness in the Nigerian banking industry. *Bull. Transilv.*, 7, 1, 161–170, 2014. [Online]. Available: http://www.palgrave-journals.com/doifinder/10.1057/palgrave/ejis/3000424.

2. Doolani, S. *et al.*, "A Review of Extended Reality (XR) Technologies for Manufacturing Training," *Technologies*, 8, 4, 77, 2020. doi: 10.3390/technologies8040077.

3. Sony, M. and Naik, S., Key ingredients for evaluating Industry 4.0 readiness for organizations: a literature review. *BIJ*, 27, 7, 2213–2232, 2019. doi: 10.1108/BIJ-09-2018-0284.

4. Rajnai, Z. and Kocsis, I., Assessing industry 4.0 readiness of enterprises. *SAMI 2018 - IEEE 16th World Symp. Appl. Mach. Intell. Informatics Dedic. to Mem. Pioneer Robot. Antal K. Bejczy, Proc*, vol. 2018-February, pp. 225–230, 2018, doi: 10.1109/SAMI.2018.8324844.

5. Kaur, M.J., Mishra, V.P., Maheshwari, P., The Convergence of Digital Twin, IoT, and Machine Learning: Transforming Data into Action, Springer International Publishing, Cham, 2020.

6. PWC, Industry 4.0: Building the digital enterprise, 2016. [Online]. Available: https://www.pwc.com/gx/en/industries/industry-4-0.html.

7. Erol, S., Jäger, A., Hold, P., Ott, K., Sihn, W., Tangible Industry 4.0: A Scenario-Based Approach to Learning for the Future of Production. *Proc. CIRP*, 54, 13–18, 2016. doi: 10.1016/j.procir.2016.03.162.

8. Jemai, A., Sadek, F., Salim, M., Talbi, M., *A lightweight Encryption Algorithm applied to a quantized speech image for Secure IoT*, pp. 1–6, 2017, doi: 10.15224/978-1-63248-138-2-01.

9. Minchev, Z., *Extended Reality Training Analytical Transcends In Future Digital Society*, pp. 151–164, 2019.

10. Wilke, W., Augmented reality projects in the Automotive and Aerospace industries. *Comput. Graph. Appl.*, 25, 6, 48–56, December 2005.

11. Ottosson, S., Virtual reality in the product development process. *J. Eng. Des.*, 13, 2, 159–172, 2002. doi: 10.1080/09544820210129823.

12. Grajewski, D., Górski, F., Zawadzki, P., Hamrol, A., Application of virtual reality techniques in design of ergonomic manufacturing workplaces. *Proc. Comput. Sci.*, 25, 289–301, 2013. doi: 10.1016/j.procs.2013.11.035.

13. PWC, New PWC Report: The Effectiveness of Virtual Reality Soft Skills Training in the Enterprise. 1–74, 2020. https://www.pwc.com/us/en/services/consulting/technology/emerging-technology/assets/pwc-understanding-the-effectiveness-of-soft-skills-training-in-the-enterprise-a-study.pdf.

14. Gavish, N. *et al.*, Evaluating virtual reality and augmented reality training for industrial maintenance and assembly tasks. *Interact. Learn. Environ.*, 23, 6, 778–798, 2015. doi: 10.1080/10494820.2013.815221.

15. Webel, S., Bockholt, U., Engelke, T., Gavish, N., Olbrich, M., Preusche, C., An augmented reality training platform for assembly and maintenance skills. *Rob. Auton. Syst.*, 61, 4, 398–403, 2013. doi: 10.1016/j.robot.2012.09.013.

16. Fernández Del Amo, I., Erkoyuncu, J.A., Roy, R., Wilding, S., Augmented Reality in Maintenance: An information-centred design framework. *Proc. Manuf.*, 19, 148–155, 2018. doi: 10.1016/j.promfg.2018.01.021.

17. Martínez, H., Laukkanen, S., Mattila, J., A new hybrid approach for augmented reality maintenance in scientific facilities. *Int. J. Adv. Robot. Syst.*, 10, 1–10, 2013. doi: 10.5772/56845.

18. Azuma, R.T., The Most Important Challenge Facing Augmented Reality. *Presence Teleop. Virt.*, 25, 2, 234–238, 2016. doi: 10.1162/PRES.

19. Masoni, R. *et al.*, Supporting Remote Maintenance in Industry 4.0 through Augmented Reality. *Proc. Manuf.*, 11, 1296–1302, June 2017. doi: 10.1016/j. promfg.2017.07.257.

20. Wolfartsberger, J., Zenisek, J., Wild, N., Data-driven maintenance: Combining predictive maintenance and mixed reality-supported remote assistance. *Proc. Manuf.*, 45, 307–312, 2020. doi: 10.1016/j.promfg.2020.04.022.

21. Henderson, S.J. and Feiner, S., Evaluating the benefits of augmented reality for task localization in maintenance of an armored personnel carrier turret. *Sci. Technol. Proc. - IEEE 2009 Int. Symp. Mix. Augment. Reality, ISMAR 2009*, pp. 135–144, 2009, doi: 10.1109/ISMAR.2009.5336486.

22. Farinha, J.T. and Galar, D., Augmented Reality and the Future of Maintenance. *Proc. Maint. Perform. Meas. Manag. Conf. 2014*, September, 2014, doi: 10.14195/978-972-8954-42-0.

23. Kaplan, A.D., Cruit, J., Endsley, M., Beers, S.M., Sawyer, B.D., Hancock, P.A., The Effects of Virtual Reality, Augmented Reality, and Mixed Reality as Training Enhancement Methods: A Meta-Analysis. *Hum. Factors*, 63, 4, 706–726, 2021. doi: 10.1177/0018720820904229.

24. Aromaa, S., Väätänen, A., Kaasinen, E., Uimonen, M., Siltanen, S., Human factors and ergonomics evaluation of a tablet based augmented reality system in maintenance work. *ACM Int. Conf. Proceeding Ser*, pp. 118–125, 2018, doi: 10.1145/3275116.3275125.

25. Masood, T. and Egger, J., Augmented reality in support of Industry 4.0—Implementation challenges and success factors. *Robot. Comput. Integr. Manuf.*, 58, 181–195, March 2019. doi: 10.1016/j.rcim.2019.02.003.

26. Funk, M., Bächler, A., Bächler, L., Kosch, T., Heidenreich, T., Schmidt, A., *Working with Augmented Reality?*, pp. 222–229, 2017, doi: 10.1145/3056540.3056548.

27. Fast-Berglund, Å., Gong, L., Li, D., Testing and validating Extended Reality (xR) technologies in manufacturing. *Proc. Manuf.*, 25, 31–38, 2018. doi: 10.1016/j.promfg.2018.06.054.

28. Siltanen, S. and Heinonen, H., Scalable and responsive information for industrial maintenance work: Developing XR support on smart glasses for

maintenance technicians. *ACM Int. Conf. Proceeding Ser.*, pp. 100–109, 2020, doi: 10.1145/3377290.3377296.

29. Masood, T. and Egger, J., Adopting augmented reality in the age of industrial digitalization. *Comput. Ind.*, 115, 103112, 2020. doi: 10.1016/j.compind.2019.07.002.

30. Funk, M., Kosch, T., Kettner, R., Korn, O., Schmidt, A., MotionEAP: An Overview of 4 Years of Combining Industrial Assembly with Augmented Reality for Industry 4.0. *Proc. 16th Int. Conf. Knowl. Technol. Data-driven Bus*, pp. 2–5, 2016.

31. Sahu, C.K., Young, C., Rai, R., Artificial intelligence (AI) in augmented reality (AR)-assisted manufacturing applications: a review. *Int. J. Prod. Res.*, 59, 4903, 1–57, 2021. doi: 10.1080/00207543.2020.1859636.

14

Use of XR Technologies for the Assessment and Training of Leadership Skills

Elena Parra*, Mariano Alcañiz, Cristina Giglio
and Irene Alice Chicchi Giglioli

*Instituto de Investigación e Innovación en Bioingeniería,
Universitat Politècnica de València, Valencia, Spain*

Abstract

Currently, in the context of leadership, there is an important compromise between training activities and evaluation methods with training focused on the skills of the 21st century (such as tenacity, resilience, social empathy, and creative problem-solving) while the evaluation continues to focus on 20th-century methodologies. As regards leadership training and assessment methods, they could be optimized using methodologies and techniques from organisational neuroscience (ON), which uses implicit measures of brain activity to gain a better understanding of the disciplines of organizing behavior and human resource management. One of the challenges of the ON is how to create complex social situations in controlled laboratory conditions that produce ecological organizational behaviors. One way is to use digital learning environments to reproduce problems that can occur in performance-based assessments. Extended reality technology (XR) scenarios can offer significant assessment playgrounds, providing students with situations that require the application of various skills. XR is increasingly used to reproduce natural events and social interaction. The advantage of XR is that it offers interactive, sensory, and multimodal stimuli. In this chapter, we will examine the latest developments in XR technology and organizational sciences. In it, we emphasize that XR is a very important tool for leadership research in particular to assess and train complex skills. This can create a new conceptualization of leadership biomarkers, called extended reality-based behavioral biomarkers (XRBBs), which can be obtained for the evaluation of leadership skills using a neuroscientific organizational paradigm based on implicit brain processes measured through

Corresponding author: elparvar@i3b.upv.es

Mariano Alcañiz, Marco Sacco and Jolanda G. Tromp (eds.) Roadmapping Extended Reality: Fundamentals and Applications, (321–336) © 2022 Scrivener Publishing LLC

psychophysiological signals and the behavior of subjects exposed to complex social conditions replication using virtual reality interfaces.

Keywords: Leadership, virtual reality, VR-based behavioral biomarkers

14.1   What is Leadership?

Uniquely defining leadership is rather difficult because different and complex are the definitions that over the years have tried to describe it. Leadership has been studied and investigated for years, resulting in different theories, styles, and principles. The effectiveness of a leader depends on the style of leadership adopted in a given situation; that is, a leader will be more effective in one situation than in another according to the characteristics that he or she satisfies within the group. More specifically, if we consider the style of leadership, four main approaches defend the different visions of the concept. The first approach is the model of traits [1] that focus on aspects such as charisma, trust, or even integrity for the definition of leadership. The second approach is based on a situational or contingency model; several authors such as Boyatzis [2] or House [3] focus on leadership concepts focused on adapting to the environment, where the organization and situations underpin the leader's effectiveness. The next approach is based on the study and analysis of the relationship between a leader and a subordinate to the definition of it. Authors such as Bass [4] or Bryman [5] assert that a leader cannot be defined or evaluated if we do so outside the context of a relationship with his group. At last, there is the approach to the concept from a model of behavior, where authors such as Likert [6], Blake and Mounton [7], or Lewin [8] speak of leadership styles focused on tasks versus people, or even democratic versus autocratic. Considering all aspects to properly define the concept of leadership, it is necessary to take into account the enormous complexity of finding a unique and unifying theory.

14.2   Leadership Assessment: Explicit Methods

As regards the assessment of leadership competencies, two broad sets of procedures for collecting leadership information should be distinguished: explicit and implicit. Most of the theoretical constructs used in organizational behavior and human resources management are based on explicit measures. These explicit measures can be included in the following methodologies:

- Competence, cognition, behavioral, and personality tests: are used to evaluate personality and behavioral styles, cognitive functions, creativity, emotional intelligence, work habits, and professional procedures and/or skills.
- Structured interview: consists of a script that the interviewer (usually a superior) has based on the main points to evaluate.
- Role-playing games or focus groups: consist of putting several participants into a group to solve a problem or do a task.
- Business games: it's a management simulation in which "players," in groups or alone, operate on virtual scenarios/markets, on which they define their action plans through their own decisions.

Thus, to date, most theoretical constructs used in management and organization are based on explicit measures, such as self-report and interviews. However, recent advances in neuroscience are showing that most of the brain processes that regulate our emotions, attitudes, and behaviors are out of our consciousness. That is, they are implicit processes that no human being can verbalize in contrast to the explicit processes mentioned above. (Barsade, Ramarajan and Westen, 2009 [9]; Becker, Cropanzano and Sanfey, 2011 [10]; George, 2009 [11]).

14.3   Leadership Biomarkers: Organizational Neuroscience

14.3.1   Leadership Assessment: Implicit Methods

There are a large number of researchers in neuroscience (e.g., [9–11]) who indicate that much of the brain processing that occurs in behavior, emotions, or even attitudes in the work context is outside the consciousness and therefore are implicit processes that often the subject itself is not able to verbalize since it is not aware of it bringing greater relevance to implicit measures when it is intended to measure behaviors in complex contexts such as in the day to day of work. This does not hold that the use of implicit measures is the only valid one, but rather that human behavior in its complexity cannot be interpreted only by conscious verbalizations and interpretations of subjects. Implicit processes can be defined as brain functions that occur automatically and out of conscious control and consciousness, whereas explicit processes occur through conscious executive control [10]. It is at this point that the concept of organizational neuroscience emerges.

14.3.2 Organizational Neuroscience and Neuroleadership

The term "organizational cognitive neuroscience" was first introduced to try to provide a framework for emerging studies that use neuroscientific methods to people's behavior within organizations. This interdisciplinary approach tries to identify cognitive and neurobiological mechanisms underlying complex social interactions, to make them quantifiable and apply the results directly at the workplace. Despite the many different definitions that are present in the literature, all include three common elements: (1) the level of brain analysis, (2) the level of organizational analysis, and (3) the interactions between the brain and an organization. It is the study and analysis of human behavior from both the individual point of view (cognitive psychology) and social, as well as keeping in mind that the analysis of the responses of the brain areas can bring us great knowledge of the implicit processes that are taken when talking about behaviors and organizational processes.

14.3.3 Organizational Neuroscience: Implicit Measures

Implicit processes can be measured by different techniques that, in some cases, will provide extra information about the real behavior of the subject. The implicit measures used to date, in organizational neuroscience, are based on brain images and physiological techniques such as functional magnetic resonance (fMRI) [12]), near-infrared spectroscopy [13], skin conductance [14, 15], electroencephalography [16, 17], eye movements or eye tracking (ET) [18], and cardiac variability [19] among others. One of the most well-known and famous techniques for measuring brain activity and making inferences about human behavior is fMRI. It is a technique that allows the direct observation of specific regions of the brain that are activated during tasks, making the spatial and anatomical resolution converge precisely [20]; by measuring small changes in blood flow that occur in brain activity, this system can study which specific areas are activated at certain times. The main limitation of fMRI is that it is a very non-ecological technique and doesn't have a good temporal resolution. An example of a technique where the temporal resolution is very good is the electroencephalogram, although it is a type of brain analysis method whose spatial resolution is much lower than the previous one (fMRI). A new brain-behavior analysis technique is magnetoencephalography, which consists of a noninvasive technique that records brain functional activity, by capturing magnetic fields. Another technique is positron emission tomography. With this technique, subjects are injected with a radioactive marker that locates changes in brain activity that occur when a task becomes automatic and changes are observed throughout learning [21]. The greatest limitation of this type of technique is the short duration of the effect of the markers that disappear quickly, and therefore, the analysis is also of short duration. Finally, we find the transcranial magnetic stimulation; this type of noninvasive technique allows a specific virtual lesion [22] that allows access to the effects of this lesion in both reactions and behaviors [20].

Although measures focused on the analysis of brain activity have acquired impressive temporal and spatial resolution in recent years and have presented increasingly detailed functional maps, there are somatic peripheral electrical measures such as electromyography or ocular follow-up or autonomous measures such as pupillometry, electrodermal and cardiovascular activity, which have been used successfully as indicators of mental reactions. Techniques such as skin conductance are effective in interpreting implicit processes such as stress, emotions, and cognitive processing [14, 15]. Another relevant technique when studying emotional behaviors and their involvement in the final behavior of the subject is cognitive variability. This type of measurement has been used to measure complex phenomena such as emotional intelligence [23], stress [24], and cognitive load [25]. Finally, about the importance of non-invasive and very realistic measurements, we find measures such as ET. This technique allows us to measure and analyze the visual behavior of the subject in a completely natural way; current devices facilitate the collection of the signal in real environments and therefore provide us with direct information from the user.

14.3.4   Organizational Neuroscience: Experimental Methodologies

In organizational neuroscience, there are a wide variety of methodologies. Currently, there are mainly two classes of methods usually used, those based on empirical data taken from a real context and those that aim to establish causality within a controlled laboratory. The first of these is the study of the behaviors of users in real environments, where not only behaviors or specific cognitive processes linked to leadership and organizations will be presented but also the naturalness of these in a real environment. On the other side, there are the experimental laboratory studies; in this case, the collection of information is quantifiable and accurate but the contextual problem is real also, that is, we are studying very detailed processes that we do not know if they are directly influencing the style of leadership or even if they are valid in the sense of influencing decision-making or critical situations.

14.3.5   Limitations

Organizational neuroscience shows some difficulties or methodological limitations. Even though implicit techniques and studies confirm the relationship between brain behaviors and certain behaviors or organizational behaviors, we see that how these measures are taken in many cases differs from completing a global experience and that this greatly impedes how behaviors or behaviors in organizations are studied and understood. The fact that a precise behavior or reaction is possible to convert it and take it to the field of neuroscience and this, in turn, links it with general concepts such as leadership styles have huge limitations in interpreting naturalness on the one hand and the other hand, the incapacity to make these metrics ecological. If we evaluate the ability to collect valid implicit information for the in-depth study of the individual's natural behaviors, we face potential experimental complications that we must overcome if we are to locate these implicit processes linked to overall leadership capacity. These behaviors that give rise to the complete understanding of the individual and his/her abilities are analyzed from two perspectives. The first of these is observation and analysis in the real world. This first methodological prospect is rich in knowledge, extracting very valuable information in a natural context but where the researcher must control many strange variables that can and directly affect the user's behavior and therefore offering a biased view and a measurement of implicit processes that are a little exhaustive but very ecological.

On the other hand, the creation of fully controlled laboratory environments where the user must carry out a series of totally guided and unnatural behaviors, which results in very limited behavior and bias by unnatural elements of the context. It is at this point that we need to seek a solution to these limitations, both context and use of quantitative metrics that give us an overview of human behavior linked to an organizational context and at the same time provide new knowledge about how within a controlled environment the subject responds to certain premises evident within work and relational environment. It is between these perspectives, an absolute control of the environment to eliminate biases in measures, and the need to have a context as real as possible so that the behaviors of the participants are as accurate as possible, where we find the possible solution of the use of virtual environments since these allow to present very realistic environments, but controlled and with the ability to collect the information in a very reliable way.

14.4   Extended Reality Technologies and Leadership Assessment

14.4.1   Extended Realities and Human Behavior

Social neuroscientists are adding social interaction variables to the development of interactive virtual environments. These are focusing their neuroimaging and psychophysiological studies during virtual social experiences to examine brain activation during the interpretation of other faces and studying users' eye movements [26–29].

In contemporary studies, XR has demonstrated its ability to regulate different human cognitive processes, with none of them analyzing in depth the individual variables of influence. One of the applications of interest for affective neuroscience is the use of virtual environments for fear conditioning studies [30, 31]. The use of virtual environments has also been used to provoke affective responses in everyday contexts [32], to the evaluation of both "cold" and "hot" processes in combat-related scenarios [33, 34], to the affective neuroscience of moral decision-making. In recent years, there has been a growing interest in the application of neuropsychological and neuroscientific methodologies to research in social psychology [35–37]. Recently, numerous studies have emerged that use VR, psychophysiology, and neuroimaging analysis of brain activity in face-to-face natural social interactions. These studies have helped to identify the brain regions implicated in the interpretation of the eye and facial movements of others. When participants were interacted by a virtual human exhibiting an expression of anger, the researchers found an activation of the upper temporal groove, the lateral fusiform gyrus, and a region of the mean temporal gyrus [27]. XR also enables the study of the embodiment of social cognition that highlights the bodily representations of the "self" and others. Since immersive virtual environments involve flexible platforms, the shape, size, or type of a virtual human body can be manipulated to represent divergent bodies of the participant's real body. This flexibility of the virtual environment and virtual human bodies can influence participants' perceptions, attitudes, and behaviors [38]; gamification; and evidence-centered design.

14.4.2   Using Serious Games for Assessment

Serious games refer to the use of game approaches and technologies to achieve training or assessment objectives that have nothing to do with the initial objectives of games (entertainment) [39]. We talk about the approach to the game about the use of strategies such as rewards or challenges. In specific cases, it is also linked to the use of technologies, namely, presenting content and the use of such strategies in immersive 3D environments, virtual reality, or even collaborative online platforms. The use of this type of methodology for evaluation has increased in different fields such as industry [30], education [40], or military [41]. This methodology can promote user participation in ratings through role-playing games, interactivity, and the realism of narratives in multisensory environments. This creates a more realistic experience and provides greater ecological value [42]. Thanks to the more interactive and fun character, users in this type of context feel more involved, and this increases the validity of ratings [43]. One more factor to take into account is the decrease in anxiety that, in many cases, more traditional techniques bring to the user. This reduction in anxiety to be evaluated is exemplified by stealthy evaluation techniques [40], or what is the same, by analyzing the behavior of the user in the serious game is evaluated so that the individual is not aware of this measurement. Anxiety is a factor that directly influences the assessment of certain competencies [44–46], does not make a real evaluation of the user in his day to day, and therefore presents certain biases that the stealthy approach decreases [37, 47]. The use of games or gamification has been used in particular in the field of management, depending on their training ability [48–52], but its use in assessing the differentiation between leadership styles is limited. In addition, the playful techniques that have been used in this regard have some limitations such as the number of studies that rely on technological resources to develop leadership is still insignificant, the lack of relationship between theoretical approaches to leadership and business games. Another major limitation is the limited evidence that game participants change their behaviors or skills. This means investing in consistent methods of evaluation and feedback because business play should not be an end in itself, but should be used as a tool. The possibility that serious games can evaluate this type of competition is the fact that they are designed based on the real world but, at the same time, take advantage of fictional contexts that cause situations that give rise to behaviors of creativity, decision-making, leadership, or teamwork at the same time that they are fully evaluable by objective measurement of the subject's conduct and performance. Another advantage of using this methodology is the ability to exploit current technologies as they are computer games that can be acquired and thus can be stored and analyzed a large amount of data to determine models of competence-related behavior [53]. Based on their technological capabilities to capture behaviors (both execution and psychophysiological) of users, serious games can be further programmed using artificial intelligence approaches to act as virtual expert evaluators of user behaviors, skills, and competencies. In this way, they can provide more impartial and precise evaluations than humans [54]. As can be seen in the literature, serious games are potentially providing more behavioral evaluations than traditional assessment approaches in psychological and implicit states [40]. OS can provide more objective and realistic contexts for evaluation using interactive immersive environments [42].

14.4.3   Evidence-Centered Design

The progress in organizational behavior research needs a more profound understanding of how leaders respond to work challenges. Developments in technology are making it possible to capture more complex performances in evaluation environments by including, for example, simulation and interactivity without asking leaders to self-report aspects related to their abilities. To develop this type of stealth assessment (stealth assessment) method, they use evidence-centered design (DEC)-based technologies as a valid and reliable reference framework for test design. This type of design considers evaluations as an evidence-based argument, that is, it is an argument from which we observe that students say or do at a particular time, making inferences about what they know, can do, or have achieved [55]. DEC is a family of practices that help test developers to clarify the inferences that they have based on their scores on those tested, thus determine how best to provide evidence to support such inferences within the limitations of the program. Thus, through DEC, an evaluation allows constructing an argument that makes it possible to defend a set of statements (about an individual's ability or trait) from specific data; that is, the tasks and behaviors of a user are observed during the execution of diverse and daily tasks. In this way and if the task design corresponds to DEC, it is guaranteed that these responses to these tasks depend directly on the subject's ability and therefore corresponds to what you want to measure. The DEC was born mainly in the educational field to improve the validity and reliability of test measures for students. The DEC framework defines three interconnected models, three of which form the core of the framework and are relevant to our discussion: the competency model, the structure model, and the task model that we will explain below.

- Competency model: This model includes the abilities, or skills that you want to measure in the exam.
- Evidence model: In this model, the objective is to find out which observations are the best by providing evidence of what you want to measure.
- Task model: The last phase of the DEC process is the task model, which is responsible for defining the characteristics of specific evaluation activities or tasks.

14.4.4   Stealth Assessment Approach

In recent times, different ways have been studied to integrate valid evaluations directly into games with a technology known as stealth evaluation [40, 56, 57]. This technology is based on the evidence-centered design framework. Each evaluation focuses on the availability of sufficient information to allow the evaluator to know what people know, can do, or to what extent they can do, known as skills. The stealthy evaluation model complements the DEC by determining game behavior that can act as evidence of this statement, that is, it provides indicators of competencies based on game execution [58]. The stealth evaluation game (SA) design approach aims to implicitly measure user performance during play. It has been shown that the SA, in comparison with traditional approaches, has greater predictive validity and reduces bias [40, 47]. SA permits creating different conditions in which participants perform a series of actions, which reduces the anxiety and bias of the test concerning the traditional evaluation and provides invisible data on various attributes and individual skills [40, 47]. These attributes and skills include constructs that have been identified as relevant in real daily life.

14.5   Future Research Agenda and Roadmap

XR makes it possible to examine brain activity during dynamic, complex, and realistic situations. Thus, XR constitutes a crucial experimental tool for the emerging field of ON that can be used to investigate new, objective, neuroscience-based methods for leadership assessment and training. VX-based assessment tools can immerse users in a virtual environment that recreates situations with key elements analogous to those of a similar situation in the real world, but the presentation of the stimuli and the measures can be synchronized in a very precise way. When the user is conveniently immersed in the virtual environment, both the adequate combination of technologies used to artificially stimulate the user's senses and the contents of the virtual environment can create a sense of presence in the user. This sense of presence creates a psychological state wherein the user has the illusion of non-mediation and hence shows brain activity very similar to what would occur in a real situation. When direct or indirect measures of brain activity are taken while the user is immersed in the virtual environment, the obtained data are the same as if they were measured in a real situation. However, the analysis of human responses in real situations is complicated because the stimuli that intervene in the experience cannot be controlled. Apart from leadership assessment methods, XR can also be used to create virtual versions of classical assessment tests. Virtual versions of such tests can be far richer in terms of stimuli, thus creating much more ecological validity than classical tests. The future of XR in leadership assessment is strongly related to technologies that increase the sense of presence, with the immersive capabilities of the hardware an important factor. The adoption of XR is likely to involve smaller, less expensive, and more portable solutions. This constitutes a very valuable condition; it enables assessment of leadership capabilities anytime and anywhere, and it advances the development of tools that allow neural activity to be understood "in the wild" and that can automatically map human responses with leadership capabilities. Overall, there appears to be a trend toward affordable XR and human activity measurement technologies that increasingly resemble the XR systems once found only in advanced XR laboratories. As these software and hardware components become ubiquitous, XR may come to be viewed as an ordinary technology for leadership assessment and training.

References

1. Northouse, P. G., Introduction to leadership: Concepts and practice, p. 352. SAGE Publications, Incorporated. Thousand Oaks: Sage Publications, 2014.
2. Boyatzis, R.E., Leadership development from a complexity perspective. *Consult. Psychol. J.: Pract. Res.*, 60, 298–313, 2008.
3. House, R.J., A path goal theory of leader effectiveness. *Adm. Sci. Q.*, 16, 321–338, 1971.
4. Bass, B.M., Free Press, New York, 1985.
5. Bryman, A., Stephens, M., Campo, C., The importance of context: Qualitative research and the study of leadership. *Leadersh. Q.*, 7, 353–370, 1996.
6. Likert, R., *New Patterns of Management*, McGraw-Hill, New York, 1961.
7. Blake, R.R. and Mouton, J.S., Gulf, Houston, 1964.

8. Lewin, K., The consequences of an authoritarian and democratic leadership, in: *Studies in leadership*, A.W. Gouldner (Ed.), pp. 409–17, Harper & Row, New York, 1950.

9. Sigal, G., Barsadea, R.L., Westen, D., Implicit affect in organizations. *Res. Organ. Behav.*, 29, 135–162, 20092009, doi: https://doi.org/10.1016/j. riob.2009.06.008.

10. Becker, W.J., Cropanzano, R., Sanfey, A.G., Organizational Neuroscience: Taking Organizational Theory Inside the Neural Black Box. *J. Manage.*, 37, 933–961, 2011, doi: doi.

11. George, J.M., The Illusion of Will in Organizational Behavior Research: Nonconscious Processes and Job Design. *J. Manage.*, 35, 1318–1339, 2009, doi: DOI: 10.1177/0149206309346337.

12. Boyatzis, R. E., Rochford, K., Jack, A. I., Antagonistic neural networks underlying differentiated leadership roles. *Frontiers in human neuroscience*, 8, 114, 2014.

13. Kopton, I.M. and Kenning, P., Near-infrared spectroscopy (NIRS) as a new tool for neuroeconomic research. *Front. Hum. Neurosci.*, 8, 549, 2014.

14. Nikula, R., Psychological correlates of nonspecific skin conductance responses. *Psychophysiol.*, 28, 86–90, 1991, doi: https://doi.org/10.1111/j. 1469-8986.1991.tb03392.x.

15. Sequeira, H., Hot, P., Silvert, L., Delplanque, S., Electrical autonomic correlates of emotion. *Int. J. Psychophysiol.*, 71, 50–56, 1009, doi: 10.1016/j. ijpsycho.2008.07.009.

16. Knyazev, G.G., Savostyanov, A.N., Levin, E.A., Alpha oscillations as a correlate of trait anxiety. *Int. J. Psychophysiol.*, 53, 147–160, 2004.

17. Pedemonte, M., Rodríguez-Alvez, A., Velluti, R.A., Electroencephalographic frequencies associated with heart changes in RR interval variability during paradoxical sleep. *Auton. Neurosci.*, 123, 82–86, 2005, doi: https://doi. org/10.1016/j.autneu.2005.09.002.

18. Meißner, M. and Oll, J., The promise of eye-tracking methodology in organizational research: A taxonomy, review, and future avenues. *Organ. Res. Methods*, 22, 590–617, 2019.

19. Lane, R.D., Neural substrates of implicit and explicit emotional processes: a unifying framework for psychosomatic medicine. *Psychosom. Med.*, 70, 213–230, 2008.

20. Kable, J.W., The Cognitive Neuroscience Toolkit for the Neuroeconomist: A Functional Overview. *J. Neurosci. Psychol. Econ.*, 4, 63–84, 2011, doi: https:// doi.org/10.1037/a0023555.

21. Jenkins, I.H., Brooks, D.J., Nixon, P.D., Frackowiak, R.S., Passingham, R.E., Motor sequence learning: a study with positron emission tomography. *J. Neurosci.*, 14, 3775–3790, 1994.

22. Lee, N. and Chamberlain, L., Neuroimaging and Psychophysiological Measurement in Organizational Research: An Agenda for Research in

Organizational Cognitive Neuroscience. *Ann. N. Y. Acad. Sci.*, 1118, 18–42, 2007, doi: https://doi.org/10.1196/annals.1412.003.

23. Craig, A., Tran, Y., Hermens, G., Williams, L.M., Kemp, A., Morris, C., Gordon, E., Psychological and neural correlates of emotional intelligence in a large sample of adult males and females. *Pers. Individ. Differ.*, 46, 111–115, 2009. https://doi.org/10.1016/j.paid.2008.09.011.

24. Thayer, J.F., Åhs, F., Fredrikson, M., Sollers, J.J., Wager, T.D., A meta-analysis of heart rate variability and neuroimaging studies: Implications for heart rate variability as a marker of stress and health. *Neurosci. Biobehav. Rev.*, 36, 747–756, 2012, doi: https://doi.org/10.1016/j.neubiorev.2011.11.009.

25. Durantin, G., Gagnon, J.F., Temblay, S., Dehais, F., Using near infrared spectroscopy and heart rate variability to detect mental overload. *Behav. Brain Res.*, 259, 16–23, 2014, doi: https://doi.org/10.1016/j.bbr.2013.10.042.

26. Schilbach, L., Wohlschlaeger, A.M., Kraemer, N.C., Newen, A., Shah, N.J., Fink, G.R., Vogeley, K., Being with virtual others: Neural correlates of social interaction. *Neuropsychologia*, 44, 718–730, 2006, doi: https://doi.org/10.1016/j.neuropsychologia.2005.07.017.

27. Carter, E.J. and Pelphrey, K.A., Friend or foe? Brain systems involved in the perception of dynamic signals of menacing and friendly social approaches. *Soc Neurosci.*, 3, 151–163, 2008, doi: https://doi.org/10.1080/17470910801903431.

28. Slater, M., Spanlang, B., Sanchez-Vives, M.V., Blanke, O., First Person Experience of Body Transfer in Virtual Reality. *PLoS ONE*. 5, e10564, 2010b, doi: 10.1371/journal.pone.0010564.

29. Rotge, J.Y., Lemogne, C., Hinfray, S., Huguet, P., Grynszpan, O., Tartour, E., A meta-analysis of the anterior cingulate contribution to social pain. *Soc Cogn. Affect. Neurosci.*, 10, 19–27, 2014, doi: https://doi.org/10.1093/scan/nsu110.

30. ALVAREZ, J. and Michaud, L., Serious Games–Advergaming, edugaming, training and more. IDATE Consulting and Research. Retrieved July, 2008, vol. 15, p. 2013.

31. Baas, J., van Ooijen, L., Goudriaan, A., Kenemans, J.L., Failure to condition to a cue is associated with sustained contextual fear. *Acta Psychol.*, 127, 581–592, 2008, doi: https://doi.org/10.1016/j.actpsy.2007.09.009.

32. Baños, R.M., Etchemendy, E., Castilla, D., Garcia-Palacios, A., Quero, S., Botella, C., Positive mood induction procedures for virtual environments designed for elderly people. *Interact. Comput.*, 24, 131–138, 1012, doi: https://doi.org/10.1016/j.intcom.2012.04.002.

33. Armstrong, T., Bilsky, S.A., Zhao, M., Olatunji, B.O., Dwelling on potential threat cues: An eye movement marker for combat-related PTSD. *Depression Anxiety*, 30, 497–502, 2013.

34. Parsons, T.D., McPherson, S., Interrante, V., Enhancing neurocognitive assessment using immersive virtual reality, in: *1st Workshop on Virtual and Augmented Assistive Technology (VAAT)*, Orlando, FL, IEEE, pp. 27–34, 2013.

35. Lieberman, M.D. and Eisenberger, N., II, Pains and pleasures of social life. *Science*, 323, 890–891, 2009, doi: https://doi.org/10.1126/science.1170008.

36. Adolphs, R. Cognitive neuroscience of human social behaviour. *Nature Reviews Neuroscience*, 4, 3, 165–178, 2003.

37. Adolphs, R., Conceptual challenges and directions for social neuroscience. *Neuron.*, 65, 752–767, 2010, doi: https://doi.org/10.1016/j.neuron.2010.03.006.

38. Slater, M. and Sanchez-Vives, M.V., Transcending the Self in Immersive Virtual Reality. *Computer*, 47, 24–30, 2014, doi: https://doi.org/10.1109/MC.2014.198.

39. Kato, P.M., Video games in health care: closing the gap. *Rev. Gen. Psychol.*, 14, 113–121, 2010, doi: https://doi.org/10.1037/a0019441.

40. Shute, V.J., Leighton, J.P., Jang, E.E., Chu, M.-W., Advances in the science of assessment. *Educ. Assess.*, 2, 34–59, 2016, doi: https://doi.org/10.1080/10627197.2015.1127752.

41. Pasquiere, P., Mérat, S., Malgras, B., Petit, L., A Serious Games For Massive Training In Assessment Of French Soldiers Involved In Forward Combat Casualty Care (3D-SC1): Development and Deployment. *JMIR Serious Games*, 4, e5, 2016, doi: https://doi.org/10.2196/games.5340.

42. LUMSDEN, Jim, *et al.* The effects of gamelike features and test location on cognitive test performance and participant enjoyment. *PeerJ*, vol. 4, p. e2184, 2016.

43. Shute, V.J. and Rahimi, S., Review of computer-based assessment for learning in elementary and secondary education, in: *Journal of Computer Assisted Learning*, United Kingdom, vol. 33, pp. 1–9, Wiley Online Library, 2017, doi: https://doi.org/10.1111/jcal.12172.

44. Cassady, J.C., The impact of cognitive test anxiety on text comprehension and recall in the absence of external evaluative pressure. *Appl. Cogn. Psychol.*, 18, 3, 311–325, 2004, doi: https://doi.org/10.1002/acp.968.

45. Egloff, B. and Schmukle, S.C., Predictive validity of an Implicit Association Test for assessing anxiety. *J. Pers. Soc Psychol.*, 83, 6, 1441-55, 2002. 20021441.

46. Horwitz, E.K., Preliminary evidence for the reliability and validity of a foreign language anxiety scale. *JSTOR*, 20, 559–562, 1986, doi: https://doi.org/10.2307/3586302.

47. Shute, V.J., Ventura, M., Bauer, M., II, Zapata-Rivera, D., Melding the power of serious games and embedded assessment to monitor and foster learning: Flow and grow, in: *Serious games: Mechanisms and effects*, U. Ritterfeld, M. Cody, P. Vorderer (Eds.), pp. 295–321, Taylor and Francis, Mahwah, NJ: Routledge, 2009.

48. Conger, J.A., *Learning to lead*, Jossey-Bass, San-Francisco, 1992.

49. Jones, P.J. and Oswick, C., Inputs and outcomes of outdoor management development: Of design, dogma and dissonance. *Br. J. Manage.*, 18, 327–341, 2007, doi: https://doi.org/10.1111/j.1467-8551.2006.00515.x.

50. Petriglieri, G. and Wood, J.D., Learning for leadership: The "engineering" and "clinical" approaches, in: *Mastering executive education: How to combine content with context and emotion*, P. Strebel and T. Keys (Eds.), pp. 140 –154, Financial Times-Prentice Hall, London, 2005.

51. Mainemelis, C. and Ronson, S., Ideas are born in fields of play: Towards a theory of play and creativity in organi? zational settings. *Res. Organ. Behav.*, 27, 81–131, 2006.

52. Rafaeli, S. and Heroti, T., Games are a serious business, T. Heroti (Ed.), 14. in: *Management leading the way*, The Marker, 2010, 14 October.

53. De Klerk, S., Veldkamp, B.P., Eggen, T.J.H.M., Psychometric analysis of the performance data of simulation-based assessment: A systematic review and a Bayesian network example. *Comput. Educ.*, 85, 23–34, 2015.

54. Bellotti, F., Kapralos, B., Lee, K., Moreno-Ger, P., Berta, R., Assessment in and of serious games: an overview. *Adv. Human-Computer Interaction*, 201, 1, 2013, doi: https://doi.org/10.1155/2013/136864.

55. Mislevy, R., Steinberg, L., Almond, R., On the structure of educational assessments. *Measurement: Interdiscip. Res. Perspect.*, 1, 3–62, 2003.

56. Shute, V.J. and Ke, F., Games, learning, and assessment, in: *Assessment in Game-Based Learning*, pp. 43–58, 2012.

57. Shute, V.J., Stealth assessment in computer-based games to support learning, in: *Computer games and instruction*, Tobias, S. and Fletcher, J.D. (Eds.), pp. 503–524, 2011.

58. Shute, V.J. and Ventura, M., *Stealth assessment: Measuring and supporting learning in video games*, MIT Press, Cambridge, MA, 2013.

15

Surgery Applications: Expanding Surgeons' Capabilities

Jose M Sabater-Navarro[1]*, Jose M Vicente-Samper[1], Sofia Aledo[1] and Pedro L. Solarte[2]

[1]Bioengineering Institute, Miguel Hernández University of Elche, Elche, Spain
[2]University of Cauca, Popayán, Colombia

Abstract

In the field of surgery, there is a consensus that XR technologies have enormous potential to achieve the goal of enhancing the capabilities of surgeons. However, this consensus does not exist regarding the usefulness of current implementations. This is due to the fact that the peculiarities of the surgical environment, difficulty of registration between models and real organs, soft organs, over-information to the surgeon, high mental load of the surgeons, mean that the solutions must have a high degree of particularization. This chapter shows the current state of XR technologies in surgery, highlighting their strengths and weaknesses, showing examples of implementations and outlining the future work that should lead us to both overcome the current weaknesses, and the achievement of giving surgeons efficient and effective tools to their work.

Keywords: Surgery, clinical procedures, registration, navigation, visualization

15.1 Introduction

The introduction of XR in surgery has become the "El Dorado" search within the realm of surgery. There is a consensus on the definition of the potential benefits that XR can introduce in the different surgical procedures; however, the real application of this technology within the operating room (OR) is still in its infancy, and there are hardly any real examples of

---

*Corresponding author: j.sabater@umh.es

Mariano Alcañiz, Marco Sacco and Jolanda G. Tromp (eds.) Roadmapping Extended Reality: Fundamentals and Applications, (337–356) © 2022 Scrivener Publishing LLC

surgeries performed using XR technologies to support surgeons. The delicate nature of surgical operations, the wide variety of surgical procedures and different approaches, and the fact that the environment is changing as the operation progresses have meant that XR technology has not yet become popular within an operating room.

The engineer R. Taylor, referring to robotic surgery, stated that the goal of robotics in surgery is "to develop a partnership between man (the surgeon) and machine (the robotic tools) that seeks to exploit the capabilities of both to do a task better than either can do alone." This too is the goal of implementing XR technology into surgery, to develop systems that enhance the surgeon's capabilities to better perform their task. In this sense, in addition to the technologies used, the aspects discussed above on usability or ergonomics take on special importance in this area. The mental load during a surgical operation is always very high, and any additional information that is provided must be balanced in terms of the benefits it provides to the surgeon. As we will see, the visualization aspects take on special relevance, and the overlay problems with soft tissues that move and deform during the operation have not yet been resolved. The anatomical knowledge that surgeons possess endows them with a very high spatial localization capacity, which has allowed several interesting studies on ergonomics of information visualization, which generally show that the most important information (3D models, vital signs, ...) should be displayed closer to the line-of-sight and minor information can be displayed outside the line-of-sight field.

This chapter first reviews the situation of XR in the area of surgery, breaking it down according to surgical specialties and subspecialties. After this brief review, the strengths and pending weaknesses are summarized to achieve a real and effective implantation in all stages of the surgical process. Examples are shown in the neurosurgery and open abdominal surgery specialties. Finally, the last section aims to outline a roadmap to overcome the current restrictions in real clinical applications.

15.2   XR and Surgery

With the improvement of computer graphics capabilities and the appearance of new miniaturized sensors, XR technology has opened up new possibilities to develop surgical techniques in the field of surgery and medical diagnosis. However, there is a wide variability in the different surgical specialties and the casuistry is very wide. Specialties such as trauma work with bones and rigid elements, which facilitates the registration and navigation processes and has allowed a greater implementation of this technology. On the other hand, other specialties such as otorhinolaryngology (ENT—ear–nose and throat) work with soft solids, and as the operation progresses, their boundary conditions change, and they suffer deformations and position changes. This problem, now a classic in surgical navigation, is immediately reflected in the XR, where visualization problems are also added when the registration is not adequate. That is, if the real tissue has moved and we have an error in the registration, it is not acceptable to visualize an object in an incorrect position, since it would not help the mental process of the surgeon.

Some surgical specialties, such as maxillofacial surgery, already regularly present different XR-based solutions. Although it was already common to use VR and CAD techniques to plan which dental implant or which dental implantology technique is the most optimal in each case. In recent times, XR is allowing new approaches beyond implantology, such as defining planes and safety zones in implantology processes or previewing the results of regenerated bone procedures. For example in [1] a clinical case of total maxillectomy is presented, in which VR is used for surgical planning and AR-guided surgery for intraoperative surgery. Other clinical examples of the use of XR in maxillectomy and orbital reconstruction can be found on [2–5].

Other specialties like the orthopedic surgery have also benefitted from data preparation, visualization, and registration/tracking technologies due to dealing with rigid organs like bones [6]. Subspecialties like spine [7], osteotomics [8], arthroplasty [9], trauma [10], pedicle screw [11], and orthopedic oncology [12] have presented use-cases with higher accuracy in surgical execution, reduction of radiation exposure, and decreased surgery time when using XR technologies. As we will see later, the particularities of orthopedic surgery, which works with rigid bones and objects, have allowed XR technology, initially developed for rigid solids, to have an easy adaptation.

Neurosurgery has also benefited from the rigidity of the skull. Many procedures that only involve bone, such as craniotomy or maxillofacial drilling, have undergone a significant advance thanks to XR technology. The scientific literature confirms that the XR is a reliable and versatile tool when performing minimally invasive approaches in a wide range of neurosurgical diseases [13]. Current neuronavigation systems present a meaningful improvement in several pathologies, like meningioma [14], angioma [15], glioblastoma [16], aneurysm [17], or arteriovenous malformations [18]. However, despite these examples, only a few XR systems have been tested and accepted for routine use in a surgical theater. The same problem that happens in neuro-navigation is that the soft tissues change shape and position as the operation progresses. This particularity of the soft tissues makes it necessary to constantly update the registration process, in addition to a reformulation of the object to be restraightened. This is the main reason why XR technology has only been applied in the first procedures of a neurosurgical operation, and as the operation progresses, this technology is no longer used by neurosurgeons.

Regarding abdominal surgery [19], several examples can also be found at the research level, although in this case it can also be said that the developments of XR in abdominal surgery have the problem of intraoperative deformation of the organs, which is disadvantageous for the registration between organs and phantom models of a patient who is undergoing preoperative reconstruction. Another reason for this delay is the existence of established modalities such as fluorography or ultrasonography in navigation surgery. A meta-analysis of open abdominal surgery using XR can be found in the work of Fida *et al.* [20], in which it can be seen that the most used viewing option is VST (video see-through) and that there is no standard registration procedure. Of special relevance, due to its real implementation in surgical procedures, are the improvements in video imaging, such as the work with Indocyanine Green (ICG) [21] where the superposition and fusion of images allow for the visualization of hidden structures. These solutions are already part of commercial teams such as the near infra-network (NIR) team from Karl Storz GmbH.

On the other hand, XR technology has also recently appeared in minimally invasive surgery, as reflected in the meta-analysis by Hua *et al.* [22]. Minimally invasive surgery (MIS) is a procedure performed through small incisions in the body, inserting a laparoscope (a thin, tubular-shaped surgical instrument with illumination and a camera) to guide the surgery. As its name indicates, it is a surgical technique whose main objective is to reduce the damage to the tissues and organs of the patient, derived from medical procedures [23]. The laparoscopic techniques of the MIS surgery represented a drastic change in surgical approaches, and consequently a break within the surgical techniques for other surgeries. The training and learning of these techniques have been a favorable scenario for the appearance of surgical simulators, many of which have incorporated different XR technologies, such as haptic interfaces, visualization with AR, or the different graphic simulation engines. For example, in [24], Fransson *et al.* present a validation study of instrument motion metrics for laparoscopic skills assessment in virtual reality and augmented reality simulators concluding that none of the motion metrics in a virtual reality simulator showed correlation with experience, or to the basic laparoscopic skills score, but all metrics in augmented reality were significantly correlated with experience (time, instrument path, and economy of movement), except for the hand dominance metric.

Therefore, it is observed in this brief state of the art that, although there is consensus on the potential benefit of the use of XR technologies in surgery, to date, there are still problems to be solved that prevent an effective implementation of these technologies, especially inside the operating room.

In general, the drawbacks to be solved in an immediate future are related to:

- – Segmentation and model reconstruction. The potential of XR makes it possible to work with individualized objects for each patient. For this, it is important to improve the automatic segmentation algorithms and optimize the reconstruction algorithms. This will allow the personalized 3D models of the organs to be integrated into the clinical workflow.

  - o Soft tissue models. A major challenge is the definition of deformable models in each case. Current works are achieving high computational efficiency for the calculation of deformations [25, 26], but in most of these models, the automatic generation of boundary conditions is an unsolved problem.

- – Registration. The ultimate goal is to correlate the pre-operative data with real-time data. Several registration algorithms work fine with rigid point sets, but no one deals when large deformations appear. A good explanation of point set registration algorithms is found on [27].
- – Haptic. Haptic technologies allow palpation of tissues, recovering tactile sensation for surgeons. This is very important due to the different mechanical behavior of the different tissues, allowing distinguishing between healthy tissues and tumor tissues. However, there are mainly two areas where improvement of current haptic solutions is required. The first would be the field of "force sensing," since current force sensors, regardless of the technology on which they are based on, are not specifically designed for surgical environments and are either very bulky or their resolution is not sufficient for palpation tasks. Systems based on indirect

measurements such as measuring deformation with structured lights [28], optical systems [29], or miniature palpation probes [30] have been tested at the research level, but they are not integrated into commercial equipment. The second improvement comes from the field of robotics, in the form of "force-based exploration algorithms." Adaptive algorithms for palpation [31] to automate the task of tumor localization and dynamically overlay the information on top of intraoperative view of the anatomy will be needed.

– Visualization and Immersive technologies. Although video see through (VST) technologies are the most commonly used in OR, allowing the surgeon to preserve the line-of-sight, it is not clear where to locate the object or how much information is the optimal to show. It is important not to interfere with the surgeons' line-of-sight. Also, the reflections or unwanted incidence of light is not desirable, and the visualization devices should take care of this. Figure 15.1 shows an illustration in which an example of positioning the organ over the patient is observed on the left, out of the surgeon's line-of-sight, but with a gentle movement of the head, he can visualize it. This option does not require registration, and the model can be visualized at any size and any location. This could be useful to provide information to the surgeon without interfering with the operation field. To the right is an overlay in which the model is displayed on the tissue. In this case, the registration issues mentioned above take on special importance. In this scenario, the size, deformation, and location of the model should be acute enough not to

Out of line-of-sight.   Overlay.

Figure 15.1 Visualization options in surgery.

Learning	Preop stage	Intraop stage
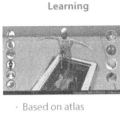		
· Based on atlas anatomy. · 3D Immersion. · Need to improve motions	· Based on preop images and reconstructions. · Automatic segmentation. · Need to improve motions (deformations)	· Automatic segmentation. · Need to improve motions (deformations) · Occlusions not solved · Registration poor, and without deformations. · Need real Intraop sensors for real navigation.

Figure 15.2 Strengths and weaknesses of XR in surgery.

distract the surgeon, and the main problem with this visualization are the occlusions.

- Tracking. Despite tracking of instruments (graspers, needle drivers) during surgery has largely evolved during last years, object tracking remains an open research problem, mainly due to motion blur, image noise, lack of image texture, and occlusion. Real-time tracking methods are time-consuming, and accuracy is diminished when high volume of information is managed.

It is true that these drawbacks do not affect all scenarios and all surgical specialties and subspecialties equally. Figure 15.2 summarizes the main achievements (in blue) and the main weaknesses (in red) that appear in the different scenarios related to surgery. In this simple scheme, it can be seen how the intraoperative scenario is the one that presents the greatest difficulty for the integration of XR technologies.

15.2.1   Education Scenario for Surgery

For decades, the apprenticeship model, in which surgical residents are extensively educated under the supervision of an experienced surgeon, was the standard. Today it has been proven that this approach is outdated due to the negative impact on the patient's comfort, such as a higher probability of complications, as well as increased operational time and cost. XR technology has the potential to increase training time to learn complicated surgical skills, such as minimally invasive surgery. Cadaveric simulators or mock-up models have played an important role in learning surgical techniques. However, it is not possible to particularize the models to study a specific clinical case, and the learning is limited to the possibilities offered by the model.

The flexibility offered by XR technologies allows the creation of a particular surgical scenario in which the pathology is shown, and the specific surgical scenario in which a certain technique is to be learned.

The level of realism achieved with Digital Anatomical Atlases is changing the way anatomy is taught. 3D immersion and the ability to navigate through the anatomy allow the student to learn using our innate sense of location. Hybrid simulators that combine Extended Reality and patient physical models such as synthetic tissue phantoms, additive manufacturing 3D printed models, which are extensively used for learning surgical techniques, deserve special attention.

However, although the level of realism is very high in these applications, the models used are always static models visualized with virtual reality (VR). Simulators that make use of augmented reality (AR) require a registration process, in which as indicated above, the case of soft tissues has not yet been resolved. An example of partial solutions to have a registry is in the use of artificial landmarks of easy identification that allow in a simple way to register the models and locate them on the user. In Figure 15.2, this case is exemplified with the image of the AR mobile apps that use the landmarks of the t-shirt to register the models.

15.2.2   Preoperative Scenario

At this point, a work carried out for navigation in a neurosurgery preoperative stage is presented. In this work, it was observed that the computational cost for the segmentation of organs and soft tissues and, in particular for the definition of neuronal tracts, is still very high, and efficient automatic segmentation algorithms are not yet available. On the other hand, although brain tissue movements were not considered in this work, the work presented in [32, 33] did show the need to improve the algorithms for calculating brain-shift deformations.

For this work, an HMD Meta II helmet from the company Metavision was used as a display; it is a device created to view augmented reality applications in real environments through its transparent screen. This device allows the user to select, grasp, and move virtual objects in 3D, in addition

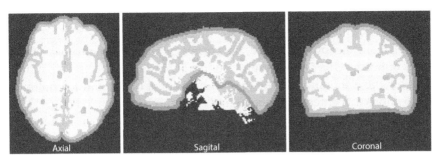

Figure 15.3 Segmentation of gray matter, white matter, and tumors.

to being able to vary their size and interact between these objects. For the implementation of this solution, the following application workflow was used: 3D Slicer, Blender, Unity3D, and Meta II SDK.

Starting from the magnetic resonance images of a certain patient, 3D models of the patient's brain were generated in 3D Slicer, an open-source software for medical imaging based on ITK and VTK, such as gray matter, white matter, and the corpus callosum represented in neurological tracts, in order to reveal these structures that are not visible to the surgeon during the development of a surgical intervention. In addition, five fake tumors were created in random areas of the brain for the development of validation tests of the system. 3D Slicer has algorithms to perform the functions mentioned previously, among which Grow Cut for the segmentation of gray and white matter, Marching Cube used for surface modeling, and UKF Tractography for the representation of matter in tracts were used. Figure 15.3 shows the segmentation for the construction of the objects.

Subsequently, the process of developing the tractography of the corpus callosum was carried out from the segmentation of this body in the same images of the previous process. Then, to show the corpus callosum in medical images, a map was created with fractional anisotropy, which is

Figure 15.4 Tractography of the corpus callosum.

the characteristic of brain tissue that depends on the integrity of the white matter fibers and the direction of its molecules of water [34]. Once said fractional anisotropy is obtained, the corpus callosum is segmented. Once this is done, the UKF Tractography module of 3D Slicer defines the parameters for the elaboration of the three-dimensional object and its multiple connections that emerge from it around the brain, as shown in Figure 15.4.

Finally, these 3D objects are imported into Unity 3D for the implementation of the environment, where the simulation parameters are defined. Figure 15.5 (left) shows the tractography and the fictitious tumors created around the brain. The colors arranged for each 3D object were defined in order to facilitate their visualization through Meta II. In Figure 15.5 (right), the finished brain is seen in pink color, and in front of it, there are three purple spheres representing the Meta II Helmet in Unity 3D. The position of the Meta II was defined so that, when initializing the augmented reality system, the brain would appear right in front of the user's eyes.

Table 15.1 shows the information on the size and relative location of the fake tumors. The objective of the experimentation was to show a new visualization in which the models of tumors and the tracts of the corpus

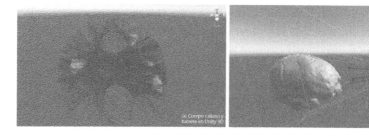

Figure 15.5 Tractography of the corpus callosum.

Table 15.1 Characteristics of tumors.

Tumor	V (mm³)	Location (X,Y,Z)
1	556	(-38.73, -6.26, 81.4)
2	500	(-5, 21.4, -35.2)
3	480	(68.2, 6.7, -12.6)
4	520	(-11.7, 29.9, -135.5)
5	540	(6.5, 0.13, -171.5)

callosum were included, in a way that helps in preoperative planning, by being able to visualize the effect on the structures of the tract that would present a given approach. Two types of tests were carried out.

In the first one, the model was static, and navigation was carried out by the user when moving in space. In this way, surgeons had a heightened sense of immersion. The procedure was as follows:

1. A timer is initialized as the user navigates within the brain to find tumor 1.
2. Once tumor 1 is found, the time used is stored.
3. The user moves to physically position himself/herself around the tumor and to define a path of access in a straight line from outside the brain, in which the least possible damage is done, compromising the least amount of neuronal tracts and white matter.
4. When the path is defined, a file of type (.jpeg) is saved with that path. In addition to that, the position and rotation values of both the brain and the Meta II are saved.
5. Tumor 1 disappears and tumor 2 appears.
6. The procedure from step 2 to step 5 is repeated for each of the five tumors.
7. When defining the access path for tumor 5, the test ends and the system returns a file (.txt) with all the data of the test development.

In Figure 15.6, you can see one of the users performing test 1 on the left and what he sees on the right. On the right of the image, you can see the tumor in green, the neuronal tracts in red, gray matter in pink, and white matter in white.

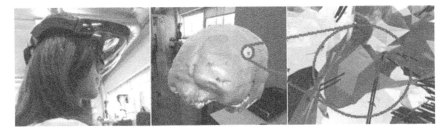

Figure 15.6 User performing test 1: Mobile user and fixed brain.

In the second of the tests, the models had the possibility of movement, and it is the user who manipulates them to place them in the position that he/she considers most suitable for the surgical approach. In Figure 15.7, a user is observed performing the second test, in which they are in a fixed position and manipulate the brain with their hands. In order to find the tumors, the user had to take the brain with their hands and visualize its interior, so that they could rotate it, move it, enlarge it, or decrease its size. At the time of the definition of the access path, the user had to move the brain away, and thus be able to capture the data of the positions and rotations from outside the brain. Once the user finds the fifth tumor and defines its respective access route, the test ends.

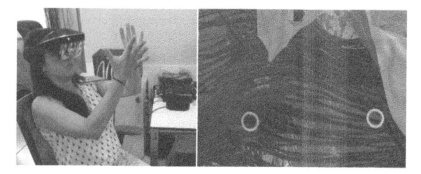

Figure 15.7 User performing test 2: Fixed user and mobile brain.

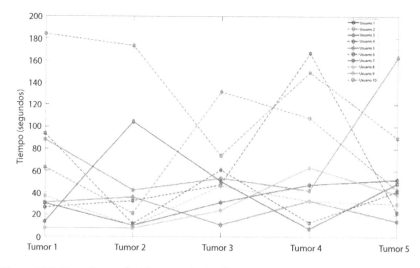

Figure 15.8 Spent time to find 5 tumors during first tests.

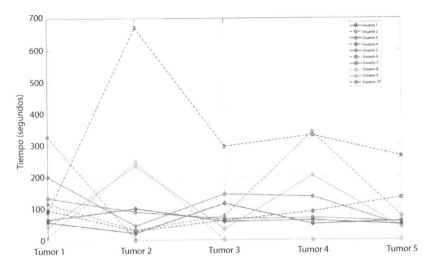

Figure 15.9 Spent time to find 5 tumors during second tests.

The graph in Figure 15.8 shows the time results in test 1 with 10 users. This graph shows a particularity in user 2, since he had the highest times to find the first tumors. This user reported feeling tired and a slight headache due to the weight of the device, generating an evident delay in time to find the first tumor (183.8 seconds) compared to the time obtained by the rest of the users, who had an average time 46 seconds. The above generated frustration in the user, making their performance in the test not the best. In addition, the user stated that wearing glasses for myopia made the development of the test cumbersome. Once 80% of the users found the first tumor, they had an easier time finding the second tumor due to a quick appropriation of the dynamics of the experiment.

The graph in Figure 15.9 shows the times in the performance of test 2. They show higher execution times, which indicates that in this type of preoperative planning, it is more efficient for the user to move and navigate through the models, rather than having to manipulate the models to locate them spatially.

15.2.3   Intraoperative Scenario

As seen previously in the review of the state of the art, there are few intraoperative scenarios in which XR technology has been used on a regular basis, beyond the numerous tests and validations carried out in surgeries, mainly maxillofacial and orthopedic. It has already been commented that the main obstacles to be solved are the registration of the models on the patient and the visualization of the models. The most widely used option is the overlay of the models on the tissue of the patient, although the problems of occlusions and partial visualization of the models have not been solved.

An experimentation carried out in our group consisted of modifying the overlay visualization by a scheme in which the surgeon's capacity for spatial orientation is exploited. Figure 15.10 (bottom) shows that the sagittal, coronal, and axial planes are presented outside the surgeon's sight-of-view. DICOM images are displayed as flat objects ("virtual screens") that can be manipulated and placed on the patient in a moment. In addition, it is possible to navigate through the different slices in each view, just like in the windows of a browser. This allows the surgeon to place the DICOM image on the patient, making a manual registration, to observe a certain detail, in addition to the image from his sight-of-view. The experimentation showed great comfort in this scheme, since the surgeons were aware

Figure 15.10 Visualization of DICOM images using AR.

at all times of the position and availability of the "virtual screens" with the preoperative images.

15.3   Future Research Agenda and Roadmap

The next steps forward are obviously related with the previously detected drawbacks: modeling of soft tissues, non-rigid registration, or improvement on overlay visualization techniques. Although many investigations using the current engineering technologies and mathematical algorithms were reported to solve the problems of organ deformation, most systems are not practical because of the complicated methods required. As illustrated in Figure 15.2, current requirements in terms of time consumption or accuracy take special importance on intraoperative scenarios. To become a routine modality, complicated preparation and time requirements should be ameliorated.

Simplicity is something that future developments should aim for. The intraoperative scenario is highly critical, and it is a requirement that the systems that will be introduced integrate perfectly with the current ones, without disturbing their current way of working and simplifying complex surgical procedures as much as possible.

The explosion of developments that are classified as artificial intelligence (AI) also presents an opportunity for working on solutions for the aforementioned drawbacks. Specifically, the automatic segmentation of organs must be approached with the application of classification algorithms that optimize the segmentation procedures, and allow this burden to be released from the current semi-automatic systems that require user intervention, for example, in the definition of the seeds. At the same time, AI techniques will make it possible to use the information from the preoperative segmentations to design new algorithms for monitoring the deformations suffered intraoperatively. This will require extensive work in deformable solid modeling. An example of this is the work of several research groups in neurosurgery in which the brain-shift phenomenon is investigated. In this type of surgery, the brain moves and deforms, changing the pre-surgical reference the surgeon had before the intervention. Among the causes of brain shift are the effect of gravity, loss of cerebrospinal fluid, location and size of the surgical objective, as a consequence of the resection practiced, and the effect of the drugs supplied, among others. A physical model of this displacement to later simulate them in any multiphysics software will help to update information to surgeons during the surgical procedure.

Therefore, it is obvious that future improvements in automatic segmentation and deformation tracking will allow an improvement in the current algorithms for surgical registration. Advances that produce simple systems to perform the surgical registration are demanded by surgeons and will allow to automate a registration process that is the main current obstacle for the entry of the XR overlay technique in surgery.

Additionally, it is undeniable that collaboration between surgeons and engineers will produce new solutions that show the potential of XR technologies in critical scenarios like surgery.

References

1. Kim, H.-J., Jo, Y.-J., Choi, J.-S., Kim, H.-J., Park, I.-S., You, J.-S., Oh, J.-S., Moon, S.-Y., Virtual Reality Simulation and Augmented Reality-Guided Surgery for Total Maxillectomy: A Case Report. *Appl. Sci.*, 10, 18, 6288, 2020. https://doi.org/10.3390/app10186288.
2. Kang, Y.-F., Liang, J., He, Z., Zhang, L., Shan, X.-F., Cai, Z.-G., Orbital floor symmetry after maxillectomy and orbital floor reconstruction with individual titanium mesh using computer-assisted navigation. *J. Plast. Reconstr. Aesthet. Surg.*, 73, 337–343, 2020.
3. Jang, W.-H., Lee, J.M., Jang, S., Kim, H.-D., Ahn, K.-M., Lee, J.-H., Mirror Image Based Three-Dimensional Virtual Surgical Planning and Three-Dimensional Printing Guide System for the Reconstruction of Wide Maxilla Defect Using the Deep Circumflex Iliac Artery Free Flap. *J. Craniofac. Surg.*, 30, 1829–1832, 2019.
4. He, Y., Zhu, H., Zhang, Z., He, J., Sader, R., Three-dimensional model simulation and reconstruction of composite total maxillectomy defects with fibula osteomyocutaneous flap flow-through from radial forearm flap. *Oral. Surg. Oral. Med. Oral. Pathol. Oral. Radiol. Endod.*, 108, e6–e12, 2009.
5. Zhang, W.-B., Mao, C., Liu, X.-J., Guo, C.-B., Yu, G.-Y., Peng, X., Outcomes of orbital floor reconstruction after extensive maxillectomy using the computer-assisted fabricated individual titanium mesh technique. *J. Oral. Maxillofac. Surg.*, 73, 2065.e1 – e15, 2015.
6. Casari, F.A., Navab, N., Hruby, L.A. *et al.*, Augmented Reality in Orthopedic Surgery Is Emerging from Proof of Concept Towards Clinical Studies: a Literature Review Explaining the Technology and Current State of the Art. *Curr. Rev. Musculoskelet. Med.*, 14, 192–203, 2021. https://doi.org/10.1007/s12178-021-09699-3.
7. Wanivenhaus, F., Neuhaus, C., Liebmann, F., Roner, S., Spirig, J.M., Farshad, M., Augmented reality-assisted rod bending in spinal surgery. *Spine J.*, 19, 10, 1687–9, 2019.

8. Kosterhon, M., Gutenberg, A., Kantelhardt, S.R., Archavlis, E., Giese, A., Navigation and image injection for control of bone removal and osteotomy planes in spine surgery. *Oper. Neurosurg.*, 13, 2, 297–304, 2017.

9. Tsukada, S., Ogawa, H., Nishino, M., Kurosaka, K., Hirasawa, N., Augmented reality-based navigation system applied to tibial bone resection in total knee arthroplasty. *J. Exp. Orthop.*, 6, 1, 44, 2019.

10. Ortega, G., Wolff, A., Baumgaertner, M., Kendoff, D., Usefulness of a head mounted monitor device for viewing intraoperative fluoroscopy during orthopaedic procedures. *Arch. Orthop. Trauma. Surg.*, 128, 10, 1123–6, 2008.

11. Elmi-Terander, A., Burström, G., Nachabé, R., Fagerlund, M., Ståhl, F., Charalampidis, A. *et al.*, Augmented reality navigation with intraoperative 3D imaging vs fluoroscopy-assisted free-hand surgery for spine fixation surgery: a matched-control study comparing accuracy. *Sci. Rep.*, 10, 1, 707, 2020.

12. Cho, H.S., Park, M.S., Gupta, S., Han, I., Kim, H.S., Choi, H. *et al.*, Can augmented reality be helpful in pelvic bone cancer surgery? An in vitro study. *Clin. Orthop. Relat. Res.*, 476, 9, 1719–25, 2018.

13. Meola, A., Cutolo, F., Carbone, M., Cagnazzo, F., Ferrari, M., Ferrari, V., Augmented reality in neurosurgery: a systematic review. *Neurosurg. Rev.*, 40, 4, 537–548, Oct. 2017. doi: 10.1007/s10143-016-0732-9. Epub 2016 May 7. PMID: 27154018; PMCID: PMC6155988.

14. Iseki, H., Masutani, Y., Iwahara, M., Tanikawa, T., Muragaki, Y., Taira, T., Dohi, T., Takakura, K., Volumegraph (overlaid three-dimensional image-guided navigation). Clinical application of augmented reality in neurosurgery. *Stereotact. Funct. Neurosurg.*, 68, 18–24, 1997.

15. Edwards, P.J., Johnson, L.G., Hawkes, D.J., Fenlon, M.R., Strong, A., Gleeson, M., Clinical experience and perception in stereo augmented reality surgical navigation, in: *MIAR*, Springer-Verlag, Berlin Heidelberg, pp. 369–376, 2004.

16. Kockro, R.A., Tsai, Y.T., Ng, I., Hwang, P., Zhu, C., Agusanto, K., Hong, L.X., Serra, L., Dex-ray: augmented reality neurosurgical navigation with a hand-held video probe. *Neurosurgery*, 65, 795–807, discussion 807–798, 2009. doi:10.1227/01.NEU.0000349918.36700.1C.

17. Cabrilo, I., Bijlenga, P., Schaller, K., Augmented reality in the surgery of cerebral aneurysms: a technical report. *Neurosurgery*, 10, Suppl 2, 252–260, discussion 260–251, 2014. doi:10.1227/NEU. 0000000000000328.

18. Cabrilo, I., Bijlenga, P., Schaller, K., Augmented reality in the surgery of cerebral arteriovenous malformations: technique assessment and considerations. *Acta Neurochir.*, 156, 1769–1774, 2014. doi:10.1007/s00701-014-2183-9.

19. Okamoto, T., Onda, S., Yanaga, K., Suzuki, N., Hattori, A., Clinical application of navigation surgery using augmented reality in the abdominal field. *Surg. Today*, 45, 4, 397–406, Apr. 2015. doi: 10.1007/s00595-014-0946-9. Epub 2014 Jun 6. PMID: 24898629.

20. Fida, B., Cutolo, F., di Franco, G., Ferrari, M., Ferrari, V., Augmented reality in open surgery. *Updates Surg.*, 70, 3, 389–400, Sep. 2018. doi: 10.1007/s13304-018-0567-8. Epub 2018 Jul 13. PMID: 30006832.
21. Boni, L., David, G., Mangano, A., Dionigi, G., Rausei, S., Spampatti, S., Cassinotti, E., Fingerhut, A., Clinical applications of indocyanine green (ICG) enhanced fluorescence in laparoscopic surgery. *Surg. Endosc.*, 29, 7, 2046–55, Jul. 2015. doi: 10.1007/s00464-014-3895-x. Epub 2014 Oct 11. PMID: 25303914; PMCID: PMC4471386.
22. Hua, J., Holton, K., Miller, A., Ibikunle, I., Pico, C.C. *et al.*, Augmented Reality and Its Role in Abdominal Laparoscopic Surgical Training. *J. Health Educ. Res. Dev.*, 7, 295, 2019. doi:10.4172/2380-5439.1000295.
23. Tholey, G., Desai, J., Castellanos, A., Force feedback plays a significant role in minimally invasive surgery: results and analysis. *Ann. Surg.*, 241, 1, 102–109, 2005.
24. Fransson, B.A., Chen, C.Y., Noyes, J.A., Ragle, C.A., Instrument Motion Metrics for Laparoscopic Skills Assessment in Virtual Reality and Augmented Reality. *Vet. Surg.*, 45, S1, O5–O13, Nov. 2016. doi: 10.1111/vsu.12483. Epub 2016 May 30. PMID: 27239013.
25. Payan, Y., *Soft Tissue Biomechanical Modeling for Computer Assisted Surgery*, Springer-Verlag, Berlin Heidelberg, 2012.
26. Kainmueller, D., *Deformable Meshes for Medical Image Segmentation*, Springer Vieweg, Dissertation University of Lübeck, 2015.
27. Myronenko, A. and Song, X., Point Set Registration: Coherent Point Drift. *IEEE Trans. Pattern Anal. Mach. Intell.*, 32, 12, 2262–2275, Dec. 2010. doi: 10.1109/TPAMI.2010.46.
28. Bandari, N., Dargahi, J., Packirisamy, M., Tactile Sensors for Minimally Invasive Surgery: A Review of the State-of-the-Art, Applications, and Perspectives. *IEEE Access*, 8, 7682–7708, 2020. doi: 10.1109/ACCESS.2019.2962636.
29. Díez, J.A., Catalán, J.M., Blanco, A., García-Perez, J.V., Badesa, F.J., Gacía-Aracil, N., Customizable Optical Force Sensor for Fast Prototyping and Cost-Effective Applications. *Sensors*, 18, 2, 493, 2018. https://doi.org/10.3390/s18020493.
30. Garg, A., Sen, S., Kapadia, R., Jen, Y., McKinley, S., Miller, L., Goldberg, K., Tumor localization using automated palpation with Gaussian Process Adaptive Sampling. *2016 IEEE International Conference on Automation Science and Engineering (CASE)*, pp. 194–200, 2016.
31. Salman, H., Ayvali, E., Rangaprasad, A.S., Ma, Y., Zevallos, N., Yasin, R., Wang, L., Simaan, N., Choset, H., Trajectory-Optimized Sensing for Active Search of Tissue Abnormalities in Robotic Surgery, in: *Proceedings of International Con-ference on Robotics and Automation (ICRA)*, IEEE, 2018.
32. Correa, K., Bermejo, N., Vivas, A., Sabater-Navarro, J.M., Performance evaluation of a computational model for brain shift calculation. *Int. J. Med. Eng. Inform.*, 13, 4, pp. 308–322, DOI: 10.1504/IJMEI.2021.115961 2021.

33. Muñoz, V.F., Garcia-Morales, I., Fraile-Marinero, J.C., Perez-Turiel, J., Muñoz-Garcia, A., Bauzano, E., Rivas-Blanco, I., Sabater-Navarro, J.M., de la Fuente, E., Collaborative Robotic Assistant Platform for Endonasal Surgery: Preliminary In-Vitro Trials. *Sensors*, 21, 7, 2320, 2021. https://doi.org/10.3390/s21072320.

34. Fedorov, A., Beichel, R., Kalpathy, J., Finet, J., Fillion, J., Pujol, S., Bauer, C., Jennings, D., Fennessy, F., Sonka, M., Buatti, J., Aylward, S., Miller, J., Pieper, S., Kikinis, R., 3D slicer as an image computing platform for the quantitative imaging network. *Magn. Reson. Imaging*, 30, 9, 1323 – 1341, 2012.

Index

Printed and bound by CPI Group (UK) Ltd, Croydon, CR0 4YY

04/12/2023